MULLAHS WITHOUT MERCY

Also by Geoffrey Robertson

Reluctant Judas

Obscenity

Freedom, the Individual and the Law

Geoffrey Robertson's Hypotheticals (Vols 1 & 2)

Does Dracula Have AIDS?

Robertson & Nicol on Media Law

The Justice Game

Crimes against Humanity

The Tyrannicide Brief

The Levellers: The Putney Debates

The Statute of Liberty

The Case of the Pope

MULLAHS WITHOUT MERCY

HUMAN RIGHTS AND NUCLEAR WEAPONS

GEOFFREY ROBERTSON

Biteback Publishing

First published in Great Britain in 2012 by
Biteback Publishing Ltd
Westminster Tower
3 Albert Embankment
London SE1 7SP

ISBN 978-1-84954-406-1

10 9 8 7 6 5 4 3 2 1

A CIP catalogue record for this book is available from the British Library.

Set in Sabon
Cover design by Namkwan Cho

Printed and bound in Great Britain by
CPI Group (UK) Ltd, Croydon CR0 4YY

For my mother

CONTENTS

Appendices:

When the air becomes uranious,
We will all go simultaneous,
Yes, we'll all go together when we go.

We were unnerved in early teenagehood by the Cuban missile crisis
– although most Australians believed they were far enough away
to survive, even if it meant moving to Melbourne. That was where
Gregory Peck faced nuclear armageddon (and decided 'armageddon
outta here'), abandoning Ava Gardner as the band played 'Waltzing
Matilda' in the final scene of *On the Beach*. Even though the chain
of maniacal coincidence in *Dr Strangelove* seemed possible, I was
never moved to campaign for nuclear disarmament: resolution of
the Cuban crisis appeared proof that possession of nuclear bombs
by great powers was unlikely to lead to apocalypse, now or at any
time soon, because the US and USSR, and later the UK and France
and China, were states controlled by rational men with wives and
children and retirement plans who would never intentionally self-
destruct: MAD (mutually assured destruction) would not happen
because these government leaders were SANE (sensible about
nuclear evisceration). Today the bomb is already in the hands of
regimes that are unstable (Pakistan), irresponsible (North Korea)
and hypocritical (Israel), and will soon be available to one that is
criminal. Nuclear devastation, from accident or mistake, has never
been more likely and there is no effective law or treaty to prevent it.
I have written this book in an attempt to show that only when the
bomb is recognised as a human rights issue – the ultimate threat to
the right to life – can we move towards its eradication.

In the 1970s I donated my youthful advocacy services to
NGOs protesting against the construction of nuclear power-
plants at Windscale and elsewhere, but out of concern that even
the slightest risk of accident, or of diversion to terrorists, would
be used by governments as an excuse for unnecessary incursions
on civil liberty. There was no connection – in my mind or, seemingly, anyone else's – between nuclear weapons and the newly
developing idea of human rights, those entitlements being taken
at the time from Pinochet's torture victims and Russian dissidents
sent to Siberia. At one point I represented the veterans of the
British nuclear tests at Maralinga: I had seen them in newsreels,

PREFACE

I probably owe my existence to the bomb. My father, an Australian fighter pilot, had volunteered to fly off aircraft carriers so he could be part of the planned Allied invasion of Japan: he was required to report to naval headquarters on the very day that news of Hirohito's surrender crackled over the wireless. Instead of reporting for duty, he telephoned the women's air force corporal he had taken out in Townsville, and proposed. It had been the mushroom cloud over Hiroshima which had given the Emperor his excuse for laying down arms because, he explained, 'the enemy has begun to employ a new and most cruel bomb'. Without it, my father would have been part of a bloody finale to war in the Pacific certain to have cost hundreds of thousands of Allied and Japanese lives, and very possibly his own. Perhaps for that reason I have been disinclined to make the facile judgements of hindsight historians who claim that dropping the bomb on Hiroshima was a crime against humanity – a crime that could not realistically have been prosecuted in 1945. But it can now, as Milošević and Mladić and Charles Taylor have discovered to their cost, and it is time to consider whether and to what extent it applies, today, to malevolent regimes which seek to gird their loins for Armageddon by acquiring nuclear weapons. Iran presents as the first test case, by which the scope of international human rights law should be tested. But it will by no means be the last.

I am from the generation that grew up in the shadow of the bomb, playing in backyard cubbies that were readily convertible into nuclear shelters and developing a sense of irony by singing, along with Tom Lehrer,

> We'll all go together when we go,
> Every Hottentot and every Eskimo,

OECD	Organisation for Economic Co-operation and Development
P5	See *'Big 5'*
P5+1	As above, plus Germany
PDKI	Democratic Party of Iranian Kurdistan
SAVAK	Organisation of Intelligence and National Security (the secret police established by Reza Shah in 1957)
START	Strategic Arms Reduction Treaty
Tudeh	'The masses' – the communist party of Iran.

GLOSSARY

AEOI	Atomic Energy Organization of Iran
AIPAC	American Israel Public Affairs Committee
'Big 5'	The five permanent members of the United Nations Security Council: US, UK, France, Russia and China (also called P5)
CIA	US Central Intelligence Agency
CTBT	Comprehensive Nuclear-Test-Ban Treaty
FKO	Fadaiyan Khalq Organization, a Marxist-Leninist Iranian organisation
HEU	Highly enriched uranium
IAEA	International Atomic Energy Agency
ICC	International Criminal Court
ICCPR	International Covenant on Civil and Political Rights
ICJ	International Court of Justice
ICTY	International Criminal Tribunal for the Former Yugoslavia
IHL	International Humanitarian Law (war law, or law of armed conflict)
LEU	Low-enriched uranium
Majlis	The Islamic Consultative Assembly of Iran, the national legislative body (parliament)
MI6	Military Intelligence, Section 6 (of the Secret Intelligence Service of the UK)
MEK	Mojahedin-e Khalq Organization, alternatively MKO or Mojahedin
NAMIR	National Movement of the Iranian Resistance
NATO	North Atlantic Treaty Organization
NPT	Treaty on Non-Proliferation of Nuclear Weapons
NSG	Nuclear Suppliers Group

in their short pants and khaki shirts, cheering with imperial pride as they observed, at much too close a range, the British mushroom cloud over the Australian desert. Whether the cancers they developed in later life were the result of radiation, or the habit of smoking a packet a day to relieve the boredom, is still disputed in the courts. But throughout the Cold War period, the duffel-coated peace marchers from Aldermaston seemed to be tilting at windmills. *Realpolitik* required that the bomb should not be banned, but rather reduced numerically in the arsenals of the five great powers that had by then acquired them. The solution to the terrible threat of atomic weapons would be to send leaders like Reagan and Gorbachev for more 'Walks in the Woods': disarmament through diplomacy was the path to nuclear safety.

By this time, after all, a Nuclear Non-Proliferation Treaty (NPT) had been put in place – a great comfort to all who feared how the 'nuclear arms race' might end. In 1968 the treaty opened for signature and was in due course ratified by almost all states. The deal was simple and seemingly sensible: the 'Big 5' UN Security Council permanent members – the US, UK, France, China and the Soviet Union – would work 'in good faith' gradually to scale down their nuclear warhead numbers, and all other states would forswear any interest in constructing the bomb in return for recognition of their right to develop, if they wished, nuclear energy for electricity, isotopes for medical treatments, and for other peaceful purposes. In 1968, however, Israel was curiously absent from this party. With shameless equivocation, it has not even to this day admitted what is now known, namely that the first of its many nuclear bombs was being secretly built at this time, by a technology it developed in cahoots with apartheid South Africa. It was not until 1986 that the whistleblower Mordechai Vanunu proved that Israel's refusal to join the NPT was because it was secretly proliferating. So were India, despite the legacy of Mahatma Gandhi, and Pakistan (responsible for a recent genocide in Bangladesh), thanks to the evil genius of Dr A. Q. Khan, who went on to design Iran's nuclear weapons programme and is today the multi-millionaire founder of a new political party and still the most popular man in the country. That this man remains free and fêted is a rebuke to the slow progress of international criminal law, which cracks down

hard on manufacturers of poisoned arrows, dum-dum bullets and land mines, but says nothing about the use of nuclear weapons and as yet seems to know of no offence of aiding and abetting the production of nuclear bombs.

It was Gaddafi who eventually ratted on A. Q. Khan, once he decided he needed the West to protect him against Al Qaeda and against most of his own countrymen. In 2003 the Colonel traded information with MI6 about his dealings with terrorists and with Khan, and abjured his quest for nuclear weapons, which had been secretly pursued in facilities undeclared to the IAEA throughout the 1980s. Ironically, had he kept his secret and continued his quest successfully, he would have had nuclear weapons to fend off NATO, and both he and his regime might still be alive today. This lesson – build your nukes in secret and don't give them up – has not been lost on other brutal regimes.

I actually had the pleasure of discussing the subject of nuclear weapons with the Colonel, whilst he was acquiring them. That a dictator quite as deranged as Gaddafi might obtain a bomb was, by 1980, already the stuff of fiction – he appeared, as himself, in a novel entitled *The Fifth Horseman* (of the Apocalypse, geddit?) in whose pages he was credited with arranging for a nuclear device to explode in Manhattan. As a practitioner at the libel bar, I had been retained by the Libyan embassy (then called 'The Libyan People's Bureau') in London to advise the Colonel on whether he could sue the publisher for defamation. I made my way to the elegant building (formerly the home of Lady Astor) in St James's Square, to deliver my opinion by telephone to the Colonel listening with a translator at his tent outside Tripoli. My advice went something like:

> Yes indeed, you have a really great case, which I would be delighted to take for a not unreasonable fee and which could bring you massive damages: this book defames you dreadfully by depicting you as a nuclear terrorist! All you have to do is issue a writ, and then you will have to come to London for a few days to testify on oath – yes, you would probably be allowed to swear an oath on your Green Book – and say that you would never dream of acquiring nuclear weapons.

I was politely thanked for this advice, and ushered out by the Libyan People's Commissar, towards the railings that now bear a plaque commemorating Yvonne Fletcher, the policewoman killed a few months later by a bullet from the 'People's Bureau' because she had refused to arrest anti-Gaddafi demonstrators. Whether it was Gaddafi's dislike of London, or wish to avoid cross-examination over his intention to acquire nuclear weapons, I do not know, but my services were not required again.

Gaddafi gave up his nuclear weapons programme in 2003, but the very fact that he had advanced so far, whilst Libya was still a member of the NPT, should have been a warning that the non-proliferation approach did not work. Further proof came in that year when North Korea, having exercised what the treaty fatally termed its 'inalienable right' to develop a nuclear fuel cycle, simply resigned from the NPT and three years later tested a nuclear weapon. This rogue state is now believed to have a dozen bombs, and missiles that can deliver them anywhere in south east Asia (although they are likely first to land on South Korea) and, in due course, through the atmosphere to the American mainland. Israel has enough plutonium for 200 bombs and is known to have made at least 80 of them; India has 100 and Pakistan 110. These four nations refuse to ratify the NPT, in order to avoid the obligation to undergo safety inspections from its watchdog, the IAEA. Pakistan's cache is certainly not safe: as I write, in September 2012, Taliban militants have just stormed the Minhas air force base that houses some of its nuclear weapons, setting buildings alight before they were beaten back. It can only be a matter of time before Islamic militants capture one of the 'Sunni bombs' bequeathed by A. Q. Khan.

And now there is Iran, with its 'inalienable right' to enrich uranium, and its power to follow North Korea by resigning its NPT membership and, within a year or two, making a bomb. Then, of course, there are all the countries that will inevitably follow Iran, and are already taking preliminary steps to set up nuclear facilities: Saudi Arabia (which says it will buy ready-made bombs from Pakistan), Egypt, Turkey, the Gulf states, Jordan, Algeria and so on. There are countries in Asia, nervous about North Korea, and Latin American states that were persuaded to give up their quests for the bomb and to join the NPT – Brazil and Venezuela, for example – and may now be tempted to reconsider. An Iranian bomb – or even the prospect of Iran lawfully developing the capacity to make the bomb – will have this knock-on consequence. The Non-Proliferation Treaty is becoming a gift for would-be proliferators.

Why concentrate on Iran? Because it is the country currently closest to the nuclear weapons starting block and its human rights record makes its acquisition of the bomb a frightening prospect – not just for Israel. This should end the complacency that has settled over a world which by luck rather than good management has gone for sixty-seven years since Nagasaki without a nuclear accident or incident. It brings into focus something that has been lost in all the debates over nuclear disarmament, namely that nuclear weapons in themselves breach the most fundamental of human rights, the right not to be arbitrarily deprived of life, and soon they will be in the grasp of men whose abuses of their own people are barbaric. For some inexplicable reason Amnesty and Human Rights Watch have never thought to campaign against the bomb, the greatest of all dangers to human rights because of its propensity to wipe out humans. As for the UN, its departments for disarmament and for human rights are entirely separate and its concern over Iran's nuclear programme has submerged any concern over its human rights abuses. I believe it is time, as the NPT begins to collapse and proliferation is about to proliferate, to bring these issues together. Not by bombing Iran (although there may in time be no alternative) but by examining its human rights record as well as counting its numbers of centrifuges and measuring its levels of uranium enrichment. If the former demonstrates a propensity for international crime, then the latter will sound an alarm that cannot be ignored. But action to bring Iran within the law must in equity be action applicable to all states in its position, which have exercised their right to a full nuclear fuel cycle and hence gained a capacity to make nuclear weapons. That is not a crime and cannot justify an attack, unless they go further and are ready to assemble a bomb. Even then, an attack must be justified – or not – by reference to an international law applicable to all states. It is in an attempt to identify such a law, based on the developing norms of human rights, and to urge a new campaign to remove the danger of nuclear weapons, that I have written this book.

It has been the perceived madness, rather than the demonstrable cruelty, of the Iranian regime that has been the main objection to its acquisition of the bomb – together with its presumed desire to nuke Israel. I consider neither assumption to be justified, but there is a much more credible reason to deny Iran's nuclear weapons, namely that its leaders are capable of crimes against humanity. Just how the mullahs who run Iran think, and what they do to their enemies as a result, was the subject of an enquiry I undertook in 2009–10, at the request of the Washington-based Boroumand Foundation, into the events in Iranian prisons at the end of the war with Iraq in 1988. I embarked on an examination of all published material relevant to the treatment of Iranian prisoners (including translations from Farsi of relevant clips from pro-government newspapers, notably *Kayhan*). I held meetings in several European capitals with over forty victims who had been in Iranian prisons at the time: in the opening paragraph of my report, I sought to incorporate the horror of what I had heard and corroborated from these survivors:

> Late in July 1988, as the war with Iraq was ending in truculent truce, prisons in Iran crammed with government opponents suddenly went into lockdown. All family visits were cancelled, televisions and radios switched off and newspapers discontinued: prisoners were kept in their cells, and disallowed exercise or trips to the infirmary. The only permitted visitation was from a delegation, turbaned and bearded, which came in black government BMWs to outlying jails: a religious judge, a public prosecutor, and an intelligence chief. Before them were paraded, briefly and individually, almost every prisoner (and there were thousands of them) who had been jailed for adherence to the Mojahedin-e Khalq Organization – the MEK. This was a movement which had taken its politics from Karl Marx, its theology from Islam, and its guerrilla tactics from Che Guevara: it had fought the Shah and supported the revolution that brought Ayatollah Khomeini to power, but later broke with his theocratic state and took up arms against it, in support (or so it now says) of democracy. The

delegation had but one question for these young men and women (most of them detained since 1981 merely for taking part in street protests or possession of 'political' reading material), and although they did not know it, on the answer their life would depend. Those who by that answer evinced any continuing affiliation with the MEK were blindfolded and ordered to join a conga-line that led straight to the gallows. They were hung from cranes four at a time, or in groups of six from ropes hanging from the front of the stage in an assembly hall; some were taken to army barracks at night, directed to make their wills and then shot by firing squad. Their bodies were doused with disinfectant, packed in refrigerated trucks and buried by night in mass graves. Months later their families, desperate for information about their children or their partners, would be handed a plastic bag with their few possessions. They would be refused any information about the location of the graves and ordered never to mourn them in public. By mid-August 1988, thousands of prisoners had been killed in this manner by the state – without trial, without appeal and utterly without mercy.[1]

These killings were suspended for a fortnight's religious holiday, and began again when the 'Death Committee' (as prisoners would soon call the delegation) summoned members of other left-wing groups whose ideology was regarded as incompatible with the theocratic state constructed by Imam Ruhollah Khomeini after the 1979 revolution. This time the issue was not their political affiliation, but their religion and their willingness to follow the state's version of Islam: in short, whether they were apostates. There was a brief enquiry into their families, with a sentence of death for those atheists and agnostics whose parents were practising Muslims, whilst women in that category and others from secular families were instead ordered to be whipped five times a day until they died from the lash or agreed to pray. This second wave of executions was genocidal in intention (because the victims were selected on religious criteria), with torture as an alternative sentence.[2] In my report, now published by the Boroumand Foundation, I concluded that these little-known and never investigated massacres were a graver human rights violation than the Japanese death marches of POWs during the Second World

War, or the killing of 7,000 Muslim men and boys at Srebrenica. And they were perpetrated by men who still rule Iran, and have been responsible – in the case of Khamenei and Rafsanjani, primarily responsible – for its quest for nuclear weapons.

'Mullahs without Mercy' seems an accurate enough alliteration for the theocrats who directed the 1988 killings in Iran and who went on to order the assassination of hundreds of dissidents, at home and abroad, to blow up a synagogue and a community centre in Argentina in reprisal for that country's refusal to assist its nuclear ambitions, and later to beat up, shoot at and torture some of the Green Movement protesters and their lawyers. The book's title is not meant to imply that other mullahs are merciless, either in Iran itself (where a few have, with conspicuous courage, opposed the regime) or elsewhere, and of course there has been no shortage of Christian clerics willing to absolve mass murder and mass murderers – the death squads at Srebrenica were blessed by Serb Orthodox priests. As will appear, I have no confidence that the bomb will be safe in the hands of anyone in the grip of a millennial religion, whether it be the book of Shia Islam or the book of Mormon.

But how can it be possible that the acquisition of a weapon, the destructive power of which cannot be limited in space or time or controlled when its ionising radiation causes exponential suffering, is lawful? This view arises from a case decided by the World Court, the ICJ, in 1996, to the effect that it was not possible *at that time* to say that certain uses of nuclear weapons – in a desert, or against enemy ships in the middle of the ocean – would be a breach of international law, so it followed that possession of the bomb could not be unlawful, per se, because of the possibility that the state possessing it might drop it lawfully. This decision struck me as nonsensical, and I sought to explain why in the first edition of my book *Crimes Against Humanity*, in 1999, the year that the arrest in Harley Street of General Pinochet alerted political and military leaders to the possibility that they might one day be punished for international crimes of torture and mass murder. Today, the *Nuclear Weapons Case* (1996) decision is ripe for over-ruling, because international human rights law has moved on, and rather quickly. Its potential for development was actually noted by the court, which stressed that its ruling was provisional and that the law was moving in the direction of banning the bomb. In 2012, it has progressed far enough to make the acquisition of a nuclear weapon an international crime, and I explain my reasoning behind this opinion in Chapter 16.

Because criminal law is not retrospective, this change would not affect the existing arsenals of the nine nuclear weapon states, but in my view they are under a legal obligation – the only obligation that can be salvaged from the wreck of the NPT – to agree on a treaty for gradual but complete disarmament. A start has been made with the New START Treaty, which effects some reduction in the bombs and missiles of Russia (which now has 10,000 nuclear warheads) and the US (8,000) but does not include the UK, which has breached that obligation (and is likely to incur up to £83.5 billion expenditure) to upgrade its 'nuclear deterrent' (224 warheads) mainly on Trident submarines. France says it will reduce to less than 300 (although experts believe it still has about 600), and China 240. Most of these devices have at least thirty times the power of 'Little Boy', the bomb dropped on Hiroshima. The prospect that some of these weapons that could destroy the world will be built in the future for delivery under the orders of the mullahs who run Iran, and then the Saudi princes and the Muslim Brotherhood in Egypt, or Assad (if he survives) in Syria, emphasises the urgency of constructing a comprehensive international law to clear what is rapidly becoming a very dangerous nuclear minefield.

The issue that Iran presents is how the world can cope with the prospect of cruel and/or irrational governments possessing the capacity to 'break out' of their nuclear fuel cycles, enrich their uranium to weapons grade, and work out the payload for a warhead on their ballistic missiles. It matters not, for this exercise, whether Iran actually wants nuclear weapons, because other states with wretched human rights records will want them in the near future. Syria certainly does, and the Assad regime would be vicious enough to use them if its survival were at stake. So might other countries, and of course the proliferation of the bomb in so many hands increases the danger that terrorists will capture – or be allowed stealthily to acquire – nuclear devices. The US and Israel think that the problem of Iran can be solved by bombing its nuclear facilities, and so do the Gulf kingdoms, whilst the King of Saudi Arabia was caught, by WikiLeaks, begging the US to 'cut off the head of the snake'. But this can only be a temporary solution, delaying nuclear weapons capability for a year or two but strengthening the nation's resolve and encouraging it to keep its facilities secret in future. Bombing Iran, at the latest 'redline' identified by Israel (spring or early summer 2013) will be plainly unlawful (see Chapter 15), and there is a danger that we will be in for a rerun of the arguments over the 2003 invasion of Iraq. The most important task for the future is to bring nuclear weapons, and the punishment of those states which seek to acquire them, within the rule of law.

The legality of the bomb is infrequently considered, and then only by reference to international humanitarian law – the inappropriate term for the law that restrains brutality in war – and rarely by reference to international human rights law, the developing doctrine that offers the best hope for banning the bomb by putting the bomb makers – the politicians and prelates, scientists and generals – in prison. Diplomacy and sanctions, and an alphabet soup of nuclear treaties, have all failed, and will fail more catastrophically in the future, whilst the US bombing that the Saudi King urges to 'cut off the head of the snake' will, to quote Macbeth, 'scorch the snake, not kill it. It will close and be itself, whilst our poor malice remains in danger of its former tooth'. Unless nuclear weapons are viewed through the prism of human rights, and the capacity to make them is denied to human rights abusers and then to all other states, sooner or later a nuclear winter will change the climate before climate change changes it. The simple fact is that Iran is run by mullahs who have already perpetrated at least three crimes against humanity. The most compelling objection to Iran obtaining a nuclear weapons capacity is the fact that this regime has already granted itself impunity for mass murder, and may do so again.

States never let courts oversee or constrain decisions made 'in the interests of national security'. But when all else has failed, international human rights law does offer some rational solutions – hard though it may be to have them adopted in our lifetimes. I am always emboldened, in advocating difficult reforms, by the words of 'Freeborn John' Lilburne, who said of the Leveller programme, 'Our cause and principles do through their own natural truth and lustre get ground in men's understandings so that though we fail, our truths prosper. And posterity we doubt not shall reap the benefit of our endeavours.' Smug-sounding, certainly, but since his cause included democracy, and a constitution protecting free speech and requiring equality, he had some reason for optimism back in 1649. It is not clear how long disarmament will take – Global Zero, the most active NGO on this issue, estimates 2030 at the earliest, and only if its recommendations are accepted. But if there is a silver lining in that mushroom cloud that hovers in our imagination as the result of the Iranian bomb, it is that this very spectacle, hopefully hypothetical, will be enough to set the world on course for progressive nuclear disarmament.

Geoffrey Robertson QC
Doughty Street Chambers
October 2012

INTRODUCTION

The existence of nuclear weapons poses some of the most profound questions about the point at which the rights of states must yield to the interests of humanity, the capacity of our species to master the technology it creates, the reach of international humanitarian law, and the extent of human suffering that people are willing to inflict, or to permit, in warfare.[3]

There is no graver threat to international peace and security than the prospect of Iran acquiring nuclear weapons. Once it has the capacity to make 'the bomb' – and it had come quite close by the autumn of 2012 – then the centre cannot hold. The NPT, which has since 1970 appeared to keep the lid on this inhumanely and insanely destructive device, will become irrelevant and a few at least of the forty countries which have already started nuclear fuel cycles will be tempted to 'break out' from them and pile up nuclear bombs in the arsenals of their armies and navies and bomber commands. On too many nervously guarded borders will missiles raise their ugly warheads, pointing towards each other in mutual enmity. As more countries follow Iran – countries like Saudi Arabia, Egypt, Jordan and Syria, with perhaps South Korea and Taiwan developing a nuclear programme to counter North Korea, which has a dozen nuclear bombs in its belt already, the risk of a nuclear accident increases alarmingly, together with the danger that bombs will get into the hands of terrorists. There will, probably in the Middle East and over disputed islands in the South China Sea, be nuclear standoffs, incidents, quarantines, some Cuban missile crises writ small. Could Netanyahu and Khamenei, Kim Jong-un or Bashar al-Assad show the same restraint as Kennedy and Khrushchev? Ancestral hatreds, based on race or religion or

previous aggression, still drive men and women to suicidally ferocious conduct, and not only in Africa (where Sudan's
President Bashir, indicted by the ICC, has been advocating an
'African bomb'). Study the judgments from The Hague about
mass murder in the Balkans, or walk down the 'line of control'
between Armenia and Azerbaijan dodging bullets, and you get
a sense of the blind blood-fury capable of unleashing a nuclear
bomb, if it is at hand, without thinking about the consequences.

The scramble for nuclear weapons that Iran has started must
be stopped. But since sanctions are not working and negotiating
is impossible with men who lie when their lips move, it appears
to many that the only way forward is force. Israel is preparing to
bomb Iran, once it achieves 'nuclear capability' (which it equates
with nuclear culpability) in the spring of 2013. President Obama
promises to attack at some indeterminate, but later, stage before
it actually acquires a nuclear bomb. Candidate Romney draws
a 'red line' somewhere in the sands of time between 'capability'
and actual possession, although he says he will 'respect' Israel
whenever it decides to attack. The use of force – unlawful force,
as this book will show – will be no solution at all.

That solution can only come about, eventually, through the
rule of international law – a criminal law which puts behind bars
the politicians who decide in future to acquire nuclear weapons
and the scientists prepared to make them. International law must
go further and enforce the duty on nuclear-armed states imposed
by Article VI of the NPT, to negotiate a binding convention for
the gradual emptying of every nuclear arsenal. This was the
prescient proposal of the first nuclear disarmers, Bernard Baruch
and 'Doc' Evatt, back in 1946, but it fell victim to the power
plays of the Cold War. There was a well-intentioned 'atoms for
peace' programme initiated by President Eisenhower, who failed
to realise that atoms for peace were the same atoms that could be
used for war. When this penny dropped, after the Cuban missile
crisis, diplomats came up with the NPT, which amounted to a
deal between the 'Big 5' nuclear weapons states (the permanent
members of the Security Council) and all the rest, the 'non-
nuclear' states which would forswear nuclear weapons and enjoy
an 'inalienable right' to nuclear power for peaceful purposes, in

return for the great powers' promise that they would negotiate a treaty for their own 'complete disarmament'. They never did, and in recent years the cracks in the NPT have become wider and more apparent. Israel, India and Pakistan never joined, so they could build bombs to their hearts' content, and then – a big crack – North Korea left the treaty in 2003 so it could build and test its first bomb. Now Iran promises to break the treaty wide open: it demands its 'inalienable right' to develop a full nuclear fuel cycle from which it could, like North Korea, divert and build, within a few years, a significant number of nukes.

But is it lawful today for a non-nuclear weapon state to acquire the bomb? The ICJ, in 1996, said that at that time it was not unlawful to use the bomb in certain limited or extreme situations, although it warned that the law was changing. The argument in the final part of this book is that international human rights not only criminalises any *use* of the bomb, but prohibits non-nuclear states from acquiring it, and requires the nine states which already possess it to agree to reduce their stockpiles, gradually, to zero.

There is a prior question, of psychology rather than law or politics. Today's nuclear weapons mostly contain at least thirty times the destructive power of the bomb that exploded on Hiroshima and provided images of human destruction and devastation as unforgettable as those pictures of Holocaust survivors at the liberation of Belsen and Auschwitz. The authors of the Nazi crimes against humanity can never be forgiven, but Allied scientists on the Manhattan Project thought and worked in a kind of moral fugue, concerned with winning a war that would be lost if the perpetrators of the Holocaust beat them to the bomb. Accepting for the sake of argument the self-exonerating mantra of amoral science – 'it is not the weapon that is to blame, it is the politicians and the generals who decide to use it' – under what circumstances could any decent human being today build or use a nuclear weapon, either for a first strike against an enemy or as a reprisal for being struck by conventional or even nuclear weapons? The very framing of this question suggests one answer, namely that some powerful men – and women – lack all decency. Iran provides a relevant example.

• • •

Iran is a nation comparatively large in size and in population (over 70 million), with inexhaustible oil wealth and a resplendent history. It was first noticed on the human rights radar in the early 1970s, when the US-backed Shah of Persia deployed a not-so-secret police (SAVAK) to torture his opponents. To many in the West, the Shah's overthrow was a case of good riddance: SAVAK was disbanded and the millions of people in the Tehran streets all seemed overjoyed to welcome home Imam Ruhollah Khomeini and they were credited with knowing what would be good for them. In 1980 the eight-year Iran–Iraq War was started by Saddam Hussein although neither side had any obvious claim to international support. The US at first plumped for Iraq, but then the Reagan administration temporarily shifted gear with the secret Iran–Contra 'arms for hostages' deals, the exposure of which forced the US to renew its support for Iraq, and to turn a blind eye to Saddam's repeated use of chemical weapons. These killed tens of thousands of Iranians on battlefields ignored by CNN and other Western media. The casualties on both sides were appalling – over one million lives were lost, and Thatcher government minister Alan Clark actually voiced the thought that Western interests were 'well served by the towel-heads killing each other in such numbers', a view which reflected Dr Kissinger's cynical hope that both sides would lose. Eventually, the UN exerted pressure on both countries for a truce, agreed in July 1988: in the general satisfaction at bringing this war to an end, nobody – a few researchers at Amnesty International excepted – noticed or cared about the mass murder, a few weeks later, of many thousands of political prisoners in jails throughout Iran.

The essential quality of the 1988 massacre was its calculated cruelty in the service of theocratic orthodoxy: unbelievers were brutally tortured and killed without compunction. That they were prisoners adds to the heinousness of these exterminations. The utter vulnerability of prisoners in times of war makes the Geneva Convention the POW's only protection against cruel and vengeful governments. The 1988 atrocity was ordered by the Ayatollah Khomeini (who died in the following year) but carried out by direction of the President (Ali Khamenei), who is now Iran's Supreme Leader, by Rafsanjani and by many others in high or middling positions in 1988. In subsequent years, following the Rushdie fatwa, they proceeded to authorise a global assassination campaign and serial killings of Tehran intellectuals (see Chapter 8). In 2009 these mullahs, in the same or higher office, approved the beating and killing of Green Movement protesters and the jailing of their lawyers (Chapter 9). This behaviour, chronicled in the first part of the book, shows that the post-revolutionary rulers of Iran lack any regard at all for humanity or human justice. International criminal law recognises now the importance of judging criminals through the eyes of their victims, so Chapters 3 to 5 include that perspective. The accounts given by fellow prisoners who survived show the true impact of the decisions by men made cruel (but by no means mad) through the intoxicating cocktail of religious belief and belief in the righteousness of their own power – hence in the rightness of killing enemies without any need to heed the consequences. Iran never bothered, for example, about damage to its reputation done by its global assassination campaigns, which made use of embassies and diplomatic bags, and it routinely breached foreign laws. This government not only believed it was right to exterminate its enemies, but that it had a religious duty to do so. It was this religious obsession which explains the frenzy with which many of its targets were murdered, and why imprisoned atheists were rushed headlong to the gallows or (if female) to the torture chambers. It explains the regime's rejection of what Khomeini called the 'Western' notion of a trial, with a defence lawyer and a right to call witnesses before an independent and impartial court. Once it was suspected that a prisoner was '*mohareb*' – an opponent of God (by which was meant an opponent of the state, since it was theocratic) he or she had to be killed.

• • •

The mullahs have excited many to believe in the re-entry to the world of the 'Twelfth Imam' – the invisible saviour called the Mahdi, who will return from his hidden existence ('occulation') once the world has fallen into a state of chaos. The Mahdi will smite all unbelievers (including Sunni Muslims, in revenge for assassinating Imam Hussein) leaving only the good Shias and their guides, the mullahs, to enjoy peace and justice after 'the end of time'.[4] President Ahmadinejad believes the Mahdi is returning some time soon, and has built a Shia theme park at Jamkaran, near Qom, where the Mahdi is expected to 'de-occulate' and take a specially built train to Tehran. This 'Twelver-Shia' belief is not based on the Koran but on the *Hadiths* (the Prophet's alleged sayings), delivered 1,300 years before the creation of the state of Israel (although one *Hadith* does urge the killing of all Jews, wherever they might be). But if religious believers are intent on creating the sort of chaos that will trigger the return of the Mahdi at 'the end of time', then one portent is a 'scream from the sky'. An atomic bomb might do the trick, and if so, Israeli hardliners postulate, the mullahs will choose Tel Aviv. Especially since Ahmadinejad has threatened – so every pro-Israeli politician, almost every newspaper commentator and most serious scholars endlessly repeat – 'to wipe Israel off the face of the map'.

Except that the President did not say this. These words were an erroneous English translation of his speech in Farsi, to an anti-Zionist conference in 2005. They appeared in an officially issued translation, so the mistake is understandable. What he actually said is 'The Imam (i.e. Ayatollah Khomeini) said, "This regime occupying Jerusalem must vanish from the pages of time."' The error has been pointed out on every anti-Zionist blog site, with hints that it must be an Israeli propaganda trick to encourage American support for bombing Tehran. In their excitement, it never seems to occur to these bloggers that the difference between being wiped off the face of the map and vanishing from the pages of time is not all that much: if Israel vanishes from time, any self-respecting cartographer will remove the country from his maps. However, the truth is that the President was invoking a prophecy by the Ayatollah about the Shia Millennium ('the end of time'), the point at which the Twelfth Imam will 'de-occulate' and wipe all unbelievers from time's pages. So, to be fair, this is not evidence that Ahmadinejad, vicious anti-Semite though he be, is building atomic weapons to bring on the apocalypse by firing them at Israel. It may be evidence – his sayings and those of the Supreme Leader are examined in Chapter 15 – of an inclination to trigger the return of the Twelfth Imam, although it hardly follows that this will be by bombing Jerusalem. It would be more likely that they are intent on provoking Israel to drop conventional bombs – 'the scream from the sky' – on their nuclear facilities, so as to bring about the chaos in which the Mahdi will return and wipe the Jews – and other non-Shias – from time's pages. (Many mullahs will, therefore, actually, welcome an Israeli strike on the Natanz nuclear facility). Ahmadinejad has certainly talked about wiping the present state of Israel off the map in the context of why it should be moved to Germany or the US or Alaska, and has proclaimed that the Zionist regime should be wiped out 'just as the Soviet Union was wiped out' – which was a relatively peaceful process of dismemberment – but he is not yet guilty of incitement to genocide. It is of some importance, when making threats of the kind which have emanated from Benjamin Netanyahu since 2006, namely to bomb a country and kill some of its people 'in pre-emptive self-defence' of Israel, to decide whether there is any imminent prospect of an attack to defend Israel against. The evidence shows that Iran certainly wants a bomb, but not to use on Israel. Threats to attack Iran at the point when it becomes merely *capable* of making a bomb are, as Chapter 15 demonstrates, irresponsible and unlawful.

• • •

The dangers of 'Twelver Shia' millennial beliefs have been exaggerated by Israel's Prime Minister in order to persuade the US to join, or at least support, an Israeli strike on Iran's nuclear facilities. But putting those beliefs aside, Iran provides an example of a class of middle-ranking states with troubled pasts where very serious human rights abuses have been committed with impunity, have never been apologised for or even regretted, and are still ongoing. Such governments may decide that they need the bomb for perfectly rational reasons: because a nuclear weapon 'puts us where we ought to be, in the position of a great power' (the reason offered by Harold Macmillan for Britain acquiring bombs that merely added to the vast stockpile of its American ally) or because a nation without a bomb 'does not control its own destiny' (De Gaulle's reason for scientifically pointless nuclear tests in the Pacific).[5] Other nations, which like Iran are unrepentant for past atrocities and present abuses, and inflamed by national pride, may claim their 'inalienable right' to enrich uranium for peaceful purposes, to a point where the bomb lies within their grasp. The simple issue which Iran presents (whether in fact it wants a bomb or not) is how the world can cope with cruel or irrational governments obtaining nuclear weapons.

Such proliferation enhances the much-discussed prospects of a nuclear accident. The US and Russia cannot even now agree to take all their weapons off 'hair trigger' alert, and memories are still fresh of that near-disastrous day in 1995 when a Norwegian weather rocket was mistaken in Moscow for a nuclear missile launched from a US submarine, and President Yeltsin's unsteady hand actually trembled over the button by which he could have launched a nuclear counter-strike and wiped out part of America. Accidents can happen, and bad luck is beyond the reach of the law. The point is that the scramble for the bomb that will follow Iran's acquisition of it would greatly increase the danger of accidental explosion, or mistaken nuclear weapon launch and consequent reprisal. The new bomb-possessing states will not have the organisational experience to keep their bombs safe, either from accident or from theft by, or diversion to, terrorists. What must be detected and deterred, if appropriate international laws and mechanisms can be put place, are not only future nuclear-vending arms dealers like A. Q. Khan, but governments whose past crimes and present intentions make their enrichment of uranium to weapons grade a threat to international peace and security.

Extraordinarily, IHL – which regulates the use of every weapon, from poison arrows to dum-dum bullets and tear gas to land mines and cluster bombs, has never outlawed possession of nuclear weapons by nation-states. It goes unmentioned, this vast elephant in every war crimes conference room, usually so as not to upset America. It is almost as if nuclear weapons are too hot for international law to handle. They have been addressed instead, nervously and unsuccessfully, by diplomats. In 1968, on the day after the Chinese first exploded their bomb, the 'Big 5', then the only nations with nuclear weapons, pledged not to use them against any other state that promised in return not to build their own nuclear weapons. That deal was solemnised in the NPT, whereby all non-nuclear states undertook to abjure any ambitions to build a bomb, in return for the nuclear powers' undertaking to pursue negotiations to end the arms race and promote a treaty which would bring about 'complete disarmament under strict and effective international control'. There are many holes in the NPT, as Chapter 11 explains. Although it now has 189 parties, including Iran (which signed up under the Shah), these have never included India, Pakistan and Israel. North Korea simply pulled out before it joined the mile-high cloud club in 2006, and now stretches its ballistic muscles to see whether they could support a nuclear warhead that could re-enter the atmosphere somewhere over the USA. (Reassuringly, its much-promoted rocket launch in April 2012 was a fizzer).

The fundamental flaw of the NPT is spelled out in Article IV:

> Nothing in this treaty shall be interpreted as affecting the inalienable right of all parties to the Treaty to develop research, production and use of nuclear energy for peaceful purposes without discrimination...

The catch-22 is that by promising this 'inalienable right', the NPT entitles every state to develop nuclear energy to the enrichment stage – a stage necessary for peaceful purposes, but which can also serve as the launch pad for a nuclear weapon, since it can provide a sufficient amount of highly enriched uranium (HEU) for use in an atomic bomb. The paradox, as Chapter 11 explains, is that the NPT encourages the use of nuclear energy for peaceful purposes, entailing uranium enrichment and fuel cycle development but to a point where a switch to fissile materials can be made swiftly and simply. The sustained fast-fissile reaction of the self-same materials (uranium 235 and plutonium 239) produces both the controlled energy release in a nuclear reactor for electricity and the explosive energy released in a nuclear warhead. There is no way to distinguish between the production of fissile materials for use in nuclear weapons and for civilian electricity generation until the end of the line, because the processes to make weapons-grade (90 per cent enriched) are the same as those performed on uranium for low (3.5 to 5 per cent) enrichment use in civil reactors, 'only one performs the process repeatedly and for a longer duration'.[6] So states wishing to make the bomb can, like North Korea, actually use the NPT as a cover, developing a full fuel cycle and low enrichment capacity, then resign from the treaty and 'break out' by enriching to weapons grade.

Iran has claimed its 'inalienable right' and there is not very much that the other parties can do about it under the NPT, which has no sanctions for any breach. They can, of course, ensure that the IAEA, guardian of the NPT under the direction of the Security Council, carries out extensive inspections, but its inspectors can be deceived – as Iran, Iraq and other countries have often deceived them before, or simply refused them entry to the country, or to a particular facility they want to visit, despite the threat of sanctions imposed by the Security Council. Iran has put up with sanctions (from the EU and US as well) since 2006, but has repeatedly lied about its uranium enrichment capacity and its secret nuclear plants, and refuses to allow the inspectors to enter its suspect military sites, fuelling the impression that its assertion of its 'inalienable right' to generate electricity is merely a smokescreen for its determination to generate nuclear warheads.

Another problem with the NPT is that it does not require – or even permit – the international community to act to destroy the arsenal of a state which declines to comply. Non-members (e.g. Israel, which has at least eighty nuclear bombs, and perhaps as many as 200) obviously cannot be touched, and members may become untouchable merely by a North-Korean style withdrawal. In short, the NPT contains no provision for preventative action against a non-party which has obtained nuclear weapons (at present, only Pakistan, India, Israel and North Korea) and no provision for preventative action again *any* state which tests or even uses the bomb.

The NPT, incredibly for a treaty of this importance, has no executive or secretariat: breaches reported by the IAEA to the Security Council may be dealt with pursuant to its powers under Chapter VII of the UN Charter to impose sanctions, or to use force, for the purpose of restoring international peace and security. But the Security Council is subject to the 'superpower veto': any one of the 'Big 5' can prevent any particular UN initiative. That is why the Council was pole-axed in 2006, when Iran demanded its 'inalienable right' to enrich, between the US and UK (which wanted severe sanctions) and Russia and China (which wanted Iranian oil and trade). By 2009, as the WikiLeaks cables demonstrated, America was being urged by Saudi Arabia and Jordan, as well as by Israel, to bomb Iran's nuclear facilities to smithereens. That's what the Israelis had done in 1981 to Saddam's nuclear facility at Osirak, to general condemnation, although this merely drove his nuclear programme underground: 'Operation Desert Storm' in 1990–91 blew away the covers on his advanced nuclear weapons programme, which had continued at multiple secret sites thereafter and had completely fooled the IAEA inspectors.

This problem arises from the ease with which atoms for peace can be turned into atoms for war, or to be scientifically simplistic, the 'few turns of the screw' between enriching at 3.5 per cent for electricity, or 20 per cent for medical isotopes, and then 'breaking out' to 90 per cent for nuclear weapons. It is a problem that will be greatly exacerbated by necessary climate change policies: the demand for 'clean' fuel to serve growing populations and industrial development and to power electric vehicles will double by 2030. The pressure to reduce greenhouse gas emissions and the rising price and falling attraction of fossil fuels has meant a surge of demand for nuclear power in Africa, south east Asia and the Middle East, in some countries dogged by political instability. The 2009 Report of the International Commission on Nuclear Non-Proliferation and Disarmament – another cluster of the good and the great, sponsored by the Australian and Japanese governments – warned that nuclear proliferation was as great a danger as climate change (greater in the short term) and said:

It is important to recognize that the establishment of even the most basic nuclear infrastructure and expertise may presage later pursuit of a full nuclear cycle, with all that implies – as we are now acutely aware with the examples of North Korea and Iran – about the capacity to move to, or toward, proliferation under cover of the right to develop nuclear technology for civilian purposes. Some have gone so far as label some recent nuclear cooperation agreements 'bomb starter kits'.[7]

• • •

Iran wants the bomb. That was the Shah's ultimate objective, and although after the revolution in 1979 the Ayatollah initially thought nuclear weapons were un-Islamic (because they were Western-made devices), he soon changed his mind after Saddam began killing his soldiers with poison gas. The only way to beat him, Army Commander Rafsanjani and President Khamenei and Prime Minister Mousavi all concurred, was to obtain nuclear weapons. So A. Q. Khan was invited to help, and later millions of dollars were paid to his network for their centrifuges and weapons designs. This secret programme proceeded apace, hidden from the IAEA until 2002, when a Washington press conference by the dissident group whose members had been massacred in 1988 (the MEK) revealed to the world an Aladdin's cave of centrifuges hidden in Natanz. The mullahs, caught bang to rights, suspended enrichment and weaponisation work for three years, before a new and aggressive President, Mahmoud Ahmadinejad, started it up again. Iran continued to deceive the IAEA, (for example, about its new enrichment facility under a mountain near Qom), and is now enriching uranium to 20 per cent, on occasion even to 29 per cent. Meanwhile, current IAEA reports suggest there is evidence it has re-started an associated weaponisation programme.

Security Council sanctions, as severe as the US can persuade Russia and China to agree to, and really severe sanctions from the US and the EU, have badly damaged Iran's economy. This has only hardened the country's resolve to claim what the NPT describes as an 'inalienable right' to a full fuel cycle, from which point it is easy to reach the 90 per cent level necessary for a bomb. The Security Council resolutions have ordered Iran to cease all enrichment, but it has ignored them. Throughout 2012 there was an endless round of diplomacy from the EU, leading the P5 + 1 group (i.e. the 'Big 5' and Germany), but Tehran is clever at buying time through aimless talk, and it carried on enriching regardless. At this rate, barring accident or Israeli/American intervention, it will be capable of making a few bombs by 2015 or thereabouts, and even an Israeli/US attack would not delay it more than a couple of years. But if possession of the bomb is not unlawful, and Israel has lots of them (as do India and Pakistan), on what legitimate basis can Iran be stopped or delayed by the murder of its scientists and the sabotaging of its computer systems, or by bombing its nuclear facilities?

• • •

Iran is a country run by mullahs without mercy, perpetrators of three separate crimes against humanity: the massacre of thousands of helpless political prisoners in 1988; running a global assassination campaign between 1986 and 1996; and torturing and killing Green Movement protesters and persecuting their lawyers after 2009. Part I of this book sets out the evidence, and explains why, to date, they have got away with it. One reason, ironically enough, is because the world's attention is now focused, indeed fixated, on their nuclear progress rather than on their human rights record. The two issues are seen as separate and the twain never meet, particularly at the UN where human rights and disarmament fall under quite separate departments. This disjunct is absurd, because the question of the lawfulness of possession or use of thermonuclear weapons is a matter, as Chapters 14 to 16 explain, of international human rights law, a rapidly developing doctrine which has now developed far enough, jurisprudentially, to make it an international crime to acquire new nuclear weapons in the future (the law cannot retro-actively apply in respect of states or statesmen who have built bombs in the past). Moreover, the pragmatic test of whether a state can be trusted with an arsenal of nukes can best be assessed by looking at its human rights record. The decency with which it exercises power over its own people is a reasonably good indication of whether it could, at some time in the future, engage in mass nuclear murder. Just as the last thing we would want to see is a nuclear device in the hands of terrorists, so the second last thing we would want to see is a nuclear bomb in the hands of a terrorist state. In Iran's case, not so much because it funnels money and weapons to political groups like Hezbollah and Hamas, but because it has already committed three crimes against humanity, and may, with the bomb, have the boosted confidence to commit more.

That is an intolerable prospect, but on what legal basis can it be stopped? There is no law against a sovereign state possessing the bomb, whatever its record for denying human rights or supporting terrorism. This follows from a 1996 decision of the ICJ, which could not say that use of the bomb was wrong in *all* circumstances – therefore states could acquire it for possible lawful use (e.g. on an enemy conveniently situated in the middle of a desert or an ocean). That this was a wrong and now anachronistic decision is the argument advanced in Chapter 14, but for present purposes it makes the point that the army of any member of the UN may quite lawfully keep nukes in its knapsack. It would seem simple, and certainly desirable, to fashion a law – what international lawyers call a 'norm' – that simply banned states with appalling and unrequited human rights records from acquiring nuclear weapons. Those states, perhaps, with leaders under indictment at the ICC, or that could be shown to have perpetrated crimes against humanity – in effect, mass murder or mass torture or widespread or systematic inhumane acts. This could be made the subject of a convention or else declared (like 'the Responsibility to Protect') as a principle upon which the Security Council undertakes to act, using force if necessary, under Chapter VII of the Charter against any criminal state, or state led by criminals, which had reached the stage at which it could assemble a bomb. But who would make the judgment call as to whether a country's human rights record shows it fit to keep nukes? Not the Human Rights Council, with its perennially politicised bias against Israel, or the Security Council, where the 'Big 5' would be judges in their own cause. Nor the IAEA, where technical experts are not experts in human rights, or the NPT, since, as we have seen, it has no permanent executive. The Human Rights Committee, perhaps, which is at least composed of jurists, not all of whom are diplomatic lackeys, or the judges of the ICC or the ICJ. Whatever test any unbiased judge could apply to grant a licence to own a dangerous bomb, Iran would certainly not qualify, for the reasons given in Part I of the book.

• • •

Iran is engaged in 'nuclear hedging' – a programme that will enable it to build atomic bombs in a few years, at a time of its choosing. The mullahs want the bomb not to drop it on Israel but to secure their merciless rule in Iran and their influence in the Middle East, and in the process they will further discredit the NPT and provoke a scramble for nuclear weapons throughout the region, if not the world. For all these reasons Iran must be stopped from acquiring nukes, but sanctions only increase its resolve and the diplomats – especially naive EU negotiators – are outfoxed by ambassadors sent abroad from Tehran to lie in their country's interest.

The way forward may in fact be the way back – to the proposal, after Hiroshima, to put all fissile material in the possession of the UN and to make those involved in producing new nuclear weapons guilty of an international crime. Acquiring the bomb is now, in 2012, contrary to an international law of human rights that has been developing in recent years to put the likes of Pinochet, Milošević and Charles Taylor on trial. The bomb is an illegal weapon of terror, because it causes intolerable suffering, it cannot discriminate between soldier and civilian, it causes unnecessary, disproportionate and superfluous injury through its long-lasting effects of ionising radiation and because of its catastrophic effects on the environment. The politicians, prelates and scientists who build new bombs are in consequence guilty of a crime against humanity. As for those countries which already possess nuclear weapons (the 'Big 5' plus Israel, North Korea, India and Pakistan), they cannot be subject retrospectively to international criminal law, but it is time to apply that part of the 1996 opinion of the World Court which interprets Article VI of the NPT as requiring them to admit their nuclear weapons stockpiles and to agree on a treaty for gradual but 'complete' disarmament. In this way, the rule of law can help to diminish and ultimately extinguish a weapon with the destructive power to put an end to civilisation.

There will be no alternative to the use of force against countries which, undeterred by sanctions, successfully and secretly cheat. But that force should be authorised by the Security Council, pursuant to a comprehensive settlement of the nuclear weapons question, preferably by a new convention. The alternative is a recognition that from now on, acquisition of the bomb amounts to a crime against humanity punishable at the ICC and that a binding Article VI agreement on disarmament deadlines must be reached by the nine existing nuclear weapons states. Otherwise, force will be used against new proliferators opportunistically and occasionally, mainly by the US and mainly against enemies of the US. If this short-term solution is applied to Iran, it will only make it more determined, and make other Middle Eastern countries more outraged at the discrepancy in their treatment compared to that accorded to the two most favoured nations, Israel and India.

There is no easy way out of the mess that international power politics and diplomacy have made by their silence over Iran's crimes against its own people and by putting in place a 'non-proliferation' regime that in fact encourages proliferation by giving states an 'inalienable right' to a nuclear fuel cycle but allowing them the freedom to 'break out' and build a bomb. But the case of Iran – which could soon be the case of other countries – demonstrates the urgency of putting in place comprehensive rules: criminal laws for would-be proliferators and deadlines for de-nuclearisation. The only silver lining in the next mushroom cloud will be if it forces the nations of the world to assert the rule of law and human rights over the weapon with the potential to destroy them all.

PART I

IRAN

The Shah of Shahs with wife Soraya, waiting nervously
for news of the MI6/CIA plot to overthrow Mossadegh.

CHAPTER 1

BACKSTORY

The earliest recorded claim that mercy must season justice comes to us from 539 BC. It is written in Babylonic cuneiform, on a baked clay cylinder now lodged in the British Museum. It is the work of a potent Iranian, the Persian King Cyrus, who styles himself 'ruler of the Universe'. He explains how, after capturing Babylon, he took pity on displaced people 'who had become like corpses'. He freed these captives so they could return to 'the homes that make them happy' – and they included Jews, whom he permitted to return to build their temple in Jerusalem. The Cyrus Cylinder has been misdescribed both by the British Museum and by the UN (where a copy is displayed) as the 'world's first charter of rights' – in fact, it was Persian propaganda. But it does express the idea that religious tolerance, forgiveness and human kindness are both goodly and Godly. These are the very virtues that the Republic of Iran despises and rejects, to an extent that makes its potential possession of nuclear weapons a danger to the world. The Cyrus Cylinder was temporarily loaned to Iran by the museum in 2010, in the hope that its symbolic power would influence the mullahs to treat more kindly the thousands recently arrested for supporting the Green Movement. President Ahmadinejad, whose rigged election had been the object of their protests, welcomed its return. He staged a ceremony in which Cyrus was depicted wearing the insignia of the Basij militia, which had brutally beaten demonstrators and infamously killed Neda Agha-Soltan.[8]

The cylinder had not been displayed in Iran since 1971, when it had been loaned as the centrepiece for celebrations at Persepolis, the grandest of all *folies de grandeur*. The Shah of Persia had chosen to commemorate what he said was the 2,500th anniversary of the Peacock Throne. He claimed to be heir to a noble line of conquerors which began with Cyrus the Great, followed by Darius and Xerxes. He was leader of a people imbued with the poetry of Omar Khayyam and the philosophy of Zoroaster (hailed by Nietzsche in *Also sprach Zarathustra* as first conceiver of the moral world). To celebrate this conceit came a plethora of potentates and plenipotentiaries: nine Kings, five Queens, sixteen Presidents, numerous Prime Ministers and even Haile Selassie, gallivanting for a fortnight in seventy ornate tents decorated by Janson of Paris, catered by Chez Maxime of Paris and served by royal courtiers dressed in uniforms designed by Lanvin of Paris. Thousands of the Shah's impoverished subjects were ordered to dress up and disport themselves as Medes and Persians, whilst guests consumed 25,000 bottles of champagne to fortify themselves for speeches about his own and the nation's glorious past.[9] Whilst they caroused, sixty-nine student activists, calling themselves the Mojahedin-e Khalq Organization (MEK), stumbled nearby in the darkness, preparing for their first terrorist act – to blow up the power station that supplied all the electricity.

Persepolis symbolised the pretensions of the Shah of Iran, descended not from Darius but from Reza Khan, a Cossack general of unprepossessing birth, who had dignified his military dictatorship in 1925 by adopting the name Pahlavi, with its pre-Islamic Persian resonance, and by having himself crowned as Shah (i.e. king). The glories of Iranian history celebrated at Persepolis had actually been on the decline ever since the collapse of the exotic Safavid Empire in the early 1700s, and Persia had entered the twentieth century as a backward backwater. Though the state was headed by an enfeebled dynasty known as the Qajars, it was effectively controlled by Britain and Russia, and its main resources – tobacco and then, crucially, oil – had been awarded by concessions to British adventurers and businessmen. A popular uprising produced some reform in 1905–7: a constitution (based on the Belgian model) which notionally survived until its Islamic replacement in 1979, and an elected national assembly (the Majlis). There was some support from the *ulema* (the clerics learned in Shia Islam's law and folklore), but they were split: the country's powerful clergy was always nervous about the secular tendencies of liberal and nationalist politicians.

The clerics themselves held sway over the intense spiritual lives of a predominantly rural people who were overwhelmingly Shia – members of the minority Muslim sect which believes that Mohammed's cousin Ali was the Prophet's true heir ('Shia' is a contraction of *Shi'at Ali*, or 'partisans of Ali'). This distinguishes them from the much more numerous Sunni Muslims, who believe that after the Prophet's death the leadership devolved upon his closest companion, Abu Bakr. According to Shia doctrines, the line of succession passed from Ali to his younger son Hussein, and after his martyrdom at Karbala (in modern-day Iraq), to a line of descendants which was extinguished at the end of the ninth century with the disappearance of the 'Twelfth Imam', who went into 'occulation' – a state of invisibility – in 874 AD. In Iran today, the ruling mullahs are 'Twelver Shias', believing that the Twelfth Imam will return from 'occulation' at the end of some future time when the world is in chaos, and will then extinguish the enemies of Allah and reward the faithful with eternal and paradisical life.

Shias are in a theological minority among the world's Muslim believers – they number only 13 per cent, but that still counts for about 200 million of them, mainly in the 'Shia Crescent' formed by Iran, Iraq and Bahrain. Their millennial belief in the return of an invisible saviour is regarded as heretical in the majority Sunni tradition, which comes in hardline form (the Taliban, and the Wahabi beliefs of the Saudis) and in the milder, more pragmatic version found in Malaysia and Indonesia. Shia beliefs arise from the myths surrounding bloody and brutal combat, but there is nothing that sets them apart from the hate-thy-neighbour battles celebrated by most religions, from the Mahabharata to the Bible. If anything, Shias are exceptional for their capacity to commemorate their historic defeats: in the holy month of Muharram, for example, the streets are full of wailing and flailing mourners, lamenting the death in 680 AD of Imam Hussein, Mohammed's grandson, at the hands of an evil Caliph. Shia passion for crying over the spilled blood of their martyrs is usually explained as a way of making the best of a bad job, although it can inculcate in the faithful a willingness to sacrifice and be sacrificed, for the greater glory that will come when the de-occulated Imam saves the good Shias and destroys the non-believers.

By the turn of the twentieth century, Iran was still considered insignificant – so poor that neither of its foreign masters, Britain and Russia, could bother to fight each other for the pleasure of colonising it, given the cost of administering and educating a country that did not have even the most basic infrastructure. It was set in the aspic of camel trains and merchant bazaars, unchanging and unyielding. As Gertrude Bell put it in 1928, 'strewn with the ruins of a titanic past, Persia ... looks to itself; it knows nothing of the greater world of which you are a citizen, asks nothing of you and of your civilisation'.[10] It was a country with no recent glories to speak of, even though the Shah would at Persepolis speak of its 'titanic ruins' as if their ghosts were coming into focus among the pillars (with all the champagne, they possibly were). But the country had by then acquired no particularly brutal culture, other than in the upper echelons of government in earlier centuries where grand viziers were sometimes thrown into pots of boiling oil. There was nothing in Iran's history to suggest that the prison massacres of August and September 1988 could come to pass.

The First World War gave Iran some significance by serving to highlight the enormous importance of its oil fields – 'a prize from fairyland beyond our wildest dreams' as Winston Churchill described the concessions exploited by the Anglo-Iranian Oil Company (later to change its name to British Petroleum), supplier of fuel to the Royal Navy. These concessions were protected and extended by Reza Shah, the low-born, poorly educated thug whose inferiority complex caused him to take the highbred name Pahlavi. He had risen through every rank to command its most modern unit, and although he became a dictator much attracted in the late 1930s to Nazism, he did unite and to some extent modernise, or at least Westernise, this quiescent nation – to the concern of the *ulema*, for example, by establishing a legal system separated from religious courts, banning the wearing of the veil and establishing schools for girls and sending bright students abroad to study. But in the end his fascist tendencies were too dangerous for Britain and Russia to risk as they hunkered down to the war against Hitler, so in 1941 they protected Allied oil supplies by invading Iran and ordering Reza to abdicate in favour of his son Mohammed. He went quietly into exile, in a British warship to Mauritius, leaving in his place a shy young man who had just finished at a Swiss finishing school. He was no match for a charismatic politician who by 1950 came to dominate the Majlis.

Mohammad Mossadegh was Iran's first, and in many eyes only, democratic hero. He was a doctor of laws from an aristocratic family who had served time in prison for opposing Reza Shah but was now the leader of the broad-based National Front, which demanded an end to the British oil concessions and a return to constitutional government by limiting the Shah's powers. He became a very popular Prime Minister, but outraged the British when he implemented the parliamentary will and nationalised Anglo-Iranian Oil, then the most profitable business in the world. It was a symbol of rampant and rapacious colonialism, paying little tax on its massive profits, which were extracted from the exertions of wretchedly paid local workers who lived in the company's slum housing, whilst British managers luxuriated in colonial mansions with swimming pools and tennis courts. The British Foreign Secretary, Herbert Morrison, blockaded Iran with gunboats and insisted that its oil was British property. His efforts to 'curb these insolent natives' (as Lord Mountbatten contemptuously characterised his attitude)[11] did not meet with President Truman's approval, and Mossadegh was hailed by TIME magazine as 'Man of the Year' for 1951, chosen not only because he had unleashed turmoil on the world's oil markets, but because he seemed the kind of politician devoted to the rule of law who might lead backward nations to democracy. His electrifying appearance at the ICJ, where he defended in person his nationalisation (with compensation) of an oil company that treated Iranians 'like animals' and had plundered their oil resources, turned into a triumph when the court, albeit on a technicality, held in Iran's favour.

It was the British, in a fit of post-imperial pique, who decided that Mossadegh must go. Gunboats were sent to patrol the Persian Gulf and parachutists were put on alert in Cyprus. Anglo-Iranian executives sabotaged the plant before departing, leaving problems for Mehdi Bazargan, who had been appointed by Mossadegh to run the nationalised National Iranian Oil Company. The British media demanded that something be done about insolent natives, or next they would seize the Suez Canal. More damagingly, Britain called in all its diplomatic favours and arranged a crippling international embargo on purchase of Iranian oil. It took the issue to the Security Council, with a pompous motion decrying nationalisation of 'a great enterprise' by a government elected by 'the deluded Iranian people'. Mossadegh himself came to New York to face down his pinstriped, blustering accuser (Sir Gladwyn Jebb) with a reasoned call for the UN to respect the freedom and legitimate aspirations of its weaker, non-aligned members. India, China, Pakistan, Indonesia and others were persuaded, and Britain had to retreat. It turned to its network of pliant academics and paid spies, and equipped them with the money and the diplomatic cover to commence suborning officials, public figures (especially leading clerics) and newspaper editors in a secret campaign to overthrow the Prime Minister.

Democracy in the West proved a fickle friend to democracy in Iran: the British security services had been unable to enlist the CIA to restore British profits, but soon found a bait which quickly hooked the Eisenhower administration. Iran had a communist party – the Tudeh ('the masses'), which had fallen under Moscow's tutelage. MI6 played upon America's Cold War paranoia: 'Mossadegh is still incapable of resisting a coup by the *Tudeh* party, if it were backed by Soviet support,' wrote 'Monty' Woodhouse, the MI6 man in Tehran, to his CIA counterparts. His proposal for 'Operation Boot' met favour with Secretary of State John Foster Dulles and his brother, the new CIA boss, Allan Dulles. Renamed by humourless Americans 'Operation Ajax', it was implemented in August 1953 by Kermit Roosevelt. It took the form of massive bribes – to newspaper editors, MPs, clerics and army chiefs – and the fomenting of paid mob demonstrations against Mossadegh (whose belief in the rule of law was such that he naively ordered police not to interfere with the people's right to demonstrate against him). The cowardly Shah removed himself and his family from the country, leaving it to CIA-financed army generals to move in and arrest Mossadegh and his government. When it was safe, he returned to a country controlled by his corrupted generals, backed by the US and Britain, which justified their coup by declaring that Iran had not been ready for democracy. In fact, 'Operation Ajax' had denied

Iran any democratic future and implanted in the hearts and minds of its politically aware people an abiding hatred for 'the Great Satan' and contempt for Britain, 'the Little Satan', which rewarded the US by allowing its oil companies a 40 per cent shareholding in Anglo-Iranian. For all the self-congratulation (both Woodhouse and Roosevelt were permitted to write books glorifying their actions) history would demonstrate how counter-productive this 1953 putsch would prove.

The Shah at least spared Mossadegh's life: he was tried on trumped-up charges by a military court, jailed and then released under house arrest until his death in 1967. If ever Iran becomes a democracy it will be infused with the memory of Mossadegh – a giant who fell because he could not bring himself to order the arrest of his enemies. His personal life was spotless, his integrity (in a country riven with corruption) unchallenged, and his humanity legendary (he outlawed *bastinado,* improved prison conditions, and on the day of his arrest was arranging to set up a refuge for the mentally ill and homeless).[12] He was not in any sense a communist, nor a fellow traveller: like his Australian counterpart, Dr Evatt (the Labor Party leader who fought against banning the Communist Party), he simply thought the Tudeh party was entitled to compete in elections. But this was more than the US – at the time, it was at war with North Korea – was prepared to permit. By overthrowing Mossadegh, the CIA ended the prospects for humane liberal reforms. It also fashioned the chip that sits today on every Iranian shoulder, over the 'arrogance' of a country that could intervene to destroy another people's aspirations.

Ironically, the mullahs who now make much of this history overlook the fact that Mossadegh was a secularist who despised Khomeini, and that it was their clerical predecessors who accepted CIA money to preach against him, organise 'death to Mossadegh' demonstrations and spread rumours that he was really a Jew. Mossadegh's followers included the future Prime Ministers Bazargan, Bakhtiar and later Bani-Sadr, and the liberals who fought – and lost the fight – for a democratic constitution after the 1979 revolution. Mossadegh's photograph featured prominently on placards waved by student activists in the street demonstrations that followed the presidential election of June 2009. Many clerics at first supported his National Front, although some who took CIA money were already opposed to him because he had refused to introduce Sharia law. One mullah who refused to join Mossadegh's coalition was Ruhollah Khomeini, who despised liberal democrats for their secular beliefs, and was busy working out how to replace the rule of law by the rule of Shia jurists.

Khomeini had been born in 1902 and had become a highly visible theologian. He was radical in his argument that mullahs had a duty to participate in – really, to run – government, as proxies for the Twelfth Imam, providing succour (which greedy secular politicians would overlook) to the poor and oppressed. As a means of improving the lot of the downtrodden, his message appealed to radicals for whom Marxism was unrealistic, and it came laced with visceral attacks on America, the 'Great Satan' whose troops had been stationed in Iran under a 'status of forces' arrangement with the Shah which automatically exempted them from legal liabilities. Although he had not at this point called for the destruction of Israel, he certainly viewed that country (rather than Britain) as 'the Little Satan', hailing Palestinian fighters as godly and urging that religious taxes (*zakat*) should fund their anti-Zionist struggle.

After the 1953 coup, the Shah consolidated his power and built a strong centralised state, assisted by oil revenues that brought him – and a small upper class – unparalleled wealth. His arms deals were legendary (he bought more Chieftain tanks from Britain than its own army possessed) and he dreamed of building a nuclear bomb: it would secure Iran against any attack from its regional enemies (the Sunni states, rather than Israel) and it would make the country dominant in the Middle East. In 1972 he announced a programme for forty nuclear reactors, replete with the uranium enrichment and the facilities that would be necessary for building a bomb, and entrusted it to a new Atomic Energy Organization. In 1970 he had ratified the NPT and in 1973 signed a safeguards agreement that permitted inspections by the IAEA. Iran, he thought, could always pull out when it wanted to make nuclear weapons.[13] More alarmingly, he strengthened internal security by establishing the National Security and Intelligence Organisation, later to become infamous under the name SAVAK. His obeisance to the Western powers inflamed the intellectual opposition – the Liberation Movement, which had gingerly picked up Mossadegh's fallen banner. Mehdi Bazargan led this freedom movement at the head of a younger generation of Islamic militants. Their spiritual guide was a doctor of theology named Mahmud Taleqani, who had been Mossadegh's most devoted clerical supporter. In contrast to Khomeini's theory of government by Islamic jurists, Taleqani would interpret the Koran consistently with democratic socialist ideals.[14] But both these mullahs were in agreement about the corruption of the Shah's regime. Their denunciations of its close military connections with 'the Great Satan', and its secular reforms which ignored or denied Islamic teachings, inspired street demonstrations on 5 June 1963 which were brutally quelled by the army at the cost of hundreds of lives.[15]

Khomeini was briefly imprisoned and then expelled from the country. He made his base in the Shia seminary city of Najaf (in Iraq), where in 1970 he delivered a set of famous lectures on *velayat-e faqih* – the guardianship of the jurist as the basis for Islamic government. He utterly rejected democracy as well as communism and monarchy, and argued that all Islamic powers reposed in the Imams, as descendants of the Prophet. After the Twelfth Imam made himself invisible, all secular power arrangements were illegitimate until his reappearance. During this interregnum, the only rightful rulers were those men (never women) versed in Sharia jurisprudence – i.e. the mullahs. Thus political sovereignty under Islam resided in the *ulema*. Ordinary people were required by God to live in accordance with Sharia law as interpreted by clerics, who were expected to guide them until the Twelfth Imam eventually returned from his hidden existence.

Khomeini built *velayat-e faqih* upon 'Twelver Shia' beliefs: Mohammed designated his nephew, Ali, to be his successor and Ali, the first Imam, possessed the illumination and divine wisdom to lead his community on the path of Allah, a divinely inspired characteristic inherited by every succeeding Imam. They were, in effect, God's regents on earth, genetically endowed not only with wisdom but with the key to the correct interpretation of the Koran. Imamry was as hereditary as medieval kingship, and it was the third Imam, Ali's son Hussein, whose martyrdom at Karbala in 680 AD is commemorated in the month of Muharram, as Muslims cry and wail and lash themselves into a religious delirium in memory of a wronged man who went to his death in full knowledge that he would die by the sword, but in the hope nonetheless that through his sufferings his followers would be saved. The Imams continued until the eleventh, who did not appear to have a child – a fact which would have spelled the end of the line. But Shia mythology explains that the politics of the time (a wicked Caliph) made it expedient that the eleventh Imam should conceal his son, disclosing his existence only to a few aunts. With the help of Allah, the small boy (who was about five at the time, namely 874 AD) was made invisible – put in 'occulation', this mystical and inexplicable state – which lasted for a lifetime (the minor occulation) when he had four emissaries who carried his messages to the faithful, but then, since 940 AD (the major occulation) the faithful have had to make do with their own holy men, until the Twelfth Imam returns. De-occulation will be preceded by chaos and turmoil, rousing the Twelfth Imam (at least 1,200 years old, although occulation apparently involves some form of diapause because he is expected to appear in his prime). He will emerge from a cave or well or cellar (all places in the mythologies where his invisible self is said to dwell) whereupon he will smite the unjust, destroy the unbelievers, and usher in peace (since no one with contrary beliefs will be left alive). At this point the returned Imam will be hailed as the Mahdi – all wise, all just, and all merciless to those of other religions, or none.

We shall see that some – notably Mr Netanyahu – discern great danger in this messianic and millennialist belief, so fervently promoted by President Ahmadinejad. The second, de-occulated coming of the Mahdi will be triggered by great chaos, and they fear that an excessively devout Supreme Leader, imbued by the spirit of Hussein (who consciously led his men to martyrdom), might one day decide to drop a nuclear bomb on Israel in much the same spirit, to create that chaos. But the real problem for Shia theologians was what the faithful should do whilst waiting for the Hidden Imam to come out of hiding. How should they arrange the government in this period, when bereft of an immortal spiritual guide? The traditional solution was to leave government alone – since politics would inevitably be corrupt and demeaning without an Imam. Why not put up with it and keep out of it until the old Imam reappeared? Another possibility, canvassed by a few Shia theologians, not very successfully, at the turn of the nineteenth century, was just the opposite: the clergy should try its hand at government. Its hands might get dirty, but then government might get clean. Khomeini took this theory to its extreme: *velayat-e faqih* meant government had to become clean, because it would be conducted by the closest person to an Imam that the wisest clerics could find. To help them identify this person, Khomeini did not discourage his students from calling him 'Imam' – the first since 874 AD.[16]

Khomeini's theory was obviously attractive to many members of the *ulema*, because it offered them political as well as spiritual power, and was congenial to the mass of Shia believers who were used to looking to clerics for moral guidance. They were beguiled by Khomeini's teaching that Sharia law required particular care for the poor and oppressed – Islam, he insisted, not Marxism, would eliminate class differences and produce a just society no longer disfigured by the Shah's obscene luxury or his attachments to the Great and Little Satan. These beliefs spread beneath the surface, uncontrollably but unobtrusively, although some of their more outspoken exponents (like Khomeini's intellectual comrade Hussein-Ali Montazeri) served terms in the Shah's prisons. SAVAK's attention, once it had demolished the old communists in the Tudeh network, turned to these Khomeini-inspired clerics, and more particularly to the armed resistance groups that formed in the 1960s and commenced their guerrilla struggle with an attack on a police station in Siahkal in February 1971.

Most of these groups were Marxist-Leninist: the Fadaiyan ('self-sacrificers') Khalq Organization (FKO) carried out the Siahkal attack and many more in the course of the decade, splitting after the revolution into a majority faction (which looked to Moscow and classic Marxism–Leninism) and a minority faction, influenced by Maoist thought. They were determinedly atheist, although an incipient anti-clericalism was put to one side whilst fighting the Shah's police state alongside revolutionary clerics. In prison, it was easy to sink differences with Islamists, although some jailed clerics (Montazeri, for example) complained about having to sit on toilets recently vacated by Marxist unbelievers.[17] There were jokes about how mullahs farewelled Marxists at the gates of Evin prison with promises to put them back when the Shah was overthrown.

The joke became much less amusing when it became true, after the revolution. Houshang Asadi, a communist, was banged up by SAVAK in 1974, in a cell with one pious young cleric, Ali Khamenei. The two became the closest of friends, sharing books and cigarettes and differing only about attire in the showers (Khamenei kept his pants on, claiming it was a sin to allow others to glimpse his genitals). But under President Khamenei, nine years and a revolution later, Asadi was arrested and tortured with a ferocity that SAVAK could never muster: his feet were beaten raw, his teeth knocked out, he was hung upside down and forced to eat his own excrement. Along with thousands of other communist and Marxist believers, he was marked for death in the second wave of the 1988 massacres: it took a letter from his wife to his former cellmate to secure a presidential intervention that saved his life.[18]

These guerrilla movements which formed among youthful intellectuals in the aftermath of the unconscionable killings of the 5 June 1963 demonstrators were not original: they shared ideology and tactics with similar groups abroad – in Latin America in particular. But the heady fusion of Marx and Islam that came to attract so many dedicated young martyrs to the Mojahedin (as the MEK was known) was a distinctively Iranian development. It has been traced back to Bazargan's Liberation Movement, formed a decade after the fall of Mossadegh, infused with the teachings of two important intellectuals, Taleqani and Ali Shariati, who radically reinterpreted the sacred texts to argue that they stood for equality, socialism and scientific progress, and that they demanded armed struggle as an 'historic necessity' to achieve these ends. To a new generation of educated teenagers (the Shah had at least invested some oil wealth in universal education) this had an

obvious attraction: they could retain the passionate Shia herit-
age taught to them by their parents whilst embracing the class
struggle and fighting the Shah's repressive state. The founders of
the Mojahedin were students of engineering and law, who read
Che Guevara, Debray and Fanon and paid special attention to a
theoretician of the Algerian FLN who argued that 'Islam was a
revolutionary socialist democratic creed and that the only way to
fight imperialism was to resort to the armed struggle and appeal
to the religious instincts of the masses'.[19] With that grab-bag of
principles and an avowed aim 'to synthesise the religious values
of Islam with the scientific thought of Marxism' these new Shia
Marxists prepared for martyrdom. It came rather more quickly
than they had wished.

Sixty-nine students formed the first Mojahedin guerrilla detach-
ment, and were preparing to blow up a power station in order to
plunge the Shah's 1971 Persepolis celebrations into darkness (see
pages 31–2) when SAVAK struck. It arrested and tortured them and
had eleven shot by firing squad after secret trial before a military
tribunal, and the rest jailed. Massoud Rajavi, a politics student
from Tehran University who later became the charismatic leader
of the organisation, survived with a prison sentence. The defiant rhetoric of the eleven executed leaders, as they courageously
condemned the Shah at their closed court hearings, received a
wide samizdat circulation. However jejune these Mojahedin theories now sound, they were enthusiastically discussed by students
at universities and high schools, especially in the years following
the 1979 revolution. Most of the Mojahedin massacred in 1988
were arrested merely for distributing or possessing this literature
after their organisation was banned in mid-1981.

In the intellectual ferment of the years just before and after
the revolution, there were many shifts in ideological positions.
Although a few radical clerics encouraged the Mojahedin, the
conservative *ulema* was overwhelmingly hostile to left-wing
reinterpretations of Islamic texts. Khomeini himself, whilst
welcoming allies against the Shah, said that he had 'smelled the
distinct aroma of anti-clericalism' after meetings with Rajavi, who
in turn had found the Imam highly reactionary. The Mojahedin
suffered its own ideological divisions as some adherents thought

that its Marxism made more sense than its Islamic fervour so they stopped praying and started reading the thoughts of Chairman Mao and further transmogrified after the revolution either into the Peykar Organisation ('the combat organisation for the emancipation of the working class') or the more orthodox Marxist Rah-e Kargar ('the worker's path'). These were some of the 'leftist' groups whose members, together with Houshang Asadi's communist comrades from the Tudeh Party, were to become victims of the second wave of the 1988 prison killings.

The 1970s was the decade of struggle between SAVAK and the militants. The Shah built new maximum-security prisons on the American model, most notoriously Evin on the outskirts of Tehran and Gohardasht some thirty miles distant. It was now torture time: random beatings were replaced by more scientific methods taught by the CIA or copied from General Pinochet, including solitary confinement, sleep deprivation, electric shocks, mock execution and even an early form of water boarding.[20] The old-fashioned *bastinado*, however, remained the interrogators' favourite: all it required was that victims be tied to a metal bed or grille, and beaten on the soles of the feet with an electric cable. The technique had the great advantage of causing excruciating pain that was only exceptionally lethal: the highly sensitive nerve endings at the soles of the feet transmitted the shock of the beating through the whole nervous system. SAVAK used *bastinado* on newly captured guerrillas to extract information about accomplices and safe houses, although they did not use torture on peaceful opponents of the regime – a practice which only became commonplace in prisons after the overthrow of the Shah. Another SAVAK technique was the 'public recantation', familiar from Stalin's show trials but capable of a new dimension with a television audience. This was to become a favourite of the Khomeini regime: its insistence that prisoners condemn their erstwhile comrades on prime-time television would manifest the apparent sincerity of their recantations and it also served to promote their subsequent psychological breakdown.

The last days of the Shah began, in 1978, when his tame press vilified Khomeini: street protests immediately elevated the absent cleric into the incarnation of resistance and of hope. The Shah's imperial guards massacred sixty-two protestors on 'Black Friday' in September – an atrocity which served to unite all factions and classes against him, notwithstanding their disparate objectives. Even his US backers, who had become sensitive to human rights violations during the Carter presidency, could not condone this. When in December the Shah in desperation turned to an old Mossadegh loyalist, Shapour Bakhtiar, as his Prime Minister, it was too late: by now the martial law curfew was defied every night by a chorus of *Allahu Akbar* from the Tehran rooftops. The army was divided and the massive street demonstrations raised the chant 'Death to the Shah', increasingly followed by 'Long live Khomeini'. The super-rich royal hangers-on had by now left with as much of their wealth as they could transfer to foreign banks. Bakhtiar ruled for thirty-seven days during which he disbanded the political police and called for elections. As in 1953, the cowardly Shah fled the country and waited for the US to act, but this time there was no Kermit Roosevelt to engineer his return. Instead, on 1 February 1979, hailed on the Tehran streets by millions as if he were the de-occulting Twelfth Imam, it was Khomeini who returned, with a steely determination to introduce Islamic theocracy. As he told the nation shortly after his arrival, this was 'not the republic of Iran, not the democratic republic of Iran, and not the democratic Islamic republic'. Islam was not to be demeaned by the Western notion of democracy. Henceforth, it was simply 'the Islamic Republic of Iran'.[21]

It took eighteen months for Khomeini and his 'gang of four' mullahs – Khamenei, Montazeri, Akbar Rafsanjani and Mohammad Beheshti – to achieve this goal by thwarting and outmanoeuvring all their opponents. They were opposed by a significant conservative faction, which held to traditional Shia teachings about the separation of church and state, but the intoxication of political power soon overcame most doubters among the *ulema*. The liberals, as in so many other revolutions, served as 'useful idiots': caretakers who could not, in the end, take care of themselves, or of the democratic ideals that they forbore to impose by force. Bakhtiar went into hiding and was replaced by a 'provisional Prime Minister' – another Mossadegh veteran, the 75-year-old Bazargan, in 1953 the supremo of Iran's briefly nationalised oil. He did his best to rein in the revenge kill-ings – virtual lynchings – of hated SAVAK officials, police chiefs and generals identified with the Shah's repression, but Khomeini denounced his proposal for open trials and defence lawyers as a reflection of 'the western sickness among us'.[22]

The bloody die of Islamic justice was cast on 15 February 1979, just four days after the end of the Shah, when three of his senior army officers were that morning dragged to a school where Khomeini had set up house, and put before a secret 'revolution-ary tribunal'. Denied lawyers, or any chance to present a defence, the day ended with their conviction for the previously unheard-of crime of 'corruption on earth'. Their appeal took the form of a clerk walking across to Khomeini's room and giving it to the leader of the revolution: he turned it down and the defendants were executed at 11 p.m. It was an ominous beginning, a portent of how the rule of law would dwindle to a rule of vengeance, barbarically afflicted on those whose politics or religion or both angered mullahs without mercy.

Iran had no recent history of primitive law enforcement: Reza Shah's greatest achievement, dating from 1925, had been to reform and civilise the penal code, enforced by a professional and remarkably independent judiciary which replaced religious judges and so curtailed the influence of the *ulema*. Mossadegh had followed by abolishing military courts and secret tribunals, and by 1978 the courts had provided some minimal protection against arbitrary arrest by SAVAK. But no longer: by the end of 1979 Khomeini had appointed Beheshti (a high school teacher of Sharia) as President of the Supreme Court, and then proceeded to remove all women from the bench (females were unfit to exer-cise power and could not be trusted whilst menstruating) as well as most of the professionals. Those who were not purged were demoted to legal advisers. Their place was taken by mullahs, fresh from the seminaries, without judicial or even forensic experience. 'It was a common sight to see a junior Islamic seminarian whose stock of legal and theological knowledge consisted of rudiments of Arabic grammar and some elementary lessons in theology' enforcing a new set of Islamic laws against sin (adultery, alcohol consumption, homosexuality), against *mohareb* (waging war on

God), corruption on earth and so on, with a new set of medieval punishments – stoning to death, crucifixion, amputation of limbs. 'Extraordinary courts', which worked hand in glove with revolutionary prosecutors, reported directly to Khomeini and continued to execute officials of the Shah, and soon other enemies of the state. In 1983 they were formally titled 'Islamic Revolution Courts', by which time their summary process was being used to despatch former allies of the Islamists to the gallows, or to long terms of imprisonment. Once *velayat-e faqih* became the state religion, a 'special court for clerics' was established to defrock and jail dissenting clergy.[23]

Khomeini was everywhere in charge – his authority was recognised by the Revolutionary Council and the revolutionary committees and he was the idol of the masses; by the end of 1979, his Islamic Republican Party had won most of the seats in the Majlis elections. A constitution drafted by the liberal politicians was referred by Khomeini to the 'Assembly of Experts', which redrafted it to make him Supreme Leader, an authority superior to both the elected President and the Prime Minister of the majority party. His liberal and Marxist opponents were blindsided when some of his student supporters, reflecting the popular fury when the Carter administration allowed the Shah to enter America for cancer treatment, invaded the US embassy and held its male diplomats as hostages: in this 'nest of spies' they found documents incriminating Bazargan by association, and his provisional prime ministership came to an early end. The hostage-taking served as a useful distraction from the challenges to the Islamists which were being mounted by their erstwhile allies, the liberals and the leftists. There is little doubt that Khomeini orchestrated the embassy invasion: he called for demonstrations outside the compound to protest against a US Senate resolution which had condemned the Revolutionary Tribunal executions, and to demand that America return the Shah for similar Islamic punishment.

It was the revolution's first major breach of international law. Nothing is more fundamental to relations between states than the inviolability of their embassies and ambassadors, a rule that can be traced back to the immunity of heralds on ancient battlefields. There is an almost universal adherence to the 1961 Vienna

Convention on Diplomatic Relations, because (as the ICJ put it, when condemning the Tehran hostage-taking) diplomacy remains 'of cardinal importance for the maintenance of good relations between states in the interdependent world of today'.[24] But this first international outrage brought the new regime national kudos and world-wide acclaim from anti-American countries, and absolutely no retaliation. American hysteria helped: the 'yellow ribbon' campaign to free the fifty-two diplomats influenced the result of the 1980 presidential election, which Jimmy Carter (seen as weak and unlucky when a desert sandstorm aborted a US rescue mission) lost to Ronald Reagan. Khomeini was able to play the providential saint, claiming that God was on his side: Allah had whipped up the sandstorm to show his approval of the revolution. Iranian television gloated, showing the eight dead American soldiers in obscene close-up, and mass chants of 'death to America' resounded throughout Iran. The release of the hostages, in time for Reagan's inauguration, was a satisfying symbol of Khomeini's contempt for liberals in America (and anywhere else). He had got away with his first international crime, and there would be many more to come.

In January 1980 Khomeini suffered a temporary setback in the presidential elections: although he used his position as Supreme Leader to veto the candidature of Massoud Rajavi, the MEK leader who had helped to topple the Shah but who had vocally opposed the redrafted constitution and its incorporation of *velayat-e faqih*, the Supreme Leader had to suffer the election of Abolhassan Bani-Sadr, another ex-Mossadegh democrat. He had only been allowed to stand – and had only won – because he had been one of Khomeini's advisers during his Paris exile. 'I ask everyone to support him as long as he acts according to the principles of Islam' was the Supreme Leader's lukewarm welcome to the nation's first elected President. Bani-Sadr's initial mistake was to go along with his clerical opponents' 'cultural revolution', launched in April 1980, which marked the beginning of the end of political pluralism: universities were closed, 'un-Islamic' professors sacked, and clerically organised vigilante thugs (forerunners of the Basij militias) organised attacks on the MEK and leftist groups.[25]

The Islamic Republic's defeat of its internal opposition by
June 1981 can be briefly traced. President Bani-Sadr began
well, showing genuine leadership in the face of a decision by
Saddam Hussein, the Sunni Arab ruler of Iraq, to declare war on
his despised Persian neighbour. But the Islamists prevented the
President from developing a power base in the army and built
up their own dedicated armed force, the Revolutionary Guards.
They replaced the old secular judicial system with Sharia judges,
led by the revolutionary radicals Beheshti and then Mousavi
Ardebili. Women were sacked and attacked for not wearing
veils, monarchists were executed and drug dealers lynched, and
the stoning of adulterers began with the revolution's new judges
throwing the first stones.[26] Backed by a propagandist media and
patrolling Revolutionary Guards, Khomeini launched a verbal
attack on the MEK ('syncretic mixes of Marxism and Islam') and
threatened those intellectuals who did not sever all ties with the
West. Bani-Sadr was isolated, and eventually his only supporters with any armed clout were the MEK, whose ranks had
swelled with recruits from schools and universities in the two
years since the revolution. They clashed repeatedly with the
Revolutionary Guards, and came out *en masse* for the elected
President in a demonstration on 20 June 1981: a hundred of them
were killed. Khomeini then deposed Bani-Sadr, who from his
hiding place among the Mojahedin called for a mass uprising. It
did not happen, so Bani-Sadr and Rajavi together commandeered
an air force plane and were flown to Paris. On 28 June 1981
a massive bomb exploded at the headquarters of Khomeini's
Islamic party in Tehran, killing Beheshti (one of the Ayatollah's
'gang of four' and Supreme Court President) and seventy other
revolutionary leaders. The Republic's 'war on terror' – especially
on the Mojahedin – then began in earnest.

My hands are clean? Ayatollah Ruhollah Khomeini, Supreme Leader, 1979–89.

CHAPTER 2

REVOLUTIONARY JUSTICE

The bomb that blasted the Islamic party headquarters a week after the big MEK demonstration on 20 June 1981 set off a 'reign of terror' in which, over the next few years of internecine urban violence, several thousand of the Islamic regime's youthful opponents, many of them high school or university students, would be gunned down, or executed after hasty trials, whilst MEK terrorist reprisals would take their toll of Islamic judges, officials and Revolutionary Guards. (In this period it became a terrorist – or 'armed guerrilla' – organisation, although it gave up violence in 2002 and was finally taken off the US terrorist list by Hillary Clinton in September 2012.) Responsibility for the 28 June bombing is still uncertain: Khomeini blamed the Mojahedin, who were not averse to the accusation (describing the bombing as a 'natural and necessary reaction to the regime's atrocities') although the first suspects were old SAVAK royalists and, years later, agents from Iraq.[27] The war against Iraq continued and created an atmosphere in which the regime could prosecute its opponents. From this point – June 1981 – the tensions between the forces that had overthrown the Shah emerged with bloodthirsty intensity. Khomeini beat his breast and blamed himself for tolerating the Mojahedin for two-and-a-half years, during which they had spread their propaganda so effectively in the schools and universities: he called upon the moderates who had supported Bazargan to separate themselves from these Muslim deviationists whom he called 'hypocrites' (*monafeqin* – this label stuck) because they did not really believe in God: 'they consider the afterlife to be here in this world'.[28] The label 'hypocrites' was not merely an insult, but a Koranic term of deep and ominous significance: an entire chapter of the holy book (the 63rd) was devoted to exposing their perfidy, and centuries-old principles of Islamic jurisprudence established that they were liable to earthly punishment as well as divine retribution. He appealed to the nation to support his policy of mass arrests, execution and summary justice dispensed in the streets by Revolutionary Guards: 'He who goes into streets armed and threatens people does not even have to kill anyone. Islam has ordained his fate. It has specified the punishment of those who scare believers and you surely know what it is.'[29]

The Supreme Leader shed tears at the memory of his close associate Ayatollah Beheshti, the most notable casualty of the 28 June bombing (which had also killed Montazeri's son), and promulgated Beheshti's theory that it was impossible to co-exist with 'warriors against God' (*mohareb*), a category which included all Marxist groups, Kurds and 'hypocrites', i.e. 'the so-called leftist Muslims or pseudo-Muslims with leftist tendencies who pray or fast and are regarded by their families as Muslims but who are hypocrites waging war against true believers and are no different from the Marxists'. At this point, the regime had not moved formally against the Marxist groups that still supported it – Tudeh and the FKO (Majority) – but they had been warned. As for the liberals who once supported Mossadegh, they were infidels because of their loose morality, their contacts with the West, their opposition to the Islamisation of criminal and other laws and their social reform programmes.[30]

The Friday sermons in this period set the ideological scene for the regime's approach to the punishment of political and religious deviation. Rafsanjani, who was Speaker of Parliament, in his first sermon in October 1981 made a brutal call to exterminate the hypocritical warriors against God: 'They must be killed, hanged, have their hands and feet cut off and be segregated from society.' It fell to the new religious judges to adopt one of these courses laid down by verse 5:33 of the Koran, because although 5:34 recognised that no punishment was due to those who repented, the Mojahedin had proved themselves to be incapable of reform after two-and-a-half years of governmental effort. Their newspapers also achieved a high circulation, especially among schoolchildren. 'Now they have turned into champions of human rights and accuse us of aggression for rightfully executing them!' Rafsanjani fumed. 'As decreed by the Koran we have decided to eradicate the armed hypocrites.'

A few weeks after Rafsanjani urged death sentences on the unfaithful, the religious judge who headed the Islamic Revolutionary Tribunals, Ayatollah Mohammadi Gilani, warned of a strict interpretation of the Sharia for religious rebellion. Death was the punishment for male apostates (i.e. those born into a family of practising Muslims who renounced Islam) and their repentance could not be accepted. But female Muslims and 'innate' apostates (i.e. those not born into a Muslim family) were not to be sentenced to death: their 'repentance' could be accepted if, after torture, they agreed to pray. Again, this was drawn not from the Koran itself, which specifies no earthly punishment for apostates, but from conservative Shia jurisprudence that dated back to the tenth and eleventh centuries.[31] As for torture, Ayatollah Mohammadi Gilani assured the nation that religious punishment which is essentially torture is not torture because it is Islamic, explaining that at Evin prison there were no breaches of Islamic rules: the floggings by cable on the soles of the feet were *tazir* (discretionary punishments permissible under Islamic jurisprudence). Such treatment was mercilessly applied to most of those arrested during the years following 1981. (As we shall see, even harsher beatings were meted out to left-wing 'innate apostates' to force them to pray during the second wave of prison executions in 1988.)

The authorities – the Ministry of Intelligence (which kept tabs on subversion) and the revolution's prosecutors – repeatedly asserted 'we have no political prisoners in our courts. These are terrorists, conspirators, traitors and savages who will be prosecuted in an Islamic court, dealt with by Islamic laws, and punished accordingly.'[32] Punishment was dispensed at secret hearings in prisons by the revolutionary courts, headed by a religious judge appointed by Khomeini himself – in Tehran, this was Jafar Nayyeri. The secular judiciary had been sacked (or had fled) shortly after the revolution and the Bar Association (an oasis of independence) had been disbanded because the concept of a defence attorney had been described by the Supreme Leader as a 'western absurdity'.[33] The Justice Ministry insisted upon seminary training in Sharia for all magistrates.

In the initial shakedown period, from February 1979 to June

1981, death sentences were regularly imposed on drug dealers, homosexuals, prostitutes, SAVAK members and other officials of the Shah, who were condemned after short and usually secret hearings for 'sowing corruption on earth'. After the events of June 1981 – i.e. the Mojahedin demonstrations and the Islamic HQ bombing – several thousand 'hypocrites' were arrested and held in the prisons in which some had recently been incarcerated under the Shah. Those whom the prosecutors implicated directly in armed terrorist activities were hanged after a short trial, whilst 'sympathisers' (e.g. protestors or pamphlet distributors) were sentenced to jail terms of up to ten years. They were regularly subjected to *bastinado* before their interrogation; their trials were brief and at Evin they were presided over by Nayyeri, whom they were to recognise again when he chaired their 'Death Committee' proceedings in 1988.[34]

June 1981 marked the beginning of a period of revolutionary terror: its chief architect, Tehran prosecutor Asadollah Lajevardi, announced on 23 June (just two days after the demonstration) that 400 had been arrested and twenty-five already executed. Two days later Ali Khamenei (a previously undistinguished cleric whose membership of the 'gang of four' Khomeini lieutenants had procured his elevation to the Supreme Defence Council) praised the people for 'executing their enemies' so quickly. After the bombing of 28 June and over the following nine months many 'counter-revolutionaries' were executed – 250 MEK members in July 1981 alone.[35] These executions fed a vicious cycle: MEK terrorist attacks cost hundreds of lives, mostly of pro-government clerics and officials.

By the end of 1981, Ali Khamenei had been elected as President. Into Beheshdi's power sandals stepped a hitherto obscure editor of a government-supporting newspaper, one Mir Hossein Mousavi. His unflinching support for the revolution earned him the post of Prime Minister, from which he fulminated against 'the Great Satan' ('Relations between America and Iran are like those between a wolf and a sheep') and, ironically, ordered the revival of the Shah's nuclear programme, which the revolution had disrupted and which Bazargan had then cancelled. For Mousavi, still Prime Minister during the 1988 massacres and who twenty years later stepped forward to lead the Green Movement, development of a nuclear weapon capacity always made strategic sense.[36]

In Paris, meanwhile, Rajavi and Bani-Sadr set up an opposition council – the National Council of Resistance of Iran – which operated as a propaganda centre, denouncing the 'medieval' regime and promising democratic freedoms of a kind that had never before been proposed by a semi-Marxist movement (or by the MEK). This helped to gather support from many socialist groups in Europe and, more dangerously, from Iraq. Saddam Hussein came to sponsor their military operations and allowed them to operate a radio station near the front lines of Iraq's ebbing and flowing war with Iran. This alignment was a Faustian bargain (Bani-Sadr wisely pulled out) which gained the Mojahedin short-term advantage, but lost – possibly forever – their chance of winning mass support within Iran, where most families had men fighting in the patriotic battle against Saddam. Mojahedin guerrilla units in Tehran and other cities were frequently betrayed, most disastrously when Rajavi's first wife and his second-in-command were killed in a shoot-out at a safe house that turned unsafe: their dead bodies were laid out in Evin prison for prime-time television with the brutal Lajevardi cuddling Rajavi's baby son for the cameras.[37]

The regime was successful in inducing repentance from some Mojahedin prisoners, especially among youngsters faced with the alternative of execution or the spur of repeated *bastinado*. When the flurry of death sentences after the frenzy following 28 June 1981 abated, a new policy was duly promulgated by the revolutionary prosecutor. He announced that interrogations of MEK prisoners had produced a 'miracle of the revolution', namely a widespread willingness to renounce Rajavi and welcome repentance. Henceforth, any judge convinced that a former armed revolutionary was sincerely penitent would grant a pardon. Those at liberty should therefore take the opportunity to turn themselves in and confess, because even those involved in military operations could now expect a reduced sentence.[38] This new penal policy had a less happy converse, however. Although opposition to Khomeini was capable of public expiation, those who completed their sentence would no longer be released unless they were expressly repentant. By 1988, many prison wards were full of *mellikesh* – those who

had served their sentences but had refused to recant and apolo-
gise for what was, in effect, a thought crime. Once again, the rule
of law had been stood on its head: finite sentence had no meaning
for political prisoners, who were subject to indefinite detention at
the discretion of the government.

The regime also became attracted to televised confessions,
which helped to demoralise the opposition and rally its own
supporters. (The technique was continued in the televised show
trials of alleged plotters against the regime after the June 2009
protests.) They became all the rage after May Day 1983, when two
Tudeh stalwarts were featured confessing to 'horrendous crimes'.
This was the point at which Khomeini turned on the Communist
Party and some of its Marxist-Leninist offshoots like the FKO
(Majority) for having advocated a truce in the war with Soviet-
backed Iraq. This served them right, the Mojahedin announced,
because the communists had 'opportunistically supported' – even
spied for – the Ayatollah's medieval bloodthirsty dictatorship.[39]
This ideological spat did not help relations between the groups
in prison, and the Mojahedin had to be separated from the
Marxists. The latter were more readily broken, and in 1983–4
much of Iranian reality television comprised confessions from
penitent ex-communists filmed in prison. Not that repentance
meant release: of the seventeen top Tudeh leaders who were
arrested and appeared in a televised mass apology in 1983, nine
were still available for execution in the second wave of the 1988
blood-bath.

The regime's true rationale for its war on ideological enemies
began to become clear in the Friday sermons of Speaker Rafsanjani.
'Today, a person who disobeys the government is the same as
a person who disobeys God and his messenger,'[40] he explained.
The statement amplified the Supreme Leader's proclamation that
'there is always a war between Islam and non-Islam'.[41] It was,
for Iran's theocracy, a war not only against the satanic West and
the godless Soviets, but against any perspective on the world that
opposed its own religious viewpoint. The war against the MEK
was therefore waged on grounds that were religious in principle,
if political in result. The group was blasphemous first, and seditious consequentially: its members' basic crime was to be hostile

unbelievers – 'moharebs', i.e. warriors against God. The point was crystallised by the Minister of Intelligence, in an important announcement which explained why the communist groups (which had previously supported the state and opposed the Mojahedin) were just as evil: both Marxist-Leninist and Rajavi's brand of class-based Islam 'confronted the political ideology of the state, denying Islam's pure (original) teachings and espousing an impure version of Islam ... encouraging the society to seek the improvement of their standard of living and welfare, as opposed to virtue and self-sacrifice for religious ideas'.[42]

After the initial surge of executions of Mojahedin prisoners in late 1981, there was internal dissention over sentencing policy. Montazeri, the most accomplished jurist among the 'gang of four', and by now nominated as Khomeini's successor, revealed characteristics that were soon to put him at odds with Khomeini's other acolytes: he gradually became a man of principle, capable of compassion. He designed an 'early release scheme' for those prisoners who had repented. He was opposed by hardliners like the Chief Prosecutor, Lajevardi, who doubted whether any repentance by MEK members or Marxists would ever be genuine. Lajevardi denounced pardons and oxymoronically extolled death sentences: 'we execute because we care for humanity'.[43]

Prison conditions in Iran in the 1980s were cruel, and discipline was much more severe than in SAVAK times. Over-crowding was extreme, certainly after all the MEK arrests in late 1981 and in the years following May 1983 when the arrests extended to communist groups, including those who had previously supported the Islamic Republic, such as Tudeh and the FKO (Majority). The prison guards were not the brightest (the best were needed at the front) and they brutally applied bastinado, which qualified as tazir – a discretionary religious punishment sanctioned by Islamic legal tradition, and used for those reluctant to pray. It was, in international law, torture, and was also applied in order to induce confessions prior to trials, which were delayed until any useful information had been beaten out of the defendant or, in cases where defendants had no, or no further, information to give, until they made an ideological confession (e.g. to 'eclecticism' – the doctrinal offence that Khomeini had detected in the MEK). Lajevardi instituted a regime at Tehran's Evin prison that was maintained throughout the 1980s and copied in other prisons. Inmates were blindfolded whenever they left their dormitories (if in a group, usually as a conga-line with hands on each other's shoulders). There were loudspeakers in all these wards for announcements and government propaganda, and prisoners had access to state radio and television (especially when confessions were playing) and to the pro-government newspapers. This was for 're-education' purposes.

Conditions in some prisons improved markedly after 1985, when Ayatollah Montazeri was put in control of penal policy. His officials permitted an increase in visits from relatives and ordered relaxation in some of the rules. In this period, the 'mini-groups' (as the leftist organisations were dismissively called by government officials) were permitted to live in separate cell blocks and to organise (on democratic lines) by electing representatives who would negotiate with prison administrators. Although maximum-security restrictions were in force, they did not prevent 'mini-group' members from maintaining solidarity or from contacting other wards by tapping messages in Morse code. The regime's prisons became a hypertensive microcosm of the political turmoil outside in the cities and in the war zones.

The war between Iraq and Iran had turned into the most brutal, pointless and drawn out of conflicts. Saddam began it, with an opportunistic land-grab in September 1980, but he had ample provocation – Iran was scheming to export its revolution to Iraq's Shi-ite community, which it would encourage to rise against the secular and Sunni-dominated Ba'athists. Iran was behind an assassination attempt on Saddam's deputy, Tariq Aziz – a Christian (at least with a capital C) who survived, eventually to be sentenced to death by his own people in 2010. The war went well for Iraq at first, but the smaller country (17 million people) later faced forces that were superior in sheer weight of numbers (Iran had then a population of 45 million). There was also a lack of fervour for Ba'athism, whilst for Iranians, their revolution was at stake as well as their religion, and they fought with the belief that death mid-jihad was a fast track to paradise. With an almost obscene disregard for young lives, Iran purchased half a million tiny plastic keys from Taiwan and hung them around the necks of its teenage soldiers, brainwashed to believe that if they were killed in battle, the keys would open the doors of heaven. 'They chant "Allahu Akbar" and keep coming. We keep shooting,' said an Iraqi officer. It was trench warfare of the like that had not been seen since the Somme – landscaped eventually with hundreds of thousands of dead bodies. 'It's a pity they both can't lose' was Kissinger's sardonic comment, but of course, both did – thanks to the West, which made sure that Saddam was not defeated by supplying arms and turning a blind eye to his outrageous use of poison gas. US policy, articulated at the time by Donald Rumsfeld, was simply to prevent an Iranian victory and to enhance trade and oil: he was at an arms bazaar in Baghdad soon after the slaughter of 7,000 Kurds by 'Chemical Ali' and his poison gas and there had been no outcry when scud missiles started to land on civilian homes in Tehran. To break out of this isolation, Khomeini was forced to ally with Assad Snr in Syria (an alliance which today survives with his equally brutal son) and to do the dirty 'Iran–Contra' deal, whereby the Reagan administration secretly bought weapons through Israeli arms dealers to sell on to Iran, which paid money that Colonel Oliver North distributed to the Contras in Nicaragua. It was a deal that damaged everyone connected with it (excluding, of course, the arms dealers) and its exposure forced the US to get back behind Saddam.

By 1988, this eight-year war had cost over 500,000 Iranian lives and a million injuries. Both sides ached for the bomb. 'These are savages!' Tariq Aziz expostulated. 'Of course we use chemical weapons. We would use nuclear weapons if we had them.' In Iran, the leaders of the Revolutionary Guards wrote to Khomeini opposing surrender, but insisting that they needed 'a substantial number of laser and nuclear weapons' to ensure victory. But for Iran, the war has never ended: most families lost a young soldier, if not two or three, and every Friday the mothers still mourn and adorn the cemeteries with fresh flowers for the martyrs of the revolution. For the revolution's clerics and the Revolutionary Guards, this is the sentimentality that maintains them in power – a culture of martyrdom among people whose loved ones died for a cause. That cause was a fight to the death against a dictator who was backed by the US with all the arrogance of Kermit Roosevelt. The conscripted war generation of the 1980s, which now leads the Revolutionary Guards and the Basij militias, cannot forget the fears of that time, or the smell of the poison gas. The use of chemical weapons by Iraq was a breach of IHL, and Iran volubly protested to the UN about it throughout 1988. Its leaders became familiar in this period with international law. They were well aware that it regarded the massacre of helpless prisoners as among the most heinous of crimes against humanity.

There were, by 1988, many thousands of political prisoners in twenty Iranian jails: they were 'prisoners of war' in the sense that they had been sentenced as fifth-columnists, sympathisers with the MEK (who were fighting alongside Saddam) or with Marxism, the godless enemy of God. As we have seen, the regime had effectively imposed a form of 'preventive detention' on political prisoners, whose actual length of sentence became meaningless: their release back into society would depend not upon the expiry date of their sentence but upon their affirmation of faith in both Islam and the Islamic Republic. This *mellikesh* category were in most large prisons segregated from the dormitories separately assigned (at their own insistence) to the Mojahedin and to the other leftist groups, although some wards (especially of women prisoners) were mixed. The classification had been confirmed in late 1987, when questionnaires were circulated to prisoners by intelligence officials, who used the information, together with prison interviews, to establish each prisoner's current political affiliation. This Ministry of Intelligence surveillance and classification of MEK and Marxist prisoners identified as a potential threat to the regime was undoubtedly an ongoing classification exercise related to their eventual disposal, whether by release or continued incarceration or by some form of 'final solution'. In 1988, the government was focused on fighting the war with Iraq, which had begun to go badly. Scud missiles were falling on Tehran and Qom, and popular support for the war effort had begun to ebb; there were demonstrations in favour of 'forgiving' Saddam Hussein and the numbers volunteering for the front fell alarmingly.[44] For the first time, public figures were permitted to appear on television to urge the acceptance of a truce on terms that had been suggested in August 1987 by the UN Security Council in Resolution 598. In March 1988, Mousavi's Budget and Planning Ministry concluded that severe cuts in public expenditure would be required were the war to continue.[45] The families who visited prisoners passed on reports that the regime was in difficulty, a fact that could be divined even from government-censored television and newspapers. Political prisoners were cheered by the news, not realising that if the war ended on unfavourable terms there might well be a reckoning with those among them who were perceived as traitors. They did not know that behind the scenes, Montazeri was losing power to the hardliners, a development that could be dangerous to them: they could be sacrificed in a factional struggle to succeed the Supreme Leader, who was stricken by cancer. Members of his inner circle, most notably Rafsanjani and Ali Khamenei, did not want the more merciful Montazeri to inherit virtually absolute power.

Meanwhile, the regime had been plotting to rid itself of troublesome dissidents who had fled abroad, mainly to Paris in the wake of Bani-Sadr and Rajavi. Diplomatic overtures to the French to banish them initially failed. So its embassy in Paris fell back on plotting individual assassinations and was behind a series of explosions which rocked Paris in 1986. The French reacted with the kind of diplomatic cowardice that rewards state terrorism: they merely declared one guilty Iranian official 'persona non grata'. After the usual exchange of polite insults, France decided that there would be commercial advantages from friendship with Iran, and so Rajavi and his MEK adherents were expelled from Paris. They relocated to Iraq, at Camp Ashraf, a place Saddam allowed them to occupy near the Iranian border, formed an expatriate fighting force and stepped up their radio propaganda. By 1988 almost 10,000 MEK members were in arms against Khomeini. The only time that Rafsanjani ordered his Revolutionary Guard to cross into Iraqi territory was to destroy their radio installations.

Montazeri continued to be referred to as Khomeini's appointed successor, although in this period he was having his role as conscience of the revolution undermined to an extent that would render him powerless to stop the prison massacres later in 1988. His emphasis on repentance had been criticised by Lajevardi, who took the view that a hypocrite's remorse was worthless, whilst other hardliners warned that released prisoners might go over to the enemy and would certainly require supervision by Revolutionary Guards at a time when all loyal men of fighting age were required at the front line. They encouraged Khomeini to warn Montazeri that 'inappropriate freedom, conferred on a few hundred hypocrites by a soft-headed and trusting group, has resulted in an increase in the number of explosions from terrorist attacks and robberies'.[46] He was criticised by the up-and-coming Ali Khamenei, a theologian of much less renown, as 'a poor judge of character' – i.e. as someone who could show mercy. His faction had also made a dangerous enemy in Rafsanjani. If he continued to protect political prisoners, the Supreme Leader might not permit him to inherit the Supreme Leadership.

At this time, there was a much clearer focus on apostasy as a crime against the regime. Since 1981, suspects had been arrested for involvement in one or other of the 'mini-groups' banned by reference to its political ideology. Now, senior clerics across the country began to demand the arrests of *moharebs* (warriors against God) – in effect, any alleged unbeliever whose disbelief the authorities chose to perceive as an outward sign of sedition. As the revolutionary prosecutor of Shiraz, Ayatollah Eslami, put it, 'those who badly veil themselves, even unconsciously, are following the path of anti-revolutionists and monarchists ... they are disrespecting the blood of the martyrs and will be dealt with radically, these boys and girls, and God's sentence will be enforced against them as corrupters and *moharebs*'.[47] Arrests of godless Marxists had brought a new influx of 'political' detainees into the prisons who were not easily assimilated with the old-timers and required further classification. This explains why the 1987–8 interrogations and questionnaires directed to imprisoned leftists probed their religious views and their attitude to *velayat-e faqih*, the Shia theory of Islamic government. For Mojahedin prisoners whose former comrades were encamped in arms on the Iraqi border, questions were directed to whether they would denounce Rajavi and fight for their country, or whether they remained steadfast in their support of the MEK.

The prison transfers and the classification procedures in late 1987 and early 1988 made the 'final solution' much easier to carry out. Survivors firmly believe they were a planned prelude to the massacres. Iraj Mesdaghi in his memoirs[48] says that Davoud Lashkari assigned colours – white to those who were broken and penitent, yellow to those no longer politically active and red to enemies of the regime. Even the latter category could be useful to the regime as guinea pigs, when Iran itself was experimenting with poison gas. An ex-FKO (Majority) member being held in ward 13 of Gohardasht prison in June 1988 recalls the appearance of a strange new group of guards. They sealed the doors, turned on the overhead fans and circulated a gas which caused severe nausea and semi-asphyxiation. It was much worse than tear gas, and when the vapour escaped underneath the doors it made the guards sick as well. No one died and the effects soon wore off, but there can be no doubt that Iran would have used poison gas on the battlefield had it been available. Likewise, nuclear weapons.

Survivors, especially those from Evin or its overflow prison Gohardasht, have described the prison atmosphere and conditions in this period before the massacres: they were aware of Montazeri's beneficent influence, and how it came to wane, and how the classification process became more intense, with Intelligence Ministry officials interrogating them about their political and especially their religious beliefs. ('They asked whether we were praying, who in our family prays, and who does not.') Nonetheless, as news from visiting relatives and perhaps smuggled radios told in 1988 of war-weariness in Iran and increased MEK activity on its borders, they became more confident – even truculent. MEK prisoners had rarely dared to admit in their interrogations or questionnaires that they were 'Mojahedin' – which would earn a severe beating. They had been forced to say they were '*monafe-qin*' – i.e. hypocrites, the Supreme Leader's designation. But in 1988, many were prepared to risk a beating by declaring their membership of 'The Organisation' – a compromise, although everyone knew they meant the Mojahedin-e Khalq Organization. Mehdi Aslani, from a Marxist faction, recalls a sense in his prison, by the summer of 1988, that the regime was about to fall. He heard them singing MEK songs in their wards, and during interrogation sometimes they would push their luck and say, when asked their affiliation, 'I am a very proud and respected Mojahedin'. The optimism spread to the Marxists, who rediscovered pride in their atheism. It was a tragic mistake, as intelligence officials in the prison grimly coloured their classification 'red'.

There was no premonition among the prisoners of the slaughter that was soon to come. Although beatings continued, conditions had improved and both Mojahedin and leftists in their (often separate) wards were in reasonable spirits, bolstered in the former case by Rajavi's little army and his radio station. They probably had access to smuggled radios in a few wards, and thus could hear MEK radio, which transmitted from Camp Ashraf, but there is no suggestion that they were receiving messages or instructions.[49] They maintained group discipline, but they remained captive and were not by any stretch of the imagination acting as spies or enemy combatants. Nor were they rioting or planning a prison uprising: there were hunger strikes and they had regained a little of their dignity, sufficient to identify themselves as members of an 'organisation' rather than to abase themselves by declaring they were 'hypocrites' (monafeqin). There was no awareness on the part of the prisoners of their impending doom, and their guards (if they knew) gave nothing away.

CHAPTER 3

THE 1988 MASSACRE

The crunch for Iran in its war with Iraq came in July 1988. Public exposure of the Iran–Contra affair had forced Washington to renew its support for Iraq and it was now pressuring Iran's other arms suppliers, including China, to desist, whilst Russia had been on Iraq's side throughout. The world looked the other way when Saddam used chemical weapons: his victories multiplied and his long-range scuds caused chaos in Tehran. Panic increased on 3 July when the shooting down, albeit through a mistake, by the USS *Vincennes* of an Iranian Airbus seemed to presage American aggression. UN Resolution 598, calling for a truce, had been on the table for a year, and suddenly appeared preferable to the prospect of an eventual surrender which would put the Islamic government in peril.

Rafsanjani, who now commanded the army, convened a secret meeting of military, political and clerical leaders on 14 July 1988 which advised acceptance of the UN resolution and this advice was endorsed by Cabinet and by the Assembly of Experts. Rafsanjani conveyed it to the Supreme Leader, who personally made the bitter, resented decision. 'Accepting this resolution was more deadly for me than taking poison. I submitted myself to God's will and drank the drink for his satisfaction,' he told the nation in a rambling ninety-minute broadcast on 20 July 1988. Three days earlier he had delegated the President, Ali Khamenei, to notify UN Secretary General Pérez de Cuéllar of Iran's consent to a ceasefire. 'The fire of war ... has gained unprecedented dimensions, bringing other countries into the war and even engulfing innocent civilians. The killings of 290 civilians (in the Iranian Airbus) is a clear manifestation of this contention,' wrote Ali Khamenei. The President's letter was the clearest admission that the country was engaged in an international armed conflict, which meant that the Geneva Conventions applied to its prisoners. The regime now had to justify the ceasefire to a people who had been whipped up by years of war propaganda to fight until death and who by now had suffered over half a million casualties.[50]

'I know it is hard on you – but isn't it hard on your own father?' was the self-pitying note struck by the Supreme Leader as he told his people of the poison still coursing through his veins. He warned them against criticising officials who had advised acceptance of the truce for the sake of expediency, but warned that it was not yet a done deal – 'we should be prepared for jihad to deflect possible aggression by the enemy'. This was a prescient warning. UN Resolution 598 required a declaration of principle, but not a formal downing of arms until the parties agreed certain conditions, so Saddam Hussein – ever the opportunist – saw an opportunity to bring down the hated Iranian regime with a final military push. Key to his misbegotten plan was Rajavi's armed Mojahedin, 7,000 strong, now grandly styled 'the National Liberation Army of Iran', stationed on the border. Misled by these fantasising expatriates, just as George Bush and Dick Cheney would be misled in 2003 by Iraqi expatriates over the likely reaction to the invasion, Saddam thought that the people of Iran would welcome the Mojahedin with open arms and strewn flowers. They would overthrow the tottering clerics and install 'the People's Democratic Government' headed by Prime Minister Rajavi. So on 25 July 'Operation Eternal Light' began with a Liberation Army advance, co-ordinated with Iraqi air forces.

The ragtag, semi-trained MEK entered Iran and set off along the highway which they thought would take them in triumph to Tehran. They captured a number of small border towns in the first two days, victories that even the state-controlled Iranian media, caught off guard, reported – to the massive excitement of all political prisoners, who imagined that liberation would soon be at hand. But when they reached the city of Bakhtaran, the Iranian forces rallied: Rajavi's poorly trained troops (many of them women) were cut to pieces by Iranian fighters and helicopter gunships. On 29 July they beat a hasty retreat, leaving several thousand dead or else facing lynch mobs.[51] Many Iranian people, bemused by the ceasefire, were suddenly infused with patriotism and with an aversion towards a double-crossing enemy among whose ranks the Mojahedin could henceforth be counted. Saddam's opportunism, at the fag-end of this war, only served to prop up Khomeini's regime. It became the trigger for his order to kill all MEK prisoners.

It takes little imagination to understand the fury which must have inflamed the leaders of Iran in that last week of July. Just who advised Khomeini to issue the fatal fatwa ordering the execution of all MEK prisoners is unclear, although the acting Commander-in-Chief of the combined forces, Rafsanjani, and President Ali Khamenei, who had been centrally involved in the decision the previous week to accept the ceasefire, must have been his key counsellors. Montazeri, the Supreme Leader-in-waiting, was not consulted, and it is unclear whether Prime Minister Mousavi was involved. The leader's son, Ahmad, to whom the fatwa was dictated – probably on 28 July[52] – was by his side. On that day, with Mojahedin victories ringing in his ears, the Supreme Leader's anguish at this new dose of poison ran through a diseased body that his doctors had warned would shortly succumb to cancer. He and his advisers were Islamic jurists, custodians of a theology based on ancient battles in which enemies were killed without compunction, although they were also knowledgeable about the Geneva Conventions and the law of war (they had constantly accused Saddam of war crimes) and they would have been aware that international law has regarded the execution of surrendered or 'quartered' prisoners as a war crime since the sixteenth century. There were more recent precedents: the Japanese generals who sent the Allied prisoners on death marches at the end of the Second World War had been condemned to execution at the Tokyo trials and the German soldiers who carried out Hitler's orders to execute the prisoners recaptured after their 'Great Escape' from Stalag Luft III were hunted down and condemned by Nuremberg tribunals. But the Supreme Leader and his acolytes deliberately disobeyed the law of nations. His fatwa, issued (ironically) *In the Name of God the Compassionate and the Merciful*, decreed:

Since the treacherous Monafeqin do not believe in Islam and whatever they say stems from their deception and hypocrisy (and since according to the claims of their leaders they have become renegades) and since they wage war on God and are engaging in classical warfare on the western, northern and southern fronts with the collaboration of the Baathist Party of Iraq, and also their spying for Saddam against our Muslim nation, and since they are tied to the World Arrogance and have inflicted foul blows to the Islamic Republic since its inception, it is decreed that those who are in prisons throughout the country who remain steadfast in their support for the Monafeqin are considered to be Mohareb (waging war on God) and are condemned to execution.

The treason of Rajavi's army was by this decree imputed to the Mojahedin prisoners, most of whom had been in captivity since 1981. *Monafeqin* ('hypocrites') was the regime's official categorisation for the MEK. Although they did believe in Islam, it was the wrong kind of Islam as far as the state was concerned because its theology would accommodate human rights, and would not require obeisance to its judge-guardians. So Mojahedin prisoners were deemed by this fatwa to be apostates: there would be no need to enquire whether they kept the faith, because their claim to do so would be the deception of the hypocrite. Since they wage war on the regime, they 'wage war on God'. The only question was whether they remained 'steadfast' in their political affiliation before the death sentence, passed on all such persons by this fatwa, was carried out. So it duly went on to establish the machinery for this life and death classification – a committee comprising a religious judge, a revolutionary prosecutor and a representative of the Intelligence Ministry.

The Tehran 'Death Committee' of Jafar Nayyeri, Morteza Eshraqi (sometimes replaced by his deputy, Ebrahim Raisi) and an intelligence official (usually Mustafa Pourmohammadi) went into immediate operation at Evin and were helicoptered to Gohardasht. There is evidence that its decisions were sometimes taken by majority, with the intelligence official invariably holding out for execution. Eshraqi was, reportedly, the member who intervened favourably on behalf of several prisoners from families descended from the Prophet. However, there were very few MEK prisoners to whom any form of mercy was extended. Understandably, because the fatwa had concluded with this chilling exhortation to cruelty:

> It is naive to show mercy to Moharebs ('those who wage war on God'). The decisiveness of Islam before the enemies of God is among the unquestionable tenets of the Islamic regime. I hope that you satisfy almighty God with your revolutionary rage and rancour against the enemies of Islam. The gentlemen who are responsible for making the decisions must not hesitate, nor show any doubt or concerns with detail. They must try to be 'most ferocious against infidels'. To hesitate in the judicial process of revolutionary Islam is to ignore the pure and holy blood of the martyrs.

On the day it was issued, the fatwa was communicated to senior figures who needed to be involved in its implementation, most notably to Ayatollah Mousavi Ardebili, head of the Supreme Court. This jurist was so concerned that he immediately telephoned the Imam's son Ahmed, seeking clarification and some limitation in its dragnet language and extra-legal operation. He asked:

1. Whether it was only for those Mojahedin in prison who had already been sentenced to death, but who had not yet been executed and were not repentant (on this interpretation, as so limited, it would not have been unlawful) or did it condemn to execution 'those who have not yet been tried'?
2. Did it condemn to death the Mojahedin who had already been tried and given a specific jail sentence by a religious judge which they were currently serving?

The Supreme Leader gave this chilling clarification:

> In all the above cases, if the person at any stage or at any time maintains his position on supporting the Monafeqin, the sentence is execution. Annihilate the enemies of Islam immediately. As regards the case files, use whichever criterion speeds up the implementation of the verdict.

There could be no going back, and the very next day – 29 July – the implementation measures began. The prisons were put on lock-down, with all family visits cancelled and radios and televisions removed from wards. The Death Committee visits commenced. Meanwhile in Qom, Ayatollah Montazeri first heard of the fatwa from clerics distressed at the prospect of having to carry it out, and made a desperate attempt to have it reversed. He wrote a letter to Khomeini which pointed out that 'it was in complete disregard of all judicial standards and rulings'. He then spelled out the reasons why the cold-blooded killing of serving prisoners would be unconscionable, unlawful and counter-productive: it would be perceived as an act of vengeance and a vendetta and the regime would be condemned by the international media. Moreover, to execute people who have been sentenced by courts to punish-ments short of execution, without any fresh court process, would completely disregard judicial standards and rulings. Under the fatwa, many people who were innocent or had committed only minor transgressions could be executed.

'It is far better for an Imam to err in clemency than to err in punishment' was Montazeri's final message, citing a holy text. But Khomeini was deaf to any appeal for mercy. The fatwa was not recalled, and the only effect of Montazeri's intervention was to set the seal on his own dismissal (Khomeini sacked him as successor a few months later, pointing out that 'the responsibility [of the position] requires more endurance than you have shown'[53]). It does, however, seem to have persuaded the regime that the docu-ment should be kept a state secret. Even today, the fatwa has never been officially mentioned. During the 2009 election campaign Mir Hossein Mousavi replied to questions about his involvement in the massacres with a nervous response that as he was the head of the civil administration he had nothing to do with them. Rafsanjani, in his unreliable memoirs, claims that Mousavi attended a session of the Expediency Council where the killings were discussed. Another opposition figure, ex-President Khatami, admitted that he and his fellow reformists should not have remained silent about this 'tragedy', but was not forthcoming further.

The Death Committee came first for the Mojahedin on 29 July. In most prisons, they were held in segregated wards. Their televisions had been confiscated before news of the defeat of Rajavi's army had come through, and they were at this point in no psychological state to renounce their political faith: they were flush with the possibility of victory. They were taken out of their cells blindfolded, and in most cases Nayyeri needed to ask only one question: 'What is your affiliation?' The proud prisoners would reply 'Mojahedin', scorning the regime's derisive appellation '*Monafeqin*'. Others would use their own defensive euphemism, 'The Organisation'. There was no further hearing: they were immediately sent outside to join the queue that led to whatever makeshift gallows had been put in place. In Gohardasht six nooses were dangling at the foot of the Hosseinieh auditorium stage, whilst at Evin they were despatched in a lecture hall or from nooses attached to the lowered – then raised – arm of a mobile crane. (Hanging in Iran is traditionally carried out by 'stringing up' rather than 'the drop' down a trap door: strangulation takes more time and consciousness remains for longer.)

Any who gave the politically correct reply ('*Monafeqin*') survived whilst their files were checked and they were required to answer further questions. Would they be prepared to inform on erstwhile prison comrades? To go on television and renounce Rajavi? To fight against his liberation army? To form the advance guard that had to clear a path through Iraqi minefields? To hang a former comrade who remained steadfast? Those few who managed to answer in ways that discharged the heavy burden of proof laid upon them by the fatwa were taken back to their wards. In ward 2 of Gohardasht only five out of 200 returned; the female ward at Evin had no returnees after fifty Mojahedin women were taken away for invigilation. Those who failed to prove that they had entirely renounced their former allegiance were directed to the execution queue, which was through the door of the tribunal at Evin and Gohardasht on the left. ('Take them to the left' served as Nayyeri's coded death sentence.) In some prisons, they were ordered to make their wills and to dress in a white sheet that would serve as their shroud.

In order to provide cover, Chief Justice Ardebili put the law courts on unscheduled vacation and announced in his sermon at the next Friday prayers (on 5 August):

> The judiciary is under very strong pressure from public opinion asking why we even put them (the Mojahedin) on trial. Why are some of them jailed and why are all of them not executed? ... The people say they should be executed without exception.[54]

By this time they were being executed, and almost without exception. The families began to panic and Amnesty International issued its first Urgent Action a few weeks later.[55] The left-wing prisoners were permitted to hear the sermon over loudspeakers in their segregated wards and suddenly the strange actions and sounds they had noticed in their prisons over the previous week made a certain appalling sense.

Few Mojahedin have survived to tell the tale of this first, atrocious wave of killings. Several managed to tap out Morse-code messages from their wards to tell other prisoners what was happening, or to carve elliptical comments on the walls of their holding cells. On 15 August 1988 Montazeri stated that between 2,800 and 3,800 Mojahedin prisoners had been executed in this first wave,[56] an estimate corroborated much later by the Mojahedin when it issued a list of 3,208 members identified as having been killed.[57] Other estimates by survivors are much higher – up to 30,000, but these take the second wave of executions into account. Left-wing prisoners soon managed to deduce what was happening in the Mojahedin wards. In their own words in statements taken for the Boroumand Foundation enquiry, a little of the dawning terror of the first massacre can be appreciated. It was carried out by the Revolutionary Guards (including Ahmadinejad according to one prisoner), who were drafted in to assist or replace the prison officers. Ebrahim Rahimi, a rare MEK survivor, recalls:

> The people in my ward were taken for interrogation and execution in batches of twenty on 5 and 7 August. I heard that on 5 August two of my sisters had been executed ... Of the 200 people in my section, only ten survived. I was taken to another ward, which overlooked the Hosseinieh amphitheatre and was next to the prison bakery. We could see what was happening by twisting a bar on the cell window. We could see that bodies had been placed in big black bags – construction trash bags rather than ordinary plastic bags.

Reza Shemirani takes up the story in his memoirs:

> They were very quickly killing everyone. In the basement of section 209 was where they were enforcing sentences. Fathollah had three daughters and Nayyeri had told the Revolutionary Guard, 'Take him and show him.' They took him to the place where the prisoners were being hanged. He saw five people hanging from the gallows. Then they took him back before Nayyeri and everyone in the courtroom was laughing at him saying, 'Well now do you want to collaborate? Or do you want to go and be hanged?'
>
> It was really hard to be taken out of the cells – each time a prisoner would be taken out they would be given a plastic bag for their belongings. The sound of plastic terrified us – if we heard it we thought it was a guard coming to take us out and tell us to pack our belongings.

Another prisoner, Shahab Shokuhi, from Marxist-Leninist group 'The Worker's Path', recalls:

> Our section was mixed with both Mojahedin and leftist prisoners. When we were outside, the guards separated us and put all of the Mojahedin into a separate queue. They said that they were Revolutionary Guards and we would be asked some questions and we should think carefully about answering because some of us would be taken to the left side of the corridor and some would be taken to the right side depending on our answers. We did not understand the significance of this at the time. For those of us who were leftist, we were basically only asked two questions at this stage, whether we were Muslims and whether we prayed. However, the Mojahedin were asked different questions. They were asked 'Which group do you belong to?' If they answered 'Monafeq' (i.e. 'hypocrite') then they might be saved. Those who answered 'Mojahedin' were taken to the left side of the corridor on the queue for execution. In my section there were seventy-two prisoners and only nine of us came back.

Mr Shokuhi accidentally saw how the Mojahedin were executed:

The guards took me away to be flogged but they were not sure where to take me. One guard went to find out and then came back and took me to the amphitheatre. When the door was opened, I was surprised and asked, 'Why is it so dark and quiet?' The guard was also surprised and told me, 'Stay here. Don't touch your blindfold until I come back.' Of course, as soon as he left I took off my blindfold. It was really dark although you could see a little light on the stage. There was a huge pile of prison shoes lying at the foot of the stage as well as piles of clothes. I looked up and saw six ropes hanging across the stage. It was obvious that they were executing everyone. At this point the guard came back and yelled at me 'What are you looking at?'

The following harrowing account is from one who got away. Mr Ashough's story has particular credibility as he is identified by name in official documents as the person who made a daring escape *en route* to the firing squad. He lived to tell a tale that described the suffering and death of Mojahedin members in one provincial prison near the war zone:

I was in my third year at university when I was arrested in 1981 after the big June demonstration and I was sentenced to ten years for being a Mojahedin sympathiser. I was taken to a prison at Dastgerd.

At the time after the Iran–Iraq War ended, the Revolutionary Guards came and told us that all visits were stopped and ordered us to put on our blindfolds and line up. There were about sixty or seventy of us. We were taken in groups of eight to the main prison office. There was a religious judge who asked me only one question: 'Would you fight the Mojahedin or not?' I tried to avoid giving a positive response by explaining that I'm not a fighter, I'm a nutritionist. But they kept pressing me, and the judge asked, 'Would you walk through a minefield and be prepared to die for Islam?' I replied that I would die if it were necessary but I could not understand why it would be necessary to walk on a mine. So I was put on the list and when I was returned to my group, I learned that it was an execution list. Of the group of eight, two were exempted from execution – both of them had said that they would fight against the Mojahedin. That left six of us condemned to death.

We six were then taken to join a line of about sixty others who had been placed on the list. The guard commander said, 'We are coming back in ten minutes and you must have written your will.' They came back with ropes and tied our hands and blindfolded us and took us out into the courtyard of the prison where we were made to sit and wait. At about 2 a.m. some mini-buses arrived and we were placed in them. The buses stopped at military barracks and we were ordered to go and wash in a bathroom and to put on white clothes of the kind that they wrap around a dead body. The washing that we were asked to do is a religious form of washing that is done with dead bodies. There were lots of other Mojahedin prisoners and there was a very tense and chaotic atmosphere. We could hear girls in the female bathrooms washing themselves and screaming.

I took a very quick shower and put my normal clothes back on – I was not prepared to wear the shroud. Several guards began to beat me severely. When I was on the ground the Commander came up and said, 'Take him and bury him as he is. Execute him as he is.' So they took me to the mini-bus and told me to sit on the back seat. Everyone else who came into the bus was dressed in white and was blindfolded with their hands tied. I think that whilst I was being beaten up, my bonds had been loosened and I was able to free my hands. By this time it was about 3.30 a.m. Everyone was screaming. The prisoners were screaming insults about Khomeini. I was determined to take an opportunity to escape. The bus was going very slowly along a bad dirt road. There was a lot of dust because of the cars and buses and there was a lot of noise in the bus. With the help of my cousin who was sitting in the seat in front of me, I took off my shoes and squeezed myself out of the bus window. I then ran for my life and I collided with some barbed wire, so I was still within the precincts of the barracks. I climbed over the barbed wire, cutting myself badly in the process, and had run about 1km to the river when I heard the shots. They were machine-gunning first and then there were individual shots. They came from an area in the distance, near the barracks, where there were lights. I had come from this area and had hunted in the nearby mountains, so I was able to make my escape.

Ashough, Mojahedin escapee from Dastgerd

Mr Ashough's evidence that the Dastgerd prisoners were executed by firing squad after being ordered to dress in shrouds and make their wills indicates that local prison authorities had some discretion in how the massacres were carried out. In another provincial prison, Shiraz, those who disavowed the Mojahedin were sometimes put to a lethal test:

> About forty-five MEK sympathisers were called out and taken away to what we later found was a detention centre run by Revolutionary Guards. Only one of them returned, my cellmate Abbas Marayan. For five days he was so distressed that he wouldn't speak to anyone. Then we finally managed to get him to talk and he explained that all the others who had been taken away had been hanged. He had been warned not to tell us, but he thought that he had been brought back on purpose to see what our reaction would be to this news. He had answered questions about believing in the Islamic Republic and was asked, 'If the Mojahedins attack Iran and we want to hang one of them, would you hang him?' And he had agreed. They had then taken him to an execution place and given him the rope to pull up and he had started to cry and say that he couldn't go through with it. Then they had brought him back but obviously he had failed the test. Two weeks after he talked to us, Abbas was taken away with another group and was executed. I believe that up to 250 of our prisoners were executed, most of them MEK.
>
> Esma'ilpour (a pseudonym), Shiraz prison

Women MEK supporters were not spared, although as a measure of what might in fanatical minds count as mercy, they were often shot rather than hanged. This was done by Revolutionary Guards who psyched themselves up by chanting 'Death to the hypocrites':

> I was arrested in 1983 for my involvement in political activities with the Workers Party and was taken to section 209 of Evin prison. I was twenty-five years old, married with a baby daughter and in the final year of an agricultural engineering course at the University of Shiraz. My daughter was taken from me and I was put in solitary confinement and given severe beatings with electric cables.
>
> ...

We had a loudspeaker in our ward and were able to listen to the radio news and we heard that the government had accepted the UN resolution. But after the ceasefire the guards came and took the televisions and newspapers and books and we didn't get any more papers and the family visits stopped. Then they came and took four MKO girls from our ward. They guessed that they might be executed because they said frantic 'goodbyes'. One of them came back to the ward later and talked to other MEK prisoners who told us 'they are killing everyone'. At night we could hear chants of 'God is Great' and 'Death to the *monafeqin*' and then we would hear shooting. They came and took more of the MEK women and they never came back. They would come each day and call a few more MEK so other prisoners would come and stand with them in the hallway to say goodbye and to cry. After a few days there was only one MEK prisoner left and then she was called and did not come back. We were in agonies during this period – we just walked the MEK girls round the ward and told them stories to distract them. The MEK girls had all packed their bags to give to their families and we discussed how to keep the packages small in case big packages were not delivered.

Fariba Sabet, Workers Party activist

Communists and other leftists – often fierce critics of the MEK and not inclined to believe them – were at this stage mostly left alone by the authorities. Only gradually did the truth dawn about what was happening in the MEK wards. The following testimonies explain how sights and sounds, rumours and unguarded remarks by guards, and the writing on the cell walls, began to add up.

We heard about the end of the war from the radio – some of the Revolutionary Guards were crying. They gave us no more newspapers and visitations were prohibited. We had no idea what was going on. Then they took the Mojahedin prisoners in groups of two or three. It took them about twenty days to take all of them away, not only those who stood by their political positions but those who co-operated as well. We did not realise at the time that they were being taken for execution, we could not believe that the regime would permit such a massacre.

We had no news until family visits were allowed and we were told the truth. Many of the Mojahedin who had been taken for execution were *mellikesh*, had completed their sentence. They executed all the Mojahedin in our section of the prison, save for two, one of whom had a close family relationship with an interrogator.

Reza Saki, FKO (Bidaran website)

The process of massacring the Gohardasht prisoners began at 9 a.m. on Saturday 30 July. From our section, nine Mojahedin were taken out that day. The executions took place inside a silo, located outside of the prison building and behind the prison wall. We could see it from the mosque of the prison. That afternoon, one of us saw Lashkari [the prison governor] with a wheelbarrow full of ropes. In the next few days we saw many Revolutionary Guards who were looking inside the silo. There was a lot of unusual movement around the area. The Mojahedin women were also executed. One of them, Zahra Khosravi, was taken to the execution section to write her will. She took advantage of this opportunity to contact the prisoners on the nearby ward by Morse code. After introducing herself, she informed them that she was condemned to death in a court that was headed by Nayyeri. On 6 August I heard that 800 were executed at Gohardasht and another 1,200 at Evin.

Excerpt from Iraj Mesdaghi's prison memoirs

The MKO left our ward and never came back. I had known that people were being executed – at night I would hear the Revolutionary Guards marching in the garden chanting 'Death to *monafeq*, death to communists'. I overheard one particularly unpleasant Revolutionary Guard telling her friends how tightly the Mojahedin women had gripped each other whilst they were waiting to be executed and how they had peed themselves in fear. She thought this was a great joke.

Maria, FKO (Minority)

A comrade overheard a conversation between the religious judge Nayyeri and one of the executioners. The executioner told Nayyeri, 'Ten minutes is not enough. When we lower the hook after ten

Mojahedin, but were reluctant to look dishonourable by agreeing to recant on television. The authorities said this meant they
must still be 'steadfast' and executed six of them. A judge from
Qom complained about the bloodthirstiness of the Intelligence
Ministry representative who had said, 'Let us kill them quick, the
Imam has delivered the verdict. All we have to do is check that
the prisoner is still holding to his views.' That question – do you
still support your group? – was asked, and when the unsuspecting
prisoner answered 'Yes', he would be marched to the gallows.[58]

Ayatollah Montazeri then hit upon a religious reason for halt-
ing – or at least suspending – the first wave of executions. On
13 August 1988 he summoned the Tehran Death Committee
in person: Judge Nayyeri, Prosecutor Eshraqi (and his deputy
Ebrahim Raisi) and the powerful man from the Intelligence
Ministry, Mustafa Pourmohammadi, and told them it was
untraditional to spill blood in the calendar month of Moharram,
which was about to begin. 'At least halt the executions during this
month.' Nayyeri replied that they had already executed 750 prisoners in Tehran and had only 200 to go in Evin. 'Once we finish
off this lot you can order as you wish...' Montazeri was dismayed
by this admission and read the four of them the lecture which
two days later he summed up in a memorandum. He began by
pointing out that he had more reason than anyone else to want
revenge on the Mojahedin as his son had been killed by them
in the 28 June 1981 bombing. But in the interests of the revolution 'I am worried about the judgment that posterity and history
will pass upon us'. The world would condemn them for massacring helpless prisoners without trial. The death penalty should
only be passed in an unemotional environment and instead they
were taking out their upset with the Mojahedin incursion on the
Mojahedin prisoners who had nothing to do with it. Besides,
executing them when they had not committed fresh crimes after
their sentence cast doubt on the legitimacy of the trial judges
who had sentenced them in the first place. How can it be just to
execute a prisoner who has already been given a lesser sentence?

Of course it never could be just, but Nayyeri and Eshraqi lacked
the integrity to admit it. So did Ayatollah Mousavi Ardebili, the
head of the Supreme Judicial Council, when Montazeri upbraided

him for making his telephone inquiry to the Imam's son: 'You should have gone to the Imam and told him that if someone had been in jail for some time and had been sentenced to five years, how can we execute them? They have not committed a new crime for which we could try them.'[59] The Chief Justice and the Death Committee members seem to have had no moral or legal qualms about carrying out the fatwa, which by necessary implication annulled the decisions of dozens of religious judges, sitting as representatives of God on earth, rendered on prisoners over the past eight years. Executing prisoners for an invasion to which they had not been party was not only illogical, cruel and unjust, but also violative of the country's constitutional order. Ayatollah Montazeri was a brave and principled man, and a distinguished jurist. But his card had been marked as too merciful and he was being elbowed aside by people who had no regard at all for taking human life – a faction led by Ali Khamenei and Ali Akbar Hashemi Rafsanjani.

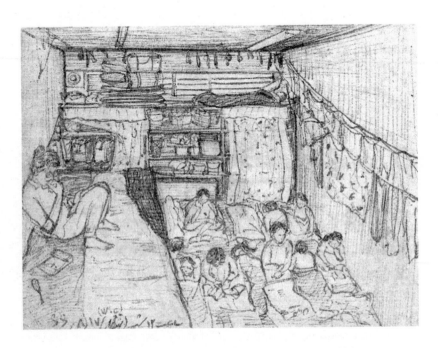

Drawing by an inmate of her cell at Evin prison, 1988.

CHAPTER 4

DEATH TO THE ATHEISTS

Prison survivors all speak of a lull in interrogations and executions for a ten-to-fourteen-day period which began in mid-August 1988. This may have been due to the beginning of the holy month of Moharram and its taboo against punitive bloodshed – a taboo that Montazeri had drawn to the attention of the Tehran Death Committee when he met them on 13 August 1988. But it may have been due to the simple fact that there were no more Mojahedin prisoners to execute: Montazeri estimated that up to 3,800 had been slain by that time. The real question is why the Death Committees reconvened, on about 26 August, and in the succeeding weeks turned themselves into courts that proceeded to try, for the crime of apostasy, all the left-wing prisoners – Marxists, Leninists, Maoists, Trotskyites and other communists, along with the odd liberal – and sentenced them either to execution, or to persistent torture until they agreed to bow down towards Mecca and say their prayers.

The fatwa cannot be interpreted as an order for the death and torture sentences inflicted on the leftists, referred to by the government as members of 'mini-groups', who were not hypo-crites – they made no secret of their disbelief in Islam. Montazeri suggests that a secret decree was issued to the Death Committees by the Supreme Leader on 6 September 1988,[60] applying to all remaining political prisoners: death for unrepentant male apos-tates, and torture for female apostates and for men who could establish that they had not been born into Muslim families. On any view, the second order was designed to break the spirit of intellectually difficult prisoners who would have to be released after the war, so that the Islamic Republic could settle back into a reign less marked than previously by ideological division.

In the second stage of the massacre period, leftist prisoners were summoned before the Death Committee for a religious inquisition, during which they were asked whether they were Muslim, whether they believed in God, whether and how often they prayed and whether they were prepared to start praying again. This time the committee more resembled a court, and sessions lasted ten to fifteen minutes, as its members had to consult the prisoners' files, probe their family backgrounds and discuss among themselves when a defendant's answers raised a fine point of theology. Most of the prisoners were Marxists and had no idea of the theological significance of their responses. For example, one communist woman who had been a high-ranking Tudeh Party official was subject to an interrogation over whether she had ever heard her father pray, and found that her denial was supported by Eshraqi, who happened to know him. She subsequently commented, 'I did not understand the consequence these answers would have for me: I did not realise the response "my father did not pray" would help reduce my sentence.'[61]

For women, the wrong response would entail a torture sentence – whippings (fifteen lashes) administered during each of the five prayer periods in the Muslim day, until they undertook to pray regularly, or died. Only during menstruation was the torture suspended – because of the primitive belief that the duty to inflict violence on women's bodies was suspended if those bodies were 'unclean'. Many second wave prisoners who received these beatings have said that they were very different and much more painful than the *tazir* beatings on the soles of their feet that they had received during earlier interrogations. The cables now drew blood, and this time they were lashed all over their body. In the case of male leftists, the inquisition would lead to a death sentence if the prisoner was judged to be an 'innate' apostate (i.e. one born into a Muslim family) and who either maintained his refusal to pray or was thought to be insincere in offering to do so. There were some questions about political party membership, but these appear to have been asked in the context of establishing a commitment to atheism – to the godlessness, rather than the class-based politics, of Marxist-Leninist thought. A number of prisoners were brought back three times to the committee before they were condemned to death – the proof of apostasy must be clear, which it is if God is repudiated thrice.[62]

In this lengthier phase, prisoners had time to understand what was in store for them; recollections of this period are clearer and more numerous than accounts of the first wave, and there are more survivors. They recall that ruses for evasion and delay were anxiously discussed in, and by Morse code between, the wards. One which appears to have confounded the committee in Tehran was for the prisoner to excuse his failure to pray by saying, hand on heart, that it was impossible to pray in the presence of unbelieving fellow prisoners, because their spiritual rankness invalidated a true Muslim's prayers. This argument seems to have been accepted by Nayyeri, until he was reminded by Eshraqi that they had heard it many times before.[63] Although the prisoners' stance towards the Islamic Republic remained relevant, it was now religious rather than political loyalty that was being tested. Membership of a godless 'mini-group' did not merely manifest seditious intent – it was taken as evidence of blasphemy.

This new emphasis on conformity in religious belief was apparent in the public pronouncements by the regime's leaders. On 1 September 1988 Ayatollah Ardebili opened the Supreme Court, after its unscheduled one-month vacation, with a diatribe against the 'mini-groups' and a demand that judges and prosecutors act with resolve in confronting them 'as though they were strictly confronting heathens'.[64] This is exactly the approach that the Death Committees took during the second wave.

On 7 September 1988 the Supreme Leader announced that he relinquished his emergency prerogative to punish, which was henceforth bestowed on the Expediency Council and the President, who would have responsibility for determining punishments for crimes against religion and for crimes against the state.[65] Rafsanjani (head of the Expediency Council) and Ali Khamenei (President) thereby became responsible in Iranian law as well as international law for the slaughter of the atheist prisoners who had done no more than exercise their rights, under conventions binding on Iran, to decide their own faith. They were fully responsible for the actions of the Death Committees, executive bodies rather than independent courts, which they allowed to investigate, try and punish by death and by torture.

Before long, reports of the first wave of executions reached the

Western press from anguished families, and on 11 September Chief Justice Ardebili made the first attempt to construct a public justification.[66] 'We are not a secular state,' he explained, so irreligion and blasphemy were not allowed in Iran. He said the regime was ready to answer the allegations by providing documents (which were never provided) at a conference (which was never convened) on 'mini-group terrorism'. These documents would, he falsely claimed, prove that those executed had all received death sentences at their trials but execution had been delayed to give them an opportunity to repent. 'These convicts who had already been sentenced to death even started to beat up prison guards thus proving their hostility to the regime.'[67] This was a thoroughly dishonest example of the tactic of confession and avoidance, i.e. acknowledging executions in passing but falsely blaming prisoners for their failure to take the opportunity to reform and falsely accusing them of committing additional crimes and so forfeiting any prospect of mercy.

These statements can be interpreted as an indication that the highest levels of the regime were aware that proceedings were being taken against 'mini-group' prisoners on account of their refusal to accept the state (or any) religion, but there was no public announcement to this effect and no such inquisition was ever inflicted upon ordinary prisoners, or upon civilians generally.

The Genocide Convention of 1948, to which Iran has been a party since 1949 and which it ratified in 1956, applies to killings of, or causing serious mental or physical harm to, members of a racial or religious group as such, with intent to destroy that group in whole or in part. It is viewed as the most heinous of all international crimes, because it is mass murder by hatred of fellow humans for something they cannot control – the fact of their race or the promptings of their consciences. The 'religious group' that the Iranian regime intended to destroy in the second wave were those in its prisons who had been born Muslim but who had later renounced Islam. Whether or not atheists should count as a 'religious group' for the purposes of the convention, it is clear that persons who are born into a particular faith that they later renounce can be so categorised. This is a feature of the second wave of killings and is one reason why they must, in international law, engage continuing attention.

There are many harrowing accounts of the 'trials', and of the death and torture sentences inflicted during the second phase. One former FKO member, a chemical engineer, testified to the Boroumand inquiry about his experience in Gohardasht:

A group of us were taken from the cell blindfolded and made to queue in a large hall. When it was my turn, I was taken into the courtroom and my blindfold was removed. I confirmed my name and was asked whether I accepted the Islamic Republic and I said I did not. I was asked whether I believed in my organisation, the FKO, and its ideas, and I confirmed that I did. I denied any belief in God – I denied that I had ever believed in God for a second, even during my childhood. I was then asked about my mother and father and whether they prayed. I said they did not. Why didn't they pray? I explained they were Kurds from Khoramshahr and were members of the Ahl-e Haq cult, a mystic group which does not believe in prayer. Nayyeri eventually seemed to accept that I had always been a non-believer. He ordered that I should go to the left. There were many people in the corridor on the left by that stage – I counted 142 – and we whispered to each other trying to figure out what was going to happen – the guards brought a trolley with bread and cheese and we jokingly called it 'the last supper'. We said goodbye to each other because we thought we were going to be executed because we had heard so many stories about the Mojahedin killings.

The prison guards called names out from a long list. All of the 142 people were called, except for me and three others who were all 'non-believers' who had never been Muslim. They were from communist families and they had never been Muslim or considered to be Muslim. Other than us, the other 138 people were taken to the Hosseinieh, the assembly hall that we knew had been used for hanging prisoners. We never saw our friends again. I believe they were taken away and hanged. Later during my torture period I was held in prison holding cells where some of them had written on the walls whilst awaiting their execution. Because there were limited ropes, and hanging took some time, those who could not be executed immediately were left in cells where they were able to open their blindfolds and scratch messages on the walls. One was signed by a friend of mine, Kasra Akbari Kordestani, and he wrote on the wall – his message causes me grief to this day – 'I offer my small heart to all the workers of Iran.' After discussion with the other survivors and information from other groups we concluded that those transferred to the right of the corridor were those who admitted to being Muslims and had promised to pray. Those of us on the left had refused to pray, and the four survivors of that queue had been confirmed as non-Muslims and so had been saved. None of us were asked any questions about our political views – the interrogation was all about our belief in God and our willingness to pray.

Although I survived execution they determined to torture us in order to make us become Muslims. The procedure was to use torture five times a day at each call to prayer. They flogged us on the soles of our feet, telling us that we had to become Muslim. We were beaten with electrical cables after being tied down to a metal bed. At each call to prayer I was given fifteen lashes. This went on for some weeks and eventually I decided to give up and commit suicide. This was on 1 December 1988 when I was unable to endure the floggings for refusing to pray, and I slit my wrists. Since suicide is forbidden in Islam, I was given good medical attention and even antibiotics.

Nina Parvaresh, in the book *Unequal Battle*,[68] recounts:

On 31 August, Naserian [the deputy governor] and the guards opened the doors to the wards, ordered us to blindfold ourselves and leave to line up in the hallway. We were taken one by one to an adjacent room to be questioned about whether we were a Muslim or not. Those who declared that they were not Muslims and would not pray were ordered to sit on the left side of the hall. They were then taken to the prison amphitheatre where they were hanged.

We were taken to ward 8 and those of us who refused to pray were laid on the bed and flogged five times a day ... after numerous beatings I told my co-prisoners that I was going to agree to pray and they told me that they were going to do the same. After we made the declaration we were sent back to ward 8 where we met some of our friends who had also survived. We hugged and we cried and we remembered those who were not with us anymore. Out of about 500 leftist prisoners in the five wards with which I was familiar, about half had been executed.

Women apostates were spared execution, but were ordered to be beaten five times a day, although in some cases with five strokes rather than the fifteen inflicted on the men. The following testimonies are typical:

I sat in front of the head judge, Nayyeri. He asked what I was accused of and I said, 'I am a member of the Tudeh Party.' He asked, 'Are you still a member?' I said, 'I have been in prison during the past five years and have no connection with them. I don't know what their position on current issues is. For this reason I cannot say whether I am or am not a member.' He said, 'She is still a Tudeh supporter. Are you a Muslim?' I responded, 'This information is personal.' He asked, 'Do you pray?' I responded, 'This information is also personal.' He then asked, 'What about your father and mother?' I said, 'My mother and father are Shia and I was born into a Shia family.' He said, 'She does not pray. She is mortad [apostate].' He added the Koran states that an apostate man must be executed and an apostate woman must be whipped until she accepts to say that she is a Muslim, or she dies. 'Take her out, brother.' The guard came and took the corner of my chador as though he were touching something dirty. They blindfolded me and let me out ... at the time of the call to prayer he began whipping me as he recited verses of the Koran relating to treatment of apostate women ... when they whipped us they spread us out on a wooden bed, but they did not tie us to it. They beat us five times a day. Everyone could hear our screams. It was *bastinado*, hitting the nerves below the swollen skin.

Fariba Sabet

The whipping sessions seemed endless. They woke us up in the morning, tied us to a bed and lashed us over and over again. They would repeat this every day at 2 p.m., 4 p.m., 6 p.m. and 9 p.m. We spent most of our time in anticipation of the next round of lashes.

It was not only the physical pain that tormented the prisoners, but the anxiety, sleeplessness and the dreadful waiting. Sleep deprivation caused many of us to break.

Witness statement of Shahla Azad (pseudonym)[69]

On the second week in September, the whipping of the leftist women began. With the first light at 4 a.m., at the sound of the muezzin's call to prayer, the cell door was opened, the prisoner was taken out, was laid on a bed in the middle of a corridor and was whipped. Five lashes. The cell door is then locked and another door opened and the second prisoner is laid on the bed. The third, the fourth and so on – it takes about an hour. The next turn is with the midday call to prayer, the third about 4 p.m., the fourth at nightfall and the last before midnight. Twenty-five lashes in all, five occasions ... The old prisoners, who had been in for several years, sent us news that they had agreed to pray – they regarded themselves as defeated. They wished they had been given a death sentence rather than a slow death. They saw no hope for an end to whippings.

Monireh Baradaran[70]

The sentences imposed on apostate men depended on the religiosity of their families, and specifically on that of their fathers. As Amnesty International reports:

At the end of August 1988 the Death Commission turned its attention to prisoners from leftist groups held at Gohardasht prison. They were asked such questions as do you pray? do you read the Koran? One eyewitness reports that a group who said that they did not read the Koran were then asked whether their fathers had read the Koran. Four of the men said yes and two of the men said no. After some discussion between the members of the commission, it was decided that those who had not been brought up in a religious family were not as guilty as those whose parents were religious, because the former group had not been brought up as believers. Consequently the two men whose fathers had not prayed were spared but the four others were executed.[71]

• • •

It is plain from the declarations of Ayatollah Khomeini, the Friday sermons of Rafsanjani and the announcements by the judicial authorities and the Ministry of Intelligence, that the Mojahedin and later the leftists were condemned not because they engaged in terrorist attacks, but because they denied the revolutionary state's idea of God. The Mojahedin were believers, but in a God who directed them to class warfare, equality and (so they later claimed) even towards democracy. The Marxists were non-believers. Neither group was prepared to obey the God installed by the revolution, whose orders were divined and declared by Khomeini. So both opposition groups were 'corrupters of the earth' and thus guilty of the Koranic crime of 'waging war on God' (Koran 5:33). As Rafsanjani and other political clerics constantly stressed in the early and mid-1980s, God's punishment for *moharebs* was death.

It follows that the massacres were not an unprincipled deviation from Islamic governance, but a consequence – almost a logical consequence – of the theocratic state constructed by Khomeini after seeing off the 'three Bs' (Bazargan, Bani-Sadr and Bakhtiar) and his erstwhile liberal and secularist allies. There was no magic about his regime's progressive elimination of political opponents – a task facilitated by the war against Saddam, which galvanised national loyalty and made it easier to justify harsh action against those who would be depicted as fifth-columnists. The consolidation of power through one-party rule, intolerance and despotism is not at all uncommon; what was unusual about this revolution's progress was that it came to treat as subversive different approaches towards Islam, as well as disbelief in general – and to regard the extermination of dissenters as a duty ordained by God. It must be said, however, that many young Iranians reject any intellectual analysis of the prison massacres or any explanation that attributes religiosity or intelligence to the killers: they regard them as a barbaric reaction to an existential threat to their power and hence a forerunner to the treatment of the Green Movement protesters in 2009.

In practical terms, this meant that 'corrupters' – whether atheists or Mojahedin – could not be allowed back into society to spread their heretical doctrines among the people, and especially the youth (the regime constantly laments not taking earlier action to stop their propaganda successes among students). For 'steadfast' prisoners, doctrinally there was, literally, no way out – which is precisely why those who completed their sentence were not let out. They were *mellikesh*, but too dangerous to release. This policy was announced by the Ministry of Intelligence in 1985: 'Henceforth, no prisoners will be released unless it is proven that they have repented and are willing to conform.'[72] Hence the choice for merciless men who could tolerate no opposition to their power: either to keep the dissidents in prison indefinitely, long after their sentences expired, or simply to kill them. The decision to go with the massacre option truly reflected the perverted views of men who shared Asadollah Lajevardi's belief that 'we execute because we care for humanity'; these true believers thought that they were paving their own path to paradise by sending God's enemies to accursed corners of cemeteries across Iran.

Families mourn where they suspect their loved ones lie,
'the place of the damned' at Khavaran cemetery.

CHAPTER 5

MOURNING FORBIDDEN

Most studies of Iranian society remark on the centrality, culturally and spiritually, of mourning. Every Friday the nation's cemeteries are attended by families putting flowers on the graves of their deceased relatives: in the martyrs' section will be found the mothers grieving at the gravestones of their sons killed by fighting in the Iran–Iraq War. It is a matter of some poignancy that the mothers whose children were killed by their own state at the end of that war have nowhere to mourn, because that state denied them the right to bury their dead, and suppresses to this day displays of grief at the sites identified as their mass graves. Those sites have been located, anecdotally, in sections of major cemeteries that are usually reserved for the corpses of criminals and atheists. They have become places of pilgrimage for the victims' families: in August 2008, the twentieth-anniversary commemoration of the massacres at a cemetery in Tehran was forcibly broken up by police, with seventeen arrests.[73] In January 2009 Amnesty International condemned the Iranian government for bulldozing the mass grave at Khavaran, alleging that it was an attempt to destroy evidence of its crime against humanity.[74] That the government refuses to answer questions about the massacres and has conducted no investigation into them is a breach of the 'right to life' provisions of the ICCPR (see page 108). That it still denies to families information as to where it buried their loved ones is a further breach, inflicting punishment on the parents for the purported sins of the children.

By November 1988 the potential threat to the regime posed by thousands of young atheists and oppositionists had been removed by taking their lives. There are no definite fatality statistics, but credible reports suggest that several hundred were killed in each of more than twenty prisons throughout the country, with up to 1,000 victims at Evin and many more in Gohardasht. Only the state knows how many lives it took, and it is not telling. Rafsanjani's claim in January 1989 that 'less than one thousand were executed in July to September'[75] is a vast under-estimate, but still remains the only official admission. There is no doubt that well over 3,000 were killed – they have been positively identified and the likelihood is that about 7,000 prisoners were massacred (comparable to the numbers killed at Srebrenica and on the Bataan death march). The MEK itself, which has transmogrified into the National Council of Resistance of Iran, estimates that 30,000 lives were lost, but this is an exaggeration unless it refers to all executions of MEK members since 1981.[76]

The regime postponed its duty to notify families of those who had been executed. All prison visits had been cancelled at the end of July, and some desperate families, hearing rumours of the killings, had rushed to Qom to complain to Ayatollah Montazeri, but he was unable to help: he was shunned by the regime after his protest in August, and removed as Supreme Leader-in-waiting a few months later. So relatives besieged the prisons. Visits resumed in November 1988 and some family members were then presented with plastic bags containing the belongings of their dead child or spouse. This callous way of breaking the news provoked these families to demonstrate, in their grief and anger, outside the prison, and so a new notification process had to be adopted. Thereafter, families received telephone calls from the prison, usually telling them to attend at a nearby Revolutionary Guard committee office to receive news of their prisoner/relative. Eventually (after a bureaucratic run-around) and inevitably, it turned out to be news of their death. They were informed that belongings could be collected in plastic bags if they attended by appointment at the prison, and families of Mojahedin victims would be permitted to collect the wills that their children had hastily made before being rushed to the gallows or put before a firing squad. Condemned leftists, however, had not been given the opportunity to make new wills because Marxists were assumed to have no interest in life after death. As one woman was told, when she asked about her husband's will and burial site:

Your husband was a communist. He did not have a will. He was an atheist so he does not have a burial spot ... what do these people know about the importance of burial? It means nothing to them.[77]

No information was provided to any relative about burial sites and all were ordered, when notified of the death or handed back belongings, that they must not hold memorials or funeral services or attempt to locate the grave. Of course rumours abounded and cemetery workers let out secrets. There are horrific stories of mothers, desperate to find the remains of their children, digging at mounds of fresh earth in these places in an attempt to identify a corpse. An Amnesty report describes how one woman 'dug up the corpse of an executed man with her bare hands' as she searched for her husband's body in Khavaran cemetery in Tehran in a part of the cemetery known colloquially as *Lanatabad* ('The Place of the Damned') reserved for the bodies of criminals. She said, 'Groups of bodies, some clothed, some in shrouds, had been buried in unmarked shallow graves in this section of the cemetery. The stench of the corpses was appalling but I started digging with my hands because it was important for me and my two little children that I locate my husband's grave.' Amnesty reported that 'she unearthed a body with its face covered in blood but when she cleaned it off she saw it was not her husband. Other relatives visiting the graveyard discovered her husband's grave some days later.'[78]

Khavaran cemetery in south east Tehran soon became a place of pilgrimage for relatives. They attend on Fridays and still meet each year on 29 July, the date that the massacres commenced in 1988. In 1996, a construction company excavating in the area came across a huge mass grave, believed to contain the remains of hundreds of executed prisoners. Family members besieged the area, but security forces dispersed them by firing in the air, and then arrested company employees whom they accused of spreading state secrets. In 2001, the National Council of Resistance of Iran claimed to have identified twenty-one mass grave sites where its Mojahedin members lay.[79]

Family members tell of the cruelty they suffered in obtaining information about the deaths of husbands and wives, or sons and daughters:

I went to Khavaran the Friday after the authorities gave me my husband's belongings. Before carrying out the 1988 massacres, the government had dug two large canals at Khavaran. When we arrived there, both canals had been filled. The ground was left uneven and rippled. You could still see pieces of clothes, slippers and combs on the ground. We were not allowed to touch the dirt or sit down on the soil. Security forces were everywhere and I could see several Revolutionary Guard vehicles parked outside. We could smell the stench of the dead...

I was told to go to the Revolutionary Guards committee office for news of my husband, who had been, even before the revolution, a member of the Tudeh Party. He was a factory manager until his arrest in May 1983 and was a *mellikesh* at the time he was killed. At the office they told me of his death and I asked, 'Why did you kill him?' The official said that he was an apostate. I said, 'Can I have his will?' And he said, 'Apostates don't have a will, the will is only for Muslims.' I asked, 'Where is he buried?' They said they would let us know later but even though we came back time and again they would never, for twenty-one years, give us an honest answer. We went with other families to Khavaran cemetery and saw that some of the holes were so shallow that you could see parts of the clothing on the corpses and bloody blankets that had been thrown down. They were greyish-coloured prison blankets that I recognised. I discovered one blanket near a wall, covered in dried blood, but we couldn't touch it – it made us feel sick. But the families became one big family, emotionally very close to each other, and always celebrated the anniversary together. I have been arrested on three occasions at these commemorations.

Rezvan Moqadam, statement regarding her
husband Ali Asghar Manuchehrabad[80]

A few months later, the family members of prisoners were called to come to the prison. It was hard to breathe; everyone wanted to find out what happened to their loved ones. They were upset, worried, waiting for a glimmer of hope whilst staring at the mouths of the prison authorities to tell the news. The air became heavier and heavier. Then the voice of the head of the prison called other names, the family members of whom were told to come forward to pick up a piece of paper. The piece of paper was a dated receipt for their relative's belongings. Suddenly people started to sob as the catastrophe became obvious. After years visiting the prisons, a piece of paper was the only thing remaining for grieving mothers and fathers, spouses who had just learned of their widowhood, and restless children.

Ahmad Mousavi, FKO (Minority)[81]

The release of the survivors – female leftists, reformed apostates, a few who had renounced the MEK – took place over the next few years. Broken, fearful and subjected to intense surveillance, some managed to leave Iran and their stories are beginning to be told, although candour is still tempered by fear; there is concern about reprisals against families back home and the threat from government assassins abroad. Khomeini's willing executioners were promoted to high positions in politics and the judiciary, where many remain today. Most are engaged in tackling a new generation of Green Movement dissidents though a few (like ex-Prime Minister Mousavi) are leading that generation. One notable absentee is Lajevardi, 'the Butcher of Evin', said to have authorised Revolutionary Guards to rape MEK women who were virgins prior to their execution, so they could not benefit from an Islamic concession which allows virgins to enter paradise. He went back to his pre-revolution day job, and was assassinated outside his tailor's shop in Tehran's bazaar by a MEK hit squad on the tenth anniversary of the 1988 massacres.[82]

• • •

News of mass murder will get out. Reports of an increase in political executions in Iran appeared in the *Financial Times* and the *New York Times* in mid-August 1988 and on 2 September 1988 Amnesty International put out an Urgent Action telegram evincing its deep concern that 'hundreds of political prisoners may have been executed'.[83] There was no conception of the scale of the massacres, but in September, the Human Rights Commission's special representative for Iran, the El Salvador diplomat Reynaldo Pohl, was deluged with oral and written complaints about a 'wave of executions'. He raised this with Iran's permanent representative at the UN, at a meeting on 29 September 1988, only to be told that the 'killings' were merely those which had occurred on the battle-field after the Mojahedin's small Iraq-based army had attempted to invade Iran in mid-July. Iran's position was complete denial, with a refusal to answer Pohl's questions on the grounds that his information had been provided to him from MEK sources and was therefore unreliable propaganda.[84] Pohl nonetheless published in October credible allegations that 860 bodies of political prisoners had been dumped in a mass grave in Behesht-e Zahra cemetery in Tehran between 14 to 16 August 1988. (This interim report may have prompted Rafsanjani, then the speaker of the Parliament, to admit unguardedly in February 1989 that 'the number of political prisoners executed in the last few months was less than one thousand'[85] – a number he appeared to think was commendably low.)

In December Ali Khamenei, who would soon succeed Montazeri as the successor to the Supreme Leader, admitted in one of Iran's conservative newspapers to executing some Mojahedin in prison who had been found guilty (or so he claimed) of being in communication with the Rajavi forces when they launched their 'Eternal Light' attack.

> Did we ever say we had abandoned executions? In the Islamic Republic we have capital punishment for those who deserve to be executed ... do you think we should hand out sweets to an individual who, from inside prison, is in contact and plotting with the *monafeqin* who launched an armed attack within the borders of the Islamic Republic...? If his contacts with such a traitorous organisation have been established, what should we do about him? He would be sentenced to death and we will certainly execute him. This is not an action that we would hide. Of course, when we say 'we' I am referring to our regime: I am not in charge of the judiciary system.[86]

The semi-official Fars news agency would much later (July 2012) seek to justify the massacre on this ground, by claiming that international law allowed prisoners in contact with the enemy to be killed without trial. This is false: the Geneva Conventions protect prisoners of war from summary execution. Moreover, there is no evidence of any two-way contact. Although the Mojahedin may in some wards have had access to smuggled transistor radios which could be tuned to MEK radio stations, this was not 'contact' of a sort that could ever justify execution. Nor is there evidence of anyone being charged with espionage or communicating with the enemy, or even a suggestion that anyone was interrogated about any such offence.

Prime Minister Mir Hossein Mousavi (who twenty years later would be the main defeated candidate in the 2009 presidential elections) was asked in December 1988 by an Austrian television reporter what he had to say about the allegations made by the Western media concerning the Mojahedin killings: incautiously, he tried to defend them with the untrue response that 'they [i.e. the MEK prisoners] had plans to perpetrate killings and massacres. We had to crush the conspiracy ... in that respect we have no mercy.' He went on to urge Western intellectuals to acknowledge the right of third world governments to take 'decisive action' against their enemies – if only Allende in Chile had done so, Mousavi lamented, he would have survived. (Mousavi must have known that anyone in an Iranian prison in 1988 with Allende's leftist views would probably have been executed.) In February 1989 Khomeini delivered an 'historical message' about his former left-wing supporters: 'We are not sorry that they are not with us. They never were with us. The revolution does not owe anything to anyone.' He inveighed against 'the liberals' who had criticised him for 'enforcing God's sentence' against 'the hypocrites' and he warned against feeling pity for 'enemies of God and opponents of the regime'. He went on, 'As long as I exist I will not allow the regime to fall in to the hands of liberals. I will not allow the hypocrites to Islam to eliminate the helpless people.'[87] Although the Iranian stance at the UN was to deny all allegations about prison executions, these veiled but menacing under-statements by its leaders, for home consumption, can in retrospect be interpreted as a defiant justification for mass murder.

To its abiding shame, the UN was well aware of the massacres shortly after they had commenced and did absolutely nothing. Professor Pohl had been appointed in 1986 to report regularly upon the situation in this country, with particular concern to investigate the credible reports of executions and torture of political prisoners and the brutal repression of those who followed the Baha'i faith.[88] His first report, in 1987, confirmed the widespread use of *bastinado* and other torture techniques (medical examinations of escaped and released political prisoners had put this beyond doubt) but did no more than call on the Iranian government to set up a human rights commission to reply to what he described as 'allegations' of mistreatment and summary executions, and to allow him into the country. He noted 'with satisfaction' the government's agreement (on which it immediately resiled) to allow Red Cross visits with prisoners.[89] The government declined to address any of the allegations and instead diverted the professor by raising academic questions about the compatibility of Sharia law with international human rights, and historical quibbles about whether there had been sufficient input from Islamic jurists in the drafting of the Universal Declaration of Human Rights. The naive academic was more than happy to ponder these questions at length in his report in 1988: he made no effort to calculate the number of political prisoners in Iranian jails, which had by this stage run into many thousands, and he dropped his request to visit prisons (despite his awareness of information that 'some prisoners were in danger of execution'). He merely suggested that 'the government may wish to initiate an urgent investigation of these complaints in order to take measures of redress'.[90] The measures of redress the government wished to take, namely the murder of all prisoners associated with the opposition, began in late July 1988 and lasted until November.

On 26 August 1988 Pohl received information that 200 Mojahedin prisoners had been hanged in the assembly hall at Evin prison. But not until 28 September ('having received information about a wave of executions that was allegedly taking place since the month of July 1988') did he write to Iran's permanent representative inviting the government's comments. He did, however, make an interim report to the General Assembly on 14 October 1988, in which he clearly set out information that 'a large number of prisoners, members of opposition groups, were executed during the months of July, August and early September'[91] and reported that on 5 August the Chief Justice of Iran (Ayatollah Mousavi Ardebili) had announced that the judiciary was under pressure from public opinion to execute all members of the Mojahedin without exception and without trial, and had added a threat that more members of that organisation and 'other groups' of oppositionists would be executed.[92] The UN special rapporteur on summary executions had already telegrammed the Iranian Minister for Foreign Affairs to the effect that the state was breaching Article 14 of the ICCPR by executing prisoners after 'extremely summary, informal and irregular proceedings, failure to inform defendants of specific accusations against them, lack of legal counsel, absence of any instance of appeal and with irregularities that contravene international standards of fair trial'.[93] It is therefore quite clear that notwithstanding Professor Pohl's failure to take any urgent action during the massacre period, the General Assembly was provided on 14 October 1988 with evidence of mass murder in Iranian prisons. It did absolutely nothing, and nor did the Security Council.

Thereafter, credible and persistent reports of the 'wave of killings' continued to reach Pohl. In his next report in January 1989, he appended a list of the names of over 1,000 alleged victims and noted that his sources indicated that there had been several thousand, mostly from the Mojahedin but also from other left-wing groups. Many of the victims 'had been serving prison sentences for several years, whilst others are former prisoners who were re-arrested and then executed ... people witnessed large numbers of bodies being buried in shallow graves'.[94] Professor Pohl concluded:

These allegations deserve to be the subject of detailed investigation and information from the government concerned, in conformity with international practice.

Notwithstanding this knowledge, Professor Pohl became lost in admiration for the ceasefire (he records 'immense satisfaction and deep appreciation' to the Iranian government), which he is sure 'will soon turn its positive attention to human rights problems' and will investigate abuses of power. With astonishing credulity, he assumed in this crucial report that the Iranian government would investigate its own abuses, despite meetings with the Iranian representatives to the UN who, with utter dishonesty, had assured him that all the Mojahedin deaths had occurred on the battlefield.[95] No truthful information from the Iranian government was ever supplied to the UN special representative about the 1988 massacres. Professor Pohl made no real investigation of the massacre allegations, although at this stage (one year after the killings) the regime had not even permitted him to enter the country.

The following year, it felt sufficiently confident of Professor Pohl's lack of detective ability to allow him a six-day visit, with five days of meetings with its officials and half a day at Evin prison, where he was welcomed with a band concert (a tactic used by the Nazis for foreign visitors at Terezin and Auschwitz)[96] but denied access to the prisoners he requested to see.[97] They paraded before him instead some alleged inmates – they may not have been prisoners at all – who told him that 'their treatment was satisfactory and the food superb'[98] and some stooges from state-backed women's organisations who explained that 'women enjoyed freedom in absolute terms and without any limitations'.[99] He was not allowed to meet Ayatollah Montazeri, who had specifically asked Pohl to visit – a request that the incurious Pohl set no store by at the time.[100] The government told him it was 'now in a position to refute the false allegations made by its political enemies'[101] and stressed 'the role played by compassion in Islam'.[102] His report ended not with a bang, but a whimper: he merely noted that allegations about human rights violations were too common to lack credibility. Prior to his visit, the regime had removed flowers and memorial stones from the suspected site of a mass grave in the main Tehran cemetery, fearing that Pohl would insist on visiting it.[103] He did not even ask permission to do so.

The UN Human Rights Commission and the General Assembly, despite having some evidence of the massacres shortly after they commenced, made no effective investigation at that time or subsequently. Astonishingly, Professor Pohl's reports from 1991 onwards do not even mention them (although they note that execution of political prisoners without fair trial continues).[104] There can be little doubt that the Islamic Republic was emboldened to flout international law so outrageously as a result of the way in which it was able to avoid accountability, or even criticism, at the UN for the brutal extermination of thousands of its prisoners. This gave a sense of impunity, and the message that goes with it: if you can get away with murdering thousands of your prisoners, you can get away with other breaches of international law, like assassinating your enemies in other countries and even, eventually, acquiring nuclear weapons. In 1988, the Islamic Republic of Iran learned the easy way, from the failure of the UN and its commissions and its member states to investigate mass murders in Iranian prisons, that international law had no teeth for biting, or even for gnashing.

The UN had abjectly failed to conduct an effective investigation, but in December 1990 Amnesty International stepped up to the plate by publishing a short but hard-hitting account of 'The Massacre of 1988'. It pointed out that 'there was awareness at the highest level of the government that thousands of summary executions were taking place without regard to constitutional and judicial procedures' and it surmised that 'the massacre of political prisoners was a pre-meditated and co-ordinated policy, which must have been authorised at the highest level of government'. Just how high was conclusively revealed in 2000, when the 'Montazeri letters' revealed the truth about the massacres. They were published in *The Diaries of Ayatollah Montazeri,* compiled by his students in the holy city of Qom, where he lived (and where he died on 20 December 2009). He alone of the regime's senior leaders had refused to countenance the massacres, and for that reason he was expelled from the mullocracy and placed under house arrest.

As the years passed, survivors of the massacres gathered courage and came forward in books and on blog sites, and the families, of course, never forgot and never ceased in their attempts to find their children's graves. References to the massacres appeared in the award-winning feature film *Persepolis* and in the widely acclaimed memoir *Reading Lolita in Tehran,* where Azar Nafisi writes:

> The victims of this mass execution were murdered twice, the second time by the silence and anonymity surrounding their executions, which robbed them of a meaningful and acknowledged death and

thus, to paraphrase Hannah Arendt, set a seal on the fact that they never really existed.[105]

Comparisons are invidious, especially in levels of evil. The most vulnerable class of human beings – and hence deserving of the highest international protection – are prisoners in or of a war. The Iran prison massacres, by virtue of their calculated cruelty designed by the political and judicial leaders of the state, are more reprehensible than their comparators, the Bataan death march (whose 7,000 starving American and Filipino prisoners were literally marched to their deaths) and the execution of a similar number of Muslim men and boys at Srebrenica. Japanese General Homma, who ordered the Bataan march, was sentenced to death by the Manila War Crimes Tribunal (he was allowed the military dignity of a firing squad) whilst General Mladić is now on trial at The Hague and others of his staff at Srebrenica are serving forty-five years' imprisonment. The two leaders who advised and implemented the 1988 massacres, Khamenei and Rafsanjani, are respectively Supreme Leader and Expediency Council head, and the Death Committee judges remain in judicial place. They deserve to be put on trial at an international court, of the kind that can only be established by the Security Council.

CHAPTER 6

GETTING AWAY WITH MASS MURDER

In 1988, the state of Iran committed four exceptionally serious breaches of binding rules of international law which entail both state responsibility and individual accountability for war crimes and crimes against humanity, *viz* the arbitrary killing of thousands of male and female prisoners pursuant to a fatwa that held them collectively responsible for the Mojahedin invasion, notwithstanding that they had been in prison for years, serving fixed-term sentences for relatively minor offences. This was not the execution of a lawful sentence, because there was no trial, no charge and no criminal act other than adhering to a particular ideological group. The right to life, guaranteed by customary international law, by treaties to which Iran is a party and by the Geneva Conventions, was quite deliberately and barbarically breached, and all who bear international law responsibility for this mass murder should be prosecuted.

The second wave of apostate killings was also a breach of the right to life, as well as the right to religious freedom. The male prisoners who were executed were given some kind of trial, but it was wholly deficient in compliance with legal safeguards and massively unfair. They were denied lawyers and offered no time or facilities to prepare their defence and were taken by surprise by questions the implications of which they did not understand. They were executed for a crime of conscience in that their only offence was to refuse to adopt the religious beliefs, prayers and rituals of the state. Apostasy is not a crime for which the death penalty is permissible in international law, as most states in the world pointed out to Iran a few months later, when its Supreme Leader purported to sentence Salman Rushdie.

The beatings inflicted on leftist women and on other men who were regarded as capable of religious compliance satisfied the definition of torture, which is absolutely prohibited even if it is consonant with national law. The beatings by electric cable on the soles of the feet, five times a day for weeks on end, together in many cases with beatings on the body, were calculated to and did cause excruciating pain and extensive suffering as well as humiliation and degradation. The mental anguish was heightened by the fact that the beatings were inflicted to intimidate the prisoners to adopt a religion that they had rejected, and thus to surrender their freedom of conscience. Again, no defence of necessity can possibly arise: the only object of the beatings was to break their will and their spirit and to make them more amenable to the state's version of Islamic governance.

The rights to know where close relatives are buried and to mourn their deaths have been and still are being denied by the state. There is no possible justification, today, for denying information about burial locations or for prohibiting gatherings of mourners: there is no evidence to suggest that these gatherings would cause public disorder or breaches of the peace. What is being denied, two decades after the deaths, is the right of parents, spouses and siblings to manifest their feelings of devotion in respect of the memory of a family member: this is a denial of their rights to respect for home and family life (an aspect of privacy) as well as a denial of the right to manifest religious beliefs. It also amounts to discrimination, since no other class or category of the bereaved has been denied the opportunity to mourn. The refusal to identify mass graves implicitly involves a refusal to allow DNA testing (which has proven reliable in war crimes investigations as a means of identifying the remains in mass graves) and, in consequence, the prevention of a proper burial.

But how – and where – could Iran's offences be tried? The ICJ might be activated by a UN organ or by a member state, but Iran would refuse to cede jurisdiction to it. That would not matter if the General Assembly or another UN organ were to seek an advisory opinion (e.g. on whether the prison killings amounted to genocide or to a crime against humanity): in such a case, the consent of Iran would not be required – the reason why Israel could not stop the ICJ from deciding the issue of the Palestinian wall. The prospect of a claims tribunal, or any other form of arbitration or negotiation under UN auspices, depends upon *real-politik*. It may, for example, be urged that any concession to Iran in respect of its right to a full nuclear fuel cycle should be contingent upon its atoning for past human rights abuses by providing information and compensation to survivors and relatives of those it has unlawfully massacred, and upon opening mass graves so that DNA testing may establish and identify the remains. It has never occurred to the EU or UN diplomats who are always negotiating with Iran over its nuclear fuel cycle or imposing sanctions because of its nuclear progress to set conditions requiring it to remedy its past human rights violations.

War law has, for many centuries, protected unarmed prisoners in times of war, because of their utter vulnerability to sudden or summary execution or to torture by their captors. By the time of the English civil war in the 1640s, the obligation to give 'quarter' – to spare an enemy who yields – was a firm rule. Any soldier or officer guilty of slaying an unarmed prisoner in his custody was himself liable to execution. At the first war crimes trial of a head of state, in 1649, the most telling evidence against Charles I was that he had supervised the torture of prisoners of war.[106] From the sixteenth century onwards, a prohibition against torture and killing captives can be found in the ordinances of most European armies. For some time it was subject to a special tit-for-tat defence of 'reprisal' (Shakespeare, to justify Henry V's notorious Agincourt order to slay his French prisoners, had to invent a French war crime – killing the boys in the baggage train – which would give the King the right to retaliate).[107] This defence was rejected by Francis Lieber, whose code for the US Army remains the basis of customary international war law, and Article 13 of Geneva Convention III now prohibits any defence of reprisal: killing captive prisoners of war constitutes 'one of the most obvious and absolute of war crimes'.[108] The government of Iran was well aware of the Geneva Convention provisions: the state had ratified them and the government constantly complained to the UN about Saddam's breach of them by using chemical weapons.

So there can be no doubt that those who carried out the fatwa knew well that they were committing an act that was unlawful as a matter of IHL. Article 75 of the First Protocol to the Geneva Conventions defines minimum standards of humane treatment and the basic standards for fair trial – what are termed the 'elementary considerations of humanity', breach of which may entail both state liability and individual criminal liability.[109] These elementary considerations of humanity were breached routinely in the course of the 1988 massacres. Prisoners were arbitrarily executed without fair or (in the case of the MEK) any trial; they were tortured and viciously beaten after proceedings of which they were given no notice and in which they were given no rights of defence. 'Elementary considerations of humanity', as we shall see in Chapter 14, governs the use of nuclear weapons. So long as Iran's breaches of these considerations remain unpunished, can it be trusted not to breach them again if permitted to obtain the bomb?

Article 75 of Geneva Protocol I (1977) reflects the position that customary international law had reached by 1988 and it informs the modern content and interpretation of human rights law in wartime. The basic prohibitions – against arbitrary execution, torture and unfair trials – are all what lawyers term '*jus cogens*' rules of international law – i.e. principles so fundamental that no nation may breach or opt out of them. They are endorsed and amplified by the provisions of the ICCPR, which Iran ratified and which applied in 1988 notwithstanding the 1979 change in government. The ICCPR lays down that the death penalty is only permissible after a proper trial and appeal with defence rights guaranteed; it forbids torture and requires public trial; it guarantees freedom of expression and of religion. All these rights, recognised as part of customary international law, were grossly and indefensibly violated by the government of Iran.

Article 32 of the 1977 First Geneva Protocol refers to 'the right of families to know the fate of their relatives'. It imposes a correlative duty on the state to identify the graves of those it has executed and to permit families to mourn in peace at burial sites. This collection of rights has been said by the Inter-American Court of Human Rights to be derived from the right to life,[110] although more logically the Human Rights Committee has treated the refusal of a government to notify the family of executed convicts of the location of their body as a violation of the prohibition on inhuman and degrading treatment,[111] and the European Court of Human Rights has taken the same approach.[112] The anguish caused by the arbitrary denial of an opportunity to mourn the dead has been recognised at least since Sophocles dramatised the mental frenzy of Antigone, forbidden by Creon to bury her brother's body. The right to bury the dead is of fundamental importance to Muslims, and the Shia have taken a particularly firm line in this regard ever since Hussein, grandson of the Prophet Mohammed, was left unburied on the battlefield at Karbala in the year 680. On this basis, the continuing behaviour of the regime is not only calculated to inflict psychological torture, but is an especially cruel kind of hypocrisy.

There are a number of features of the 1988 massacres which would justify the establishment of an *ad hoc* court with a prosecutor tasked to investigate and issue indictments if appropriate. Firstly, the nature of the atrocity: there has been no comparable act of state slaughter of so many prisoners since the Japanese death marches. (The Muslim men and boys rounded up at Srebrenica were briefly taken hostage and were not serving prisoners.) Secondly, the embarrassing fact (for the UN) that Professor Pohl's investigation was stymied, partly because of lies and lack of co-operation from Iran (although he found out enough to put the General Assembly on notice of the crime, if not of its full magnitude). Thirdly, despite the passage of time, many of the men responsible for the massacres are (with the exception of Ayatollah Khomeini) still mainly in place or in higher place: there are survivors who remain alive and neutral witnesses available, and some members of the regime who are now living abroad are beginning to speak out, although sadly, Grand Ayatollah Montazeri died in 2009, so he cannot give the evidence that he asked to give to the incurious Professor Pohl. Member states whose concerns have been much focused on Iran's nuclear pretensions should investigate the human rights record of a regime which asks to be trusted in respect of undertakings to the international community not to develop nuclear weapons. Whether Supreme Leader Khamenei can be trusted to comply with international law should be pondered in light of his conduct in 1988 – conduct that makes him an international criminal.

Moreover, as a matter of international law, Iran has a duty to provide 'adequate compensation' to victims' families and survivors, and especially to victims' children.[113] In *Aloeboetoe* v. *Suriname*, the Inter-American Commission found the defendant state responsible for its soldiers, who arrested and tortured a group of fishermen and ordered them to dig their own graves before shooting them. It was ordered to pay US$500,000 to the benefit of each of the victims' children and relatives. These reparations were made up of actual damage (compensation for the trauma of having a close relative assassinated) and moral damage (compensation for the terror suffered by the victims in the hours before their death, the right to which becomes enforceable by their heirs). This latter head of damage is particularly appropriate in the case of the Iranian massacres, where the right to life was extinguished after torture and terror. The difficulty, however, is in finding a forum where such a claim could be adjudicated, since Iran refuses to accept the decisions of international courts.

CRIMES AGAINST HUMANITY

The crime against humanity entered international law by way of Article 6(c) of the Nuremberg Statute, which spelled out an offence of which Nazi leaders were convicted on 30 September 1946. The statute provided a law against

> murder, extermination, enslavement, deportation and other inhumane acts committed against any civilian population, before or during the war, or persecutions on political, racial or religious grounds in execution of or in connection with any crime, within the jurisdiction of the tribunal, whether or not in violation of the domestic law of the country where perpetrated. Leaders, organisers, instigators and accomplices participating in the formulation or execution of a common plan or conspiracy to commit any of the foregoing crimes are responsible for all acts performed by any person in the execution of such plans.

This definition would plainly cover the extermination of the MEK and the inhumane actions committed against the atheists, at the end and in the aftermath of the Iran–Iraq War, which actions in any event amounted to persecution on politico-religious grounds (in respect of the Mojahedin) and on religious grounds (in respect of the atheists) whether or not the fatwa was constitutional or the floggings were in compliance with Sharia law. Article 6(c) was the basis for convictions of Nazi government officials for the killing and torturing of their own nationals in concentration camps – German Jews and homosexuals who were not 'prisoners of war' – and the judgment at Nuremberg provides an authoritative basis for holding individuals at all levels, whether Revolutionary Guards, prison governors, political leaders or powerful theologians, liable for crimes against humanity. Torturers cannot rely on the defence of 'superior orders' any more than commanders can rely on the privileges and immunities of the states they serve.

In 1988, the crime against humanity existed in international law, as a result of the judgment at Nuremberg. The Iranian leaders could not therefore complain of being victims of retrospective law, if they were put on trial for the 1988 massacres. Crimes against humanity are too heinous to be barred by the passage of time.

The most authoritative contemporary definition of crimes against humanity is provided by Article 7 of the Rome Statute of the ICC. Such crimes include

> any of the following acts when committed as part of a widespread or systematic attack directed against any civilian population, with knowledge of the attack[:]
> Murder
> Extermination ...
> Imprisonment or other severe deprivation of physical liberty and violation of fundamental laws of international law
> Torture ...
> Persecution against any identifiable group or collectivity on political, racial, national, ethnic, cultural, religious, gender [grounds] ...
> Other inhumane acts of a similar character intentionally causing great suffering or serious injury to body or to mental or physical health.

The government policy towards the Mojahedin and the atheists in 1988 plainly satisfies this definition. The acts of murder and torture suffered by individuals were indubitably 'part of a widespread or systematic attack': they occurred almost simultaneously in at least twenty prisons throughout the country and they were organised and synchronised in the days after 28 July by the cancellation of prison visits, the denial of access to the media, the questioning of the Mojahedin and then of the leftists, the hangings or shootings and alternatively the beatings five times a day to force prisoners to pray. Although *murder* may seem an inapt way to describe any judicially sanctioned killing, the crime of *extermination* fits the facts, implying 'by its very nature' both a 'direction against a group of individuals' and 'the element of mass destruction'.[114] *Persecution* on political and religious grounds is also an accurate description of the fate inflicted upon the Mojahedin and the atheists.

Article 7(2)(a) goes on to say that the attack must be 'pursuant to, or in furtherance of, a state or organisational policy to commit such attack'. The overarching impression from the evidence is that of a policy to destroy or neutralise any religious dissenter who would pose a political problem for the Islamic regime after the war, and that this was implemented in two separate waves. This must have taken a great deal of expeditious organisation, building upon the information analysis that had accrued over previous years. The massacres were without doubt 'pursuant to a state or organisational policy to commit such attack'.

DEFENCES

Could any individual official involved in the massacres advance a credible defence to a charge of committing a crime against humanity? The death penalty *per se* is not contrary to international law and many other states, Islamic and secular, have penalties that include caning and whipping. But before any defence of 'lawful execution' could be sustained, it would have to be demonstrated that the death penalty was carried out in accordance with international law – after a fair trial process for a serious offence. And in the case of corporal punishment, it would have to be shown that the beatings did not exceed the severity threshold that amounts to torture, or to inhuman or degrading treatment or punishment.

So far as the Mojahedin executions are concerned, no defence of lawful execution could possibly be advanced. There was no 'trial', but merely a classification process by which all who were identified as adherents were immediately and arbitrarily killed. Many were available for execution because they were serving uncompleted fixed-term sentences for their minor acts of adherence or support in or after 1981: the fatwa simply annulled those sentences and replaced them with the sentence of death. The rest – the *mellikesh* – were in prison despite having completed their sentence for minor offences: the fatwa sentenced them anew, for no crime other than irreligion or disfavoured religious and political views, to death without trial. Under Article 6(2) of the ICCPR, capital punishment must be reserved for serious crimes with lethal or exceptionally serious consequences: the Human Rights Commission has consistently held that they cannot be imposed merely for political or religious allegiance[115] nor can capital punishment be imposed for crimes committed when the individual was aged under eighteen – and many of these victims had been arrested for offences committed when they were high school students.

There was a complete and utter disregard of all international law safeguards: the 'defendants' had no right to defend themselves, to be defended by a lawyer, to call evidence or to testify on their own behalf or to appeal. These denials of fair trial rights were very much more extensive than in *Öcalan* v. *Turkey*, where the Kurdistan Workers' Party leader's death sentence for the gravest terrorist crimes was held to have been vitiated by failure to provide him with adequate time and facilities to prepare a defence or allow him access to a lawyer.[116] The Iranian jail hearings lasted for no more than a few minutes during which the Mojahedin prisoners were merely identified as persons subject to a mandatory death sentence by fatwa, imposed as a measure of collective responsibility once they admitted to membership of or sympathy with that organisation. The hearings were in secret and the sentence was not pronounced publicly. Every safeguard required by international human rights law for the infliction of capital punishment was absent.

The 'second wave' death sentences on the apostates were also indefensible. There appears to have been in most cases a very short 'trial', in the sense of questioning by the panel to establish whether the defendant's parents were Muslim and whether he was a practising Muslim or not. There was no charge or indictment and they had no idea of the significance of their answers in respect of the theology being applied by the judges. The complete absence of any fair trial guarantees, essential for the imposition of capital punishment in international law, negates any defence of 'lawful execution', quite apart from the fact that the sentence was imposed for a crime – apostasy – which is not in the category of 'exceptionally grave offences' for which the death penalty must be reserved. The Human Rights Committee has specifically held that international law does not permit capital punishment for apostasy – a 'thought crime' which directly contradicts the right to change religion that is guaranteed by all human rights conventions and by the Universal Declaration.[117]

There is an interesting precedent afforded by the decision of the Iraqi High Tribunal in the *Dujail* case. That town – a haven for oppositionists – was the site of the attempted assassination of Saddam Hussein in 1982. Although attempted by only a few men, Saddam's officials rounded up 148 citizens: they were tortured and then executed without proper trial by a revolutionary tribunal. Saddam, who confirmed the sentences, the judge who imposed them, and the officials who organised the torture and executions were all convicted of crimes against humanity. The Iraqi Tribunal rejected the defence of necessity, i.e. that the prisoners were terrorists aligned with Iran, the wartime enemy, because their deaths were 'not necessary to stop an immediate and imminent danger' and the executions were disproportionate to any actual threat. The revolutionary judge who conducted the sham trial argued that he was under a legal obligation to do so, but the tribunal ruled that he had no justification for enthusiastically 'following the whims and moods of those that outranked him in power'. Like the Nazi judges convicted in the *Altstoetter* case, 'the dagger of the assassin was concealed beneath the robe of a jurist'.[118] The Iraqi High Tribunal was not an international court, and its bias and vulnerability to political manipulation undermines the authority of its actual verdicts,[119] but there is a general consensus among commentators that it was correct to reject the defences of 'necessity' and 'superior orders' proffered by the judge and the security officials.

TORTURE

Those excepted from executions were subjected to *bastinado* – severe beatings by electrical cable on the soles of their feet, five times a day until they agreed to pray or else died from the ill-treatment or committed suicide in pain and despair. Was their suffering capable of a justification defence based on a proviso to the 1984 UN Torture Convention, which excuses suffering 'arising only from, inherent in or incidental to, lawful sanctions'?

No sanction can be lawful, at least in international law, if it arises from torture, which is absolutely prohibited and was defined in 1975 by the UN's Declaration Against Torture as

> any act by which severe pain or suffering, whether physical or mental, is intentionally inflicted by or at the instigation of a public official on a person.

The punishments inflicted on apostates undoubtedly reached the severity threshold that constitutes torture. This is not a judgment that is made on individual cases in isolation: as the Hague courts ruled in relation to the Omarska concentration camp, punishments inflicted in a prison 'where detainees were kept in inhuman conditions and an atmosphere of extreme mental and physical violence pervaded the camp' (an apt description of the wards in Iranian prisons where political detainees were kept in August and September 1988) must be taken into account.[120] Whippings and beatings in this environment produce an intensity of suffering that is absent from the routine administration of corporal punishment in some other countries. Moreover, as early as 1969, in the landmark *Greek Case* brought against that government by other European states, the European Commission found that the use of *falange* (involving beating on the soles of the feet which is excruciating and causes swelling but leaves no other physical trace), amounted to torture and ill-treatment. In a series of cases from Turkey, where this technique is known as *falaka,* the European Court of Human Rights had no hesitation in treating it as torture.[121]

Although the jurisprudence on the definition of torture widened somewhat in the years after 1988, this does not alter the fact that the treatment of the second wave of prisoners amounted to 'torture' as it was well understood at that time. It would, of course, satisfy the current definition, which takes account of whether the acts were 'such as to arouse in the applicant feelings of fear, anguish and inferiority capable of humiliating and debasing him and possibly breaking his physical and moral resistance'.[122] This was exactly the purpose of the beatings – to break principled moral resistance to the religion of the state and to require five manifestations each day of grovelling obeisance to it.

• • •

So who would be – and is, because international crimes have no time limits – liable to prosecution for the 1988 crime against humanity? The Supreme Leader signed the fatwa, but it was advised and implemented by his two most powerful lieutenants, President Ali Khamenei and Commander Rafsanjani. They are equally responsible, followed by Chief Justice Ardebili, the Death Committee judges, the prison officials and the diplomats who aided and abetted the crime by lying to the UN. In such cases, international criminal law imposes a duty to prosecute those who bear greatest responsibility: the Revolutionary Guards who killed without compunction – some with evident enjoyment – could be spared a trial, on condition that they were prepared to testify against those who gave the orders. Any developed system of international justice should see the major perpetrators in the dock, but retribution was unavailable in 1988. There is still time for nemesis to catch up with Tehran's mass-murdering mullahs, many of them still running a government that is on the brink of acquiring a nuclear weapon capability. One way to stop the bomb falling into the hands of international criminals, of course, would be to put those criminals in jail.

This could happen, as it did with Saddam, as a result of foreign intervention and regime change, although as the Iraqi and Libyan experience shows, regime change justice can be difficult to distinguish from revenge. Where a great crime has been committed in the past, and its perpetrators have enjoyed impunity, it is proper for the Security Council to establish an 'ad hoc' tribunal to investigate, issue indictments if that is justified by the evidence, and if possible to try the perpetrators. This has been done in the Balkans, Rwanda, Cambodia, East Timor, Sierra Leone and Lebanon: in each of these countries, the Security Council deployed its power under Chapter VII of the UN Charter to establish tribunals before which international crimes could be prosecuted, called 'ad hoc' to distinguish them from the ICC, to which the Security Council may refer cases from any country, but only in relation to crimes committed after mid-2002. So although the ICC does not have jurisdiction over crimes committed before then, there are ample precedents for the Security Council to establish an 'ad hoc' tribunal with a prosecutor charged with investigating and indicting, whether or not these indictments are able to produce an immediate arrest. As we shall see in the next two chapters, these same perpetrators went on to commit further international crimes, notably an assassination campaign which ended the lives of several hundred dissidents and the bombing of a synagogue in Argentina; more recently (and within the jurisdiction of the ICC, if referred to it by the Security Council) they have turned Evin prison into a torture camp and have encouraged their agents to kill peaceful protesters from the Green Movement and to jail their lawyers. It is time – before Iran does obtain the bomb – for the world to examine, through a prosecutorial investigation, just how much blood is on hands that could soon grasp nuclear weapons.

Many still-powerful individuals appear to have been directly responsible for approving the death and torture sentences that they must or should have known to have been contrary to international law. On the well-known principle established by the *Altstoetter* case (dramatised in the film *Judgment at Nuremberg*) judges who contribute to crimes committed in the guise of legal process cannot themselves escape prosecution: as the Nuremberg prosecution put it, 'men of law can no more escape ... responsibility by virtue of their judicial robes, than the General by his uniform'.

Those defendants were convicted for 'administering legislation which they must be held to have known was in violation of international law'.[123] That would apply to those judges, still in office, who sat on the 'death committees', and to the 'guardian jurists' such as the President. In considering the complicity of professionals in crimes against humanity, there is no good reason to exclude diplomats who, knowing the truth, nonetheless lie about them to UN bodies to whom they owe a duty of frankness.

The international community has never conducted or demanded an investigation into the 1988 crime against humanity, and has never threatened sanctions unless Iran ends impunity and tells the relatives of victims where they have been buried. Sanctions galore for enriching uranium, no sanctions at all for putting thousands in mass graves. The Security Council would be perfectly entitled under its Chapter VII powers to establish an international court with a prosecutor who can quickly collect the incriminatory evidence and obtain access to the relevant state witnesses and records.

Many obvious suspects are still alive and well. They were men in Khomeini's inner circle; ministers and diplomats who knew what was happening; judges who betrayed their calling by zealously sentencing prisoners to death and torture without trial; prison governors and intelligence officers who shepherded the blindfolded victims to the queue for the gallows. There are many more who have been identified by survivors and are listed on dissident websites.[124] Although most of those judges and officials worked at Tehran's prisons, Evin and Gohardasht, where the main massacres took place, it is evident that there were hundreds and possibly thousands of prisoners killed in the provinces: Shiraz, Dezful, Tabriz, Qazvin, Arak, Khoramabad, Qom, Rasht, Esfahan, Mashhad, to name but ten local prisons. All would have had their trio of implacable judges, and their willing executioners from among the prison officials and intelligence operatives and Revolutionary Guards.

International law obliges all states to acknowledge and comply with their obligations under a human rights law which is fundamental and universal. It abominates systematic torture and summary executions – but that is what happened in the prisons of

Iran in the middle of 1988, as the result of orders that came from the very pinnacle of state power. Notwithstanding overwhelming evidence in the Boroumand Foundation and other reports, and from published accounts of survivors, Iran has drawn an iron veil over the prison massacres and has never admitted or been obliged to account for them. However, the pressure upon it has mounted, and on 1 August 2012, to mark the anniversary of what was termed 'the redeeming and lifesaving fatwa', the semi-official Fars news agency issued a statement purporting to 'prove the legitimacy of the 1988 executions from the perspective of international law'. It argued that the prisoners had been in contact with the MEK force in Iraq, and so became 'effectively a unit of the enemy military, in prison'. On this basis, the article absurdly suggests, they became liable to summary execution without the right to lawyers or to a defence or to appeal. It went on to applaud the Supreme Leader for establishing a 'three-member board' (i.e. his death committees) to investigate so as to make sure that individual prisoners had been in contact with the MEK before they were executed ('an innovation that deserves strongly to be applauded'). This statement, translated from Farsi by the Boroumand Foundation, is factually false in several respects: the prisoners may have been aware of Rajavi's army in Camp Ashraf but they were not part of it and the death committees did no investigation. There is no attempt to defend the killing of all the Marxists and atheists who were not MEK members. But the essential fraud is to suggest that international law permits the execution of prisoners who are members of an enemy force. On the contrary, the most basic rule of international humanitarian law is that prisoners of war – i.e. enemies in custody – must be treated humanely and can never be summarily executed. That is the whole point of Geneva Convention III, and by claiming that the MEK members in Iranian jails were prisoners of war, this Fars agency release implicitly concedes that their killing pursuant to the fatwa was a grave breach of the 1949 convention – a war crime that all state parties to that convention have a duty to prosecute by tracking down suspected perpetrators and putting them on trial.

I know that my blasphemer liveth: Salman Rushdie, 1988.

CHAPTER 7

GLOBAL ASSASSINS

A s the evidence of the 1988 mass murders began to leak out, the government of Iran was placed on the back foot. Prime Minister Mousavi dodged the question in December and then Rafsanjani pretended that the victims had numbered less than 1,000. If there is cunning in deflecting suspicion about a past atrocity by proposing another in the future, then the dying Ayatollah possessed it: on St Valentines Day, 14 February 1989, Khomeini unleashed the mother of all fatwas on the British writer Salman Rushdie:

> I would like to inform all intrepid Muslims in the world that the author of the book entitled *The Satanic Verses,* which has been compiled, printed and published in opposition to Islam, the Prophet and the Koran, as well as those publishers who were aware of its contents, have been sentenced to death. I call on all zealous Muslims to execute them quickly, wherever they find them, so that no one will dare to insult the Islamic sanctions. Whoever is killed on this path will be regarded as a martyr.

There could be no plainer incitement to murder. To the offer of a place in paradise was added a reward of $2.6 million for Iranian would-be assassins or $1 million for non-Iranian criminals if they managed to accomplish the murder of the writer or his publishers. This outrage drew almost unanimous condemnation from Western states, which Mousavi was quick to ridicule, whilst the Supreme Leader repeated that 'as long as I am alive, I will not let the state fall into the hands of the liberals'.[125] He was not alive for long (Khomeini died three months later) but his successor at Supreme Leader, Ali Khamenei, and Ali Khamenei's successor as President, Akbar Hashemi Rafsanjani, saw to it that the state did not fall into the hands of liberals, royalists or communists by the simple process of killing their leaders, wherever in the world the Iranian intelligence services could find them.

Between 1989 and 1996, the government's global assassination campaign claimed over 160 individual victims. Once again, the UN's special rapporteur, the impotent Professor Pohl, failed to sound a loud enough alarm, and it should also be said that certain countries – notably France and Austria – connived in allowing assassins to escape in order to retain trade with Iran. Nonetheless, Iran's conduct in this seven-year period, when Supreme Leader Ali Khamenei and President Rafsanjani are said to have spearheaded a secret committee which drew up the hit list and approved the murder plans, amounted to a further crime against humanity, in addition to the prison massacres of 1988. In this period, too, Iran killed foreign-based leaders of its Kurdish separatist movement, sponsored Hezbollah and later Hamas, and experimented with terrorist operations in Latin America, bombing Jewish targets and killing over a hundred civilians. Its international conduct, followed by 'chain murders' when state officials killed a number of locally based writers and intellectuals, constituted a widespread and systematic plan to liquidate opponents of the theocratic government. Almost all of the perpetrators of this second international crime – Khamenei and Rafsanjani themselves, the Ministry of Intelligence officials, the Revolutionary Guard leaders, diplomats (Iranian embassies helped shelter some of the assassins) and those actual killers who escaped arrest – are alive and well and living in Iran today.

THE RUSHDIE AFFAIR

The most interesting, yet least remarked, aspect of *The Satanic Verses* is that it is not as the fatwa claims, 'in opposition to Islam, the Prophet and the Koran'. Misled by the Ayatollah's misreading of the book (he was virtually blind by this time, and unlikely to have read it at all) many thousands of Muslims throughout the world demonstrated against its publication, and twenty-two were crushed to death when a protest in Bombay turned into a riot. Hitoshi Igarashi, who had translated the work into Japanese, was assassinated, stabbed over and over in the face and the arms in the frenzy that would mark so many other assassinations instigated by the state of Iran. The book's Italian translator and its Norwegian publisher were severely injured in assassination attempts. Almost a quarter-century later the fatwa required the cancellation of Rushdie's visit to a literary festival in India. Yet when an attempt was made in London in 1991 to prosecute the author for blasphemy, the thirteen Muslim barristers who worked on this forensic *jihad* were hard put to find anything to charge in the indictment. The book is the fictional story of two men, infused with Islam but confused by the temptations of the West. The first survives by returning to his roots. The other, Gibreel, pole-axed by his spiritual need to believe in God and his intellectual inability to return to the faith, finally commits suicide. The plot, in short, is not an advertisement for apostasy. The Muslim prosecutors could only allege six blasphemies in the book, and each one was based either on misreading it or upon theological error.

- God is described in the book as 'The Destroyer of Man'. *As He is similarly described in the Old Testament and the Book of Revelation, especially of men who are unbelievers or enemies of the Jews.*
- The book contains criticisms of the prophet Abraham for his conduct towards Hagar and Ishmael and their son. *Abraham deserves criticism and is not seen as without fault in Islamic, Christian or Jewish traditions.*
- Rushdie refers to Mohammed as 'Mahoud'. He called him variously 'a conjuror', 'a magician' and a 'false prophet'. *Rushdie does nothing of the sort. These descriptions come from the mouth of a drunken apostate, a character with whom neither author nor reader has sympathy.*
- The book grossly insults the wives of the Prophet by having whores use their names. *This is the point. The wives are expressly said to be chaste, and the adoption of their names by whores in a brothel symbolises the perversion and decadence into which the city had fallen before it surrendered to Islam.*
- The book vilifies the close companions of the Prophet, calling them 'bums from Persia' and 'clowns', whereas the Koran

treats them as men of righteousness. *These phrases are used by a depraved hack poet, hired to pen propaganda against the Prophet.*

- The book criticises the teachings of Islam for containing too many rules and seeking to control every aspect of everyday life. *Characters in the book do make such criticisms, but they cannot amount to blasphemy because they do not vilify God or the Prophet.*[126]

The case against *The Satanic Verses* was really contrived for domestic reasons, to rally the faithful to maintain the revolution after the imminent death of the Supreme Leader Ayatollah Khomeini, whose cancer was now far advanced. To this extent, it worked: hysterical mass grief was on display at his funeral as mourners clung to his open coffin as it bobbed and lurched on a sea of undulating and wailing humanity, tearing at the shroud and exposing a scrawny white leg. With the media distracted, the regime managed to translate Ali Khamenei, the mediocre Islamic jurist, to the position of Supreme Leader. The loyal Prime Minister, Mousavi, explained that international outrage over the fatwa proved that the West could not be trusted, and exulted as radical Muslims in countries throughout the world took the bait and zealously burned the book at protest meetings, whilst the new Supreme Leader demonstrated his revolutionary credentials by demanding that Rushdie 'must be handed over to British Muslims to be killed for committing blasphemy'. President Rafsanjani added that the death sentence was irrevocable and supported by 'the entire Muslim world'.[127] The consequence of his incitement to a terrorist murder, even with respect to European states that wanted friendship and trade with Iran, were calamitous for his country, which was severely damaged by the ensuing sanctions. In 1992, President Rafsanjani tried to placate European states by explaining that the government would not itself 'despatch commandos to kill Salman Rushdie' (although apparently other organisations were free to do so). Even this measly concession caused uproar in Tehran, where hardliners insisted that the fatwa was valid forever, and religious foundations promised to pay the declared bounty. Rushdie was not an Iranian and had no connection with the country, which added to the international outrage over his *in absentia* death sentence. This incitement to murder was a UK crime, but not of itself a crime against humanity, although it could be used as evidence of predisposition to such a crime along with other assassination plots, many of them success-ful, which were targeting leaders of the Iranian dissident diaspora at this time. MI6 later discovered that there had been a meet-ing of the 'Special Affairs Committee', at which Rushdie's death had been ordered by the new Supreme Leader, and a plan for it had been drawn up by the intelligence ministry chief, Ali Fallahian.[128] The writer had to stay in hiding under the alias Joseph Anton for many years. The UK caught some Iranian diplomats who were plotting an assassination although they had no luck infiltrating Rushdie's intellectual circles (one dangerous gang of English criminals were attracted by the bounty, but lost interest when they studied the small print: they had to prove their entitlement by being found guilty of the murder, by which time they would be serving life imprisonment). In 2005, long after the danger seemed to have passed, the Supreme Leader described Rushdie as an apostate who deserved to die, whereupon government agencies confirmed that the fatwa was still in force.[129]

THE GLOBAL ASSASSINATION CAMPAIGN

The government of Iran, operating through its highest officials and making use of its diplomatic embassies, conducted a global assassination campaign against Iranian dissidents that led to over 160 murders between 1989 and 1996.

After Ayatollah Khomeini's death, the most powerful mullahs established a 'Special Affairs Committee' chaired by the new Supreme Leader, Ali Khamenei. It usually met at one of the Shah's former residences, the Turquoise Palace.[130] Its members included the new President; Rafsanjani; Mohammad Reyshahri, who had been Minister of Intelligence at the time of the prison massacres; his deputy and successor, Ali Fallahian; the Revolutionary Guard leader Mohsen Rezai, who had asked the Ayatollah's approval for the country to develop nuclear weapons; the Foreign Minister, Ali Akbar Velayati (predicted to be the regime's candidate for the 2013 presidential election); and Ayatollah Khazali, a brutal jurist. Another member was said to be Ali Larijani, much later to become the regime's chief negotiator on nuclear weapons and currently the Speaker of the Majlis. Recommendations to assassinate individuals were canvassed at their meetings, and once the Supreme Leader approved, a committee member would be charged with implementation, using resources from the Intelligence and Foreign Ministries, and sometimes involving the Revolutionary Guards and their new Qods force, an elite unit trained for secret foreign missions. In some cases, Hezbollah operatives were used as proxies. A 'licence to kill' would be signed by the Supreme Leader and shown to leaders of the particular operation.

One gruesome feature of these assassinations was that most were carried out as brutally as possible – the victims died from multiple stab wounds or repetitious gunfire, inflicted by frenzied killers. Another sickening aspect of the campaign was the way in which the killings were not merely condoned but publicly celebrated by top clerics in Iran. Ali Fallahian, the Minister of Intelligence, who was in operational command of most of the death squads, boasted about his success on television and was publicly congratulated by new Supreme Leader Khamenei for 'uprooting the enemies of Islam, inside and outside the country'. Although Fallahian has been identified as the director of a number of killings, and has in consequence collected three Interpol 'Red Notices' which still confine him to Tehran, this executioner-in-chief remains influential – he was recently a security adviser to the Supreme Leader. His impunity serves to remind all oppositionists that their days of opposition may well be numbered: this is a government which continues to terrorise its opponents. Throughout the assassination period, co-terminous with Rafsanjani's presidency (1989–96), the regime found it more satisfactory to terrorise its opponents and their families than to avoid reprisals from outraged states whose laws they had violated. These reprisals were never serious enough, or so well co-ordinated, as to deter the regime from savouring the fear it was spreading among its enemies.

The executions commenced soon after the revolution, in January 1979, with the Shah's captured generals and SAVAK officials shot by firing squad on the roof of the Islamic Girls High

School in Tehran, following a brief hearing before a religious judge (Ayatollah Khalkhali) and an appeal, invariably refused a few hours later by the Supreme Leader. 'Criminals should not be tried,' he declared. 'Human rights demand that we should have killed them in the first place when it became known they were criminals. Our belief is that criminals should not be tried and must be killed.'[131] This was the mentality which infused the mullahs from the outset: critics of the Islamist government were enemies of God (*mohareb*) and should be killed whenever and wherever possible, without the need for legal process.

It followed from the logic of 'execution after identification as God's enemy' that any Iranian nationals who declared themselves hostile to the regime could be liquidated wherever they might be found: they were condemned as apostates who had rejected the true Islamic rule of *velayat-e faqih* enshrined in the Constitution. By rejecting the state they were treasonable, and by rejecting God they were blasphemous: in the theocratic republic, there was no difference and death was the automatic decree. As the regime's revolutionary judge, Ayatollah Khalkhali, announced after the first foreign murder, 'if we cannot arrest them, we will assassinate them'.[132] That was his way of celebrating the shooting in Paris of the Shah's nephew, Shariar Shafiq, as early as December 1979, whilst he was on his way to visit his mother, Princess Ashraf Pahlavi. 'We were lucky,' joked this judge. 'We were after his mother, but we got him instead.'[133]

With this gallows humour, the overseas assassination campaign began; an agent of the regime next struck in Bethesda, Maryland, shooting Ali Tabatabai, a former diplomat who had set up a foundation to work for a secular democracy. His killer escaped to Geneva, where he was harboured by the Iranian embassy and spirited back to Tehran, to be personally congratulated by Ayatollah Khomeini.[134] Another early target was General Oveisi, a Shah loyalist who was organising a royalist opposition movement in Paris. Khalkhali publicly sentenced him and others – including the Shah's last Prime Minister, the liberal Shapour Bakhtiar – to death *in absentia*, announcing outrageously that 'any Iranian who kills one of these people in foreign countries is considered an agent executing a court order'.[135] The killing of Oveisi was hailed in Iran as a 'revolutionary execution' and others followed – in Pakistan, Turkey, the Philippines, India and Austria. In 1987 the Revolutionary Guards claimed credit for killing a dissident and his son in their home in Wembley, a suburb of London, whilst in Geneva they shot Ahmad Talebi, an air force officer who had been Rafsanjani's private pilot and had left Iran to protest against the barbarity of his employer.

After Ayatollah Khomeini's death, the newly formed Special Affairs Committee under his successor proceeded to authorise more high value targets. Their first successful assassination was of Dr Abdul-Rahman Ghassemlou, secretary general of the PDKI, and two other supporters, in a Vienna apartment to which they had been lured for 'peace talks' with Iranian government officials. The meeting had been instigated by Iraqi Kurd leader Jalal Talabani, an unwitting dupe of Iranian intelligence. The three unarmed Kurds met with Mohammed Sahraroudi, an official of the Intelligence Ministry, and several government agents: afterwards, their bullet-riddled bodies (each having received a *coup de grâce* in case they managed to survive multiple wounds) were discovered. The police had no doubt that the Iranian ministry-men had assassinated them, but in a sorry display of cowardice the Austrian government arranged for the suspects to leave the country after Iran threatened reprisals if they were arrested. Once safely back in Tehran, Sahraroudi was promoted to brigadier general and became head of the Qods force intelligence directorate. Austrian prosecutors indicted him when it was safe to do so three months after the government had arranged his escape and had signed a lucrative weapons deal with Iran.[136]

The Special Affairs Committee took heart from this pathetic behaviour and in 1992 arranged a more spectacular strike against the PDKI, whose leaders were to meet at the Mykonos Restaurant in Berlin. Evidence at the trial of the assassins established that the committee's approval of the assassination received the written authorisation of Ali Khamenei and was entrusted by Fallahian to Abdul-Rahman Banihashemi, who had led the hit team which had killed Rafsanjani's disaffected pilot in Geneva in 1987. The Ministry of Intelligence supplied him with an Uzi sub-machine gun, an automatic pistol and a team of local agents on loan from Hezbollah. The hit squad burst into the private dining room of the restaurant, led by Banihashemi, who shouted 'Sons of whores' and opened fire with the sub-machine gun, killing the four PDKI leaders and wounding others of their party. The assassins escaped, but their weapons were recovered and linked with weapons used in previous assassinations of Iranian dissidents in Cyprus and Hamburg. Although Banihashemi fled Europe with the help of Iranian embassies, and was reportedly rewarded with a Mercedes and shares in companies run by Revolutionary Guards, three members of his squad were arrested and put on trial. Ali Fallahian flew to Berlin three weeks before the trial opened to demand that the charges be dropped. His colossal effrontery cut no ice with the Germans, even after orchestrated demonstrations outside the German embassy in Tehran. The trial went on for three years, and its evidence exposed the structure of the Iranian government's machinery for liquidating overseas dissidents.

The most important witness was Abolghassem Messbahi, ex-intelligence chief for western Europe, and the highest-ranking defector from the Ministry of Intelligence so far, who identified the membership of the Special Affairs Committee at the Turquoise Palace and explained in detail how the Supreme Leader had authorised Fallahian to order the 'hit'.[137] (Messbahi, last heard of under protection in Germany, remains a vital witness if ever the Supreme Leader and the Special Affairs Committee members are brought to international justice.)

Iran's first elected President, Abolhassan Bani-Sadr, took the witness stand to explain that the Mykonos murders had been authorised by Supreme Leader Khamenei. Iranian television tapes of Ali Fallahian boasting of strikes his ministry must have planned against the PDKI raised the question of why he had not been arrested when he came to Berlin to demand the release of the defendants. Only one organiser and one gunman were convicted in 1997 and jailed for life. The judge concluded:

> The political leaders of Iran gave the order for the murders ... The evidence makes it clear that the Iranian rulers not only approve of assassinations abroad and that they honour and reward

the assassins, but that they themselves plan these kind of assassinations against people who, for purely political reasons, become undesirable. For the sake of preserving their power, they are willing to liquidate their political opponents.[138]

• • •

There could be no clearer verdict upon a regime. But Germany merely recalled its ambassador from Tehran, as did fourteen other European states together with Australia and New Zealand, but the breach was shortlived and purely symbolic. Both Rafsanjani and Ali Khamenei made dishonest statements denying government involvement. Nobody believed them, because by this time the role of the Intelligence Ministry in over one hundred similar political assassinations had become clear. Kazem Rajavi, for example, the diplomat brother of Massoud who frequently led MEK delegations to international conferences, was driving to his Geneva home when two cars blocked his path. One assassin sprayed his windscreen with machine gun bullets, and two gunmen drew alongside and shot him five times at point blank range. One of their cars was hidden at the Iranian mission to the UN and could not be inspected. Arrest warrants were issued, and two suspects were later arrested in Paris. The Swiss applied for extradition, but the cowardly French government, in fear of threatened terrorist reprisals, sent the suspects back to Tehran.[139] Once again, craven compliance with the demands of a terrorist state had allowed assassins to go free. The Swiss were rightly outraged, but nothing could be done. In 2006 they decided to issue a warrant against Ali Fallahian, alleging that he ordered the murder.

It might be said of the MEK in this period that it was still engaged in guerrilla warfare against the regime, and had not shed its early Marxist influence. That was not the case with NAMIR, the rallying point of those the mullahs hated most – the liberals who exposed their crimes and their intellectual deficiencies and were genuinely in favour of democracy. They were led by Dr Shapour Bakhtiar, once a minister in Mossadegh's legendary government, who had later been imprisoned by SAVAK for criticising the Shah's autocratic rule. As opposition to that rule increased in 1978, he had agreed to head a government which would introduce democratic reforms: it lasted only thirty-seven days (in which it dissolved SAVAK, freed political prisoners and lifted press censorship) before it was swept away with the return of Khomeini. The brutal Judge Khalkhali had sentenced him to death *in absentia* and the regime made several unsuccessful attempts to kill him at his refuge in Paris – on the first occasion its agents murdered a policeman and a neighbour who got in their way. Police identified the organiser of the attack as an agent working undercover as a translator at the Iranian embassy, in which he sought asylum. The French officials demanded his surrender, but after the French embassy in Tehran was surrounded by protesters they allowed him to fly home.[140] (The would-be assassins were jailed for life, but pardoned a few years later and allowed to return to Iran as part of a deal by which Iran used its influence to secure the release of three French hostages held in Lebanon by Hezbollah.)

Next came a poison plot. The would-be poisoner (who claims he was incited personally by Fallahian) was supplied with a vial of powder to mix with Bakhtiar's vodka, and promised a reward of $600,000 and a house in Tehran.[141] The recruit, a member of the ragtag group of displaced Iranians who collected around Bakhtiar in Paris, got cold feet and sought political asylum in America.

But NAMIR was easy to infiltrate, and the Iranian Intelligence Ministry had better luck with one of its top spies, Fereydoun Boyer Ahmadi, who wormed his way into the leader's trust, to such an extent that he was one of the few who was permitted to pass without objection through the police guard at Bakhtiar's residence. In April 1991, an Iranian assassin murdered Bakhtiar's friend and colleague, Dr Abdorrahman Boroumand, a fellow veteran of Mossadegh's National Front who had helped to found NAMIR. He was stabbed to death in the lobby of his apartment, after which Bakhtiar told his friends (including his false friend Boyer Ahmadi) that he was planning to move to more secure premises. The Ministry of Intelligence acted quickly, using the Telecommunications Minister to obtain entry visas to France for two of the most accomplished assassins from the Qods force. Security officials of Iran Air at Orly airport were used to provision the assassination team and assist their escape. Some of the assassins' calls were made to the Iranian mission at the UN in Geneva (evidently tasked to assist them), and they reported to the Iranian embassy in Bonn. A British GCHQ monitoring station in Cyprus on the night of the murder picked up a chilling telephone enquiry from the Ministry of Intelligence in Tehran, asking its Bonn embassy to confirm Bakhtiar's death. A relative of Rafsanjani was accredited to the Iranian mission in Switzerland, ostensibly as an archivist although his undercover job was to help the two assassins to escape. They were both subsequently identified as senior Intelligence Ministry officials attached to the Qods force.[142]

The killing was as daring as it was brutal, of a man guarded around the clock by an elite police protection team. The spy Boyer Ahmadi called Bakhtiar to arrange a meeting with two men he said had urgent information. These three came to the home, presented their passports to the police guards and were searched. They proceeded to meet with the 76-year-old Bakhtiar, whom they stunned with a blow to the head and strangled by tearing out his vocal cords. With a bread knife obtained from the kitchen, these frenzied killers stabbed him numerous times (to a 7-inch depth) and then jumped on his chest, breaking his ribcage. When his assistant came in with tea, they suffocated him and stabbed him thirteen times. Then Boyer Ahmadi coolly went down to the police guarding the house and retrieved the passports, taking the bloodstained assassins out the back door and into his BMW. They drove off, dumping their passports and their clothes in the Bois de Boulogne, where they were later discovered by a passing prostitute. This was the assassination of which the Iranian government was most proud: a scholarly democrat, butchered by professional killers on a mission ordered by the Supreme Leader and the most powerful clerics in his government. In Tehran, the tame press rejoiced in Bakhtiar's death, quoting President Rafsanjani: 'We must show that we are powerful and stable by assassinating people from the opposition.'[143]

One of the assassins and several of the accomplices were convicted, but the spy and the other assassin escaped with the help of Iranian diplomats. Throughout the assassination years (1989–96) Ministry of Intelligence killers struck again and again at leading dissidents, in drive-by killings or by the infiltration technique used on Bakhtiar. There was compelling evidence, in some of these cases, of government direction and of the complicity of Iranian embassies, which abused diplomatic immunity to organise equipment and escape routes for assassination teams. Occasionally, exposed diplomats were declared *persona non grata*, but this was no substitute for punishment – back in Tehran, they wore expulsion as a badge of honour. It is a sad reflection on the lack of human rights concerns in Europe at the time, at least in respect of oil-rich Middle Eastern countries, that only Rushdie and the Mykonos murders produced diplomatic reactions in the form of sanctions, which were polite and short lived. There was, of course, a double standard: the threat to the celebrated literary figure was roundly condemned, whilst the murder of distinguished Iranians like Boroumand and Bakhtiar was largely ignored.

THE BUENOS AIRES BOMBINGS

The regime's anger at Argentina, which under US pressure pulled out of a deal to help it develop nuclear power, was in all probability the motive for revenge attacks in this period on Jewish targets in Buenos Aires – joint operations between the Ministry of Intelligence and Hezbollah. The first attack, in 1992 on the Israeli embassy, took twenty-two lives. The second, in 1994, was a bombing at a Jewish community centre which left eighty-five dead. There is evidence that this later attack had been approved by a Special Affairs Committee meeting at Moshad in August of 1993, as a way of venting the regime's fury at Argentina's nuclear pullout, encouraged by the fact that the previous Israeli embassy bombing had been a success.[144] This time, however, Iranian fingerprints were left – notably those of Ali Fallahian and an Iranian intelligence official, who was hastily given diplomatic cover by masquerading as a cultural attaché.[145] The ten-year Argentinian prosecution investigation was beset by incompetence and in its early stages by a desire to cover up for corrupt policemen who had been bribed to assist the plotters and other corrupt police who were bribed to tamper with evidence. Eventually, a respected

Argentinian judge characterised the bombing as a crime against humanity and issued international arrest warrants for Fallahian, Mohsen Rezai (the former commander of the Revolutionary Guards), the cultural affairs officer and the third secretary at the Iranian embassy. He drew the line at indicting President Rafsanjani and the Supreme Leader, although it was clear that the evidence justified charges against them as well.[146]

This mass murder was an unusual and dangerous targeting decision, which could have had serious consequences (and may do yet). That the Special Affairs Committee could authorise it – and the Argentinian prosecutors and judge had no doubt that they did[147] – indicated a desire for revenge over loss of the Argentinian nuclear deal. As we have seen (on page 38) the Shah had an ambitious civilian nuclear programme which he had dreamed would in due course produce nuclear weapons. It had been abandoned by the revolutionary government soon after Khomeini came to power, but Saddam's deployment on the battlefield of chemical weapons was one reason why, in the mid-1980s, the regime became suddenly very interested in acquiring a bomb. It turned to Argentina, which had an advanced nuclear power programme and the added advantage, at the time, of having refused to sign the NPT. So in 1987 lucrative agreements were put in place for Argentina to supply 20 per cent HEU, to train Iranian nuclear scientists and to complete the reactor at Bushehr. When at the end of 1991 the Argentinians agreed to assist in further uranium enrichment, the US decided that enough was enough. The President, Carlos Menem, was persuaded to cancel the contracts.[148] Had this been a routine commercial setback, Iran would have taken no reprisals, certainly not reprisals so deadly and dangerous as detonating 275 kilograms of explosions in a community centre. But the need to acquire nuclear weapons had taken hold among the mullahs, who believed, almost as an article of faith, that Saddam had forced them into a humiliating truce because he had used unlawful chemical weapons – weapons that in any future conflict could only be trumped by the bomb, which Iran's security would ultimately require. Hence Argentina deserved an unpleasant punishment for obliging 'the Great Satan', and forcing Iran to look elsewhere for technical assistance – which it was to obtain from the A. Q. Khan network (see page 199).

THE CHAIN MURDERS

International criminal law is designed to protect people against persecution by their own rulers should that persecution reach such a pitch that it constitutes a crime against humanity. The mass murder of prisoners in 1988 clearly qualifies, as does the subsequent assassination campaign against dissidents residing abroad. A further set of systematic offences, which came to light during the 'Tehran Spring' which followed the election to the presidency of the reformer Khatami in 1997, may also qualify, if it is properly investigated and its most powerful perpetrators uncovered. It is called 'the chain murders', i.e. serial killings by the state, and concerns – so far as has been admitted – the stabbing and strangling of a number of leading Iranian intellectuals and political theorists by a group within the Ministry of Intelligence led by a senior official, Saeed Emami. To everyone's amazement, under pressure from a newly free press, the Ministry of Intelligence actually admitted, in January 1999, that 'the despicable and abhorrent recent murders' were committed by 'a small number of irresponsible, misguided, headstrong and obstinate staff within the Ministry'.[149] They had, it said, been led astray by foreign agents, although they had in fact been led astray by life in a ministry that paid no attention to the law. Some of the group were jailed, and Emami, the principal scapegoat, soon died unpleasantly in prison so that he could never identify Fallahian and Khamenei, from whom his orders were most likely to have come. It is now believed that there were up to eighty victims and that those responsible occupied higher offices than Emami. The case should be reopened, although it is one of the very few in which any officials of the regime have been held to account in Iran.

The inability of the mullahs – for all their theological pretentions, most were men of mediocre intelligence – to tolerate the intellectual or the scholar or the poet is one of the most telling features of the governance which followed Khomeini's revolution. *Velayat-e faqih* was not a particularly interesting idea, and has been rejected by many Shia scholars and by some of its originators (Montazeri, for example). Ali Khamenei succeeded Khomeini as Supreme Leader because he was always in the right place at the right time (even as a target of an MEK attack, after which his injuries gave him standing) but no one regarded him as a good jurist. Rafsanjani, certainly, was clever and cunning and politically astute (except in his later years) and utterly amoral when it came to murdering enemies and taking public money for his personal use, but he has added nothing to Shia theology other than some bloodthirsty Friday sermons. These men and their clerical allies were clearly aware of their own intellectual limits, and their insecurity may have contributed to a wish to eliminate those of superior intellect or learning. Although the killings of leftists in the 1980s were fuelled by hatred, there was always a fear of Marxism, in any of its forms. Now it was the fear of genuine Shia scholarship which might weaken popular belief in the de-occulation of the Twelfth Imam or argue for separation of church and state. Oppositionists in 1988 were murdered because they were atheists and apostates, but ten years on, they were killed because the regime feared the intelligence of their opposition to it.

This fear of the intellectual showed up in the chain murder targets, chosen not because of their political clout or advocacy of regime change, but because their writings, drawing on a history of Persian literature and scholarship, put the regime to cultural shame. In the 1990s it turned on its own writers and artists – those who had stayed in Iran, mostly supportive of the revolution, although later expressing doubts. Some victims were Sunni theorists who challenged the brand of Shia religion promoted by the regime, whilst others were writers and teachers who were organising to demand relaxation of censorship. Some 'disappeared' – their bodies later found, dead from strangulation, on deserted roadsides. Others were taken into prison where they died, invariably from 'cardiac arrest' – a consequence, it was later alleged, of potassium suppositories or cyanide. In one blackly comic occasion that could have turned into a major tragedy, the Writers' Union hired a bus to carry twenty-one of its members to a literary seminar in Armenia. The chain murder plotters in the Ministry of Intelligence arranged a switch of drivers to one of their own men – Khosrow Barati. When the bus approached a deep ravine on the Havrun Pass he suddenly jumped out, leaving its scholarly passengers to plunge to their deaths. Luckily one of them jumped into the driver's seat and jammed on the brakes.[150]

After the stabbing to death of a surviving Mossadegh minister, Dariush Forouhar, and his wife, in 1998 and the discovery of the strangled bodies of several other writers, the recently elected President Khatami set up an inquiry and the press, newly and briefly liberated, investigated as well: all the trails led to the door of the Ministry of Intelligence. As the evidence mounted, the ministry made its unique public confession, identifying Emami, one of its deputy directors, as the person who bore responsibility. He was taken to prison, where he conveniently died – from 'cardiac arrest', brought on, so the ministry said, by 'suicide from drinking a depilatory compound'. ('It is impossible for Saeed Emami to have killed himself with the compound,' said Shirin Ebadi, the lawyer for Forouhar's family.)[151] Several men in Emami's team were given lengthy prison sentences (including Khosrow Barati, who confessed to the plot to run the writers' bus over the cliff) but his death prevented an investigation into the higher-ups, as high perhaps as the Supreme Leader, who would have given this well-known ministry thug his orders. As for the investigative journalists whose work kept up the pressure on the ministry, the regime marked their cards and several were in due course jailed for sedition. Shirin Ebadi, later to receive a Nobel prize, was targeted as the next link in the lethal chain: the murderers had been ordered not to kill her until the holy month of Ramadan had passed – by which time their activities had been exposed. This would have been a precursor to the attack on lawyers which became such a marked feature of the regime's response to the Green Movement in 2009.

NUCLEAR TENSION: THE CAMPAIGN REVIVED?

The international terror campaign, in which the Argentinian bombings may be counted, as well as the chain murders, was called off (with the exception of continuing support for Hamas and Hezbollah) by President Khatami, elected President in 1997 as leader of a reform movement which for a time faced down the hardline clerics and even muted the hatreds in the heart of the Supreme Leader. Khatami's government forswore any action over the Rushdie fatwa, and promised not to assist or encourage anyone to implement it. They expressed regret for causing the hostage crisis, and US Secretary of State Madeleine Albright made a reciprocal apology for the CIA's part in the 1953 coup against Mossadegh. Come 9/11, Iran was among the first states to express sympathy and provide invaluable assistance to the US in its invasion of Afghanistan to dislodge Iran's Sunni enemies, the Taliban. Iran lent its ports and its airspace to the invaders, used its influence with the Northern Alliance and even sent a Qods brigade from the Revolutionary Guards to help America overthrow Mullah Omar.[152] But for all these improvements, rapprochement with America was impossible whilst Iran supported Israel's enemies, Hezbollah and Hamas, and began to edge towards a nuclear weapon. For these reasons George W. Bush placed it on 'the Axis of Evil', which gave the Supreme Leader an opportunity to vent some vintage spleen. ('The Islamic Republic of Iran is proud to be the target of the rage and hatred of the world's greatest Satan.'[153]) His hardline faction, dominant in the press and the parliamentary committees, prevented much domestic liberalisation during the Khatami period. In 2005, Ahmadinejad won the presidency from the untrustworthy and corrupt Rafsanjani, who had by now fallen out with his long-time partner in power and in international crime, the Supreme Leader.

Ahmadinejad had served in the Revolutionary Guards during the war with Iraq, and had possibly been involved in the massacres of 1988. (One survivor says he was tortured by him in prison at this time, but there is no corroboration of the claim.) As Mayor of Tehran he had presented himself as a politician of utmost piety, notable for his unshatterable belief in the de-occulation of the Twelfth Imam, a miracle that he thought (like other superstitious Shias) would occur at Jamkaran, a shrine situated south of Tehran. He spent mayoral funds on building a rail link to speed the reincarnated Mahdi's return to the city. Ahmadinejad represented the veterans of the war with Iraq, a conservative class which had risen to middle age and power with him and were uncompromising in reaching for violent solutions to internal dissent, and the religious poor from whose ranks the volunteer thugs, called the Basij militia, were recruited. Although he did not revive the assassination campaign, there was a curious echo in 2011, when the US accused Iran of a flagrant violation of international law by attempting to blow up the Saudi ambassador at a Washington restaurant.[154] A large sum of money had been despatched, apparently by a Qods force operative, to pay a Mexican drugs cartel to carry out the attack, although details await the trial of the US-based Iranian alleged to have been the middleman. Saudi Arabia has certainly earned the ire of Iran: WikiLeaks cables reveal how its King urged the US to bomb Iran's nuclear facilities 'to cut off the head of the snake', but it is not clear how a reversion to terrorism (the bomb would have killed many in downtown Washington at lunchtime) would help Iran unless it really did want to provoke a US attack.

By this time, Iran had probably identified the US as being behind the 'stuxnet worm' virus attack on its nuclear computer systems (admitted by the White House in June 2012) and could therefore have reasonably suspected US assistance to Mossad in assassinating five of its nuclear scientists. This may have been the motive – i.e. revenge – for other 2012 attacks on Israeli embassy staff in India and Georgia and a bombing campaign that was about to begin in Thailand had not three Iranians – allegedly a terrorist cell – managed to blow themselves up when their explosives accidentally detonated.[155] A number of Iranians separately involved in the terrorism planned in Thailand and executed in India (where a bomb attached to the car of the Israeli military attaché seriously injured his wife) had begun reconnaissance operations shortly after nuclear scientist Majid Shahriari had been killed in Tehran by a bomb attached to his car.[156] These recent, largely botched attempts at terror involved Iranians but not necessarily Iran – many commentators thought them too amateurish for the Qods force, although perhaps they were just out of practice. A more devastating suicide bomb attack on Jewish tourists at a Bulgarian Black Sea resort in July 2012 killed eight and injured around thirty others: Israel immediately accused Iran working through Hezbollah as its proxy, although the accuracy of this kneejerk allegation remains open to question.

THE LEGAL CONSEQUENCES

Putting these recent events aside, at least until further evidence links them more clearly to the Iranian government, it remains the case that this government has conducted, quite openly, an international campaign of murder and terror against Iranians resident in foreign states who disagreed with its politics or theology. The attacks that it ordered, sponsored, controlled and supplied military agents or Revolutionary Guards to carry out were all murder or assault under the law of the place of commission, but were also a crime under international law: a crime against humanity, because between 1989 and 1996 they amounted to a widespread and systematic attack directed against a civilian population, namely the civilians who were opposed to their regime. It was essentially an attack to exterminate dissenters, and in that sense a continuation of the prison massacres of 1988. It featured murder, torture and disappearances as the various modes of committing the offence, all of them 'pursuant to or in furtherance of a state or organisational policy to commit such an attack'. This is the definition of a 'crime against humanity' in the ICC statute.[157] Those open to prosecution for it, in respect of the assassination campaign, are the members of the Special Affairs Committee who approved the targets – Khamenei and Rafsanjani, Ali Fallahian and the Revolutionary Guard leaders, and the ministry officials and diplomats.

Could there be any defence for these men, were they to be indicted for a crime against humanity committed between 1988 and 1996, comprising targeted assassination and the Argentinian bombings? The right to life is the most fundamental of human rights, an inherent right contained in Article 6(1) of the ICCPR, which Iran ratified under the Shah and still pretends to honour. Partly as a result of its sponsored assassination programme, the General Assembly in 1996 roundly condemned state-governed violence and extrajudicial killings, making it clear that perpetrators were guilty of international as well as national crimes.[158] Of course, an exception is made for 'lawful execution' – because many countries retain the death sentence. This regime at first sentenced its targets to death, in their absence, by way of a fatwa granted by the Supreme Leader or some other convenient ayatollah (like the revolutionary court judge Khalkhali) and passed an official warrant on to the Intelligence Ministry officials and Revolutionary Guards who would be involved in the killing. One such 'licence to kill' a former minister of the Shah, signed by the Prosecutor General, has come to light: it recites allegations that he 'bamboozled the masses' and 'questioned the sincerity of the religious authorities' so that 'spilling his blood is permissible' and that at a Special Commission meeting 'it was unanimously decided that his execution is necessary'. It concluded, chillingly:

> The agents that successfully discharge this duty and kill the corrupted in accordance with the Islamic Sharia decree will receive a significant monetary sum as a bonus, in addition to rewards in the afterlife.[159]

This does not amount to any kind of authority in international law, which denies the right of a state to execute its nationals unless there has been proof of guilt before an independent and impartial court. It is no more than a blood-money certificate, an incitement to murder, offering a financial incentive to break the law of another state and the law of nations. The carefully nurtured notion that the clerics on the Special Affairs Committee were sitting in solemn judgment and were entitled to hand down *in absentia* death sentences which would absolve the executioners – and themselves – is absurd.

They are all still in Iran, alive and well, if growing old. They are international criminal suspects, allowed impunity so far for their international crimes. But such crimes are not time barred: a crime against humanity is considered to be so heinous that perpetrators deserve punishment before they die and the international community has a duty to ensure that suspects are prosecuted. General Mladić, who killed his prisoners at Srebrenica, was put on trial in 2012 after seventeen years on the run. The top Iranians who ordered the assassinations never had to run (although some of the assassins ran to Iranian embassies to effect their escape). The main perpetrators are living happily ever after their crimes: the families of their victims are still anguished by the brutality of their loved ones' end. Shahintaj Bakhtiar's grief and suffering was so prolonged and extensive – she has worn black ever since her husband's death – that a US court awarded her $12 million for pain and suffering after a civil case which she brought against Iran.[160] An award of civil damages may provide some token solace although they are fiendishly difficult to collect, and they do not provide retribution or deterrence. If the Security Council believes in international criminal law (sometimes it does, sometimes it doesn't: compare its responses to Gaddafi and Assad) then it should establish an *ad hoc* tribunal to consider the crimes of the Iranian regime from 1988 onwards. The prosecutor would collect evidence (there is plenty available from survivors of prison and assassination) and prepare indictments. A state's 'inalienable right' to enrich uranium up to weapons grade might become very alienable if its ruler turned out to be an international criminal indictee.

Neda Agha-Soltan: the Green Movement's martyr.

CHAPTER 8

CRUSHING THE GREEN MOVEMENT

Despite what many think, there is freedom of speech in Iran. Only, there's no freedom after speech.

Hadi Khorsandi, Comedian in exile and fatwa recipient[161]

The surprise victory of Khatami and the reformers in the 1997 presidential elections had put the hardliners on the defensive, exemplified by the incomplete yet remarkable confession by the Ministry of Intelligence to responsibility for the 'chain murders' (serial killings of intellectuals). The theocratic construct of *velayat-e faqih* was not yet at stake – President Khatami himself was an ayatollah and most of his supporters wanted greater liberty and less corruption but within the existing theocratic structure. Rafsanjani in his second term as President had shown a more pragmatic side, playing down the Rushdie fatwa, for example, against the wishes of the Supreme Leader and showing a willingness to engage with 'the Great Satan' in the form of the Clinton administration. From this point he becomes a powerful but more enigmatic presence, his political positions dictated by opportunism and his increasingly apparent attraction to wealth. He had supported Khatami (his former Culture Minister) in the 1997 presidential election, against the wishes of Khamenei and the conservatives, who now found a philosophical shake-up necessary after their electoral defeat. They restated *velayat-e faqih,* making particular use of a 1989 constitutional change (engineered, ironically, by Rafsanjani) that had added the suffix 'absolute' to the title of Supreme Leader. It had been intended to shore up the authority of Ali Khamenei when he took Khomeini's place, but now it was adapted by the conservative ideologist Ayatollah Mesbah-Yazdi as a means of challenging the reformers by demanding blind obedience to Khamenei as the 'absolute'

Supreme Leader. These hardliners called themselves 'Principle-ists', and demanded a return to theocratic first principles.

The first of all such principles was to believe in the hidden Twelfth Imam, who had as a child in 874 AD made himself invisible, but who would at some point in the not-too-distant future 'de-occulate' and emerge as the Mahdi (the promised one) and reward the faithful, whilst wiping all infidels from the pages of time. In the meantime, his absolute power was to be exercised by the representative with whom he communicated, the Supreme Leader, 'absolute' under the constitution. Elections, in other words, might come and go, and throw up politicians of different ideological shades, but 'Islamic democracy' was always subject to the *velayat-e faqih* first principle, the guardianship (i.e. ultimate control) of the Supreme jurist. It was a totalitarian theory that many other leading Shia theologians rejected (Montazeri, one of its originators, would later point out that it made the 'Islamic republic' neither Islamic nor a republic) but it played well to the masses, at least in the hands of a clever populist who could arouse their religious as well as their political passions. That man was the Mayor of Tehran, Mahmoud Ahmadinejad.

The apocalypse would begin at Jamkaran, or so the Mayor believed. Over $500 million was spent, from Tehran taxes and a generous donation from the Supreme Leader, on building a spectacular shrine complex to await the emergence from hibernation of the Hidden Imam, by now 1,238 years old. This shrine served as the focus of his cult, and had the added benefit of diverting attention from the devout from clerics in Qom, hitherto the theological capital of Islam, who doubted the principalist emphasis on the likelihood of this re-emergence coming sometime soon.[162]

Ahmadinejad was elected President in the unappealing contest in 2005 with Rafsanjani. This victory was helped by George W. Bush, whose war-mongering in Iraq and inclusion of Iran on 'the Axis of Evil' seemed to require a more belligerent President. Ahmadinejad represented the generation which had fought US-backed Saddam and whose half-million fallen comrades were mourned as martyrs at prayers every Friday. They were still angry and intolerant of opposition, and were now filling the leading offices in the police force, the army and the Revolutionary

Guards. They represented the country's new middle management of its security apparatus, the cadre which provided the bosses for the Basij and the officers of the Revolutionary Guards. During the 2009 elections, a Green Movement supporter gave a neat pen-portrait of a member of this class, 'the man from the Ministry', who came to close down a Mousavi campaign office:

> He's a squat, muscular man about forty-five, bearded and covered in sweat, wearing a white shirt and has a perfectly centred disc of calloused skin from excessive contact with the prayer brick. This man is a member of Iran's military security complex. He fought in the war with Iraq, has been on the pilgrimage to Mecca a dozen times, considers himself a front-line soldier on behalf of the Hidden Imam, and has hit and tortured people. He inhabits a constellation of atmospheres – the Revolutionary Guard, the *Basij,* the police, the Ministry of Intelligence and the judiciary. The people in these worlds grew up together, fought together and were corrupted together. They are brothers-in-law and buy companies and houses on each other's recommendations. They attend memorial services for each other's parents and help each other's children enter university or get a passport. They worship together and breakfast together during Ramadan. They all enjoy the favour of people close to President Ahmadinejad ... Before, the Mullahs were in charge of everything. Now they are being superseded in public affairs by the Revolutionary Guard. The officers don't need their intervention in divine matters because they have a direct line to the Hidden Imam. And he, in turn, is God's representative on earth.[163]

Another example of the class was Tehran's brutal Chief Prosecutor, Saeed Mortazavi, who had overseen the torture and murder of photojournalist Zahra Kazemi in 2003 for taking pictures of a demonstration outside Evin prison. The case received international attention and criticism from a parliamentary enquiry, but Mortazavi survived to be promoted by Ahmadinejad to Chief Prosecutor of the nation and to play a leading part in directing the deaths of demonstrators after the 2009 presidential elections.[164]

What was less noticed, but emblematic of the paranoia in the hearts of Ahmadinejad and the principle-ists, was the arrest of three academics in 2007, accused of laying plans for a 'velvet revolution' inspired by the books on passive resistance by a Harvard professor, Gene Sharp, in league with two unlikely co-conspirators, George Soros and John McCain. The Ministry of Intelligence even produced a 'public information' television programme about the plot, which was widely derided at the time. After the 2009 election protests, however, it became a fully fledged conspiracy, advanced at a series of show trials designed to show the Western-induced malice behind the Green Movement.

The 2009 presidential elections were held on 12 June. Hundreds of candidates had been whittled down to four by the Expediency Council, the device that, ever since Khomeini vetoed Rajavi's candidature in 1980, had ensured that only candidates with a *velayat-e faqih* imprimatur could run. Ahmadinejad was up for re-election, against Mousavi, the former Prime Minister, who had lived quietly (as an architect and painter) since his post was abolished in 1989. His revolutionary credentials were unassailable, although his platform called for abolition of the 'moral police' and promised greater freedom of expression. His candidacy was endorsed by Khatami, who presented him with a sash of green – the colour of Iran and now, the colour of the reform movement.

Mehdi Karroubi, the former speaker of Parliament, was also a candidate in favour of reform. Representing hardline but more orthodox conservatism was Mohsen Rezai, former head of the Revolutionary Guards and advocate of nuclear weapons, and a former member of the Special Affairs Committee, which ordered targeted assassinations. He had reinvented himself as a free-marketeer – an economic position close to the heart of his Revolutionary Guards, who had been allowed to take over corporations and were now active in the economic life of the country.

Ahmadinejad was a strong contestant, especially in television debates when he tarred the reformers with the corruption he imputed to their fickle friend Rafsanjani, but on election day most observers thought Mousavi had won – none more certainly than Mousavi himself, who declared his own victory. The turnout was exceptionally high, which should have favoured the reformers, but to widespread disbelief the Electoral Commission announced that Ahmadinejad had won with a massive 63 per cent of the votes. There were many reasons to think that the numbers were rigged – not least because Rezai, the hardest of hardliners, also disputed the result.

Street protests erupted spontaneously, featuring the cry 'Where is my vote?' Less spontaneous was the action of the Basij militias, the volunteer vigilante section of the Revolutionary Guards whom the Supreme Leader had put on standby to 'deal with threats from internal enemies'. The Basij had been the brainchild of Ayatollah Khomeini in the 1980s – he had organised ex-soldiers, unemployed men and hoodlums into neighbourhood squads to hunt down fifth-columnists. The Basij have been compared to the fascist 'blackshirts' and Nazi Stormtroopers, a lumpen squad that can be used for violent action without implicating the government. By 2009, however, they had been given official leaders (one an army brigadier) and placed under the direction of the Revolutionary Guards. The Iranian equivalent of the *sans-culottes,* they wore shirts with tight collars and baggy trousers and were armed with batons, knives and guns.[165] After the protests erupted on 13 June they were quickly on the scene, working to break up the demonstrators, at first by beating the protesters but later by shooting at them. On the following night they broke into student quarters at the University of Tehran, throwing tear gas canisters and beating six students to death with batons and electric cattle prods.

The following day – Monday 15 June – saw over a million protesters take to the streets, again to suffer casualties from Basij shootings and beatings. Nevertheless, the peaceful demonstrations continued for the rest of the week. 'Where is my vote' was not followed by 'Where is my gun?' Instead, protesters shouted '*Allahu Akbar*' from the rooftops, as they had in 1979. ('Everyone realises that in 2009 "*Allahu Akbar*" means something different from "*Allahu Akbar*" in 1979. No longer is it a call for religion. It has become a call for truth. And it is a mischievous call, for it dares the authorities to declare "*Allahu Akbar*" a counter-revolutionary slogan!')[166] Obama sent a message: 'The world is watching, and inspired', although it would never be inspired enough to go to their aid. On 19 June came the Friday prayer sermon, an occasion for important speeches, this time delivered by the Supreme Leader himself. He read, grimly, from a script hailing Ahmadinejad's 'victory' as legitimate and condemning public protest as 'the beginning of a kind of dictatorship'. He ordered the organisers to bring demonstrations to an end – 'the political elite' (i.e. Mousavi and other leaders of the reform movement) would be liable for any bloodshed if they did not desist. 'Responsibility for the chaos which follows will be on their shoulders.' He ended by summoning up the invisible Twelfth Imam:

> Pray for us for you are our master, you are the master of this country and of this revolution.[167]

He began to cry, a signal for his audience – mullahs, judges, generals and war veterans – to burst into tears, wailing and beating their breasts. It was also the signal for a reign of terror, which descended upon demonstrators the next day.

The 20 June massacre lives on in infamy, now a world-wide day of commemoration for those who fell on the streets of Tehran to bullets and knives from government forces, the atrocity captured on cellphone snaps and video records posted on Facebook. Over twenty were killed, but none so mercilessly and publicly as Neda Agha-Soltan, a music and philosophy student of no political affiliation who was shot in the chest by a Basij militia-man on a motorbike, and died whilst being taken to hospital. Her blood-stained death agonies at the kerbside were photographed and posted on YouTube within hours, and she became the human symbol of the barbarity of the regime. Ironically, the crowd captured the killer, but resisted the opportunity to lynch him ('We are not like them, we can't kill him.') Fearing to hand him over to the police – who would be likely to arrest them instead – they let him go, having taken his identity.[168] Instead of arresting him and launching an immediate enquiry, the regime arrested Neda's boyfriend, threatened her parents and insisted it was a 'media murder' (featuring an actress and fake blood) arranged by the BBC to give the republic a bad name. Later, this ridiculous story changed to blame subversive 'mini-groups' (i.e. the MEK) for her death: there was no investigation of the Basij militia-man who had been captured by the crowd, to whom he confessed. Neda became a hate figure of the theocracy, the example that proved it had become a thugocracy. (They should instead have viewed her as their guardian angel: the strongest argument against bombing Iran is that this action would kill civilians like Neda.)

This brutality deterred some other demonstrators, although on 9 July police returned to Tehran University to beat up protesters and to take 145 of them to Kahrizak detention centre, a stinking collection of cells in which they were beaten and raped under the blind eye of Prosecutor General Saeed Mortazavi. A number of them died, including one young man whose father, an influential figure in the Revolutionary Guard hierarchy, found his dead son and demanded a parliamentary enquiry. Other families were not so lucky: they were not informed for weeks about the deaths of their children, and were denied permission to take their bodies from the morgue until they agreed to sign forms releasing the authorities from all liability for the deaths. This was contrary to the Islamic law requirement that bodies should be buried immediately. The Green Movement publicly alleged what has been described as 'the most notorious public secret of the Theocratic state',[169] namely that some protesters had been sexually abused in prison – a taboo subject in this puritan culture, but a practice which was widely known to occur, to males as well as females. Evidence soon emerged, from courageous detainees prepared to be named, that they had been raped. This crime was regarded by the Basij as doubly gratifying: a form of torture for their victims and reward for their own loyalty.[170] The parliamentary enquiry in due course blamed Mousavi and Karroubi for 'inciting the emotions of the people', but at least criticised Saeed Mortazavi for using the centre and for pretending that the student victims had died of meningitis rather than police torture.

It was the regime's dishonesty, as much as its cruelty, which caused the replacement of 'Where is my vote?' with the catch-cry 'Death to the Dictator'. This was blasphemous, given Khamenei's intimacy with the Hidden Imam, as well as subversive (the two crimes were interchangeable), and pictures and murals of Khamenei were torn down or defaced in public places.[171]

Unsurprisingly, demonstrations were banned for the rest of the year. They occurred, of course, and hundreds of protesters were arrested, joining some 4,000 who had been detained in June. On 19 December Grand Ayatollah Montazeri died in Qom – a hero both of the revolution and of the counter-revolution, he (much more than Mousavi) had been the inspiration of the Green Movement and had maintained a barrage of criticism of the government over its harsh treatment of the demonstrators until the day of his death. There were funeral processions all over the country, and the seventh day of mourning for him coincided with *Ashura* – the holy day when Hussein was killed in his strug-gle against Yazid, the evil Caliph. The Basij were out in force, and killed thirty-seven demonstrators, shooting and driving over them. Once again, bodies were only returned to families for burial on condition that they should not publicise the cause of death or publicly criticise the government.

Then the Twelfth Imam raised his mysterious head. A public letter was addressed to Him by the Chief of Police, General Firuzabadi, who assured Him that the violence He was witness-ing (perhaps his hidden cave was equipped with television) did not come from the security forces, because they had no guns. As if this lie were not embarrassing enough for the Holy One, the letter went on in terms that seemed to deify Khamenei, or at least to suggest that he might even be the de-occulated saviour. Khamenei, in his next sermon, shocked many of his senior clerics by inclining towards this supposition. Some mullahs in Qom disagreed with his 'sacralisation' of politics, and his attempt to bring forward the date of the Hidden Imam's emergence. Ahmadinejad's supporters were not above suggesting that the chaos arising from the rigged election was the kind of chaos predicted by the *Hadiths* as the prelude to the world's end, although they suggest that something rather more apocalyptic is in store – for example, a devastating war.[172] There is another Shia belief that worried the protesters rather more – it is that rules of law and humane conduct may be ignored in a battle with the *moharebs* – the enemies of God. This was the explanation, they thought, for the bestial behaviour of the Basij at Kahrizak detention centre, and for the beatings and shootings on the street.[173]

Meanwhile, the regime had to construct a story to justify the rapes and the killings, the beatings and the 4,000 arrests, some suffered by journalists who were merely observing the protests, or by academics and politicians who were sitting – safely, so they thought – at home. The chosen vehicle was the show trial – reminiscent of Stalin's purge trials of the 1930s – which recited a vast and unlikely conspiracy between the defendants and George Soros, Facebook, MI6, the BBC World Service, the BBC Persian Service, *Newsweek,* the MEK, the Royalist Society, the Shell Corporation, Nobel laureate Shirin Ebadi, Harvard academic Gene Sharp, the Voice of America, Mossad, the British embassy, the British Council and even the long-deceased sociologist Max Weber. The alleged object of the conspirators was a 'velvet revolution', which the regime (in a flash of self-recognition) likened to the overthrow of the Stalinists in Czechoslovakia by Havel and his band of philosophers. As one detainee was told by his interrogator, 'You are worse than any saboteur or killer. You destroy minds and provoke people against the leader.'[174] The lengthy and convoluted indictments exuded the regime's fear of intellectuals, and the power of their ideas to turn minds against the illogical pretentions of *velayat-e faqih.*

The trials themselves, however, were sad and boring affairs. The defendants appeared on television, beaten and cowering, in prison pyjamas and without lawyers. It took hours for the prosecutors to read the barely coherent indictments, punctuated by calls upon particular defendants to make pre-arranged confessions. Several of those confessors have explained, once released and out of the country, how they were beaten and told what to say (the invariable sign of a coerced confession came when they paid gratuitous tribute to the kindness of their jailors and the excellence of prison food). They confessed to avoid further beatings, and in the hope that nobody who knew them would believe what they were saying. Thus Maziar Bahari, a Canadian-Iranian journalist for *Newsweek,* who was detained for 118 days and routinely beaten, was threatened with torture and execution unless he confessed: under that duress he stumbled before a press conference to explain that the foreign media had agreed to incite a 'velvet revolution'. The unethical conduct of the government's propaganda station, Press TV, in putting out this interview and pretending that it had been freely given, was contemptible but typical of the Iranian media.

The global velvet conspiracy was an absurd construct, of course: although many NGOs had friendly links with the reform movement, such connections as were alleged in the indictment had only come after the election, in order to report on the demonstrations, and could not be responsible for fomenting them. Many of the defendants were forced to plead guilty – and receive prison sentences – merely for posting images on Facebook or providing them to Western television services. It was certainly true that BBC Persian TV and its website became the most trusted provider of daily news about the uprising, but this was a measure of the need for independent and accurate coverage, unavailable from the state-owned television services. In due course the regime would react in its typically vengeful way, by terrorising relatives of BBC Persian Service broadcasters still living in Iran, and by arresting six documentary makers whose films had been acquired by the service.[175] An amusing aspect of the conspiracy theory, reflecting Ahmadinejad's personal Anglophobia, was how this time it identified Britain as 'the Great Satan': the newly elected Obama was too popular, and George W. Bush was regarded as too stupid, to be credited with a diabolical plot to brainwash the Iranian people. It was these cunning perfidious British, the brains behind the bringing down of Mossadegh in 1953, who still yearned for the days when British Petroleum (i.e. Anglo-Iranian) ran the country. But Ahmadinejad, although he preened himself with the comparison, was no Mossadegh. At Friday prayers, the faithful were exhorted to shout 'Death to Britain' at the gates of the UK embassy. Many were not fooled: they shouted instead 'Death to Russia', because they had not forgotten how a grinning Medvedev was first to congratulate Ahmadinejad on his rigged victory.[176] Russia, meanwhile, was supplying Iran with its nuclear power plant at Bushehr, and had provided crowd control training to its Revolutionary Guards.

The events of June 2009 constitute the third serious violation of international criminal law by Iran, after the prison massacre of 1988 and the targeted assassination campaign of 1989–96. The essential crime is that of beating up, torturing and killing peaceful protesters, by unleashing untrained paramilitaries to disperse them by using unreasonable and lethal force. The actual casualties are still unclear – the regime admitted thirty-six dead in the June demonstrations, although the Green Movement counted seventy-two, and a further thirty-seven in December, but the figures are under-estimates and the fate of some who disappeared at this time has still not been uncovered. There is evidence that the Basij violence was premeditated, and it was 'adopted' by the regime's regular forces – the police, army and prosecuting authorities, which themselves resorted to violence and torture when arresting and imprisoning protesters.[177] One such attack does not constitute a crime against humanity – 'Bloody Sunday', when British paratroopers killed thirteen demonstrators in Northern Ireland in 1972, was not an international crime. But a month of bloody Sundays, of the kind that the Green Movement experienced, most certainly was. International law allows demonstrations to be dispersed by proportionate force – tear gas, water cannon and rubber bullets may be used if demonstrations turn violent – but it cannot excuse the pre-planned use of paramilitaries to kill and terrorise. The evidence – much of it unanswerable, because captured on video footage – shows the vast majority of demonstrators to have been peaceful. Unarmed members of the public, exercising their right to assemble, were chanting 'Where is my vote?' but otherwise constituting no danger to public security. They were set upon, beaten, knifed, stabbed and some were shot, at times when they were unthreatening. There was no calculation here of reasonable force to disperse a disorderly crowd: the object of the violence, spurred by Khamenei's Friday sermon, was to punish protest against the government by widespread and systematic assaults. There was a deliberate breach of the right to life, constituted by arbitrary killings by the security forces and their semi-official proxies, the Basij.

Added to this international crime – although in effect a part of it – was the torture and rape and denial of medical treatment that was a feature of the detentions. Women who were raped by the Basij have said their molesters spoke of this as their 'reward' promised by their leaders. Some of the beatings appear to have been motivated merely by anger, whilst later they had the objective of coercing confessions. The behaviour of the police and Basij at Kahrizak detention centre, where prisoners were raped and sodomised, burned with molten tar and subjected to mock executions, has been authenticated by the parliamentary enquiry established because one victim was the son of a VIP. The centre was urgently closed by order of Khamenei (who was derided by Montazeri for thinking that the blame could be attributed to a building). The treatment of detainees, many of whom were eventually released without charge, certainly passed the severity level for torture, which international law absolutely prohibits. There were many cases of 'forced disappearances', where protesters were killed or incarcerated without notice to their families. Khamenei must again bear command responsibility – he suffered these crimes to take place and did nothing to stop them or punish the perpetrators other than to close the building where they were perpetrated. He should be joined in the hypothetical dock by Saeed Mortazavi (responsible for the atrocities in Kahrizak), the heads of the Basij militia, the Chief of Police and the head of the Revolutionary Guards.

The show trials may have been a farce, but they were not amusing to those who, behind the scenes, were beaten into making public confessions. Mortazavi seems to have taken the show trial part of Vyshinsky (choreographer of Stalin's show trials) by orchestrating the conspiracy charges and selecting defendants who were denied most of their due process rights – to be represented by a lawyer, or to call witnesses in their defence. Ayatollah Montazeri, throughout this dangerous period the voice of sanity and courage, posted on his website:

> The confessions that have been extracted in prison have absolutely no religious or legal value and cannot be the basis for the punishments that have been issued ... Those who are responsible for such confessions and their accomplices are religiously and legally guilty and criminal.[178]

The regime, perhaps in recognition that the show trials had not shown very much, displayed some leniency in sentencing, at least compared to earlier cases. This was not mercy, but a ploy in support of the conspiracy theory that the defendants had been corrupted and brainwashed by MI6 and George Soros. Most sentences were of five or six years, and the half-dozen death sentences were confined to defendants who were found guilty of membership of the MEK or the Royalist Society.

The 2009–10 show trials, along with the detention, torture and the killings of protesters, amount together to a widespread and systematic attack on civilians, and persecution by intentional and severe deprivation of their rights, 'pursuant to or in furtherance of a state or organisational policy to commit such an attack' – a crime against humanity under Article 7 of the Rome Treaty, and may as such (having been committed after July 2002) be prosecuted before the ICC. Iran, of course, is not a party to the ICC treaty, but the Security Council could refer the case to the court's prosecutor in circumstances where it regarded the impunity of the perpetrators as a threat to international peace and security. The impunity from prosecution for crimes against humanity of the head of a state about to obtain a nuclear weapon might well be thought such a threat to international peace and security.

The Green Movement was a civil rights movement. It went into a kind of occulation itself after its brutal suppression in 2009, whilst prosecutors picked off its leaders and its lawyers. Both Mousavi and Karroubi were placed under house arrest and denied access to the outside world, and in 2011 it was announced that they would face prosecution. Astutely, the mullocracy and its new apparatchiks recognised that the main threat from a civil liberties movement would come from its lawyers, so from 2010 onwards they became the main targets for revenge, by way of prophylactic detention and long jail sentences. Many are protégés of Shirin Ebadi, the Nobel Peace laureate and Iran's only Nobel prizewinner. Nasrin Sotoudeh (formerly Ebadi's own lawyer) was arrested after defending some of the detained Green Movement protesters. Her offices were searched and her files seized: she was taken to Evin prison, held in solitary confinement, and denied all contact with her children and not allowed to attend her father's funeral. After a short, secret trial in 2011 she was jailed for eleven years (reduced to six on appeal after an international outcry) and banned from leaving Iran or practising law for twenty years, for the crimes of 'damaging national security' and 'spreading propaganda'. Her real crime, of course, had been to represent her clients. In a moving letter to her infant son, smuggled out of prison, she expressed her anguish at separation from her family but asked him to pray that Iran's judges and prosecutors rediscover the meaning of justice so that 'he too can some day be allowed to live in peace like in so many other countries'.[179]

These merciless prosecutors and judges are, of course, immune to prayer: the next human rights lawyer who came before Revolutionary Court judge Pirabhesi, hammer of the Green Movement, received eighteen years (reduced to thirteen on appeal). Abdolfattah Soltani, once Ebadi's partner at the Centre for the Defence of Human Rights (closed down by the government in 2008), had been warned that he faced arrest and a long sentence if he continued to defend protesters: at the age of fifty-eight, his courage in continuing to do so was heroic. The deputy head of the centre, Narges Mohammadi, received eleven years (reduced to six) – even after her health was seriously damaged by a lengthy period of solitary confinement in Evin.[180] Fifteen defence lawyers in total were jailed or exiled in the 2010–11 period, three of them merely for signing a letter asking for the release of Nasrin Sotoudeh.

But it was the sad, cruel case of Sakineh Ashtiani that captured world attention, and led to the capture of her lawyers as well. She had nothing to do with politics but had been arrested in 2006 and charged with complicity in killing her husband, and with adultery. The court acquitted her of murder, but convicted her of the lesser crime and sentenced her to be lashed ninety-nine times and then subjected to death by stoning for adultery. This medieval punishment, which requires a convict to be dressed in a shroud and buried up to her head, whereupon she is pelted with large rocks until she dies, was approved by the Supreme Court. She suffered the lashing but her lawyer managed to publicise her plight to the world before the death sentence could be carried out. He was charged with 'spreading propaganda' and fled the country. Her second lawyer, Javid Kian, was not so lucky: he was arrested and sentenced to eleven years in prison for the same crime. His defence lawyer, Naghi Mahmoudi, saw him in prison: teeth smashed, nose broken, and cigarette burns up and down his legs and on his genitals. At Kian's courageous request, Mahmoudi left the country to tell of his torture, whereupon Mahmoudi's wife was immediately arrested and held in solitary confinement in the sinister Section 209 of Evin prison.[181]

Meanwhile, an international campaign to save Ashtiani from death was met by the regime with its usual truculent dishonesty, forcing her to confess to a murder plot – of which she had been acquitted – by beating her for two days in Chamber 37 of Tabriz prison (revealing this fact caused Javid Kian's arrest). Then the Ministry of Intelligence made a propaganda film using the video-taped confession, which was transmitted by the government's tame television station to show that she deserved to die.[182] Her alleged partner, who had been convicted of the murder, had by this time been released because her children had pardoned him. Not so fortunate was a German television journalist, who was jailed for interviewing Kian. Although he had suffered torture (electric shock administered through the lips) he was released after a year of German diplomatic pressure, and spoke publicly of regular use of the torture chamber. He had been in the same prison as Ashtiani, and related how, after six years on death row, she had become a shadow of her former self.[183] She is, at the time of writing, still alive – thanks entirely to international action. Her plight at least scuppered Iran's bid to take a seat on the new UN agency to promote women's rights, and prompted the Human Rights Council to appoint a special rapporteur on the country's human rights abuses, notwithstanding the speech by Iran's UN ambassador in which he claimed that his country had 'an inherent, genuine and deeply rooted respect for human rights'. He was supported by only three other countries: Pakistan, Russia and Cuba.[184]

The regime's urge to see Sakineh Ashtiani stoned to death reflects a mentality among its mullahs, MPs and officials that can fairly be described as primitive. Stoning to death is not a punishment mentioned for adultery in either the Koran or the *Hadiths* of the Prophet – it is a Sharia accretion with no clear theological basis. Nonetheless there have been as many as 100 women stoned to death since the revolution – nine in 2006–7. This may be a small number compared with the 6,000 women put to death by hanging or by firing squad in that period, or indeed the 94,000 men who have been executed.[185] But there was a determination to justify it in the case of Ashtiani, although as Azar Nafisi points out,

> she was hardly Westernised or in any sense political. Like most victims of stoning law, she was from a poor traditional religious background, one that the regime claims to defend. This is a good time to ask apologists for the Islamic regime, who degrades Islam? Who imposes stoning, forced marriage of under-age girls and flogging for not wearing the veil?[186]

Punishments devolving from the practices of ninth-century Arab tribes are, like practices common among other religions in that time, in many cases unfit today for any civilised society – such as the death penalty for homosexuality and apostasy and the amputation of the hands of thieves. Yet the hardline Islamists want to keep these punishments, which Javad Larijani, the regime's representative at the Human Rights Council, refuses to admit constitute torture. The regime almost relishes its defiance of civilised values, and uses this defiance to retain the support of the right-wing clergy and their congregations. In 2011, it attracted further Western obloquy by trying to hang a Christian minister for apostasy: he had been sentenced to death, but the Supreme Court offered him a reprieve if he would renounce the Christian faith. As the Archbishop of Canterbury pointed out, this was an outrageous demand contrary to every human rights convention, but it suited the government precisely because it outraged the likes of the Archbishop of Canterbury.[187]

In 2012, Iran pretended to the world that it was abolishing death by stoning. But its 'new' law merely omits reference to stoning, but requires sentences to be in accordance with Islamic law and fatwas – which include stoning! There has been no reform of Islamic rules which value a woman's evidence at half the weight accorded to a man's, or which set the compensation for women in civil claims as half of that awarded a male. Despite the horror of Western human rights NGOs at these sexist beliefs and practices, Larijani defends punishments such as cutting off hands and feet, severing arms and gouging out eyes as 'a very real part of Iran's judicial law – retaliation and punishment are beautiful and necessary things'. (His judicial opinion is apparently based on Koran 8:12: 'I will cast terror into the hearts of those who disbelieve. Therefore strike off their heads and maim them in every limb.') He defends stoning as much kinder than execution because there is a slim chance that 'the defendant can actually survive' and his sarcastic view of gay marriage is that 'in the near future in the West, a human being will be allowed to marry a cat'.[188]

The massive human rights violations recounted in this chapter – and there are many more – demonstrate that the present Iranian regime is still run by officials who should stand trial for crimes against humanity. The international sanctions that have been imposed on Iran – and they are increasingly severe for its economy – are related (with a few US exceptions) only to its development of a nuclear weapons capacity. There has been, to this point, an almost complete disjunct at the UN in viewing its human rights record and its nuclear pretentions, although it is surely obvious that a state which mass-murders its own people is more likely to misuse a weapon that can mass-murder its enemies. It is, perhaps, the failure of international law to condemn the acquisition of nuclear weapons, notwithstanding its conventions against chemical weapons and land mines, that produces the irony whereby Iran has been called to account for every centrifuge it adds to its stock in an underground bunker, but not for the thousands of political prisoners it tortures, tries unfairly (or not at all) and then kills. There has never been any suggestion that its Supreme Leader and ruling mullahs should face justice – a striking contrast to all the ICC indictments issued against African leaders. But before any regime can be allowed to build its own bomb, it must demonstrate a capacity either to treat its own people with humanity, or else to make amends for the occasions in the recent past when it has failed to do so. The focus on the nuclear threat, to the exclusion of the humanitarian threat, has served the regime well and may even provide a reason for its endless diplomatic evasions: as Hamid Dabashi points out,

> from mid-summer 2009, the nuclear game became perhaps the single most important ploy in the hands of Ahmadinejad's government and the regime at large to shift global attention away from the domestic Iranian scene towards the regional implications of a nuclear Iran.[189]

These implications are serious enough, precisely because of the nature of the regime that is revealed by its domestic behaviour. It is run by mullahs without mercy, not merely towards those of their own people with political or religious objections to theocratic rule, but towards the rest of the non-Shia (or non-Twelver Shia) world. As the West frightens itself with film scenarios based on the unlikely event of a bomb falling into the hands of terrorists, there is a failure to realise the consequence of a bomb near to the hands of a terrorist regime. Although this book has thus far summarised the evidence for that characterisation of Iran, there are other governments which might answer that description: the Syrian regime, for one topical example, which has admitted to stockpiling unlawful chemical and biological weapons which it threatens to use against its enemies, just as it would most likely use a nuclear bomb against them if it had one. Then, and always, there is the problem of Israel, with its surreptitious bomb store and its nuclear-armed submarines, a country that has shown itself willing to strike its enemies disproportionately (the Gaza incursion, 'Operation Cast Lead', in 2010, for example). But Iran, because of its defiance of Security Council orders to stop nuclear enrichment, is now the exemplar of a much wider problem, namely how the world can deal with nuclear proliferation. Having established that the Islamic Republic of Iran is responsible for a series of international crimes, we now turn to examine the nature of the weapon it appears to be seeking and the international arrangements, short of force, which are capable of stopping it.

PART II

THE BOMB

'Little Boy': Frankenstein on the slab.

CHAPTER 9

HIROSHIMA

Unless some agreement about the control of the use of the new active materials can be attained in due time, any temporary advantage, however great, may be outweighed by a perpetual menace to human security.

Niels Bohr, memorandum to President Roosevelt, July 1944

There has been no spectacle more terrifying – and more fascinating – in recorded history than the mushroom cloud that rose over Hiroshima on the early morning of 6 August 1945, after a lone B-29 bomber, called 'Enola Gay' (after the pilot's mum), dropped a large atomic bomb absurdly named 'Little Boy'. At 1,900 feet the uranium fissured and the chain reaction produced a noiseless flash that blinded and burned, decapitated and disembowelled everyone beneath, in hospitals, schools and shops. This (primitive by today's standards) nuclear weapon wiped four square miles of the city off the map, immolating 70,000 immediately and killing a further 70,000 thereafter who died in the agonies of radiation sickness, succumbing to its fevers, ulcers, gangrenous flesh and leakage of blood from every orifice. Pregnant women survivors all miscarried, whilst tens of thousands died later from leukaemia. The *New York Times*, to its everlasting shame, tried to cover up the horror: 'No Radiation in Hiroshima Ruin' screamed the world's most dishonest headline. An intrepid Australian journalist, Wilfred Burchett, was the first Westerner to enter the city to refute this American propaganda: his reports for the *Daily Express* of the 'frightening devastation' and of the reality of radiation poisoning were syndicated throughout the world.[190] And so began the debate over the morality and legality of a development hitherto known only to scientists sworn to secrecy, and to a handful of Western political leaders.

But the advent of the bomb – atomic and then hydrogen and thermonuclear – was inevitable. It had, quite remarkably, been first envisioned and accurately described as an 'atomic bomb' by H. G. Wells, in a science fiction novel, *The World Set Free* – inspired by turn-of-the-century discoveries about the radioactivity inside uranium, which might be induced into a chain reaction to produce a blinding inferno. In Wells's prescient novel, published in 1914, it takes a nuclear war before a wise king determines that the metal must be locked up forever – a utopian solution actually broached in the months after Hiroshima and startlingly necessary to revisit today, as rogue states are close to getting their hands on the bomb. It took just twenty-five years for a series of famous physicists – Ernest Rutherford, James Chadwick, Niels Bohr, Otto Frisch, Enrico Fermi, Mark Oliphant and others, in particular Leó Szilárd, to bring Wells's nightmare within reach. (Szilárd in fact credits Wells's book for giving him the idea of how to split the atom and invoke a chain reaction.)[191]

As Europe slid to war, Wells published his most influential work, *The Rights of Man* (1939), which helped to inspire the post-war Universal Declaration of Human Rights: 'It is time we recognised fully that the making of any lethal weapon larger than what may be required for the control of big animals, is a matter of universal concern…'[192] Leó Szilárd, however, came to a different conclusion. He wrote a letter to the President of the United States, and rushed to Long Island to ask Albert Einstein to sign it. It warned that in the immediate future 'it may become possible to set up a nuclear chain reaction in a large mass of uranium, by which vast amounts of power and large quantities of new radium-like elements would be generated … extremely powerful bombs of a new type may thus be constructed'[193] – by Germany, the letter hinted. Einstein signed the letter – the only mistake, he said years later, that he had ever made in his life.[194]

Yet in August 1939, with the world on the brink of war, telling the President what would soon become clear to experts in other countries from the published scientific literature was not a moral mistake. Churchill heard it from Cambridge scientists, Stalin from his Cambridge spies and Japan soon became aware and made some experiments. Hitler was averse to 'Jewish physics', joking, 'If the dismissal of Jewish scientists means the annihilation of German science, then we shall do without science for a few years!' So Germany did without Jewish scientists, who later helped to build the bomb for the Allies (Szilárd and Teller most notably), and Germany did not exploit the uranium stocks it captured in Sudetenland. The Allies were not to know this, and were right to fear the clandestine development of a Nazi bomb under the over-rated physicist Heisenberg. The Manhattan Project, the top secret $2 billion operation authorised by Roosevelt in 1942 to build the bomb, and run by General Groves and J. Robert Oppenheimer, was a sensible precautionary step to counter a real threat. It was not a direct result of the Einstein letter, but came rather from pressure by British government scientists, who after the outbreak of war developed the most advanced plans for the bomb, and the most advanced fear that the Germans would build it first. As their MAUD Committee report explained in 1941, after the detonation of a moderate amount of uranium isotope 235, 'the cloud of radioactive material will kill everyone within a strip of several miles'. The report concluded: 'It is quite conceivable that Germany is, in fact, developing this weapon.'[195] One of its members, Australian scientist Mark Oliphant, a protégé of Rutherford, flew to Washington and California to alert American physicists, including Robert J. Oppenheimer, to America's responsibility to lead the free world in making the first bomb.

The US alone had the financial and human resources, and the peaceful skies, to do so. After Pearl Harbor, in December 1941, the US needed no second bidding, and Churchill was now avidly urging them on. Germany was not, as it happened, minded to embark on the project: in 1942 Heisenberg reported to Albert Speer, Minister for Armaments, that the bomb could be built within four years. Speer thought that the war would be over by then, and declined to inform Hitler, fearing his 'tendency to push fantastic projects by making senseless demands'.[196] One of history's abiding ironies is that if Hitler had not made life in Germany and its occupied countries so impossible for Jewish physicists, they might have corrected Heisenberg's miscalculations and produced an atomic weapon by the time the Führer was raving in his bunker. At that point, the object of the Manhattan Project – an Allied bomb to deter a Nazi first strike – would have been meaningless: with the survival of Germany at stake, its demented leader would have wanted nothing better than to end his own life, and the lives both of the German people who had failed him and the Russian enemies at Berlin's gate, by a nuclear *Götterdämmerung*.

There can be no doubt about the justification for Roosevelt's decision in 1942 to establish the Manhattan Project, and none was expressed by the scientists – nineteen of them from Britain and others from Europe – or the military and political leaders let in on the secret. There were no moral qualms: the Nazis had begun the obliteration of cities and the mass killings of civilians by blitzing London and Coventry, whilst actual Japanese atrocities were more bestial than even Allied propaganda could make them: thousands of prisoners of war had been marched to their deaths at Bataan after the fall of the Philippines; fallen airmen were usually beheaded; 160 Australian POWs had been lashed to trees in Rabaul and then bayoneted. This war was fought in an ethical vacuum: to win it, research on a 'super bomb' was simply – and understandably – not a moral problem for military men who were soon to order the carpet-bombing of Dresden and Tokyo. It was not a problem for Churchill, or the more fastidious Roosevelt. On 18 September 1944, they reached agreement (subsequently written down and secretly signed as the 'Hyde Park Declaration') that 'after careful consideration, the atomic bomb should be used on Japan'. The die was cast, and the Manhattan projectionists were given a year to produce a spectacle they accomplished eleven months later.

There is one glaring omission, in all the hundreds of books, and the thousands of documents on which they are based, dealing with the decision to make and then drop the bomb. No one seems at any stage to have consulted lawyers, or even to have wondered whether a weapon of such unique power might contravene the laws of war.

This collective amnesia is a measure of the failure to enforce international law, at a time when it applied only to states and not to their political and military leaders. The first Hague

Convention, in 1899, had laid down the overriding war law principle:

> That the right of belligerents to injure the enemy is limited by their duty to avoid doing so by methods which cause unnecessary suffering, and which are either novel or generally perceived as dishonourable.

The novel atomic bomb, known (certainly after the test in mid-July 1945 of a plutonium bomb in the New Mexico desert) to cause unnecessary suffering, obviously attracted this principle. It was not 'generally perceived as dishonourable', but only because it was not perceived at all by the public until it was dropped on Hiroshima.

At the second Hague Peace Conference in 1907, forty-four states endorsed as a fundamental principle that 'the right of belligerents to adopt means of injuring the enemy is not unlimited', and proceeded to forbid weapons 'calculated to cause unnecessary suffering' or 'the diffusion of asphyxiating or deleterious gases'. A few years later these rules were broken by both sides in the First World War, competing in the noxiousness of the poison gases they blew at each other across 'no man's land'. Afterwards, of course, their representatives attended a conference in Geneva in 1925 to produce a protocol prohibiting the use of poison gas, immediately ratified by Italy (which then gassed the Ethiopians) and Japan (which used gas on the Chinese in Manchuria). The League of Nations had utterly failed to deter these breaches of international law, and in the absence of any international criminal jurisdiction over national leaders it could scarcely be described as 'law' in any meaningful sense. It did not deter either Britain or Germany from seriously considering the use of chemical weapons at various stages of the Second World War – they declined, not so as to comply with the protocol but out of fear that the other side's chemical weaponry, unleashed in reprisal, might do them more damage than they had inflicted. Another rule that emerged in this period (from The Hague, in 1923) was meant to limit the future use of aerial warfare: bombing was only legitimate 'when directed at a military objective' and not when used 'for the purpose of terrorising the civilian population'. Yet causing civilian terror was precisely the purpose of Luftwaffe, RAF and US Air Force fire-bombing of cities, and of Hitler's last effort to fend off surrender by the reckless V-bombing of Britain. It might be said that the purpose of dropping the A-bomb was a military objective, namely the terrorising of Japan's Emperor and his military leaders into surrender, to be accomplished by massive civilian suffering ('Little Boy' in fact exploded directly over a hospital: its doctors, patients and nurses were the first to be incinerated).

The truth – which seems to have eluded all the retrospective mock trials which keep finding Roosevelt, Truman, Oppenheimer and the pilot of the 'Enola Gay' guilty of a crime against humanity for Hiroshima – is that in 1945, international human rights law barely existed and political leaders had immunity from trial, hence the Kaiser had been allowed to live happily ever after the First World War without being prosecuted for invading Belgium and authorising unrestricted submarine warfare. Arms treaties did not identify and ban this unique new weapon, and 'state practice', which determines whether a rule is binding on states as part of 'customary international law', was silently approving: the four main belligerents, the US, UK, Germany and Japan, were all secretly researching nuclear weapons possibilities. The most fundamental legal principle is the rule against retrospectivity – you cannot be guilty of a crime if there is no law against it at the time you are alleged to have committed it – so on this basis Truman's soul can rest easy. (As it did. When Oppenheimer, 'the father of the A-bomb', told the President in a fit of remorse that he felt he had blood on his hands, Truman proffered his handkerchief: 'Here, would you like to wipe it off?')[197]

That time was early August 1945. Truman had inherited the Presidency when Roosevelt died on 1 April, and clearly felt that he was Roosevelt's nuclear executor. But the Hyde Park agreement had been one of principle, made when Germany and Japan were both dangerous enemies, and did not tie his hands. The case for dropping the bomb had weakened with Germany's surrender on 8 May. Until this point there had been no qualms in the multi-national scientific community at Los Alamos: with hind-sight, some have explained their moral quiescence by the fact that 'events were moving just too incredibly fast' – they had dedicated two to three years of their lives to an all-absorbing quest to win a war against barbarism, and no second thoughts could be allowed to intrude to rob them of its climax.

They had been idealistically engaged on a frantic mission to build not one but two kinds of atomic bomb. The first was a simple device ('Little Boy') in which a nuclear explosion was triggered by firing one piece of uranium-235 into another, resulting in a fission chain reaction within the torpedo-like gun barrel casing. 'Little Boy' was expected to work, but was an only child – it had used up all the purified 235 available for the Manhattan Project. The second – codenamed 'Fat Man' (an affectionate reference to Churchill) – was more complex, but could readily be replicated. It was indeed fat, and within its balloon-like casing was a sphere of metal, plutonium-239, surrounded by packs of high explosives which, when detonated, would compress the plutonium to a critical density to set off a chain reaction.[198] It was uncertain whether this implosion device would work, hence the need for a secret test, in the middle of the New Mexico desert, for Oppenheimer's scientists and some security-cleared officials. At 5.30 a.m. on 16 July 1945 they were first to witness the flash (many were temporarily blinded) and mushroom cloud and a force equivalent to 18,000 tons of TNT. Oppenheimer, the bohemian genius, Rhodes scholar and lover of communist women, recalled – with something like satisfaction, because he had devoted body and soul to this outcome – Krishna's reflection in the *Mahabharata* that 'I am become death. The shatterer of worlds,' to which the test site manager standing beside him replied prosaically, 'Oppie, now we're all sons of bitches.'[199]

It was in a last-minute effort to exempt themselves – and all nuclear physicists – from that category that the very next day Leó Szilárd, the brilliant Hungarian émigré who had done more than anyone else to bring the bomb to birth, wrote another letter to the President, which sixty-nine Manhattan scientists were prepared to sign. (More might have done so had Oppenheimer been prepared to circulate it – 'Scientists have no right to use their prestige to influence political decisions,' he told its author.) It pointed out that the original impetus to develop atomic bombs had passed with the defeat of Germany, and that 'a nation which sets the precedent' of using this new force of destruction 'may have to bear the responsibility of opening the door to an era of devastation on an unimaginable scale'. It begged Truman not to drop the bomb on Japan until that nation had refused surrender terms, and even in that event to think about 'all the other moral responsibilities which are involved'.[200]

Harry Truman did not think at all, not about morality and certainly not about international law. By this time he was in Potsdam, sorting out Europe's future, and Hiroshima was a straightforward military decision like the fire-bombing of Tokyo. It had already been made by Roosevelt and he endorsed it on the basis that it would bring an end to war with fewer casualties than by the alternative route of an invasion of mainland Japan. This was his almost unanimous advice, supported by Churchill and Attlee, and only doubted by the fastidious Henry Stimson, Secretary of State for War, and possibly by Eisenhower (whose much later, self-serving claims to have opposed Hiroshima are not supported by the slightest evidence). It should in fairness be said that none of the politicians, and few of the scientists, had any idea of the appalling effect of the radiation fall-out: increased levels had been noted at the test in the New Mexico desert, but had not been thought significant enough to raise alarm or to evacuate nearby towns (the locals were told that an ammunition dump had exploded). Attlee said that he and Churchill were told nothing about the possibility of long-term fall-out, and the definitive history of Britain's role in the bomb by Margaret Gowing finds little evidence that scientists antici-pated the genetic effects of ionising radiation on the civilian population.[201] Nor did they appreciate the full devastation of the superbomb: Oppenheimer, who chaired the 'Targeting Committee', honestly believed that Hiroshima would suffer a maximum of 20,000 victims, many of them soldiers and sailors or munitions workers, in a city that was a major military and industrial target. This was a casualty rate less than one night's bombing of Hamburg (45,000) or Dresden (35,000) or indeed the fire-bombing of Tokyo, where on one night 90,000 were immolated.

But the real issue for these decision takers was the Benthamite calculus: would dropping the bomb save more lives – Japanese as well as American – than it would take? The US military had scheduled their invasion of the main south island of Japan for 1 November, and their 'Ultra' intercepts had picked up the Japanese plans to defend it with two divisions dug into bunkers in the mountains, and with *kamikazes* suicidally bombing the invaders on the beaches. This was *ketsu-go* – the defence of the homeland to the last man, and the Americans knew what that would mean. They had suffered 42,000 casualties at the Normandy landing, 31,000 in taking back Luzon, and 7,000 deaths just to extricate the Japanese from the tiny island of Iwo Jima. From April till June, 150,000 American marines, with naval and air support, had been engaged in the battle for Okinawa: it cost 110,000 Japanese lives and left about 70,000 Okinawans dead. The US suffered a massive 35 per cent casualty rate (52,500), as well as substantial naval losses. A 35 per cent casualty rate in the 766,000 American troops needed for the November mainland invasion would leave 270,000 Americans – not to mention Australian and British allies – dead or wounded. (An independent assessment, pointing out in July that Japan was still capable of fielding two million soldiers, reckoned that 150,000 pints of blood would be needed to cope with 395,000 US casualties, a third of them battlefield dead and wounded. [202])

What made even these figures seem an under-estimate was the ferocity of men fighting for their homeland and the mentality of the Japanese leadership: the stubborn, utterly self-centred Emperor Hirohito, his amoral Prime Minister Suzuki and his immoveable hardline Commanders, for whom 'honour' required that the Japanese fight 'to the very end'. Japan had been beaten – and the Commanders and Emperor knew it – by the beginning of 1945, yet their response was to launch several thousand *kamikaze* missions which caused great loss of allied lives. As late as June, the Supreme Council of the Imperial Army committed the nation to fight to the last Japanese – 'without reservation, compromise or quarter'. This was monstrous of course: a fanatical military nationalism prepared to condemn millions of civilians to death for the 'honour' of a spineless Emperor and an army whose barbarism exceeded any other in the twentieth century (only 3 per cent of prisoners of war died in German or British custody, unlike the 35 per cent worked or marched to their deaths by the Japanese). The Allies were well aware, thanks to their Ultra intercepts, of Japan's determination to fight invading forces to the very end.

At Potsdam, where the victors gathered at the end of July, Churchill noted how the responsibility for 'unlimited effusion of American blood' in this projected land invasion was weighing on Truman. A call for Japan's unconditional surrender was made by Churchill and Truman on 26 July: they promised democracy, with freedom of speech, religion and assembly and resettlement of soldiers, in return for permanent disarmament and 'stern justice' on war criminals, who might (and certainly should) have included Emperor Hirohito. 'The alternative for Japan is prompt and utter destruction,' said the Potsdam Proclamation: it did not say how, and even if it had spelled out the threat, this would have made no difference. The Japanese Cabinet, fully and indeed wickedly aware that they were signing the death warrant of countless civilians who would be killed in the anticipated invasion, decided to ignore the ultimatum, whilst their government-controlled media derided it. In these circumstances, it must have seemed to Truman that there was no alternative but to proceed.

Critics have picked over his decision ever since, but it is difficult to imagine the head of a democratic state with responsibility for the lives of his people making a different judgement call. It is said that he should have waited for possible peace overtures that might have been forthcoming through the Russians, but these were tentative, low level and deniable. It was said he should have waited for Russia to declare war on Japan and invade it from the west through Manchuria, thus obviously relieving some of the dangers to the US from its projected land invasion, but the Russians waited until after Hiroshima to make their move, and in any event the Japanese army would have fought desperately on both fronts, adding tens of thousands of Russians to the casualty list. It is said that Japan was about to surrender anyway, but this was belied by the Ultra intercepts and is unsupported by records of top-level meetings which show consistent and fervent military refusal even to think about surrender. It is said that the Potsdam terms should have been spelled out more clearly, and the Japanese assured that the Emperor would be allowed to stay on the throne. But it was for the Japanese government to come back seeking clarification and instead they decided to treat the offer with contempt. Finally, and most powerfully, it is said that the bomb was so horrific that it should not have been dropped at all, irrespective of how many lives might have been saved.

At this point, it is only right to consider the alternatives – as Oppenheimer's Target Committee did. It concluded – reasonably enough – that a warning of what might be in store would not impress Japan's military leaders, who would consider it mere bluff and propaganda. Dropping the bomb on an uninhabited island would only leave an 'unimpressive crater', which would be even less impressive if the bomb did not work or if the Japanese shot down the aircraft carrying it. The conclusion that only the devastation of a city, of great military and industrial significance but consequently full of workers, would provide the kind of spectacle which might shake the samurai spirit: nothing less than proof of its annihilating power would do the trick. This was true, to the extent that Hirohito surrendered eight days after Hiroshima, citing the 'most cruel bomb' as his excuse for a surrender to avoid 'the total extinction of human civilisation'. Where Truman's critics have a point (although few make it) is that the defence of 'military necessity' which runs for Hiroshima does not apply with the same force to the Nagasaki bomb – 'Fat Man' – delivered only three days later. This plutonium device had been tested in New Mexico and its immediate destructive capacity was known, if not its radiation consequence. (In fact, it caused 39,000 immediate deaths, and perhaps 60,000 from radiation sickness thereafter.) It is difficult to resist the conclusion that other considerations were taken into account in the dropping of 'Fat Man': scientific curiosity about the effect of a plutonium bomb on a city centre, the desirability of sending a signal to Russia against messing with America after the war, and the inevitable American desire to get their money's worth from the $2 billion cost of Manhattan, as well as the military purpose of ramming home the message that Japan had no option but to surrender.

That this message may well have needed to be rammed home is given some support in hindsight by records of deliberations by the Emperor, his Foreign Minister Tojo and Prime Minister Suzuki. These men, even after Hiroshima, lacked the courage to tell the military it was all over, and the Emperor, with utter selfishness, still wanted to wait until his post-surrender survival as 'Head of State' could be assured. They temporised on the day of the bomb, but two days later (7 August) came Russia's opportunistic declaration of war. Some revisionist historians suggest this was the real reason for the surrender, but this is unconvincing: the Japanese politicians on 8 August knew that they were beaten by the bomb, and would not otherwise have quailed at the prospect of a land war with the Russians – their military had already embraced the death-and-glory prospect of a land war with the Americans. The delay was caused by a power struggle with the fanatical military leaders, who even after Nagasaki still opposed surrender. 'Even if one hundred million people have to die, Japan would fight to the last man,' insisted War Minister Anami, supported by army chief Umezo and Privy Council president Hiranuma. It took the Emperor to assert his divine authority and insist, not on surrender but on a surrender offer, not made until the day *after* Nagasaki (i.e. on 10 August), that Japan would accept the Potsdam Declaration on the understanding that it did not 'prejudice the prerogatives of their Majesty as a Sovereign Ruler'. The man who had authorised Pearl Harbor, and all the major atrocities of war in the South Pacific, was primarily concerned not for his people but to save his own skin.

Anami and the militarists were not deterred: 'Even though we may have to eat grass, swallow dirt and lie in the fields, we shall fight on to the bitter end,' he announced on 11 August. But the two bombs had given the surrender faction the leverage they needed to override the army – they were 'in a sense, a gift from the Gods,' said Admiral Yonai, the moderate Minister for the Navy and the first Japanese to credit the bombs with bringing peace. As for Emperor Hirohito, the most responsible war criminal of them all, after receiving a signal from the US that he might be given immunity, he prepared to speak on the radio, for the first time ever, to his people. It was a thoroughly dishonest speech ('the war situation has developed not necessarily to Japan's advantage') but his sacred personage and his portentous excuse for surrendering, namely that thereby Japan would save the world from nuclear destruction, carried the day. Anami committed *hara-kiri*, as did over 2,000 fellow fanatics. Their crazed minds had not been changed by the bomb, but it had aroused an instinct of self-preservation in others – most notably, in the cowardly Emperor. If it did not force the surrender, Hiroshima at least provided the excuse without which a surrender would not have been forthcoming on 15 August 1945 (when the terms were accepted), or possibly at all.

For that relief, some thanks, although it did come at the terrible cost of two dead cities, expressed in the haiku of one survivor, the poet Sadako Kurihara:

> Hiroshima: nothing, nothing –
> Old and young burned to death,
> City blown away,
> Socket without eyeball.
> White bones scattered over reddish rubble;
> Above, sun burning down:
> City of ruins, still as death.[203]

If there was a small comfort in Hiroshima's suffering, it was that the spectacle of exponential death and devastation caused by recklessly pushing science to its limits could never, in a rational universe, be repeated. It would require states in future to summon all the arts of diplomacy, and failing that all the sinews of international law, to remove the temptations of nuclear weapons in human hands. In fact, diplomacy produced only a temporary and now ineffectual solution, a treaty which has failed to stop North Korea, India and Pakistan from piling up nuclear arsenals and is failing to stop Iran. International Human Rights law, which guarantees the right not to be unjustly deprived of life, may deserve a try.

There had been one moment of black comedy at Potsdam. Truman – only three months into his presidency – was advised by Stimson and Churchill, after they had received reports of the successful New Mexico test, to inform comrade Stalin of at least the possibility that they possessed a powerful weapon, so that he could not accuse his allies of deceit when it was dropped. So Truman found an opportunity to take the dictator and his translator aside, and to whisper that the US had 'a new weapon of unusually destructive force'. 'I'm glad to hear it,' replied Stalin without missing a beat, 'I hope you will make good use of it.' The rookie President was taken in by the dictator's feigned ignorance – Stalin knew all about the Manhattan Project (thanks to the diligence of his spies Klaus Fuchs and David Greenglass) but had not yet heard the result of the New Mexico test a week before – which Truman's comments had just revealed to him. He was immediately on the phone to Beria, his intelligence chief, cursing the lack of information and ordering the Russian bomb – already in development – to go full speed ahead. The Russians had infiltrated both Los Alamos and the British intelligence service in Washington (Philby, Burgess and Maclean), but they had their own very capable nuclear physicists, and despite the confident belief of American scientific advisers that the Soviets would not have a bomb until the mid-1950s, their first test in 1949 would have come even earlier had they been able to access a sufficient quantity of uranium. Unbeknown to the West, the nuclear arms race began with Truman's aside to Stalin, at Potsdam on 24 July 1945.

Once Wilf Burchett's despatches from Hiroshima broke the horrifying truth, and the pictures and survivor stories took hold, public gratitude in the West for an early end to the war turned to apprehension about a nuclear future. Journalists throughout the world all hit on 'Frankenstein's Monster' as their metaphor for the bomb, without bothering to read Mary Shelley's book about how kindness and culture could have prevented the creature from turning on his creator. If there was any novelist responsible for the bomb it was the amazingly imaginative H. G. Wells, with his 1914 story of how a 'central Europe' axis makes nuclear war on the democratic West, dropping a nuclear bomb on Paris before a French pilot drops two on Berlin, eviscerating the city but not before the Germans have bombed Holland and destroyed the British Houses of Parliament, whilst China bombs Moscow, the US destroys Tokyo, and Japan just misses San Francisco but destroys Delhi. By this time a few sensible statesmen meet in the unscarred olive groves of north Italy and agree to criminalise the future production, possession and use of atomic bombs.

A utopian ending, perhaps, but by 1945 Wells's *The Rights of Man* was one of the sources being used for drafting the Universal Declaration of Human Rights. In 1940 this slim book had been translated into German and dropped by the RAAF on German army tanks that were speeding through France. They did not stop to read it, but Roosevelt did and it inspired his 'Four Freedoms' speech after Pearl Harbor, and his insistence, in the Atlantic Charter, that human rights was an Allied war aim. At the end of *The World Set Free*, the prescient author writes: 'The moral shock of the atomic bombs had been a profound one and for a whilst the cunning side of the human animal was overpowered by its sincere realisation of the vital necessity for reconstruction.' This is a cynical but not entirely unfair description of the post-war posturings of the United States, the Soviet Union and other powers with nuclear potential.

• • •

'The hope of civilisation', said Truman, 'lies in international arrangements looking, if possible, to the renunciation of the use and development of the atomic bomb.' This was self-evident, and a new international law arrangement was getting underway in October 1945 with the trial of the Nazi leaders in Nuremberg. This would be necessary, as H. G. Wells envisaged: in his novel, the New World Government punishes severely the Head of State who is found to be secretly hoarding atomic bombs. The United Nations was now available for that purpose, and humankind's nuclear future – in effect, how to put the genie back in the bottle – was top of its first session agenda. Its very first resolution established an Atomic Energy Commission responsible to the Security Council that would supervise the sharing of scientific information for peaceful nuclear purposes, encourage the elimination of atomic weapons, and use inspectors to check for evasion of safeguards. Its first chairman was Dr H. V. Evatt, the Australian Foreign Minister, who had emerged as a leader of the middle-ranking member states. All this was premature of course, because the US remained the only nuclear power. Nonetheless there was a remarkable movement in mid-1946 when the United States actually offered to put all its atomic weapons – there were only three of them at the time – under UN control and to join in a treaty by which all nations would forswear the bomb and punish any state or statesman or scientist who tried to build another.

This was a plan developed by Dean Acheson, with the support of Stimson and Attlee, and unveiled at the UN by Truman's new nuclear spokesman, an old Woodrow Wilson hand, the conservative financier Bernard Baruch. The *quid pro quo* for America putting its bombs at the disposal of the UN and not producing any more would be that other states must first agree to establish an agency with the power to inspect all nuclear establishments, anywhere, and to prosecute and severely punish states or individuals caught in the commission of a new set of international crimes, notably the possession or separation of atomic material for use in a nuclear weapon, and the crime of engaging in dangerous nuclear projects without the agency's licence. Most importantly, the Baruch plan insisted that the superpower veto in the Security Council would not be used 'to protect those who violate their solemn agreement not to develop or use atomic energy for destructive purposes'. Baruch was nothing if not dramatic. Addressing the United Nations in June 1946, he told them, 'We are here to make a choice between the quick and the dead.'

But the dead arose, in the form of Soviet Foreign Minister Gromyko, who objected that abolishing the superpower veto was 'incompatible with the interests of the UN' – by which he meant, of course, the interests of the Soviet Union, secretly rushing to build its own bomb, and determined to veto any inspection of its facilities. Besides, said Gromyko, the Baruch plan put the cart before the horse: the Gromyko plan was for the US to destroy its bombs before other states would agree to forswear building theirs. And there could be no international criminal laws, only an agreement to introduce domestic legislation – a watering down to the point of impotence of the Baruch plan, since no violating government would ever prosecute

itself. Gromyko, harbinger of the Cold War, would accept no dimi-
nution of Soviet sovereignty, and denounced the Baruch plan as a
breach of Articles 2(4) and 2(7) of the UN Charter, which enshrined
the sovereign rights of member states to have no interference in their
internal affairs. Gromyko was wrong, of course – these sections are
subject to the Chapter VII powers of the Security Council to intervene
in the interests of international peace and security, the elimination of nuclear weapons being such an interest *par excellence*.
Churchill joined with progressive American lawyers like the later
Supreme Court judge William O. Douglas to support the Baruch
plan, although right-wing US senators were aghast that it would give
away America's weapons superiority and the US military establishment undermined Baruch's position by conducting an atomic bomb
test at Bikini Atoll, as if to suggest that it would carry on regardless.

It was left to the chairman of the Atomic Energy Commission,
Dr H. V. Evatt, to attempt a compromise between Baruch and
Gromyko. He suggested an international treaty, whereby all
nations would undertake never to use the bomb (whether or not
it came into their possession) in a war.[204] The treaty would set
up a commission which would buy up all available uranium and
other relevant raw materials, would prosecute those who failed
to comply or tried to enrich private supplies, and would encourage the peaceful use of nuclear energy. The commission would
be empowered to fix a future time to end bomb-making and
require existing bombs to be dismantled – a time that, in 1946,
the Soviets did not want to come until long after they had made
some bombs.

The debate continued in committee after committee, with the
Soviet Union (and its puppet, Poland) abstaining, and then in
1948 it eventually vetoed a Security Council resolution which
would have endorsed a version of the Evatt plan (thus proving
that abolition of the veto is essential if nuclear proliferation is to
be stopped). The Baruch and Evatt plans and their variants finally
came to naught in September 1949, when the Soviet Union tested
its A-bomb, and the Atomic Energy Commission was wound up
shortly afterwards, a victim of the Cold War. The Baruch plan
was before its time, and still is: the states of the world have not
yet agreed that they should all belong to a treaty which empowers

an international agency to inspect all their nuclear facilities and stockpiles of relevant raw materials and to prosecute and punish them – and their individual leaders and officials – for violations of its rules. The best they could do was to establish the IAEA in 1956, to encourage nuclear energy for civil purposes. (In 1970 it would be attached to the NPT as an inspection unit.) After 1949, the approach was limitation rather than elimination, to be regulated by an unempowered and voluntary inspection regime rather than by international crime and punishment. In this choice, of self-regulation rather than law, lies the root cause of our current discontents as more states turn to the bomb to solve their security problems and to boost their prestige. International law, absent from the calculations over Hiroshima, was never, after rejection of the Baruch plan, allowed to influence its aftermath. The future of the only force that could destroy the world was left to fate, and to the shifting self-interests of large nation-states.

The man who made the Islamic bomb, Dr A. Q. Khan,
and his protector, President Musharraf.

CHAPTER 10

PROLIFERATION

Nuclear destruction is mass destruction, both of persons and of things. It signifies the simultaneous destruction of tens of millions of people, of whole families, generations and societies, of all the things that they have inherited and created. It signifies the total destruction of societies by killing their members, destroying their visible achievements, and therefore reducing the survivors to barbarism. Thus nuclear destruction destroys the meaning of death by depriving it of its individuality. It destroys the meaning of immortality by making both society and history impossible.

Hans Morgenthau[205]

So the Cold War arms race began, at vast expense to governments which might have put their billions to better use and at a vast squandering of the human spirit and potential of three generations of scientists (including Andrei Sakharov, a Soviet hero for making its bombs bigger and better). Oppenheimer lost his security clearance because of his pre-war communist dalliances and his post-Hiroshima philosophical *tristesse*, and perhaps, most of all for his scepticism about nuclear competition between the US and USSR ('two scorpions in a bottle, each capable of killing the other but only at the risk of his own life'). But there were plenty of ideological warriors to take his place and press on with Truman and then Eisenhower's approval – to what Einstein soon condemned as 'an arms race of an hysterical character'. Thousands of atom bombs, and hundreds of tests, were followed by the 'super', i.e. hydrogen bomb, and later thermonuclear devices with many times the destructive force of 'Little Boy'. The H-bomb was first tested in 1952 on the Pacific atoll of Eniwetok, which it destroyed with an explosive force equivalent to 10,400,000 metric tons of TNT (compared to the first New

Mexico test, which had an equivalent of only 18,000 metric tons). The Soviets were, this time, only a year behind, and both nations were test-dropping H-bombs on or under god-forsaken parts of the world throughout the 1950s.

This was the era of the backyard fall-out shelter, school 'duck and cover' drills, and films like *On the Beach* and later *Dr Strangelove or: How I Learned to Stop Worrying and Love the Bomb* – a satire on the vast sums being spent on 'mutually assured destruction', which could not exclude the destruction that might be occasioned by accident or by the madness of someone with a finger on the nuclear trigger. Or, indeed, by some stark staring sane military leader who wanted a quick victory. General MacArthur asked for forty nuclear weapons to drop on the Chinese during the Korean War, and in 1954 the French formally requested that Washington supply them with a bomb to drop on the Vietnamese forces at Dien Bien Phu. The danger of such requests was not only that they might be accepted, but that they were turned down, and thereby provided a spur to France and other countries to develop their own nuclear weapons – in the jargon that is now commonplace, to proliferate. The roll call of proliferators, for reasons invariably to do with national prestige and a false sense of security, went (after the US and the Soviet Union) as follows:[206]

GREAT BRITAIN

The nation whose scientists did more to set up the nuclear era than any other had a residual pride in their achievement and saw the 'British bomb' as a means of recovering some of the military power that had been drained by its long and eviscerating battle with Nazi Germany. There was also the egregious argument (later deployed by Tony Blair to convince his Cabinet they should join the US invasion of Iraq) that 'we have to be in it to exercise a moderating influence on the Americans'. Foreign Minister Ernest Bevan told Cabinet: 'We've got to have the thing over here, whatever it costs. We've got to have the bloody Union Jack on top of it.' So the UK rebuilt the bomb (the Manhattan expertise of Klaus Fuchs was particularly helpful, until he was taken off to jail for spying for the Soviets) and then replicated the already dated US tests, in islands off and deserts in Australia, leaving local Aborigines and British servicemen prone in later life to radiation-induced cancers.

There was never any point in the UK having an 'independent nuclear deterrent' – its few bombs add nothing to the US arsenal available to NATO, but as Harold Macmillan told a television audience in 1958, the bomb 'puts us where we ought to be, in the position of a great power'. Ah, the nostalgia for Empire! 'The whole thing is ridiculous,' Macmillan admitted in private whilst renegotiating with America to buy Polaris missiles in 1962, but 'countries which have played a great role in history must retain their dignity'.[207] Harold Wilson's government, although virtually bankrupt, maintained the pretence, giving the US Diego Garcia and the rest of the Chagos Islands and cruelly extirpating the Chagossian people, in return for a discount on the price of Polaris.[208]

Britain now has about 220 nukes, 180 of them aboard four Trident submarines. These will be replaced by 2025 at a massive price. The government admits it will cost £25 billion but a more realistic estimate by Greenpeace UK is that total costs will be close to £95 billion. The country cannot afford the Trident replacement, which was authorised by Tony Blair and approved by the present Coalition government. The only point of this 'independent deterrent' is to provide black humour at the Monty Python-esque ritual played out on the first day in office of every British Prime Minister: they must write a top-secret letter to the four submarine commanders, sealed and kept in the submarine's safe, not to be opened until it is clear that a nuclear war has wiped out the British government and people (this will be clear, say the instructions, when the BBC no longer broadcasts). They will open the letter to receive their final orders from Her Majesty's Government: whether to shoot their nuclear missiles in retaliation at the enemy capital or to drop them in the ocean and hightail it for Tasmania. The contents of these 'Letters of Last Resort' have never been revealed, and only one Prime Minister (Jim Callaghan) has ever said they should be. It is said that Margaret Thatcher ordered that the last nuke should be fired so as to cause maximum destruction to the enemy, and that Gordon Brown was the only Prime Minister to refuse to sign (so post-Britain use of the British deterrent was, during his prime ministership, presumably left to a direction from the First Sea Lord).

FRANCE

French scientists had worked with British and Canadian counterparts on wartime nuclear projects in Montreal, and France had uranium stocks in its African colonies Niger and Madagascar. A certain Gallic moral disdain slowed the nuclear project until the sudden desire to drop a bomb on the Vietnamese. After this defeat, Prime Minister Mendès France muttered that 'a country is nothing without nuclear arms' and de Gaulle, echoing Macmillan, said that 'a great state does not command its own destiny' without the bomb. It tested first in Algeria in 1960, and when that colony rose up France inflicted radiation on its colonies in the South Pacific. So prickly was France, after Australia took it to the ICJ in an effort to stop testing at Mururoa Atoll, that its secret service actually planted a bomb on a Greenpeace boat – the *Rainbow Warrior* – in Auckland harbour, murdering a crewman. The French tests, in the atmosphere and underground, have added nothing to scientific knowledge and its 'independent deterrent' is surplus to NATO's requirements: what its tests have caused is a degree of pollution, both of the atmosphere and the ocean, which is increasingly blamed for cancer in people and malformation in fish. France has been the most irresponsible of the 'Big 5' in relation to its nukes, and even today will not come clean about their numbers: it pretends to have less than 300, but British intelligence suggests it has more than 600. It is the most resistant of the 'Big 5' to giving 'no first strike' guarantees or to welcoming disarmament agreements.

EUROPE

The North Atlantic Treaty Organization (NATO), headquartered in Brussels, has since its inception after the war welcomed the stationing of US nukes in Europe, with vast arrays of missiles facing the even vaster Soviet short-rage strategic missiles stationed in Warsaw Pact satellites. It was a different kind of Soviet satellite – Sputnik – launched in 1957 that put the wind up the West and heralded Moscow's introduction of intercontinental ballistic missiles, soon to be matched by US counterparts. Europe in a sense was 'piggy in the middle' – nobody really thought that the Soviets would target Paris or London, when they had new rockets that would take only half an hour from launch to hit America. Nonetheless, the US convinced its European partners that packing their countries with nukes was a 'risk and responsibility sharing arrangement' – although it became clear that Europe would take the risk and the US the responsibility, threatening 'no nukes, no troops'. Cold War paranoia meant little opposition other than from pacifists, and the lingering camphor of pacifism dogs the anti-nuke movement to this day. After the end of the Cold War and the break-up of the Warsaw Pact, there was little point in stationing US nuclear missiles on the continent, as an increasing number of cost-conscious congressmen pointed out. However, they were silenced in 2008 by a report from James Schlesinger, which said that they 'failed to comprehend ... the political value our friends and allies place on these weapons'.[209] In the UK, CND veterans in the Blair Cabinet like Margaret Beckett and Des Browne meekly went along with the extortionately expensive replacement for Trident, whilst in Germany the coalition government which had come together in 2009 on a platform of removing nukes from the country soon went to water after a NATO 'Group of Experts' chaired by Madeleine Albright reported that 'the retention of some UN forward-deployed systems on European soil reinforces the principle of extended nuclear deterrence and collective defence'.[210] But is there any point in reinforcing a principle of deterrence when there is nobody to deter?

The European Union and Council of Europe are, it must be said, utterly hypocritical in respect of nuclear weapons. They have never advanced a vision for 'Europe without Nukes' on the basis of the right to life in the European Convention on Human Rights, and have done nothing to request removal of NATO weapons or to chivvy the UK and France to live up to their Article VI obligations to agree a disarmament treaty (see page 207). The excuse has been the numerical disparity between US and Russian short-range non-strategic nuclear weapons, but the removal of the remaining US weapons would spotlight Russia's laxity in this respect and perhaps embarrass it into reciprocating. The point is that there is no prospect that they will be fired in anger at Europe. The only incident that has caused any alarm was in 2008, when Georgia irresponsibly provoked the Russian Federation by invading South Ossetia, and found itself facing SS-26 ballistic missiles which might have been carrying nukes (but probably were not – the Russians refused to say). This is hardly an incident which makes out the case for US nukes on European soil – quite the contrary, since the US automatically and at first belligerently took Georgia's side (it was George Bush's favourite European country). Now, the nuke retentioners can point to the danger of Iran firing a missile towards Europe, although were this to happen, conventional bombing of its military bases would be the appropriate retaliation. The continuing argument does show how the very prospect of Iran going nuclear is being used as a reason to maintain existing nuclear stocks in Europe.

CHINA

The People's Liberation Army, the largest land force in the world, has never needed to bolster its sheer manpower by nuclear bombs. It was Eisenhower's veiled threats (and MacArthur's demands) to use the bomb against Chinese military targets during the Korean War which alerted Mao to the need to have an 'equaliser', as much as a matter of status as of military use. In 1964 an A-bomb was tested and several hundred were built before the test of a thermonuclear device (in 1967) rendered them old-fashioned. China is a rational nation with a mere 240 bombs, and is more than willing to give 'no first strike' guarantees, but was irresponsible in giving assistance to Pakistan – with advice, blueprints and a supply of weapons-grade uranium – to help A. Q. Khan to build a bomb with which to threaten their mutual enemy, India.

INDIA

Its first test came in 1974 – 'a peaceful nuclear explosion' as Mrs Gandhi oxymoronically described the 'Smiling Buddha' nuclear device from a government that had pretended it was guarding Mahatma Gandhi's legacy of non-violence. It had been galvanised by China's first nuclear test in 1964 – an enemy which had invaded India just two years previously. Psychological factors were at play too, in the country's stealthy pursuit of nuclear technology, at first assisted under the 'Atoms for Peace' programme by the US and UK, taken in by Nehru's pretence that India needed nuclear power only to provide electricity for its teeming masses. There was also a bitter anti-colonialism behind India's duplicity: its rulers were fed up with Western condescension and contempt for the sub-continent's scientific skills, so they built the bomb for status as much as for acquiring an equaliser with China and power over Pakistan. The 1974 test had a domestic purpose as well, namely to boost Mrs Gandhi's low rating in the polls, which it did quite remarkably. This was the first clear sign of how extremely popular nuclear weapons are with the people in developing democracies. This became even more apparent in 1998, when a nationalist party (the BJP) came to power and tested more complex devices ('We have a big bomb now,' gloated the Prime Minister). India was one of only three countries to refuse to sign or ratify the NPT, driving the first nail into the coffin of this centrepiece of international nuclear co-operation.

India now has at least 100 nuclear weapons, and is so excessively proud of its achievement that the date of its 'big bomb' test – 11 May 1998 – has been declared a national holiday, 'National Technology Day'.[211] Going public about its stocks of nuclear weapons has boosted both its international prestige and its self-image, and it has been quite blatantly allowed to avoid the NPT regime without suffering sanctions or very much criticism. This is largely because of its protection by the Bush administration, which secured India's exemption from bans imposed on non-NPT members by the Nuclear Suppliers Group (see page 212). The 2008 India–US agreement liberated India from nuclear and 'dual-use' technology prohibitions. This was in part a reward for India's support for Bush's decision to pull out of the Anti-Ballistic Missile Treaty (India too wanted to move its nukes from bombers to ballistic missiles) and in part to enlist India's support for moves against Iran and possibly against Pakistan.

India has some reason to regard its acquisition of nukes as the key to accession to power in the world: its ambition is to be admitted to permanent membership of the Security Council, as part of the 'Big 6'. Indians can (and do) reflect that nuclear weapons have so far served them well. Whether they will continue to do so is another matter.

PAKISTAN

Zulfikar Ali Bhutto made no attempt to hide his nuclear bomb plans: Pakistanis 'will eat grass or leaves – even go hungry – but we will get one of our own'. And they did, thanks to Dr Abdul Zadeer Khan, a spy who worked at URENCO, a supposedly safe facility in Europe – the only one licensed by the IAEA to enrich uranium for civil nuclear power plants. In 1974 he persuaded Bhutto that he could steal materials and blueprints from URENCO for a uranium-based A-bomb, and he did – getting them out of the country with assistance from the Pakistani embassy in Amsterdam. In 1976 Khan opened his own company, and with the support of successive Pakistani governments and its military (which formed most of those governments) and some assistance from China, he worked to circumvent IAEA restrictions on necessary materials, purchasing mainly from greedy Swiss and German companies prepared to turn a blind eye to the prospect that these dual-use items would be used to build the bomb. There is no doubt that many of his suppliers deliberately evaded export restrictions, some in the arrogant belief that 'third world scientists', lacking the sophistication and intellectual breadth of a Robert J. Oppenheimer, were just not up to the job of producing a bomb. This was one reason, of course, why Khan was determined to produce it – so that 'nobody can undo Pakistan or take us for granted'.[212]

The government continually lied about its nuclear ambitions and capacities, and was the grateful recipient of billions of dollars in US aid for its secret intelligence service (the ISI) to back bin Laden and the Taliban in the war against the Soviets in Afghanistan. When Pakistan eventually broke cover, in 1998, with tests underneath a mountain which generated seismic evidence that it had become the first Islamic member of the nuclear club, Khan became a national hero: Bhutto's estimation of his people's pride had not been amiss. It was not until 2003 that it became clear just what Khan had really been up to since 1986, when he had opened his clandestine 'nuclear Wal-Mart', selling the blueprints for the bomb (and centrifuge parts) to pariah states

– Iran first, then Libya and North Korea. It was Gaddafi, as a result of his 'deal in the desert' with Blair, who squealed on Khan, who had by that time brought all three countries a long way towards a nuclear weapon.

American pressure forced President Musharraf to take some action against the popularly revered 'father of the Islamic bomb' but it was no more than to place Khan under house (in fact, mansion) arrest and furnish him with a pardon after he had made a brief apology on television in 2004 for causing embarrassment to his beloved nation. This secured his safety and ensured that the IAEA would never have access to debrief him and track down the full consequences of his avarice. Three of his foreign accomplices have been prosecuted under their domestic laws, but most remain free, and Pakistan, disgracefully, has never made available his confession, or the notes of his sympathetic debriefing. Khan has sometimes suggested that he acted out of hostility to the way the NPT discriminated against Islamic states, but this excuse cannot be squared with his greed-driven sales to North Korea and the meeting his representatives had with Al Qaeda. He is the archetype of the scientist who belongs behind bars for the rest of his life, in any scenario for future control of nuclear weapons.

SOUTH EAST ASIA

There are two very different views about the consequences of the proliferation in south east Asia. 'If India and Pakistan have kept each other in a nuclear stalemate, why would Iran not be similarly deterred?' asks the complacent Bill Keller in the *New York Times*.[213] The answer is that whilst neither have dropped their nukes on each other, yet, the sub-continent is a much more dangerous place – not only because of the greater risk of accident or seizure by terrorists, but because possession of bombs has emboldened Pakistan's military and intelligence services to support insurgents in Kashmir and wage asymmetric warfare on India, requiring India to prepare aggressive war plans for possible reprisals. Given the long history of hatred between the two countries – going back to the time of partition, when Pakistan was bequeathed only 23 per cent of British India and 18 per cent of the population, and when up to one million people were killed in Hindu–Muslim violence, it may only be a matter of time before one of their many border conflicts develops into fully fledged war, with nukes available to reverse the fortunes of the likely loser.

True, there has been no such war on the sub-continent since nuclear weapons were introduced, but a screaming match over Kashmir almost provoked one in 1990, with both sides puffed up by their unrevealed bombs. Pakistan realised it could get away with funding and supplying the anti-India separatist movement in Kashmir because India would fear to retaliate. The conflict in Kargil in 1999 was a consequence of Pakistan adopting a much more aggressive policy towards India in Kashmir after successfully testing six nuclear weapons in 1998. At the end of that year, Pakistani soldiers disguised as local Kashmiri militants invaded across the 'line of control' separating the two countries, in due course provoking a bloody counter-attack: it was stopped only when the US put pressure on Pakistan to withdraw, fearing that it might launch nuclear retaliation if India counter-attacked with conventional forces and advanced too far into the country. The damage that nuclear weapons did, within a year of the 1998 tests, was both to regional stability and to the lives of a thousand Indian and Pakistani soldiers: Pakistan would never have been emboldened to undertake the Kargil invasion without its bombs as a back-up. Pakistan's nuclear-inspired aggressive confidence has caused it to sponsor a number of terrorist groups, 'sorcerer's apprentices' that it could not in the end control, most notoriously *Lashkar-e-Taiba*, which conducted the murderous assaults on Mumbai in 2006 and 2008. The Indian government has in consequence massively boosted its conventional forces and constantly war-games 'Operation Cold Start', a planned reprisal offensive against Pakistan calculated to fall just short of triggering a Pakistani nuclear response. That calculation is India's: Pakistani military experts say that 'Cold Start' will instead, by lowering the nuclear threshold, force the weaker country to rely on its nuclear weapons.[214] India's intentions to acquire a ballistic missile defence system will also exacerbate tension, not only with Pakistan but with another historic enemy, China, which is likely to respond with ballistic missile transfers to Pakistan, its longstanding ally. And so it goes on...

SOUTH AFRICA

Nuclear bombs had great attraction for apartheid South Africa. It had lots of enemies and lots of uranium, which it sold to the US and the UK in return for assistance with its 'Atoms for Peace'. The weapons side of that development was kept dark, of course, at facilities which employed 900 workers, none of them black.[215] Before A. Q. Khan was in the market South Africa was in business with Israel, which it cultivated as a secret collaborator in the 1970s, by the end of which it had six workable A-bombs of the Hiroshima gun-barrel type. It was only stopped from testing them in the Kalahari when the Russians identified the purpose of the site from a Sputnik image and blew the international whistle. But the six bombs were available for use for another decade, until apartheid's days were numbered and F. W. de Klerk ordered their destruction – a remarkably bold decision, which can to some extent be cynically explained by Afrikaner reluctance to see half a dozen nuclear bombs in the hands of the ANC. In 1993, Mandela's parliament passed a law making it a crime for any South African citizen to aid or abet the development of nuclear weapons – a breakthrough hastened by the scientific experiments of Dr Basson, who had been working on the quintessential apartheid weapon, which would eradicate blacks but not whites.

ISRAEL

The story of – and problem with – the Israeli bomb (of which there are now at least 80, and possibly as many as 200) is told in Chapter 13. It provides yet another example of how Eisenhower's 'Atoms for Peace' were turned into atoms for war. It was embarrassment about Jewish passivity during the Holocaust that determined the Israeli leaders, as soon as they had a nation, to protect it with nuclear weapons. So they took advantage of Eisenhower's offer, and the French built them a reactor at Dimona and supplied the first uranium, later supplemented with supplies from South Africa. David Ben-Gurion solemnly pledged to President Kennedy that they were not out to acquire nuclear weapons when they were trying desperately to do so, and Shimon Peres uttered the great lie (which is maintained to this day) that Israel will not be the first to 'introduce' nuclear weapons into the Middle East.

By the time of the Six Day War in 1967 Israel already had a nuclear device, which it thought hard about 'introducing' and would have done so if the war had not gone their way. The following year 'the Plumbat affair', where it was caught secretly trying to import enough uranium for thirty bombs, gave the game away, although proof had to await until Mordechai Vanunu's revelations to the *Sunday Times* in 1986. Even so, Israel maintains rigid censorship of any media information about its nuclear weapons programme. Its international posture is neither to confirm nor to deny – 'nuclear opacity' or 'ambiguity' as it is officially called, rather than by its proper name, 'nuclear hypocrisy'. It bombs the reactors of neighbours which might go nuclear – Iraq (Osirak) in 1981 and Syria (Kibar) in 2007, and now threatens Iran. At least Israel has stopped short of 'nuclear dishonesty' – it did not join the NPT as a non-nuclear state, and now refuses to do so because it would have to declare its nuclear-related facilities at Dimona. Paradoxically it has been permitted to join the IAEA, although it does not permit inspection of its nuclear facilities.

NORTH KOREA

North Korea is described by American diplomats, with good reason, as 'the impossible state'. It was carved out in 1948 as the communist half of the Korean peninsula and the Soviet Union installed Kim Il-sung, a loyal apparatchik, as its leader. He quickly liquidated all opponents and then, in 1950, dragged his other protector, China, into a war to reclaim the capitalist South. In that conflict 2.7 million Koreans were killed, together with 33,000 American servicemen and 800,000 Chinese. It may have been MacArthur's threat to end it by dropping nuclear bombs that inspired Kim's quest to make nuclear weapons. He sent his scientists for nuclear training in Moscow, which in turn built him a reactor at Yongbyon but did not trust him, so insisted it should be inspected by the IAEA and that the country should join the NPT. As the Cold War ended, China made clear to Pyongyang that it could not necessarily hide under its nuclear umbrella, so 'the Great Leader' went shopping in A. Q. Khan's nuclear Wal-Mart, purchasing centrifuges, enrichment machines and technical data and drawings. North Korea joined the NPT in 1985 but still pushed on with its secret weapons programme, thinking it could fool the IAEA inspectors and hide the plutonium it was reprocessing from spent fuel rods at the reactor. But the inspectors took 'swipe samples' from the equipment and discovered that North Korea had amassed enough plutonium for two bombs. The state refused future inspections and in 1994 IAEA chief Hans Blix reported North Korea to the Security Council.

The Clinton administration seriously considered invasion at this point (Iran is close to it today), but was horrified by the estimated cost: $100 billion, and a million casualties.[216] War was averted by the single-handed diplomacy of Jimmy Carter, who went on a private visit to meet the Great Leader and negotiated an 'Agreed Framework' under which the inspectors could return (although not necessarily to the facilities they wanted to visit) and the US would supply light-water reactors for electricity. It is fair to say that neither side lived up to the bargain but the North Koreans began cheating from the outset, making more plutonium from their spent fuel rods and diversifying their bomb-making capability by enriching uranium. Despite the so-called 'six-party talks' where from 2002 North Korea sat around a table with the US, China, Russia, South Korea and Japan, it still kept enriching and reprocessing and testing missiles that could carry a nuclear payload, one of which may one day carry a payload to America.

In 2006 North Korea broke cover with a plutonium-based bomb, exploded underground, adding insult to injury by conducting this test on 4 July, American Independence Day. (Puerile provocation is second nature to the North Koreans – the next, more powerful, test was on American Memorial Day, 2009.) In 2010 it dropped all pretences and admitted it had a fully operational enrichment facility at Yongbyon, and it now is estimated to have built a dozen bombs.

After the tests, Security Council resolutions expressed 'gravest concern', condemned North Korea 'in the strongest terms' and imposed non-proliferation duties on other states, requiring them to inspect ships with North Korean cargoes.[217] These resolutions, significantly, were supported by China and Russia, North Korea's traditional allies, but that did not deter it: the tests were needed, it explained, 'to help settle scientific and technological problems arising in further increasing the power of nuclear weapons'.[218] As if testosteroned by possession of the bomb, North Korea's recent behaviour has been outrageous: in 2007 it was caught building a secret nuclear reactor for the Assad regime at Al-Kibar in the Syrian desert; one of its submarines torpedoed a South Korean naval vessel in 2010 (with the loss of forty-six young lives); its army fired on a South Korean island, killing four and injuring more. It now openly boasts of its operational uranium enrichment facility at its Yongbyon nuclear site. It gets away with all these provocations despite the fact that they provoke China and Russia as well as the West. Perhaps this is because North Korea is misperceived by the US as a sad and slightly ridiculous totalitarian state that can always be carpet-bombed if it seriously threatens to nuke its neighbours. But in a few years, when it perfects the ballistic missiles that can deliver its bombs to America, the prospect of a nuclear reprisal will not make the bombing of North Korea an easy option. The very fact that it gets away with its lethal antics serves as an encouragement to Iran, whose antics are not so far advanced but are, in the long run, even more dangerous.

Meanwhile, and despite the collapse of the Soviet Union, which freed eastern European states from various forms of Stalinism, North Korea remains totalitarian and has become a human rights black hole. It is a dictatorship of the Kim family – the Great Leader died in 1994 and was followed by 'the Dear Leader', Kim Jong-il, and in 2010 by 'the Great Successor', Kim Jong-un. The Kims are kept in power by a clique of geriatric generals at the head of a one-million-strong army goose-stepping in a time-warped country disconnected from reality and close to economic collapse. Its people have the least freedom of any in the world, and the most censorship: citizens have been jailed for not dusting pictures of the Great Leader in their homes or for whistling South Korean pop songs; history textbooks make no mention of the fact that the US won the war against Japan and rather indicate it was through the heroism of the Great Leader (who in fact had no war record to speak of). Those citizens who are not successfully brainwashed are sent to gulags – there are seventeen at least – where they are worked, in some cases, to death. Starvation is endemic outside

Pyongyang – it has claimed a million lives in recent years, despite aid programmes (the largest, ironically, from the US). The elite live in luxury, as elites usually do, although the Dear Leader resided in medieval splendour in eleven palaces, their lights kept blazing all night, perhaps to demonstrate the nation's need for electricity. Its human rights record is atrocious, although the allegations lack detail because of North Korea's isolation and secrecy. It does not seem to kill its political prisoners, for example, although it did blow up a South Korean passenger airliner over the Andaman Sea in 1987 (in protest against the Olympic Games going to Seoul), and its recent torpedoing of a South Korean destroyer demonstrates its unfitness to possess nuclear weapons. It has not threatened to use them, but when in a few years' time it makes a missile that could deliver them the US mainland, Bill Clinton may think that his projected but rejected 1994 invasion, costing $100 billion, would have been cheap at the price.

North Korea is a Cold War anachronism, but despite its gulags and its food shortages it is good at building bombs and missiles, and at selling them to opportunistic allies: Pakistan and Iran have copied its Nodong range of rockets, which are available for purchase by other countries which are not in alliance with America. It will be capable of a nuclear attack on the US once it perfects a design for a nuclear warhead, completes successful development of a three-stage missile launch (which it tested in 2009) and works out how to make a re-entry heat shield for a long-range ballistic missile (to prevent it from exploding when it re-enters the earth's atmosphere). All it will need to reach Hollywood is a good reason to go to war. That would be provided by a US land invasion or carpet-bombing, so the path not taken by Clinton in 1994 will be permanently closed within a few years, which is all it will take for North Korea to develop these capacities.[219] Those nearby countries which are under the US nuclear umbrella – South Korea, Taiwan, the Philippines and Japan – may therefore want to develop their own nuclear bombs. Even Australia might accept the stationing of US nuclear weapons permanently on its territory. Under the recent Gillard–Obama agreement, there will be new American bases in Darwin and the Cocos Islands, within the range of the latest North Korean 'dong'.

North Korea has not been deterred by UN sanctions, imposed unanimously by the Security Council after its last bomb test, or by decades of what passes for diplomacy. It wants to be admitted to the NPT as the sixth (or seventh after India) nuclear weapon state, but that is resisted by the existing five on the basis that it would be a reward for cheating. It may, however, be the only way, short of force, to impose any constraint on this country of the personality cult, which the Great and Dear Kim family wants to rule forever. Recognition as a nuclear power and readmission to the NPT with that status would at least impose upon it a duty to disarm eventually, albeit a duty on which it would be likely to cheat.

THE MIDDLE EAST

A report published in 2012 warned of the proliferation conse-quence of the Iranian quest for nuclear weapons:

> In a region racked with open warfare, persistent interstate rival-ries, powerful non-state actors and ominous interstate tensions, countries throughout the Persian Gulf and Middle East now seem united on at least one issue: the need to develop their own nuclear power programmes. In regional capitals such as Rabat, Algiers, Cairo, Riyadh, Abu Dhabi, Manama, Doha, Muscat and Amman, political leaders announced their intention to start development of indigenous nuclear programmes and have been beating a path to the IAEA's door, seeking information on creating a significant nuclear research programme.

Does this mean that Iran's neighbours, frightened by its progress, are grasping their 'inalienable rights' to nuclear energy as a pretext, or at least a first stage, in their development of nuclear weapons? Egypt is a particular danger, now it has elected a Muslim Brotherhood President, whose party spokesman said in 2006, with echoes of Bhutto's 'we will eat grass', that 'we are ready to starve in order to own a nuclear weapon that will represent a real deterrent and will be decisive in the Arab–Israeli conflict'.[220] The Muslim Brotherhood opposed Mubarak's policy of making the Middle East a nuclear-free zone. The Gulf Cooperation

Council announced its intention to develop nuclear energy, and Saudi Arabia – the main counter-balance to Iran – said in July 2012 that it would purchase a nuclear weapon from Pakistan, if Iran reached nuclear capability. (The two countries are currently reported to be exchanging nuclear 'know-how and expertise'.) WikiLeaks cables showed that in 2009 King Faisal was begging the US to bomb Iran, which has Shehab-3 medium-range missiles capable of carrying a nuclear warhead as far as Riyadh.

It really does not matter whether Iran is developing a nuclear weapon or not: to the extent that other countries within its range think that it is, they will be tempted to use their newly acquired nuclear reactors for high-enrichment programmes, resigning from the NPT as soon as they feel it necessary to assemble a nuclear device. Once, countries like Saudi Arabia, the Gulf states and Morocco could rest assured that the US would come to their aid, as it did when Saddam invaded Kuwait in 1990. But thanks to George W. Bush's benighted invasion of Iraq, the US in the Middle East today has much less political influence, a good deal less military clout and very little public approval. Iran has a new and potentially powerful ally in Iraq, whilst Israel and the US are deprecated throughout the region (a recent poll showed 70 per cent of Middle Easterners regard them as the most serious threat to regional stability).[221]

ELSEWHERE IN ASIA

Here, the most provocative role has been taken by North Korea, which remains a menace, although China has also frayed regional nerves. The Peoples' Liberation Army, with over a million soldiers, has developed a sophisticated electronic warfare capacity with air force and navy capability and missiles that can hit – with nuclear warheads – any target in the region. Taiwan is an obvious target for a Chinese 'decapitation strategy' and hence an obvious candidate to seek 'deterrent' nuclear weapons, although it has a strong anti-nuclear movement which wants to confine the island to its present security, based on cruise and long-range ballistic missiles and alliance with the US. President Obama has announced a new 'Pacific Strategy' to contain China and North Korea using bases in Australia (Darwin and the Cocos Islands) which may soon have nuclear-tipped ballistic missiles pointing northwards.

Vietnam is also hostile to China, with which it is locked in a potentially inflammable dispute over the Spratly Archipelago. Its government is already exercising (with US assistance) its 'inalienable right' to nuclear energy to supplement its unsatisfactory hydro power. The tight communist control of Vietnam could keep any nuclear development secret. Japan could 'break out' and build a bomb within a month or so, and is having increasingly bitter disputes with China over small islands, although a very strong anti-nuclear movement, strengthened as a result of Fukushima, would make this a last resort. Indonesia is less of a problem, although its military was cruel enough to use chemical weapons in East Timor, and would not scruple, if beyond civilian control, to develop nuclear weapons. In that event the real danger may not be that it will use them but that it will lose them – its safety record is low, and the terrorist group that set off the Bali disco bombs that killed over one hundred tourists remains a threat.

Burma is firmly under the control of its generals, notwithstanding the release of Aung San Suu Kyi. It has purchased a reactor from Russia and is reported to have had secret talks with North Korea about nuclear weapons diversion. In 2007 it announced a 'nuclear research centre', the location of which remains secret, although its technicians are being trained in Russia and possibly in North Korea. Stories abound about A. Q. Khan's trips to Burma, although there are few hard facts extricable from this secretive military stronghold. Its past human rights record suggests that it would not hesitate to lie to the IAEA about its intentions to attain nuclear weapon capacity, or to build some bombs.

LATIN AMERICA

The bomb always appealed to Perón's nationalist movement in Argentina and to the brutal military regimes which followed: it had developed a nuclear fuel cycle under the armed forces junta led in the late 1970s by General Videla, whose moral outlook is showed by in the fact that he is currently serving fifty years in prison for having pregnant leftists killed in childbirth and their children adopted by loyal army families. Argentina was willing to make deals with Iran in the early 1990s, until the US stepped on Carlos Menem's toes and Iran attacked the Jewish community centre in Buenos Aires in revenge. Its relations with Tehran have been strained ever since it sought Interpol warrants for the arrest of the Iranian Intelligence Ministry chief responsible. But Argentina's renewed sabre-rattling over the Falkland Islands may yet make it keen to acquire the bomb: it feared that Mrs Thatcher might hit Buenos Aires with a missile from a Trident submarine during the Falklands War back in 1982. Brazil, the new South American dynamo, has a Vice President who openly demanded the right to develop nuclear weapons to obtain, he said, more 'respectability' in world affairs – a new form of 'honour killing', so to speak. The President overruled him, claiming that he had personally renounced nuclear weapons, although Lula is a constant critic of the NPT and is building a nuclear-powered submarine. Venezuela is currently seen as a likely proliferator, given the introspective populism of the Chávez government and its attacks on judicial independence and freedom of speech. He has 'reportedly' (which means not verifiably) allocated funding for a secret nuclear programme, and has publicly supported Iran's development of nuclear arms – thus providing some evidence that it *is* developing nuclear arms, given his closeness to Ahmadinejad. The two leaders have met a dozen times, and the latter has approved technology transfers to the Chávez 'nuclear village'. Chávez maintains that he is not interested in uranium enrichment but he fervently supports what he calls Iran's 'sacred' right to enrich. It may be that some stories about his nuclear weapons aspirations are (as he claims) CIA propaganda, but his constant support for Ahmadinejad and the man he describes as his 'humanist brother', Syria's Bashir al-Assad, do not inspire confidence.

DR KHAN RE-EXAMINED

The major problem with the Non-Proliferation Treaty has been proliferation, caused particularly by Dr A. Q. Khan. His network only came to public knowledge when revealed by Gaddafi in 2003, by which time it had kick-started nuclear weapons quests not only by Libya, but by Iran, Syria, Iraq and North Korea, and perhaps others. There is now a mounting number of states that, whilst members of the NPT, have attained 'nuclear weapons capacity', the ability to enrich their uranium to weapons grade and make bombs within a few months of a decision to do so. The greater availability of nukes, to states locked in regional rivalries, undermines the theory of 'stable deterrence' – the perception that any first use of nuclear weapons would be met with a sufficiently large retaliation to make that first strike, if not suicidal, at least lethally counter-productive. This was a logic that could be appreciated by the US and the Soviets in the 1950s, when a nuclear reprisal against a first strike had to be virtually automatic. But it does not work a half-century later by which time human rights law has condemned any use of nuclear weapons, including a second reprisal nuclear strike, which would in any event be an exercise in futile revenge, especially if the first strike had been by accident or by an enemy which had a third strike up its sleeve. Once nuclear bombs were available to lesser states with their own strategic standoffs – to India and Pakistan and Israel and then to states like North Korea, and then potentially to Iran and Syria, 'stable deterrence' became very unstable indeed, when a first strike in a regional war would bring in second and third strikes from great-power allies, when radiation would drift with the wind across borders and the lights would go out all over continents.

It was the exposure of the A. Q. Khan network which called into question both the assumptions behind the NPT and the prospects that even with a more intensive inspection regime it could detect or stop proliferation. The IAEA uncovered 1,300 separate cases of illicit trafficking through Dr Khan's nuclear bazaar, netting him over $400 million.[222] Khan, as 'the father of the Pakistani bomb', had enough cover from his hero-worship in that nation to sell nuclear designs and material to other states, without his sponsor government necessarily knowing what he was up to. 'Necessarily' in that sentence comes freighted with suspicion – it is likely that elements in the government (notably sections of its army and security service) knew what he was up to, and either gave him encouragement (as in the case of North Korea, where his assistance was given in return for purchase of Nodong rockets) or turned a blind eye, perhaps in return for a greased palm.[223]

Khan obtained his start through insecure security facilities at URENCO, a British, German and Dutch commercial consortium which had the European monopoly on developing advanced centrifuge technology for enriching uranium. This is the most crucial stage of the nuclear fuel cycle, which increases the uranium-235 isotope to 5 per cent by spinning it in centrifuge cylinders at very high speeds – the same process that can be used to increase it to a weapons-grade 90 per cent. Khan possessed no skill in nuclear physics: he trained as a metallurgist, and should not have been given clearance by the incompetent Dutch security service and should certainly not have been allowed the run of the URENCO premises, from which he stole its secret designs and data, smuggled out of the country with the help of Pakistani diplomats with their diplomatic bags and other immunities. It is ironic that a humble metallurgist from the third world was not perceived as a threat by his European superiors, who thought that Pakistan would never be up to making a bomb – it was this very condescension that drove Khan to prove them wrong. He was an extreme Pakistani patriot, who had witnessed his nation's defeat by India in 1971 and offered his services to the nation in a letter to President Bhutto. It was the government, then the army (which formed later governments) which provided and protected his status in Pakistan and his use of diplomatic bags in which to carry his nuclear shopping.

In the course of his purchases for the secret Pakistani nuclear bomb programme, Khan found many suppliers of dual-use material who would not ask questions about which use was intended. As for the 'crucial yellowcake', (partially refined uranium ore), it helped to have the backing of the state to do a deal with Gaddafi, who purchased it from Niger and shipped it on to Pakistan beneath the IAEA's radar. After the Russian invasion of Afghanistan in 1979 the Americans became Pakistan's best friend, and President Zia assured Ronald Reagan that Pakistan would not develop nuclear weapons. ('I have said it at the top of my voice ... we are not developing a bomb! But it is the right of any developing country to acquire nuclear technology for peaceful purposes.')[224] It was a common refrain of dictators who protest too much, and it was heard from Zia, and later Musharraf, whilst they knew very well that A. Q. Khan was enriching as fast and as much as he could. In 1984 President Reagan wrote to General Zia warning him not to enrich beyond 5 per cent, and Zia of course agreed, knowing that enriching to 5 per cent is the really difficult part: it takes only a few months, after the cascades are reconfigured, to enrich to 90 per cent.

A. Q. Khan was not publicly unveiled as a nuclear smuggler until 2004, when he made a televised confession and received a pardon. He was placed under house arrest for the next five years but remained a national hero, legally untouchable, allowed to keep most of the proceeds from his double life as a smuggler and seller of state nuclear secrets. It was the ease with which he had developed his nuclear network under the nose of IAEA inspectors that was most disconcerting. It is likely that the first contacts with Iran began when he was invited to inspect Bushehr in 1986, after Saddam had bombed it. In 1987, there was a meeting in Dubai between Khan's associates and government scientists with a shopping list to begin building the bomb. It is known that later, a deal worth $3 million for centrifuge designs material was struck with Iran. By that time Khan had already done a deal with Iraq. In relation to both governments, his deals seem to have gone undetected (although IAEA inspectors gleaned some evidence of his dealings with Iraq from a defector in 1995).[225] His dealings with North Korea had government support – Pakistan bought its Nodong missile and renamed it the Ghauri, after a medieval Muslim warlord who smote Hindus. This semi-official operation, although secret and in breach of the NPT, gave Khan the opportunity to build up a supply network which he began to use in 2000, to equip Libya with bomb-making equipment. It continued until Gaddafi exposed him.

Khan acted as a Pakistani patriot infused with hostility to India, and greed was responsible for his offer of nuclear services to other, not necessarily Islamic, countries. He was not a religious fanatic, although documents left in Kabul by fleeing Taliban did show that Pakistani scientists who were members of his network had met with Al Qaeda to discuss nuclear devices.[226] Since greed was Khan's major motivation, it would not be surprising if the meeting was followed up, but the very fact that it happened at all sent shivers down American spines. He also had links with Saudi Arabia and, more worryingly, with Syria – a regime which would have been quite capable of using a bomb to gain the upper hand over the Free Syrian Army, with whom it was locked in struggle in 2012. Had Khan not been stopped – and that he was stopped is largely to the credit of Colonel Gaddafi, who decided to blow his cover – Khan would have gone on to aid and abet proliferation in more than half a dozen NPT member states.

The A. Q. Khan network was shocking. It demonstrated a loss of control over nuclear know-how, and 'all the keys to a nuclear weapon – the supplier networks, the material, the enrichment technology and the warhead designs – were out of state oversight and control'.[227] Although he constructed an impressive nuclear weapons operation in Pakistan which did produce bombs, he was not selling weapons himself on an open market, but rather expertise and assistance to develop the URENCO technology he had stolen and was now marketing, already tried and tested in Pakistan, to Pyongyang, Tehran and Tripoli. There are further links in the nuclear weapons chain: the enrichment process involves constructing centrifuges and positioning them into 'cascades' of machines – the first point at which detection becomes likely, and then fissile material, once obtained, must be converted into uranium metal and machined into a nuclear explosive device. Khan was selling his assistance with all these steps in the process, through the company he had established to share production of the Pakistani bomb. This corporate autonomy enabled him to operate unobserved, buying and selling on the nuclear black market he had created. He worked through many companies in thirty countries (particularly South Africa, Malaysia, Germany and the UAE), buying from businessmen of different nation- alities and often paying in large cash amounts which banks, to their discredit, were happy to process. The network used familiar devices – front companies, ships chartered by companies which did not know their customer, and banks which declined to find out. Nuclear know-how, once upon a time locked in the brilliant minds of Manhattan Project scientists, is now available to metal- lurgists from the University of Karachi – or of Tehran – where an undergraduate degree in nuclear physics will bestow the secrets of Fermi and Szilárd.

The worst feature of the A. Q. Khan network is simply that its members, both individual and corporate, are still in place and not in prison. They are 'merchants of death' in the most accurate

sense of that over-used phrase. Even Khan's 'house arrest' was
a form of state protection from the extradition claws of the US.
Only three members of his network have been prosecuted and
their sentences for breach of export controls (which carry a
maximum of two years in many countries) were light. Unless it
becomes illegal to make and process the bomb, and aiding and
abetting that crime carries up to life imprisonment in an international court, there will be no satisfactory protection against
future Dr Khans, perhaps inspired by religious fervour as well as
greed and national pride.

Ayatollah Ali Khamenei, President of Iran, 1981–89
and Supreme Leader, 1989–present.

THE NPT PARADOX

Atoms for peace and atoms for war are Siamese twins.

Hannes Alfvén[228]

Mohammed ElBaradei, the head of the IAEA from 1997 to 2009, draws three morals from the saga of Dr A. Q. Khan:

First, proliferation begets proliferation. Secondly, whilst export controls should be significantly stronger, they can no longer be considered a remedy: the technology is out of the tube and third, so long as nuclear weapons exist and bring power and prestige to their owners we will continue to see proliferation, especially in countries and regions that continue to see themselves under threat.[229]

To what extent is this a counsel of despair about the NPT, or the IAEA, which has been attached to the treaty as a verification mechanism, or the Nuclear Suppliers Group (NSG), the forty advanced countries that refuse to sell dual-use equipment to potential proliferators or to states outside the NPT? What we are observing, in the endless diplomatic shuffle between nuclear weapons states (the five 'haves') and non-nuclear weapons states (the 184 'have nots') is the consequence of a mismatch between the technology to be regulated and the method chosen to do the regulating. It is also the consequence – a very common one in other areas of competitive and lucrative endeavour – of putting too much faith in 'light touch' regulation, where regulators are provided with insufficient legal power and financial resources to investigate and there is no real deterrent for disobedience.

By the time of the NPT in 1968, it was feared that some twenty-six countries, in addition to the present 'Big 5', would have the bomb by the turn of the century, and the fact that only four have acquired it so far is some credit to the treaty, although some of these prospective nuclear powers have come in under the NATO umbrella and others on the list – like Taiwan, South Korea, Canada and Australia – were prepared to accept nuclear defence commitments from the US. Iran's current nuclear preoccupations have brought such lists back into vogue. Middle East countries in particular are suddenly clamouring for help for their civil nuclear programmes, for which a need (e.g. for 'clean energy') has been felt just as Iran is about to reach nuclear capability. This is the way Israel, Pakistan and India started off, with dual-use technology and a full nuclear fuel cycle which could secretly be switched to high enrichment. The danger is epitomised by Assad's Syria, which had its newly acquired nuclear reactor facilities hit by an Israeli air strike in 2007, which prevented any prospect of a nuclear weapon in Assad's hands by 2012, when his forces were attacking Homs and Aleppo. A regime with no powerful friends except Russia, and one that does not scruple to threaten to use its illegal stockpile of chemical weapons, would have had no compunction in threatening to use nuclear weapons on a relatively isolated city like Aleppo, were it to fall to the Free Syrian Army.

THE NUCLEAR NON-PROLIFERATION TREATY

The NPT grew out of the notion that nuclear power was not a Faustian bargain, but rather a gift that humankind was morally and intellectually capable of managing for exclusively peaceful purposes. This was the 'Atoms for Peace' philosophy, 'how to destroy the curse but retain the blessing' of nuclear energy. It was revived after the Cuban missile crisis, as states cast around for some alternative to nuclear Armageddon. In 1968, they came up with a treaty based on three pillars:

1. Peaceful use of atomic energy was an 'inalienable' state right and would be encouraged.
2. There must be no new nuclear states, other than the extant 'Big 5'.
3. These existing nuclear states were under an obligation to negotiate a treaty for 'complete' disarmament.

The preamble of the NPT (see Appendix B, page 353) refers to the devastation of nuclear war and the consequent need to avoid it at all costs. Because proliferation of weapons would 'seriously enhance' the prospects for such a war, state parties declared 'their intention to achieve at the earliest possible date the cessation of the nuclear arms race and to undertake effective measures in the direction of nuclear disarmament'. This was not envisaging early abandonment of the bomb, but rather a move 'in the direction of nuclear disarmament', and to promote peace and security 'with the least diversion' (i.e. with *some* diversion nonetheless) 'of the world's human and economic resources'. Article VI of the treaty lays a duty on the 'Big 5'

> to pursue negotiations in good faith on effective measures relating to the cessation of the arms race at an early date and to nuclear disarmament and *on a treaty on general and complete disarmament under strict and effective international control.* [emphasis added]

This was more than just a 'best endeavours' duty – as the ICJ pointed out in 1996, it was a legal undertaking to negotiate a treaty for 'general and complete' disarmament – i.e. a world without nukes. There was no requirement to do so at an early or any date – the time stipulation for ending the arms race had no deadlines – but the treaty itself was to run out after twenty-five years unless extended (it was – indefinitely – in 1995), which was some indication of the time its over-optimistic authors thought it might take to bring about global disarmament. Nonetheless, Article VI was a solemn and binding obligation on the 'Big 5', which for many years they ignored.

Article I constitutes an undertaking by 'nuclear weapons states' (i.e. the 'Big 5') not to assist any other state to manufacture or acquire nuclear weapons (although China was to help Pakistan, and Canada and the US helped India). Article II is an undertaking by all the other parties not to 'manufacture or otherwise acquire nuclear weapons ... and not to seek or receive any assistance in the manufacture of nuclear weapons'. This is precisely what Iraq did in 1990 and Libya in 2001 whilst both were NPT members: it is what Iran did in 1994, paying $3 million in cash in Dubai to the A. Q. Khan network, and what it did afterwards, at least until its Natanz site was exposed in 2002, and it is what a good deal of evidence suggests that it is continuing to do. Unfortunately, the treaty provides no sanction for breach of its own terms and is silent on one very important question – does the breach of Article II by Iran lose it the 'inalienable right to enrich' bestowed by Article IV? (see page 219)

THE INTERNATIONAL ATOMIC ENERGY AGENCY

Verification is the province of Article III, by which parties undertake to accept 'safeguards', namely inspection of their nuclear facilities by the IAEA, in order to verify that they are not diverting energy for military purposes. The IAEA predates the NPT (it was established in 1956) and is responsible for administering the 'safeguards system' – whereby its experts examine the design of equipment, facilities and nuclear reactors, receive state reports on facilities, and travel to member states to inspect the sites they 'declare' to be part of their peaceful nuclear programme. The IAEA will approve a facility only if it does not further any military purpose, and if it complies with health and safety standards.[230] States are obliged to notify the IAEA of the source of all fissionable material for peaceful activities within their territory and under their jurisdiction. The problem is that the NPT itself gives the agency very limited inspection authority: it is only expected to inspect, i.e. to 'verify', what a country has already declared and to concentrate on finding 'material unaccounted for' at nuclear facilities which might have been diverted for military purposes.

In their work, IAEA inspectors appear more like accountants than detectives. 'They are accustomed', Mohammed ElBaradei has admitted, 'to looking for and pointing out quantitative and qualitative discrepancies' – usually by matching data supplied by the state with externally available information. They are obliged to respect state parties to the treaty under which they operate, and cannot make use of the usual spying techniques – intercepts, planted informers, unannounced inspections and the like. They are reliant on permission from the state party with which they negotiate an agreement, and some states insist on a week's notification of an inspection, or deny inspectors entry to particular parts of a plant. When North Korea was a member, for example, secretly and busily planning its bomb, it simply refused a request by the IAEA for a special inspection.[231] Iran refuses admission to its Parchin military base, claiming that the inspectorate could observe and leak its military secrets and that in any event military bases were beyond the IAEA's mandate.[232] States can refuse inspectors entry for long enough to 'clean up' the suspect site of any nuclear debris (soil sample analysis can be of particular value in exposing nuclear use of allegedly 'non-nuclear' sites). Nor can the IAEA do 'deals' with intelligence agencies like Mossad or the CIA – whilst it can receive information from anywhere, it cannot reciprocate and risk being seen as a 'stooge'. (This was the fate of UNSCOM, the verification agency with special powers set up to monitor Iraqi weapons of mass destruction in the lead-up to the US invasion in 2003.)

After the IAEA Iraqi fiasco in 1991, when post-Gulf War inspections revealed that Saddam had a well-developed nuclear weapons programme that the organisation had failed to discover despite its access to harmless 'declared' sites close by, there came the realisation that the IAEA was a watchdog looking in the wrong direction. It had spent most of its time 'inspecting' the safety of nuclear plants in industrial countries like Italy and Germany and Canada and Japan, co-operative states unlikely to be secretly developing nuclear weapons, and had spent less time targeting countries like Iraq and Iran which had little or no nuclear infrastructure, but obviously craved a bomb. As the result of the 1991 Iraq debacle an 'additional protocol' was adopted in 1997, giving the IAEA greater powers of inspection and to search for undeclared facilities. But the additional protocol is not compulsory and only 117 NPT members have signed up to it. All NPT members have a duty to enter into a comprehensive safeguards agreement with the IAEA, but it has no power to require them to do so, and seventy-two have not. The NPT is a creature of its state parties – all 189 of them – and they have not, collectively, been prepared to give the IAEA powers essential to verify compliance, such as the power to enter at will (its inspectors still require visas) or to make unannounced inspections without prior permission at any site it chooses, or to demand information about, and access to, undeclared sites, or to conduct interviews with scientists and technicians outside their own country. Until it is vouchsafed these legal powers, there will always be a suspicion that it has been misled and outfoxed, as it was by the Iraqis until 1991, by A. Q. Khan since 1987, by the North Koreans and by the Syrians until the Israelis bombed Al-Kibar in 2007.

Despite these failings as a detective and serious under-funding, the IAEA is one of the more efficient and respected of the UN's technical bodies. It is headquartered in Vienna, and its director general is responsible to a board of governors who may in turn refer an issue for action to the Security Council. From 1997 to 2009 it was directed by the Egyptian lawyer Mohammed ElBaradei, who was rather too respectful and protective of potential proliferators for America's liking: he was succeeded by the Japanese diplomat Yukiya Amano, who made a disastrous start by failing (and perhaps fearing) to contradict his own government when it was pretending that the Fukushima meltdown was not particularly dangerous. The agency was attached to the NPT at the latter's inception, but its work since then has been focused on verifying compliance by non-nuclear states, rather than verifying compliance with Article VI (disarmament) by the 'Big 5' permament Security Council members (known in arms-control jargon as the P5). It has, in this respect, been an easy target for those who claim the NPT is biased against the global South: the Article VI 'grand bargain' of a 'complete' disarmament treaty has never been implemented so there is no weapons destruction timetable for the agency to verify, and the P5 have never had to suffer the indignity of intensive inspection. This is a fair criticism – of the NPT and the P5 – not of the IAEA. If a disarmament convention were ever to be ratified the agency would be the obvious candidate to check that the nine nuclear weapons states really were reducing their nuclear arsenals in compliance with the treaty.

The level of deception of the IAEA perpetrated by Iran since 1987 – twenty-five years of lies, half-truths and failures to declare nuclear facts and facilities – demonstrates how easy it is to deceive an inspectorate that can only investigate facilities that it can see on Google maps and is given permission to enter, and which cannot deploy the full range of surveillance and detection tactics available to less scrupulous agencies like Mossad and the KGB. The CIA has virtually admitted having 'assets' in the Iranian scientific hierarchy, no doubt well paid for inside information, whilst Mossad uses honeytraps (see the Vanunu case) and *agents provocateurs*. The IAEA rages when these agencies do not pass their information on, but the simple fact is that it is not trusted to make the best use of it. Thus the US, Britain and France decided to keep their knowledge of Fordow – which secretly opened in 2006 – from the IAEA, which first heard of it when Iran, believing that the US would go public, confessed to its existence in 2010. Outsmarting the IAEA has not only been the prerogative of Iran: South Korea, Iraq until 1991, Libya and Syria all led it a merry dance. ElBaradei, between 1997 and 2009, was a rigorously fair lawyer who resented American pressure and gave these countries the benefit – too much benefit, as it turned out – of the doubt.

There is a concern that his successor, Amano, may be over-anxious to please the US. In the course of lobbying for his appointment, against strong competition from anti-apartheid hero Abdul Minty, he told the US chargé d'affaires (so WikiLeaks reported) that 'he was solidly in the US court on every key strategic decision, from high level personal appointments to the handling of Iran's alleged nuclear weapons programme'.[233] This revelation has helped to keep Amano honest – the IAEA under his stewardship since 2009, whilst being prepared to publish more of its suspicions about weaponisation, has not indulged in scare stories. ElBaradei had been reluctant to publish unproven allegations for fear they would give the Bush administration and Israel arguments to use force, but this approach denied information to analysts outside the IAEA, who had a more sophisticated political perspective than its inspectors. Although Joseph Cirincione of the Plowshares Fund says that 'the main beneficiaries of the Amano regime have been US policy and the Japanese power industry',[234] it is only reasonable to point out that ElBaradei's efforts to be fair to Iran were rewarded by serial dishonesty and a refusal to accept diplomatic solutions.

This history casts doubt not only on the IAEA as an effective investigator but on the NPT as a satisfactory anti-proliferation device, and upon any future convention that purports to ban the bomb. As H. G. Wells predicted in his prescient novel, some sovereign states will find it hard to resist the temptation to cheat. Condign punishment, including invasion and regime change, was Wells's answer, although if the cheating state threatened to drop its bombs on any invaders, this might not work. The IAEA's record demonstrates that it will not be enough for every state in the world to sign up for bomb-banning: there will have to be a regulator with inspection powers going well beyond the IAEA's additional protocol.

The IAEA has been subjected to continual criticism by non-aligned countries (notably Cuba, Iran, Syria, Venezuela, India and Egypt) for strengthening nuclear safeguards at the expense of their national sovereignty (a desire to avoid the agency's scrutiny on this ground is itself some indication of a desire to acquire nuclear weapons). The P5, however, tend to stand together: during the Cold War, the danger of proliferation was one issue upon which the Soviets and the US could agree, and it is notable that at a time when Russia and China have refused to join the US, France and the UK in Security Council action against Assad's military exercise in Syria, they have agreed to some sanctions against Iran.

THE NUCLEAR SUPPLIERS GROUP

The IAEA's work was supplemented in 1974 by an informal but vital regulatory body, the Nuclear Suppliers Group (NSG). It was set up unofficially and outside the NPT structure, but it represented forty states involved in the export of nuclear-related goods and services, which agreed on guidelines that restrict the exportation of dual-use equipment and technologies to states suspected of seeking to proliferate or that were subject to UN sanctions, or stayed outside the NPT regime. Non-aligned critics accuse the group of operating a cartel, which of course it does. It can, however, play a crucial role in deciding which items should be subject to export controls, if only its forty member states (which include members of the non-aligned group such as South Africa, South Korea and Turkey) could always agree on what to put on the export control lists. As one expert comments, export control regimes are malfunctioning because states are not consistent, serious and unanimous about non-proliferation. A sense of futility is dooming the efforts to control nuclear technologies and especially dual-use technologies. Enforcement agencies in most states are not equipped to control the export of proliferation-sensitive dual-use items. In many cases they often fail to appreciate the purpose of dual-use goods that evade export controls.

It is difficult to enforce export controls on dual-use items through criminal laws, because it is hard to prove that the exporter had positive knowledge of the particular weapons-related use to which they would be put. And in the *Matrix Churchill* case in the UK, which exposed 'Iraqgate' (the secret and illegal UK assistance to Saddam during the 1980s), the CEO of a machine tool manufacturer escaped conviction although he knew that the dual-use tools he was sending to Iraq were calibrated to make bombs: he had been encouraged to make false entries by Mrs Thatcher's Trade Minister, anxious that British companies should trade with Saddam and insouciant about the consequences.[235] The subsequent judicial enquiry resulted in the quashing of the convictions of other arms exporters, because the law had been selectively applied.[236]

Nonetheless, the NSG has been crucial to the credibility of the NPT/IAEA system, at least until 2008 when its members were put under enormous pressure (to which they succumbed) by the Bush administration to exempt India from the rules. They decided that material relating to nuclear weapons could be sold to India, although it was not an NPT member and refused to subject itself to international safeguards. This was one of the most irresponsible actions of the Bush administration (although it was egged on by France and Russia, anxious for commercial profit). They did not even exact a *quid pro quo* (e.g. by insisting that India ratify the CTBT). If India can get away with building 100 nukes outside the NPT, with no safeguards and no IAEA inspections and no restrictions from the NSG, why should North Korea, Iran and other states not be treated equally?

IAEA SAFEGUARDS

Israel (an IAEA member despite the fact it is outside the NPT) showed what it thought of the organisation's safeguards system in 1981 when it bombed Iraq's research reactor at Osirak, even though it was under IAEA safeguards. This encouraged Saddam to develop a weapons programme from 1982 onwards that was so clandestine that the IAEA inspectors did not discover it. (Israel was condemned by the Security Council and asked to compensate Iraq and subject its own nuclear facilities to IAEA inspection – demands it ignored.) Nor did the IAEA have any truthful picture of Libya's progress towards nuclear weapons until this was publicly revealed by Gaddafi in 2003. It had no idea of Iran's centrifuge cascade at Natanz, until this was revealed by the MEK at a Washington press conference in 2002. ElBaradei always insisted that the IAEA show respect rather than suspicion when inspecting Middle Eastern states, but in the cases of Iraq and Libya and Iran, his organisation was over-respectful and his decency repaid by dishonesty. It should have treated these countries with greater cynicism and suspicion, precisely because of their human rights record. ElBaradei's mistake was to fail to recognise that they were governed by men who could not be trusted – Saddam Hussein, Colonel Gaddafi and Ali Khamenei.

The 1997 'additional protocol' strengthened its safeguards regime by requiring access to all parts of a state's fuel cycle, permitting collection of environmental samples at requested locations and requiring access at short notice to suspect sites. The additional protocol provides for increased transparency, but it is not a treaty or an amendment to the NPT – it is a voluntary commitment by individual member states, and those member states under suspicion simply do not commit.[237] Iran did so, under Security Council pressure, in 2003, but withdrew on the advent of Ahmadinejad in 2006. The additional protocol should be mandatory for all IAEA members, but countries like Brazil, Egypt, Israel and Pakistan adamantly oppose any such move. Australia, so far, is the only country to insist that it will not supply uranium to states that have not adopted the additional protocol. Otherwise, states which have not signed up – the very states suspected of harbouring a wish for nuclear weapons – cannot be subjected to 'complementary access inspections' which would allow the agency to check for evidence of an enrichment programme.

Despite the technical competence of its staff and the respect in which the agency is held, it remains perfectly possible for a state to develop a nuclear weapons programme clandestinely, under the noses of inspectors allowed to enter only the innocuous facilities that it has 'declared' to the IAEA. Until the additional protocol becomes mandatory, and the IAEA is given further powers for its inspectors to enter without visas and without notice, to inspect anywhere in a suspect country, and to interview its nuclear scientists (if necessary outside the country in question), it is difficult to have confidence that a determinedly duplicitous government will not give it the slip, just as they have in the past. It must have power to operate its own intelligence service, rather than to rely on being drip-fed information by state intelligence agencies when that serves their purpose. It must develop expertise in associated subjects (such as weapon design and ballistic missile warheads, which provide vital clues as to whether a nuclear weapons programme is afoot); it needs to be empowered to offer special protection and rewards to scientists prepared to 'blow the whistle' on their own governments; and it must be prepared to take into account a government's human rights record, a fairly sure guide to whether it is capable of the duplicity required for building up a nuclear weapons capacity and of the barbarity involved in dropping a nuclear bomb. These powers are essential if the IAEA is ever to prove capable of monitoring a treaty requiring complete disarmament, and their acquisition will require substantial amendment to its constitution. It has already come under fire for acting beyond its mandate by looking at Iran's weaponisation studies, although this is an obvious clue to whether it intends to build a bomb.[238]

The IAEA has no power to punish, and the NPT has no enforcement mechanism (other than by reference of disputes to the ICJ) but the agency's board of governors may report to the Security Council, which can impose duties on the state suspected of building or harbouring weapons, or impose sanctions on that state if it fails to co-operate, or even use its power under Chapter

VII of the UN Charter to authorise use of force against the state in the interest of international peace and security. Resolutions in respect of Iraq, Iran and North Korea have placed the onus on these suspect states to show unequivocally that they are not involved in a cover-up. This has been somewhat grandly called BPSP – the transfer of the Burden of Proof to Suspected Proliferators – and it provides the answer to states which claim they are 'innocent until proven guilty' and should not be singled out or sanctioned until the IAEA comes up with hard evidence. It is commonplace in evidence law to place the burden of proving a fact on the party which has direct access to information about that fact: governments know very well whether they have a clandestine weapons programme and should be placed under a duty of transparency. If they continue to obstruct IAEA inspectors, then the agency should be entitled to draw an inference that the reason why they are obstructive is that they have something to hide. Once that inference is drawn, however, and the Security Council has imposed sanctions, which do not deter countries like North Korea and Iran, what then? It is the utter failure of the Security Council to indicate any preparedness to use force to stop a country acquiring nuclear weapons that encourages would-be proliferators. Their sovereignty is safe no matter how many bombs they make.

The reluctance to use force was most apparent at the 2010 NPT Review Conference, which singled out North Korea for a particularly contemptuous paragraph in its report, deploring its proposed further nuclear test explosions and angrily pointing out that it could not have what it really wants, namely the prestige and the status of a nuclear power under the treaty. But North Korea took heart from the fact that the conference rather pathetically said it 'remained determined' to resolve issues with Pyongyang through diplomatic means – a coded signal that there would be no use of force, which is the only language that the North Koreans have ever understood.

THE FATAL FLAW

The fatal design flaw in the NPT is that 'atoms for peace' can all too easily become atoms for war, once a full nuclear fuel cycle is operational. That is the point at which conversion to a nuclear weapons programme becomes feasible within a matter of months. So far as Israel is concerned in relation to Iran, this is the point of no return. It is the point at which a state can be said to have a 'nuclear weapons capacity', although whether it can take any step to develop that capacity will depend on whether it is also developing a nuclear 'weaponisation' capability, e.g. by designing and manufacturing nuclear warheads for its ballistic missiles. Most media discussions of this problem focus on uranium enrichment as the key to determining whether a country has opted to 'break out' of the fuel cycle in order to weaponise: a nuclear reactor which enriches to 3.5 per cent is all that is needed for most civil uses (energy, pest control, ground water management etc.). Enrichment up to 20 per cent is not overly suspicious, but a level above that is described as 'weapons usable' HEU and if the level reaches 90 per cent the result is 'weapons grade', although the fuel might also serve a benign purpose, by producing medical isotopes. The actual enrichment process is done in a line (a 'cascade') of gas centrifuges – high metal cylinders which spin at incredible speed (more than 20,000 revolutions per minute) for months to produce small amounts of enriched U-235. The central problem for NPT compliance is that

> in order to produce HEU, even up to weapons grade, one essentially performs the exact same processes upon a quantity of U-238 as one performs to make HEU for use in civilian reactors, only one performs the process repeatedly and for a longer duration.[239]

There are seven stages of a fuel cycle:[240]

1. **Mining** of uranium ore. Only 0.7 per cent of natural uranium is U-235, i.e. 'fissile' in the sense that it can sustain a nuclear chain reaction. The rest is U-238.
2. **Milling** – The ore is processed to produce 'yellowcake', a partly refined uranium ore.
3. **Conversion** – Yellowcake is converted, by a series of chemical processes, to uranium hexafluoride (UF_6) gas, which will be fed

into the centrifuges to separate out the fissile U-235 from the
U-238.

4. **Enrichment** – As the UF_6 gas is fed through the spinning centrifuges, the concentration of U-235 is increased, and U-238 is
   dispersed.

5. **Fuel fabrication** – The enriched uranium is processed into pellets
   and inserted into fuel rods, to power the core of a reactor.

6. **Storage** – The depleted fuel, mostly U-238, is stored as 'spent
   fuel'. It will contain about 1 per cent plutonium, created as a
   by-product.

7. **Reprocessing** – The spent fuel can be recycled, a process which
   separates the uranium and plutonium for reuse.

None of these seven steps in the nuclear fuel cycle is weapons
specific: stage four (enrichment) and stage seven (reprocessing)
require the closest monitoring, to ensure that all relevant facilities
for them are declared by the state, and that all nuclear material
is accounted for, and has not been diverted for use in weapons. A
number of countries which are industrialised NPT members have
such a fuel cycle, which for safety reasons requires IAEA inspections, and all members of the NPT are accorded by Article IV the
'inalienable right' to develop such a cycle. Because the production
process is the same, whether fissile material is being produced for
a nuclear warhead or for civilian power generation, it is difficult
until the very end of the process to identify a facility as being
dedicated to production of weapons. A clandestine intention
to 'break out' from the cycle can only be inferred – e.g. from a
contemporaneous interest in designing nuclear warheads, or from
information passed by defectors. Thus the 'grand bargain' of the
NPT allows parties like Iraq and Iran to exercise their 'inalienable
right' to have nuclear energy technologies supplied without questions asked: a decision to switch to nuclear weapons will be made
secretly, at a top political level, and will not necessarily become
apparent to the IAEA until too late: until the bomb is tested (as
in the cases of India and Pakistan and North Korea) or dropped.

The Bush administration decried this paradox as a 'loophole'
in the treaty. As George W. Bush explained, with uncharacteristic
clarity, in 2004,

the NPT was designed more than thirty years ago to prevent the spread of nuclear weapons beyond those states which already possessed them. Under this treaty, nuclear states agreed to help non-nuclear states develop peaceful atomic energy if they renounced the pursuit of nuclear weapons. But the Treaty has a loophole which has been exploited by nations such as North Korea and Iran. These regions are allowed to produce nuclear material that can be used to build bombs under the cover of civilian nuclear programmes.[241]

But it was not a 'loophole' at all – the treaty was designed not to ban the bomb, but to keep it in the hands of five countries, in return for which those countries agreed to reduce their stocks – eventually to zero – and would help all other parties to acquire or access nuclear energy for peaceful purposes. It was a deal that failed, in the sense that the 'Big 5' did not proceed to disarm, but it permitted and indeed encouraged a number of other countries to develop a fuel cycle. What the treaty did not provide was any mechanism for drawing a distinction between states that would be permitted to develop a fuel cycle to the full, and those that could not be trusted with the nuclear weapons potential that a full fuel cycle would provide. States such as Libya, Iran, Iraq and Syria could not be trusted (unlike Germany and Japan) for a number of reasons, notably because their human rights record shows them to be run by international criminals. But as members of the NPT, they are entitled to exercise their 'inalienable right' and only a new convention or a new rule of international law could prevent them from becoming nuclear weapons capable.

IS THE 'INALIENABLE RIGHT' ALIENATED BY MISCONDUCT?
There is a legal question that requires clarification, and should be made the subject of a Security Council or General Assembly reference to the ICJ, because on one interpretation the US will claim a right to bomb Iran. It turns on the meaning of Article IV read with Article II, to determine whether Iran's breach of the latter (by which it has undertaken not to manufacture or seek assistance in manufacturing nuclear devices) deprives it of its

much touted 'inalienable right' to enrich under Article IV. That article reads, in full, as follows:

> Nothing in this Treaty shall be interpreted as affecting the inalienable right of all the Parties to the Treaty to develop research, production and use of nuclear energy for peaceful purposes without discrimination and in conformity with Articles I and II of this Treaty.

Article IV is badly drafted and the use of the term 'inalienable right' is utterly ill judged and inappropriate. It is a term that applies (most powerfully in Jefferson's Declaration of Independence) to human rights that are fundamental – 'life, liberty and the pursuit of happiness', which is a far cry from the right of a state to generate electricity. It must be interpreted as referring to a power attached to the sovereignty of a state, which can always be overridden by international law. 'Inalienable' does not (as Iran seems to think) mean 'unchallengeable', but merely undetachable from a state other than by force of its international obligations. There is no comma after 'develop' so the right protected by Article IV is to research, produce and use nuclear energy for 'peaceful purposes' (e.g. for producing electricity or medical isotopes) as distinct from warlike purposes, including the enrichment of uranium to 90 per cent). The 'research, production and use' must be 'in conformity with Article II of this Treaty', which prohibits seeking or receiving assistance to manufacture bombs. There is no doubt at all that Iran, prior to 2002, sought and paid for and received exactly such assistance from the A. Q. Khan network. Does this deprive it from enjoying the benefits of Article IV? Or does such misconduct simply have no effect on the 'inalienable right' since 'nothing ... shall be interpreted as affecting the inalienable right...' This is a real question of law, an ambiguity in a treaty which might be interpreted either way, although the powerful opening line ('*Nothing* in this Treaty...') and the fact that there are no penal provisions or any other consequences flowing from default or any time provision (Khan's assistance was last rendered ten years ago) means that Iran's position that it has a right to enrich is probably correct. In that case, of course, coaches and horses can be driven through the NPT – it carries no punishment for disobedience, states may withdraw at any time, subject to the question posed below, and America cannot claim that force is justified to stop Iran exercising its Article IV rights to enrich merely because it has broken Article II of the Treaty.

CAN IRAN WITHDRAW FROM THE NPT?

But can Iran withdraw so easily from the NPT? The other aspect of the Treaty that urgently demands a definitive interpretation is the meaning of Article X:

> Each party shall in exercising its national sovereignty have the right to withdraw from the Treaty if it decides that extraordinary events related to the subject matter of the Treaty have jeopardised the supreme interests of its country.

This is not a normal treaty, from which states can resign at any time or on giving a few months' notice. 'Extraordinary events' must have happened, related in some way to proliferation, which have put in jeopardy the state's 'supreme interests' – i.e. its interest in existing as a state. Nothing short of a threatened use of nuclear weapons against it would justify withdrawal, and there is no such threat to Iran. The problem is that North Korea was allowed to withdraw in 2003, when there was no such threat that it could reasonably apprehend. The withdrawal was accompanied merely by a belligerent press statement attacking the IAEA for requiring it to 'co-operate fully and urgently with the Agency', after evidence had emerged of its secret programme to enrich uranium for weapons use. North Korea said that the US had 'instigated' this IAEA resolution and its 'vicious hostile policy' had 'seriously violated our nation's sovereignty'.[242] (It added a barefaced lie, 'we have no intention to produce nuclear weapons'.) This fell far short of jeopardising North Korea's supreme interests, but Article X makes North Korea the judge of that. The Security Council could – and should – have rejected North Korea's reason for its purported resignation, and required it to accept inspections at the peril of sanctions or, failing that, forcible closure of its reactors. Instead the Security Council merely expressed 'concern' and said it would keep following developments, but the next development was the A-bomb test, in October 2006.

Although the NPT, absurdly, has no full-time secretariat or governing directorate, Article X requires the resigning state to give written reasons to the Security Council and to all other member states, with the implication that they could reject them if they failed to show jeopardy to the 'supreme interests of the country'. This could provide a basis for holding Iran to its Article II undertaking, by force if necessary, and preventing it from leaving the treaty membership. But this would not square with the unfortunate precedent of North Korea. It was folly for the Security Council to ignore the inadequacy of that country's reasons for withdrawal. There were no 'extraordinary events' which jeopardised its supreme interests, other than a belief that the supreme interests of the Kim dynasty would be jeopardised if they did not have the bomb as soon as possible. On this precedent, Iran would have a more acceptable reason to resign than North Korea – the threats of attack from Israel presage 'extraordinary events' that do threaten its sovereignty.

CAN THE SYSTEM BE REFORMED?

George W. Bush, in his 2004 speech, proposed a way to 'close the loophole', namely to prevent states that were not already among 'the world's leading nuclear exporters', i.e. the forty members of the Nuclear Suppliers Group, from developing a full nuclear fuel cycle. 'Enrichment and reprocessing are not necessary for nations seeking to harness nuclear energy for peaceful purposes,' he declared. All such nations would have to sign up to the additional NPT protocol: refuseniks would not be allowed to import material for their civil nuclear programmes. But in return for accepting more intrusive inspections and renouncing rights to a fuel cycle, these not-so-developed states could then, said Bush, 'have reliable access at reasonable cost to fuel for civilian reactors' from the Nuclear Suppliers Group. This was, in fact, a sensible proposal, which harked back to the Baruch–Evatt plans for an international fissile fuel bank to supply developing countries, but it was expressed in condescending language which made 'developing' countries – now members of the non-aligned group – smell a capitalist rat. The 'reasonable cost' would be price-fixed by a cartel from the military-industrial complex of the US and Europe, and their sovereign and 'inalienable' right to a nuclear fuel cycle would be extinguished.

The proposal had a better reception recently when recast by Obama's nuclear envoy, Rose Gottemoeller, as a multi-lateral fuel ban that would 'reassure countries embarking on or expanding nuclear power programmes that they could reliably purchase reactor fuel ... it is not necessary to pursue expensive enrichment and reprocessing facilities to exploit nuclear energy for peaceful purposes'. But the NPT review conference in 2010 gave this rephrased Obama proposal for a multi-lateral fuel bank a lukewarm welcome, promising only discussions 'without prejudice to fuel cycle policies'. The non-aligned movement (which has 120 state members) continues to be suspicious of any Bush-originated proposal because 'they fear that the new tone of the Obama administration only puts sheep's clothing on the original wolfish idea'.[243] Its future will depend on sourcing it back to the Baruch plan, rather than a George W. Bush speech, and removing its administration from the Nuclear Suppliers Group cartel.

The other proposal in the 2010 US Posture Review, that all NPT members should adopt the additional IAEA protocol, providing extra powers of detection (for example, inspectors have to be given multi-entry visas, so they cannot be stopped from entering a member state without notice to look at suspect facilities), was not unreasonable either, but because it is voluntary many states stand on their sovereignty, refusing to be inspected without notice or by inspectors that they cannot vet and veto before they arrive. For similar reasons, powerful but non-nuclear supplier states like Brazil, South Africa, Turkey and South Korea have blocked the Nuclear Suppliers Group from more restrictive rules on the export of dual-use technologies, and the non-aligned group maintains its hostility to the 'Big 5' over their failure, for forty years, to honour the disarmament obligation in Article VI.

This stalemate, a mixture of pride, truculence and sovereignty obsession on the non-aligned side and arrogance, power-play and truculence on the other, has failed to make the NPT/IAEA anti-proliferation system an effective security for the world.

Whether the US-driven reforms – the multi-lateral fuel bank and the compulsory IAEA protocol – will be enough to provide nuclear safety, or will even be agreed, is most unlikely. There is some slight cause for optimism – after all, the world is down to 19,000 nuclear warheads from a Cold War high of 70,000, and the 2010 Prague Treaty (or 'new START') obliges both the US and Russia to reduce to 1,550 warheads each, by 2018, with only 700 launchers and delivery vehicles such as B-52 bombers.[244] But the treaty's bizarre 'counting rules' make it less impressive than it sounds (one B-52 counts as only one bomb, although it carries twenty).[245] The US and Russia are still capable of destroying each other many times over, and the treaty does nothing to reduce the arsenals of China, Britain and France, let alone of India, Pakistan, Israel and North Korea. Given the stand-off between the non-aligned group and the 'Big 5', and the inability of the NPT/IAEA to enforce disarmament or verification, the non-proliferation system now serves the interests of proliferators.

CHAPTER 12

IRAN'S NUCLEAR HEDGE

This chapter advances five propositions:

1. There can be no doubt that the government of Iran craves nuclear weapons, and is positioning itself to make them when the time is opportune.
2. This policy is not motivated by an intention to use the bomb to destroy Israel: on the contrary, the bomb is intended to balance Israel's, to protect Iran from American, Israeli or Saudi attack, and enhance its power and prestige in the region.
3. Iran is some distance from 'breaking out', which will then have to be followed by further work on weaponisation and a missile delivery system. One bomb will not be enough, in any event. If Iran reaches 'nuclear capability' in 2013, it will not have a bomb to assemble until 2015.
4. Iran cannot be permanently deterred in its quest by sanctions, however harsh, which can destroy the economy but will rally the people behind the national nuclear enterprise.
5. Diplomacy is futile. The time spent talking allows Iran the opportunity to enrich further. It has outmanoeuvred diplomats from the EU, the P5+1 and the IAEA.

THE QUEST
It was the Shah, always one for grandiose gestures, who established a massive nuclear energy project in Iran as early as 1957, taking advantage of the 'Atoms for Peace' offer to obtain a small research reactor from the US, the beginning of a plan to establish twenty-two reactors for generating 23,000 megawatts of electrical power throughout the nation. He was first to sign up to the NPT on the very day it opened for signature in 1968, and to ratify it in 1970 just as soon as it became ratifiable. America

was a happy ally at this point: only after India's nuclear test in 1974 did the penny drop in Washington over how 'Atoms for Peace' could in the hands of the Shah become atoms for war. The Ford and Carter administrations reined in his dual-purpose plans, which envisaged eventual weapon development in co-operation with apartheid South Africa, from which he bought $700 million worth of yellowcake.[246] He commenced construction of a light-water reactor at Bushehr and established the AEOI in 1974. Its former head, and others close to the Shah in this period, have subsequently told of his plans for nuclear weapons.[247] Ironically, it was the revolution which put paid to them: the Ayatollah initially denounced this Western-devised weapon as 'un-Islamic'. Once the war broke out Saddam's air force bombed Bushehr, just in case.

It was the war, and especially the casualties caused by Saddam's use of chemical weapons, that convinced the Revolutionary Guard leaders, Rafsanjani and Rezai, and Prime Minister Mousavi, that nuclear weapons were essential for Iran's security: Rezai wrote to Khomeini before the truce, telling him they would win in five years' time, once they had acquired a 'substantial number' of atomic weapons.[248] As early as April 1984, President Ali Khamenei told his top officials that the nuclear programme would be reactivated, in order to safeguard the Islamic revolution. They were sent out to shop in the black marketplace, and in these shadows they soon encountered Dr A. Q. Khan. They invited him to a visit to Bushehr in 1986, and later signed a secret nuclear co-operation agreement with Pakistan and another with North Korea, and reconnected with South Africa. As soon as the war ended, Rafsanjani urged Iranian nuclear scientists who had left after the revolution to return, and openly called for them to develop nuclear weapons.[249] Khan provided centrifuge and weapons designs that he had stolen from URENCO, and a payment of $3 million was made to him in 1994.[250] In this period, Iran had been receiving assistance from Argentina, which was withdrawn under American pressure, hence the Buenos Aires revenge bombings (see Chapter 7). US pressure even managed to deter China from co-operating, although Russia rebuilt the civil plant at Bushehr and there is some evidence of an inter-government agreement with the Pakistani military as well as with Khan's network. The 'research budget' rose to $800 million per year.[251]

It is now clear that throughout the 1990s, until the revelations of 2002, Iran had a civil nuclear programme declared in detail to the IAEA and a secret military programme running in parallel, never reported to the Majlis (parliament) or to the IAEA and funded by a special budget allocated by the Supreme Leader, which paid for the uranium enrichment facility at Natanz and the heavy-water facility at Arak. Although nominally under the control of the AEOI (which reports to the President), the military programme is directed by the Supreme National Military Council, chaired by the Supreme Leader.[252] It was this secret programme that acquired from Khan a starting kit for a gas centrifuge plant, a set of technical drawings for a P (for Pakistan)-1 centrifuge, samples of centrifuge components and instructions for enriching uranium to weapons-grade level. It received drawings for the sophisticated and weapons-only-related P-2 centrifuge in 1995.[253] It had obtained uranium hexafluoride (UF_6) gas from China, which it fed into centrifuges at a secret facility (the Kalaye Electric Company) in 1999, and it began constructing a cavernous underground enrichment facility near the city of Natanz. All these weapon-related operations were conducted in total secrecy. All should have been reported, either under the verification requirements of the NPT or under Iran's safeguards agreement with the IAEA. None were reported, and it seems idle to ask: why not?

In 2002, it was the MEK that returned to haunt the mullahs, in the form of a press conference in Washington by the National Council of Resistance of Iran, an organisation into which the MEK had transmogrified, led by Madame Rajavi. (Massoud Rajavi, its charismatic leader, had avoided assassination, and is said to be still alive but in hiding.) It revealed details of the nuclear facility at Natanz, to the great embarrassment of the IAEA, which had, over the past fifteen years, been comprehensively lied to by Rafsanjani and Khatami about Iran's nuclear programme. ElBaradei, who had believed and defended them, was told by Mubarak that they had been practicing the Shi-ite ideological concept of *taqiyya*, meaning the right to lie e.g. for a good cause or to protect your fellow Shias from harm.[254] He was eventually allowed to visit Natanz, where he found a gigantic underground bunker built to house 50,000 centrifuges. He asked to inspect the Kalaye Electric Company, but was refused. Because Iran had not declared it pursuant to its safeguards agreement, he had no right under the NPT to insist on seeing it.[255]

Eventually the Iranians agreed to allow him to take some soil samples at Natanz, but only after they had cleaned up the area. To their fury, the IAEA's extremely sophisticated tests were able to show the presence of enriched uranium. Iran's lying diplomats and politicians had been caught out – and further inspections, under pressure from the Security Council, exposed more lies, relating to the secret construction of a full nuclear fuel cycle, and attempts to test the advanced P-2 centrifuges. Why had Iran lied so long and so constantly, breaching its obligations under the NPT and to the IAEA? Because, quite obviously, it was pursuing the secret path that had brought Pakistan to the bomb in 1998, and which would produce a bomb for North Korea in 2006. For the first time, and in some earnest, the Bush White House began to contemplate regime change in Tehran.

But Iran's exposure, in the course of IAEA inspections in 2003, came towards the end of the Khatami presidency, when the country still valued its international reputation: its diplomats had been severely embarrassed. More importantly, its military – especially the senior Revolutionary Guards, who were developing a profitable stake in the country – were terrified that the US really would follow up its invasion of Iraq with an invasion of Iran. It was to avoid this that Iran agreed to suspend all nuclear activities, and provisionally to sign the additional NPT protocol, permitting further and more intense inspections. Even so, and despite some confessions to earlier deceptions, the regime could not bring itself to disclose what it thought it might still get away with. For example, in October 2003, it pretended to make a 'full' disclosure of enrichment activities 'to remove any ambiguities and doubts about their exclusively peaceful character'. There was no mention of building and testing the advanced P-2 centrifuges, which the IAEA discovered after the inspection. It asked for an explanation for this inexplicable oversight, and was told it was the result of 'time pressure in preparing the declaration'.[256] Even the indulgent ElBaradei found this 'deplorable' and 'difficult to comprehend' – although it was in fact all too easy to comprehend. Iran had been deliberately concealing its latest steps towards enrichment.

In 2005, Ahmadinejad was elected. The new President was a populist, well aware that defying the West and the IAEA would add to his popularity in a country which had for years been led to believe that the nuclear programme was a matter of great national prestige – as important, in its way, as Mossadegh's nationalisation of Iranian oil. He began to play up this image of himself as the new Mossadegh, and revelled in defying the IAEA and the Security Council by recommencing enrichment. Iran henceforth refused to implement the additional protocol, refused to allow some inspections and some inspectors, or to answer IAEA questions about past or ongoing experimentation on nuclear weaponisation and the development of nuclear warheads for missile delivery systems.[257] Ahmadinejad confessed to – and boasted of – the P-2 tests and ordered around-the-clock work at Natanz. By April 2006 he was able to announce, at a triumphant celebration, that they had successfully enriched LEU to 3.75 per cent. 'Iran has joined the nuclear countries of the world.'[258]

In the same year, Ahmadinejad made public an old letter from Ayatollah Khomeini, in which he referred with approbation to the projection by Mohammed Rezai, the Revolutionary Guard commander, that Iran would need 'atomic weapons' to win the war with Saddam. Given this authority, it could no longer be contended that the bomb was 'un-Islamic'. At this time his main spiritual adviser, the 'principle-ist' theoretician Ayatollah Mesbah-Yazdi, wrote that Iran needed to acquire the 'special weapons' that only a few countries possess – a fairly obvious reference to nuclear weapons.[259]

In 2009, the leaders of Britain, France and the US discovered that Iran was up to its old tricks: they had found a clandestine uranium enrichment plant at Fordow, underground and just north of the holy city of Qom. It was ideally suited for a 'break-out' facility that would quickly enrich to weapons grade and be safe from surface bombing. Again the question: why hide this facility, (especially since Iran was already under mounting UN sanctions for failure to comply with IAEA requests) unless it really was part of a weapons programme?

Despite these escalating sanctions, enrichment continues unabated. By 2010, the 3.75 per cent enriched uranium had been further enriched to 20 per cent, at both Natanz and Fordow. The only reason for the latter site to have been built, some experts concluded, had been 'in order to provide Iran with the ability to quickly and securely make highly enriched uranium in the event of a breakout to make nuclear weapons'.[260] This indicates a 'hedging strategy' – building a full fuel cycle pursuant to its 'inalienable' NPT right, but stopping short of enriching to weapons grade (90 per cent), until a time when Western backs would be turned. In 2011 the IAEA, usually cautious, reported that it had 'reason to believe' that Iran was developing a nuclear payload for a missile, the Shahab-3 – and a successor that could reach Israel. It had carried out activities 'relevant to the development of a nuclear explosive device', had been designing blueprints for nuclear warheads and still refused to allow the IAEA the access that it had repeatedly demanded to the military site at Parchin. The suspicious new information in the 2011–12 reports related to research and experimentation with nuclear warheads – the actual explosive device in a weapon. There were immediate claims that the IAEA had gone beyond its mandate by gathering evidence about plans to carry nuclear devices on missiles, but this was pettifogging.[261] The fact that Iran is working out how its missiles can be designed to carry nuclear payloads is obviously relevant to the question of whether it intends to acquire nuclear weapons.

Iran lied to the IAEA about its nuclear-related operations between 1986, when it first dealt with A. Q. Khan, and 2002, when Natanz was exposed. It told some truth between 2003 and 2005 because it feared a US invasion, but in 2006 under the new and aggressive President, it retreated into deception (failing to declare the Fordow facility for example) and refused to accept inspections. For this defiance, its people have suffered increasingly severe sanctions, whilst its diplomats, playing for time, have never been prepared to reach an agreement that will persuade the US or the UN to lift them. Given this record, the burden of showing that it does not want nukes must be placed on Iran, and it is a burden it cannot discharge. Its conduct is only referable to a determination to obtain a nuclear weapons capacity, i.e. a 'hedging strategy' that will enable it to 'break out' with weapons production in the future, when US attention is distracted and the time is propitious.

THE RATIONALE

One reason that stands out as bogus is Iran's claim that it needs massive enrichment facilities to supply its people with electricity and the means for treating cancer. So far as energy is concerned, it has a nuclear power station at Bushehr, built by Russia and using Russian fuel, so it has no civil rationale for enrichment, certainly beyond 3.5 per cent. So far as its need for medical isotopes from its Tehran research reactor is concerned, the required 20 per cent U-235 has always been available from abroad. The P5+1 offered to supply all its needs in return for some of its LEU – an offer that Iran refused. Mark Fitzpatrick, director of the Non-Proliferation and Disarmament Programme at the International Institute for Strategic Studies, points out that '72 per cent of the effort to produce weapons-grade uranium is accomplished by the time the product is enriched to 3.5 per cent and nine-tenths by the 20 per cent mark'.[262] Another 10 per cent lift and it will be there.

The other evidence of military preparation gathered by the IAEA – Iran's work on uranium metal (directly related to producing missile cores for nukes) and on detonation systems and payload chambers relevant to nuclear bombs, and the procurement of dual-use items by its military – all suggest plans to build nuclear weapons at some future time.[263] The nationalist fervour which followed the nuclear tests in India and Pakistan shows how politically popular the bomb – a Shia bomb (Pakistan has a Sunni bomb) – will be in the 'Shia crescent'. (This explains why Iran's regional enemies – Saudi Arabia, Jordan, Bahrain and the Gulf states – have been egging the US on to bomb Iran.) Domestically, Ahmadinejad has played on the popularity of his defiance of the US and the UN, to the extent of celebrating it with bumper stickers.[264] The Iranian opposition dares not question it.

Washington wisdom – so often half baked – has it that Iran

wants the bomb in order to destroy Israel. There is little hard evidence of this: everything points to the common-sense conclusion that Iran wants the bomb for prestige and for security, in a region – and a world – where it is surrounded by enemies. Israel is 2,000 kilometres distant and barely within reach of Iran's existing ballistic missiles (adapted from the North Korean Nodong missile) and any failure to destroy Israel on a first strike would have Israeli missiles raining down on its cities and its military facilities, and even the complete destruction of Israel would not save Iran from a similar fate at the hands of the US. Rafsanjani's much-quoted comment that destruction would not be mutually assured – 'even one nuclear bomb inside Israel will destroy everything' whilst a few million Muslims would be left after its reprisal attack on Iran – was a musing rather than a serious calculation: he was not counting second and third strikes by the friends of Israel. There is no history in Iran of any rooted hostility to Jews (who are numerous and protected throughout the country); Ahmadinejad's anti-Semitism is vicious but his star is waning as his presidency is coming to an end (in June 2013), and the Supreme Leader has recently distanced himself from this erratic protégé, whose economic mismanagement is blamed, even more than sanctions, for the dreadful state of the country's economy.

The only circumstance in which Iran could decide to obliterate Israel would be if its Revolutionary Guard leaders deferred to a dying or dementia-ridden Supreme Leader who wanted to create the state of chaos necessary to trigger the de-occulation of the Twelfth Imam by despatching a bomb Tel Aviv-wards, in the expectation that the Mahdi would reappear and smite all remaining unbelievers. There are plenty of historical examples of millennialist morons going to their death believing that their messiah would return at the last moment to save them (the fate of several hundred 'fifth monarchy' men in London in 1660, who thought a de-occulating Jesus Christ would interpose himself between their bodies and King Charles II's cavalry). True it is that Ayatollah Khomeini behaved outrageously when he knew he only had a few months to live, by issuing the Rushdie fatwa, and Ali Khamenei, the second-rate Islamic jurist who has lasted for over two decades as his replacement, may want to go down in history in a truly historic way. But for all the religiosity of the mullahs, they are unlikely to hazard all their wealth, possessions and stake in the country by obeying his orders to advance towards Armageddon. As one of Iran's oldest politicians, Jahangir Amuzegar (the Shah's last Minister of Finance), puts it, 'a cursory look at the ruling clergy's way of life – multiple wives, spacious living quarters, luxury cars, foreign bank accounts – protests their love of life and fear of death. Shi-ite clerics in Iran may reject certain aspects of Western culture, but they are hardly suicidal.'[265] The prospect that Iran will unleash nuclear weapons on Israel in the future – other than perhaps in self-defence were Israel to mount an attack on Iran – is very low risk.

What Iran will do with the bomb is boast of it. The first reason to acquire it is for domestic political purposes: just as nuclear weapon tests produced an outburst of patriotic joy in India and then in Pakistan and then in North Korea, so they will in Iran. There is a folk memory about the war with Iraq and the tens of thousands gassed by Saddam's chemical weapons: there is a rooted belief they would have won the war had they been able to respond by dropping a nuclear bomb on Baghdad. So the first nuclear test explosion will be an occasion for rejoicing by a people who have sacrificed so much under sanctions. Then Tehran will pump its chest in the region, and in the world: the first Shia Muslim state with nukes that terrify Israel. This will, of course, spread panic among Sunni Muslim states – Saudi Arabia has already said it will buy bombs from Pakistan to save the time and trouble of developing its own, whilst Turkey, Egypt, Algeria, Jordan and several of the Gulf monarchies are likely to proliferate as well. There will be very little point in the NPT once this happens, and Middle East proliferation will disincline the 'Big 5' to carry through on their disarmament promises. Nuclear fever will spread to Asia and Latin America: countries will be keen to acquire the bomb, even though it will wipe them out in a reprisal attack should they use it. For this reason, Iran may not be the first to use the bomb, although it may be tempted to supply 'dirty bombs'– weapons of mass panic if not mass destruction – to a terrorist group like Hezbollah. This is unlikely, however: the nuclear thumbprint on such devices would trace them back to Tehran and a conventional war would follow. Iran was extremely careful in 2003–4 not to provoke a US invasion and will not do so by arming US enemies with terrorist devices – unless the US attacks.

TIMING

Iran has adopted a strategy of 'nuclear hedging', i.e. 'maintaining, or appearing to maintain, a viable option for the relatively rapid acquisition of nuclear weapons, based on an indigenous technical capacity to produce them within a relatively short time frame'.[266] This means: (i) it must acquire enough fissile material – uranium enriched to 90 per cent concentration of U-235 isotope (or plutonium reprocessed from spent reactor fuel), (ii) this must be placed in a weapon which can trigger the chain reaction, and (iii) it must have a delivery vehicle, such as a ballistic missile.[267] It has enriched – to 3.75 per cent and then to 20 per cent – enough fissile material to make a bomb once this is enriched to 90 per cent (a process it does not seem yet to have begun and which would be detected if done at Natanz, which is monitored by the IAEA). The second step – weaponisation – involves converting HEU into metal and working out how to pack it into a warhead with high explosives: the IAEA report in November 2011 indicated that prior to 2003 Iran had obtained the necessary designs, purchased from A. Q. Khan, but may not have experimented before the process was suspended in 2003. In its August 2012 report, it published its suspicions that the process had been restarted with explosives tested at Parchin military base, which the IAEA had asked to inspect but had been refused for no good reason (and therefore, by inference, for a bad reason). Thirdly, although it is developing two missiles that could (just) reach Israel, the Ghadr I and the Sagil II, it has not worked out how to integrate a nuclear payload and has not completed their test flights. Both have very small warheads and it is not certain that Iran could build a bomb that would sit inside them.

As of September 2012, estimates of when Iran would be nuclear-ready once it decided to 'break out' varied widely: it would not only need to solve these problems but would have to obtain more uranium or yellowcake to provide an arsenal of six to eight bombs that would allow for tests and failures. Moreover, despite the latest IAEA report at the end of August 2012 which showed a steady expansion in its nuclear programme with hundreds of newly installed centrifuges at Natanz and Fordow, and up to 20 per cent enrichment, any decision to 'break out' by enriching to 90 per cent would be detected (very quickly at Natanz under round-the-clock IAEA surveillance). It could well trigger an Israeli attack, and even if its bombs could not penetrate the underground cavern at Fordow, this would certainly damage associated facilities and delay the programme. Iran would therefore need another secret facility and one that could stay secret from the prying eyes of the CIA, Mossad, the MEK, MI6 and the KGB, for the several years that would be needed to solve the delivery system problem and to acquire more yellowcake. There are suspicions that this secret facility may already exist at or under Parchin military base, hence the reason that Iran repeatedly refuses to allow the IAEA to inspect. Another theory for the refusal is that a steel chamber at the site has been used to experiment with implosion techniques, which could only be relevant to nuclear weapons.[268]

'Experts' have predicted, every year since 2006, that Iran would have nuclear weapons within two to three years, but the reality is that progress has been slowed by sanctions and export bans on important dual-use equipment. The Mossad-contrived murders of five of its nuclear scientists do not appear to have slowed Iran's progress – nuclear scientists are more replaceable now than they were in the days of Szilárd and Oppenheimer – but US computer trickery has achieved some disruption. Although the 'stuxnet worm', a computer malware virus which caused centrifuges in Natanz to crash, produced limited damage, it is likely that there will be more cyber-attacks, authorised (as was the stuxnet worm) by President Obama himself – unlawful as well as dishonourable, but no doubt justified as the lesser evil, clipping Iran's nuclear hedge rather than uprooting it.[269] It took North Korea three years from 'break-out' to make and test a nuclear warhead, and a similar time may be expected before Iran has the weapons-grade fissile material, the fully designed weapon and the systems to deliver it. It is on course, but that is a course to reach nuclear capability – Israel's 'red line', drawn at spring 2013 – which is too early for a Democratic President to join or support an Israeli attack. A Republican President might decide otherwise.

SANCTIONS

International pressure has been exerted on Iran over its development of nuclear energy, taking the form of the carrot of diplomacy and the stick of sanctions. It is startling how little pressure has been brought to bear to stop its human rights violations: the 1988 prison massacres were met with silence and then an inept follow-up by the Human Rights Commission's special representative, Professor Pohl (see Chapter 6). No sanctions have ever been imposed, even to require the regime to tell families where their children's bodies were buried. The Rushdie fatwa in 1989 did produce some trade bans, at least from Europe and America, and some Western diplomats were withdrawn as a result of the Mykonos restaurant killings, but the other global assassinations were ignored, as were the 'chain murders'. The killings and torture of protesters after the 2009 election-rigging scandal saw the US impose some visa bans and financial sanctions on officials of the Ministry of Intelligence and on Tehran's prosecutor general, Basij commander, Revolutionary Guards leader and Saeed Mortazavi. The UN Human Rights Council recently appointed the Maldives lawyer Ahmed Shaheed as its special representative: he has maintained dialogue, but only of the deaf, in relation to the imprisonment of Green Movement leaders and lawyers.[270] The Iranian government refuses to co-operate with him and will not allow him into the country. Sanctions as an effective means of combating human rights abuses no longer interest the international community with respect to Iran, but from 2006 onwards they became the solution of choice to force the country to cancel its enrichment programme. The UN has passed eighteen resolutions on Iran for its nuclear disobedience over the past ten years, whilst the EU has frozen the funds and bank accounts of thirty state officials.[271] The lack of interest in human rights, and the obsession with denying Iran any enrichment rights at all, has led to the failure of both sanctions and of diplomacy, separately and in tandem, to produce any 'solution' short of a threatened resort to bombing.

Sanctions of course are a blunt instrument likely to harm the civilian population and to rally its support behind the sanctioned government although they are attractive for politicians who do not want to resort to war with intransigent states. Hillary Clinton speaks of 'crippling sanctions' on Iran and even Israel has been prepared – without much hope – to give them time to work, at least until early 2013. They were ineffective when imposed at the behest of Jimmy Carter to release the US hostages in Tehran, although they contributed to bringing apartheid to an end in South Africa. There, the victims – the black majority – were already at subsistence level and could not suffer much more, whilst financial sanctions persuaded the wealthier whites that they had no future, and the men found sporting bans on cricket and football particularly demoralising. Those circumstances were not present in Iraq, where the 'oil for food' programme meant that the poor starved and the corrupt rich stole their share. Other rogue states have managed to survive severe sanctions – Zimbabwe, North Korea and Cuba, for example – and collective punishment is never attractive when imposed on a people whose elections are rigged. As Gary Sick concludes, 'sanctions do not persuade dictatorial regimes to abandon projects that they think are central to their security and survival, and even self-image'.[272] The sanctions on Iran, beginning with a ban on WMD-related imports and a freezing of the assets of Revolutionary Guard leaders, now prohibit banks from doing business (British banks have been heavily fined in the US for non-compliance) and have frozen the assets of the Iranian Central Bank as well as government-related corporations. The OECD discontinued its purchase of oil from 1 July 2012 and other customers have cut back under US pressure. This has certainly damaged the economy: it is facing a serious shortage of hard currency and an escalating devaluation of its currency (the rial).[273] But this mostly affects the educated middle classes, who are the main supporters of the pro-democracy movement.

At a political level, Mousavi and Karroubi cannot welcome sanctions – not only are they offensive to Persian pride, but they are being imposed on the regime for doing pretty much what the reform movement would do if given the chance. Mousavi himself, when Prime Minister, had nurtured the atomic energy industry and had later been a member of the Supreme National Security Committee, which approved the secret development of Natanz during the reform presidency of Khatami. The Green Movement has no quarrel with Iran's right to enrich – the absurdity of the current European position is that they are imposing 'crippling' sanctions on the country for exercising a legal right, but not for killing protesters or mass-murdering prisoners.

The Nobel laureate and human rights heroine Shirin Ebadi told the BBC 'We oppose economic sanctions because that's to the detriment of the people' but her voice fell on deaf ears in Israel – which does not seem to care about the people of Iran – and on US senators and congressmen whipped into a state of fury by AIPAC over Tehran's determination to enrich, if only to 3.5 per cent at first. The Obama administration succumbed to heavy pressure from Congress to punish Iran for nuclear enrichment and the European Union followed, and so to some extent did Russia and China, which voted for Security Council Resolution 1929. Iran was not permitted to bring back the crude oil that it had been sending abroad for refining into petrol (this caused substantial economic damage), or to deal with international banks (which caused even more). Its people were, by late-2012, suffering severely for their government's claim to an 'inalienable right to enrich'. That was a right given by Article IV of the NPT that at least forty other countries were exercising without difficulty: the Iranian people were not only suffering, but regarded themselves (with good reason) as suffering unfairly. It has made some of them question whether the nuclear game is worth the candle and recent opinion polls have been censored by the government because they show some anxiety over whether it was being sensible to be pushing the claim at the expense of the public welfare. But sanctions will not cause Iran's economy to collapse. Its growth may have slowed to 1 per cent, but that is still growth. It has reserves of $120 billion in cash and gold, a balance of payments surplus, and an estimated $100 billion in export earnings for 2012. Despite its vulnerability, its chaos and lack of gas, Iran is well practised in smuggling and China remains its biggest customer, whilst countries beyond US influence will still line up for cheap oil. After several years, sanctions were having the counter-productive effect of toughening the regime's resolve not to give in or make concessions, and had enabled the commercial divisions of the Revolutionary Guard to take over core sections of the economy – those parts that were dependent on foreign investment.[274] By October the economy was in such a dire state that bazaar traders led street protests, but not against the real villain – the Supreme Leader – and not against the nuclear programme. Ahmadinejad was made the scapegoat, for his economic mismanagement and his decision to squander an estimate $5 billion on propping up the Assad regime in Syria.

DIPLOMACY

Diplomats must exercise their craft within an extremely limited, indeed claustrophobic, space, the 'wriggle room' left after governments have taken into account their domestic political imperatives. The US government could not resist the power of Congress, worked up by the Jewish lobby to favour severe sanctions on Iran unless it suspended all enrichment; whilst the Iranian government in 2006 had to start enriching again as a result of the nationalist pressure which had produced Ahmadinejad's election – unrigged on this first occasion. It was this narrow space within which creative solutions had to be found, for example an offer that other states would enrich uranium for Iran in return for it abjuring a fuel cycle. There was always the possibility, which increased as the negotiations dragged on, that Iran was delaying these talks without any real intention of accepting a compromise, but in order to give itself more time to enrich. In 2012, as war drums beat in Israel, echoed up to an uncertain point by the US, the European Union took a hand, leading what was called 'the P5+1' (the 'Big 5' plus Germany) in a series of much-publicised but entirely unproductive meetings, which moved in a diplomatic caravanserai from Israel to Baghdad and thence to Moscow.

The first time that the West could sensibly reach out to Tehran had been in the reform period of 1997, with the election of President Khatami. There were some tentative approaches, and the prospect of a rapprochement emerged after 9/11, when Iran helped the US to defeat the Taliban – their joint enemy – only to be slapped in the face by President Bush who placed it on 'the Axis of Evil'. It was Tehran's good luck that Bush destroyed Saddam, Iran's other long-standing enemy. Either in embarrassment or in fear (until the occupation of Iraq turned into a disaster, there was serious talk in Washington of invading Iran), the mullahs suspended their enrichment programme after it had been exposed by the MEK, and actually made an offer to end their support for Hamas and Hezbollah and to hand over some Al Qaeda captives if only the US would give them the 3,500 MEK members ensconced at Camp Ashraf, over the border in Iraq.[275] This was an extraordinary offer: Iran owes much of its prestige in the rival Sunni Arab world to its funding and facilitating of anti-Israeli fighters, and its willingness even to talk about abandoning them in return for getting its hands on the MEK was an indication of the depth of its hatred of the group that had exposed Natanz, and which it had tried to exterminate back in 1988. The approach came to nothing: Dick Cheney and Donald Rumsfeld decided that 'we don't speak to evil'.[276] The fate likely to await any Camp Ashraf members surrendered by the US would certainly have been evil, but in other respects the rejection was the last opportunity for dialogue before the onset of Ahmadinejad.

The Mayor of Tehran, with his disgusting anti-Semitic rhetoric, disbelief in the Holocaust and crude anticipation of the advent of the Twelfth Imam, who would wipe non-believers in general, and Israel in particular, from the pages of time, was a gift for Israeli propaganda obsessed about mad mullahs with fingers on nuclear triggers. What intelligent Israelis fear is that nuclear capability alone will give Iran a boost in credibility and in prestige, and greater confidence in its support for Hamas and Hezbollah. Hence Israel's initial 'red line', promoted through its US lobby and described for some years as 'the point of no return', is not a capacity to 'break out' but a capacity to enrich at all, notwithstanding that this is its right as an NPT member (which Israel is not). Nonetheless, Israel encouraged the US to push for the severest economic sanctions, leaving Israel's military option 'on the table' if sanctions fail to stop Iran enriching. This was just about the most counter-productive position that Israel could take – the very fact that an attack by Israel was 'on the table' was calculated to make Iran want nuclear weapons as soon as possible, to deter that attack by the threat of 'mutually assured destruction'. But in 2009, it put the Obama administration – which wanted to reverse the Bush years of non-engagement in order to find a solution to Tehran's nuclear aspirations – in a bind. The Israelis would not accept Iran's right to enrich, and Iran refused to suspend enrichment. Diplomacy offered a lose-lose result.

And so it turned out. Ratcheting up sanctions at the same time as trying to find a diplomatic solution was hopeless – it meant that the mullahs would be humiliated if they appeared to climb down under threat, in the eyes of a people they had keyed up to believe in their nation's 'inalienable right'. Obama's emollient speeches, one of them uploaded on YouTube so Iranians could judge his genuineness, could not hide the fact that he too was powerless to stop the sanctions his congressmen insisted on piling up, and he could not even unfreeze the assets frozen by the US government at the time of the 1979 hostage crisis. He could not stop Benjamin Netanyahu visiting the US, exciting Congress with speeches about the peril of a nuclear Iran and announcing more Jewish settlements on the West Bank. Obama declared that he would be prepared to begin discussions after the 2009 Iranian elections – in the hope, of course, that he would be dealing with President Mousavi. His weak reaction to the election fraud and the ensuing 'where is my vote?' protests ('the world is watching') was no doubt diplomatically tailored to protect future dialogue with President Ahmadinejad, but it struck many Americans as a pathetic abandonment of democracy and human rights. It was certainly appreciated by the mullahs, who hurriedly put Britain in place of the US as 'the Great Satan' in their show trial indictments, but it disappointed the Green Movement and the international human rights movement, and gained no favours from the mullahs. To make matters worse, the US sanctions targeting communications equipment helped the regime to close down the internet, which had become the reform movement's main tool of communication.[277] The reformers were not bothered by the regime's progress towards a nuclear fuel cycle: this was not an issue. As Trita Parsi concludes in his perceptive study of the failures of Obama's diplomacy in Iran, *A Single Roll of the Dice*, 'the balance struck between the nuclear issue and human rights tilted too far in the direction of the nuclear talks and tended to neglect the gravity of the human rights abuses in Iran'.[278]

In other words human rights were sacrificed to naive diplomats' hopes that a government which was abusing them would act decently and trustworthily when it came to negotiating over nuclear weapons. At least Nicolas Sarkozy pointed out that 'it is the same leaders in Iran who say that the nuclear programme is peaceful and that the elections were honest. Who can believe them?'[279] The Iranians toughened their negotiating position and insisted on enriching to 20 per cent for their research reactor in Tehran, taking the stance – backed by ElBaradei – that they had the legal right to do so, just like Japan, Germany, Brazil and the dozen or so other members of the NPT which had a full nuclear fuel cycle. The difference, of course, was that these countries did not mass-murder prisoners or protesters, nor did they cheat, as Iran did, all the time. As the P5+1 prepared for its opening round of talks with Iran in Geneva, the US learned of the existence of the Fordow facility near Qom – another undeclared and underground enrichment cavern, which could be used as a secret 'break-out' facility, or (as the Iranians were belatedly to insist when the secret was out) as a contingency facility if Natanz was destroyed by the Israelis.

The diplomatic dance began in Geneva in October 2009 and continues still, a seemingly endless round of tantalisingly prospective agreements, then retreats from these agreements by the Iranian negotiators on the dual track of sanctions and sweeteners that psychologically cancel each other out. At Geneva, for example, Iran tentatively agreed to 'swap' half its existing research reactor fuel by sending it for enrichment abroad, and to allow the IAEA access to its newly discovered facility at Qom. But at the next meeting Iran went back on the swap proposal and found a reason to object to French participation: the talks collapsed after the Supreme Leader told his negotiators that the request for Iran's research reactor fuel had become 'an insult to the nation', and so it would only be released in small batches.[280] Later, in the hope of warding off more severe sanctions at the UN, he reversed his position and tentatively agreed to allow half of the research reactor fuel to leave the country for enrichment in Turkey and Brazil. This was hailed by Tehran, by ElBaradei (recently retired from the IAEA), and by some non-aligned states, as the way out of the impasse, but by this time it was too late to take Iran seriously, and their tentative agreement was in any event subject to a future confirmation. Tehran would still have enough fuel left to make a bomb and it then confessed triumphantly that whilst the talks had been 'progressing', it had been enriching to 19.75 per cent – in contravention of several Security Council resolutions. So once again the Security Council (significantly, with Chinese and Russian support, although they watered down the resolution) imposed more sanctions, and the P5+1 meetings in 2011 made no advances – Iran petulantly refused even to reconvene until sanctions were lifted and its right to enrich was recognised.

The latter demand could not be denied on the legal basis argued by the French, i.e. that Article IV of the NPT did not include the right to enrich. This argument was unsustainable, because Article IV speaks of the 'inalienable right to develop research, production and use of nuclear energy for peaceful purposes without discrimination', and 'production' must include enrichment. A better argument was that the right could only avail those states which complied with their Article II undertaking not to seek assistance to manufacture nuclear weapons, and Iran was therefore disqualified from the right given by Article IV because it had sought assistance from A. Q. Khan (this argument is evaluated earlier – see page 219). The standoff continued for a year, during which Iran moved its nuclear programme forward by building a few hundred more centrifuges, testing ballistic missiles and mulling over warhead designs. It ignored the Security Council resolutions, and in fact quite openly defied them: Ahmadinejad publicly and proudly announced 'a very big new achievement' in February 2010, of producing nuclear fuel rods to enable enrichment to 20 per cent.[281] Netanyahu condemned his televised boast as aggression, and called on the Security Council to draw a 'red line' against it.[282] Sanctions and diplomacy had achieved nothing, other than to give Iran time – several years – slowly and surely to advance its nuclear programme, with a brinkmanship quite breathtaking in its audacity and in its success.

• • •

In November 2011 came the IAEA's report of 'credible' evidence that Iran had recommenced its nuclear weapon programme, which prompted more angry Israeli threats to bomb its nuclear facilities. Defence Minister Ehud Barak came up with the concept of 'the zone of immunity' – the Rubicon point beyond which Israel, acting alone, could not stop or substantially delay Iran's progress by means of a military strike. And Iran would reach that immunity zone, said Barak, if it installed more centrifuge cascades at Fordow, which lay under a mountain that would protect them from conventional bombs. Iran replied with theological denial from its Supreme Leader: 'We consider developing nuclear weapons unlawful. We consider using such weapons a big sin. We also believe that keeping such weapons is futile and dangerous, and we will never go after them.'[283] Few believed this international criminal, who had lied so often before, and assumed this was another example of the Shia doctrine of *taqiyya* – the duty to lie in the interests of advancing the faith. Since delay was permitting the advance of Iran's nuclear programme towards the 'zone of immunity' which would engage an Israeli attack, another roll of the diplomatic dice was called for.

The 2012 talks were convened by Catherine Ashton, the EU's foreign policy chief, who led the P5+1 into the conference room to go head to head with Iran's chief negotiator, Saeed Jalili, secretary of the Supreme National Security Council. Ms Ashton was no match for the wily Iranians, experienced at hide-and-seek games with the IAEA such as pretending a willingness to talk, and then spinning out the meetings with devices to delay (such as constant calls for prayer breaks) and occasional threats to close the Strait of Hormuz (which would force oil prices to a level beyond the comfort of most Western states). The P5+1 had their own fractures – Russia wanted Iran to have a full fuel cycle under intensive inspections, whilst the US, revved up by AIPAC, did not want it to enrich at all. Meanwhile the Iranian delegates just talked whilst their scientists continued to build more centrifuges to boost enrichment levels to 20 per cent – and in May the IAEA found that at Fordow they had actually enriched to 29 per cent. Meanwhile the talks made no progress other than to agree to talk again at Istanbul in April and at Baghdad in May, where again no progress was made. The European Union's face was saved by an agreement to talk again in Moscow in June.

What was achieved in Moscow? In a hilarious deadpan press release, the Russian Ministry of Foreign Affairs announced: 'The frequency of talks with Iran regarding its nuclear programme has never been higher than now. This is a very significant achievement.'[284] It was the only achievement. The Moscow conference ended with an agreement to send some boffins back to Turkey in July, but not to talk turkey, only technologies. And so it goes on – and on, whilst Iran continues to approach the nuclear threshold and Israel continues to pressure Washington to approve or to join a bombardment by spring 2013, and at least five other countries in the Middle East contemplate the need for nuclear weapons. Meanwhile the conference on a nuclear-free zone in the Middle East, arranged at the 2010 NPT review conference to take place in December 2012, is still (in September) without an agenda. Says its facilitator, the Finnish Under-Secretary of State:

> The political environment is difficult but certainly the commitment is there which makes me pretty confident we can make progress.

The only progress that is ever made on this issue is by Iran, stealthily and steadily adding centrifuge cascades, enriching up to and occasionally beyond 20 per cent, and studying weaponisation designs, whilst the diplomats talk.

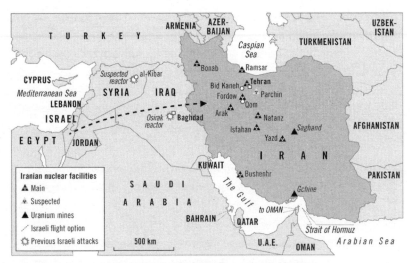

Distance between Israel and Tehran, approximately 1,500 km.

A map from which President Ahmadinejad would like to wipe
Israel, showing the flight path to his nuclear facilities.

CHAPTER 13

THE PROBLEM WITH ISRAEL

It is 1938 and Iran is Germany. And Iran is racing to arm itself
with atomic bombs.

Benjamin Netanyahu

History teaches us that overreaction is preferable to under-reaction.

Shimon Peres

The most powerful argument from the *vox populi* in favour of
Iran's right to nuclear weapons is that Israel has so many of
them: estimates range from 80 to 200, some of exceptional
destructive capacity which make use of tritium, a hydrogen isotope
produced at Dimona. At discussions on the Iranian question in
2012, from seminars at the Hay-on-Wye book festival to televised
debates in Sydney, critics of the Iranian nuclear programme were
interrupted by angry voices from the floor: 'What about Israel
with its 200 nuclear bombs?' These were not anti-Americans or
anti-Zionists (who make the point consistently and belligerently),
but people with a sense of fair play. On the face of it, it does seem
preposterous for the US even to contemplate war with Iran to stop
it from making a few rudimentary nuclear bombs, when Israel
has for about a half-century had a large stockpile, mounted on
missiles and recently capable of delivery from its submarines. The
obvious answer – that Israel, unlike Iran, is not run by international criminals – does not altogether convince. There have been
too many targeted killings of Palestinians[285] ('Operation Cast
Lead' killed over 1,000 of them in the Gaza Strip in 2009, including 700 civilians of whom 400 were women and children);[286]
the unlawful storming of the Turkish ship MV *Mavi Marmara*;
abusive treatment of children in military custody;[287] and the

assassinations of Iranian scientists (undoubtedly engineered by Mossad): in these respects, Israel is its own worst enemy, and although it will only use its nukes in the face of a threat to its existence, the problem is that Israel itself will be the judge of that threat. The judgement of its Prime Minister in 2012, that Iranian nuclear facilities should be attacked (preferably by or with the support of America) was so unwise and unlawful as to cast doubts over any judgement he might make about the threat from Iran, or from anyone else. Israel's determination never to give up the bomb, and to use violence against any near or far neighbour which comes close to acquiring nuclear weapons, constitutes a serious stumbling block to regional security and to the prospect for international disarmament.

'The Jews of Israel will never be like the Jews in the Holocaust. Israel will be able to visit a terrible retribution on those who would attempt its destruction.' David Ben-Gurion, its first Prime Minister, for this reason wanted the bomb as an ultimate security blanket, or at very worst to provide Israel with the 'Samson option' of pulling down the roof on the Philistines – its Arab enemies – if they were on the verge of capturing the country. So the quest for the bomb began as soon as possible: a secret deal was put in place with the French, who provided some uranium and built a reactor at a site just south of Dimona in the Negev (where Ezekiel had prophesied 'the blazing flame that will not be quenched'). It was disguised as a textile factory, and funded through a South American corporation by wealthy American Jews who knew that their 'charitable donations' were going to no ordinary charity. They were well aware that Dimona would make bombs for dropping, if an Israeli government ever thought it necessary, on Arab cities. Further supplies of uranium were readily acquired with the help of sympathetic diasporians who arranged for the purchase of yellowcake from a Belgian corporation on behalf of an Italian paint company. It was a simple matter for Mossad to buy a tramp steamer and supply a crew to pick up the yellowcake (labelled as plumbat, an inert and harmless lead product) and arrange for it to be transferred, on a dark night in the middle of the Mediterranean, to an Israeli freighter. The 'Plumbat Affair' in 1968 supplied Israel with sufficient uranium for its first thirty bombs.

When President Kennedy found out about Dimona, back in 1961, he immediately recognised the danger that Israel would go nuclear and never come back. At a meeting with Ben-Gurion at the Waldorf Astoria Hotel, he extracted a pledge that Dimona would be used for peaceful purposes only. Kennedy remained suspicious, and insisted on US inspection to check on Ben-Gurion's pledge. Shimon Peres gave an equivocal promise to Kennedy that Israel would not be the first state to 'introduce' nuclear weapons to the region.[288] However, the nuclear weapons programme was hidden from the US visitors and was well advanced by 1968, when Israel resisted US pressure to sign the NPT. (It had hastily assembled a makeshift nuclear device in 1967, on the eve of the Six Day War, but decided not to use it.)[289] In 1969, the perspicacious Dr Kissinger reported to President Nixon that 'our interest is in preventing Israel's possession of nuclear weapons [but] since Israel may already have nuclear weapons, the one objective we might achieve is to persuade them to keep what they have secret … the international implications of the Israeli program are not triggered until it becomes public knowledge.'[290] In that year, Kissinger brokered a secret agreement between Golda Meir and President Nixon: the US agreed to protect Israel's nuclear weapons programme and support its position as a non-signatory to the NPT, so long as Israel did not test its nukes or publicise the fact that it possessed them.[291]

This Machiavellian, or at least Kissingerian, pact has still not been made public, although it is the basis of Israel's policy of 'opacity' or 'nuclear ambiguity' (in Hebrew, *amimut*) by which it refuses to confirm or deny that it has the bomb, and threatens any whistleblower with brutal treatment of the kind meted out to Mordechai Vanunu, who exposed its programme in 1986. It still repeats its promise that 'Israel will not be the first to introduce nuclear weapons to the Middle East', which it maintains with a straight face, apparently on the basis of the explanation Yitzhak Rabin gave to arms negotiator Paul Warnke, that 'an unadvertised, untested nuclear device is not a nuclear weapon' – which of course it is.

It was another secret agreement, this time signed in 1975 by P. W. Botha and Shimon Peres, which provided for an unholy nuclear alliance with apartheid South Africa. Israel received 500 more tons of yellowcake – enough for its future weapons needs – in return for assisting South Africa with warhead design and missile technology and even some radioactive tritium, used in the construction of 'boosted fission' nuclear bombs.[292] This deal with the apartheid devil would have been ferociously condemned had it been exposed at the time, but details did not leak, even to America, until an atmospheric explosion over the South Atlantic was interpreted by the Carter administration as a South African nuclear test – until they investigated, and concluded that it was an Israeli nuclear test with South African assistance.[293]

By this time a young Moroccan immigrant, Mordechai Vanunu, was working at the Dimona nuclear reactor, and taking some photographs of secret sections of the plant. In 1986, after ten years' employment, he was sacked for joining a pro-Palestinian rally: he moved to Australia and converted to Christianity. His story about Israel's 'bomb in the basement' did not interest the Australian press, but London's *Sunday Times* came to hear of it and brought Vanunu to London for debriefing. A week before it planned to publish, the newspaper showed his story to the Israeli embassy – and left its source alone and unprotected. The very next day he was approached in Leicester Square by 'Cindy', an attractive American who chatted him up and soon enticed him to bed – the bed in question being in her sister's apartment in Rome. The lonely whistleblower fell for the honeytrap, and accepted Cindy's generous offer of a business class ticket: in the bedroom in Rome were three men from Mossad who beat and drugged him, and transported him to a waiting Israeli naval vessel, disguised as a merchant ship and hovering offshore, just inside international waters. The *Sunday Times* published his story, with the photographs that were evidence of Israel's nukes.

Kidnapped and brought before an Israeli court, Vanunu was sentenced to eighteen years, the first twelve to be served in solitary confinement. There was no fuss made in Israel about this brutal sentence, and no discussion at all in the press about the policy of 'nuclear opacity': Prime Minister Shimon Peres appealed to media editors not to cover the subject, and they complied.[294]

Vanunu was made to serve his full term: on release in 2004 he was denied a passport and banned from talking about his kidnap or using the internet or contacting journalists, or leaving the country for Norway, which was prepared to grant him asylum. In 2006, Microsoft informed on him for using his Hotmail account to reply to foreign journalists so he was jailed again, and put back in solitary confinement. In 2012, the Israeli High Court refused him permission to renounce his Israeli citizenship. His honey-trapper, Cheryl Bentov, a.k.a. Cindy, turned out to have trained as a 'fighting pioneer' in Israel where she had married a major in military intelligence. She now sells real estate in Florida.[295]

The conspiracy to kidnap Vanunu was a breach of UK law, but the British government took no action. Western nations generally turn a blind eye to Israel's revenge attacks, unless they involve its nationals: when Mossad murdered Hamas operator Mahmoud al-Mabhouh in Dubai in 2010, Britain protested – not about the murder, but about the use of stolen British passports by the murderers. The enemies of Israel are generally regarded as fair game: Mossad's execution of those it suspected (in a few cases, wrongly) of involvement in the killings of Israeli athletes in Munich in 1972 has Hollywood's seal of approval, and its drone killings in Gaza which have taken many civilian lives have gone largely uncontested. 'Operation Cast Lead' – Israel's 22-day war of bombing and shelling the people of Gaza by sea and land, killing over 1,000 citizens and destroying 3,000 homes, together with factories, hospitals and mosques – was condemned by an independent UN inquiry as an illegal exercise in self-defence (it was a disproportionate reprisal for unlawful Hamas rocket attacks). Only one Israeli soldier has been convicted – for stealing a credit card. (There have of course been no prosecutions of Hamas rocketeers in Gaza.)

The murders of Iranian nuclear scientists – five so far – cannot be so easily overlooked, although the Western media almost delights in the daring of the murders, as endless articles attest:

'The motorbike moved through the heavy Tehran morning traffic...'[296] is a typical beginning: 'the motorcyclist, ubiquitous in the capital's traffic jams, often wearing a surgical mask for protection against heavy pollution and able to move close to the target between the lines of stationary cars without attracting attention'.[297] This is followed by a dramatic account of how the pillion passenger will reach out and attach a small plastic magnetic bomb to the car of a nuclear scientist, and then rev up and away. Less attention is given to the consequences of what is invariably described as a Mossad 'drive-by killing' – the public grief and fury which transmogrifies into support for the nation's nuclear programme. There is no evidence that the death of the victims has damaged the progress at Natanz or Fordow, although the killings have certainly caused righteous anger and a determination that the 'martyrs' should not die in vain. In the non-aligned world, the murders provide even more contempt (if that is possible) for Israel, and an understandable sympathy for the families of the victims. For that reason, they were seated in the front row for the Supreme Leader's address to a non-aligned summit on 30 August 2012, holding up large pictures of their murdered relatives. Outside the hall, bombed and burned-out cars were on macabre display, with photographs of the bereaved children.[298]

It was tear-jerking propaganda, but Israel deserved it. The killings are as despicable, in their way, as the Iranian global assassination campaign. Israel has not admitted responsibility for them, of course, but has not denied it. The only other possible candidate, the MEK, was on its best behaviour – at the time of its desperately sought delisting as a terrorist organisation in the US, having been previously delisted by court order in the UK and Europe. The decision was in Hillary Clinton's lap throughout the period of the assassinations, and would have been doomed by evidence of any return to violence. (She eventually delisted the MEK in September 2012.) There have been other mysterious bombings and explosions, most notably one at an army base which killed the general who headed Iran's ballistic missile programme and sixteen Revolutionary Guards. This did real damage, although whether by accident or design is not clear (Iran says it was an accident, which means that it may well have been an Israeli attack the success of which it did not want to admit).

One assault on Iran which President Obama has been prepared to admit that the US assisted involved 'the stuxnet worm', a cyber-weapon inserted into the computer systems at Natanz which put hundreds of centrifuges temporarily out of operation. These centrifuges were the A. Q. Khan P-1 models, also supplied to Libya, which were handed over by Gaddafi and have been fully analysed by American scientists, who were thus in a position to design the malignant worm. This 'malware' would have had to be introduced into the Natanz computers by a hand-held USB device, presumably by a security-cleared Iranian physicist in the pay of Mossad or the CIA.[299] The US involvement was revealed by a White House leak to the *New York Times*, to convince the Jewish lobby that President Obama was not 'soft on Iran', as his detractors claimed in the run-up to the presidential election. Although the cyber-attack was not lethal, it was certainly unlawful: a deliberate attack on the property of another state.

It was in his address to the AIPAC Convention in February 2012 that Obama laid down his policy pitch: 'Iranian leaders', he said, 'should understand that I do not have a policy of containment. I have a policy to prevent Iran from obtaining a nuclear weapon.'[300] Although he warned against 'loose talk of war' he added that 'when the chips are down, I have Israel's back'. His audience was encouraged to assume that this meant that if sabotage, sanctions and diplomacy all failed, America would bomb Iran, but Netanyahu wanted him to be more specific about the stage that would trigger the US attack. On *Meet the Press* in September he demanded that Obama 'place that red line before them now, before it's too late. You want these fanatics to have nuclear weapons?'[301] Obama will wait at least until Iran starts to 'break out', i.e. to turn its nuclear weapons capability into an unequivocal attempt to build them. Israel has made clear that it cannot wait that long – achievement of nuclear weapons 'capability' was its red line, and Netanyahu, having urged the US to bomb Iran in the course of 2012, 'blinked' when he addressed the UN in late September and said that Israel would be 'on the brink' by spring or early summer 2013. He has received a more supportive promise from Mitt Romney – that as US President he would use 'any and all measures' to curb what he called Iran's 'existential threat' to Israel. 'We recognise Israel's right to defend itself, and it is right for America to stand with you,' he told his old friend

Netanyahu – the two had made money together in the 1970s when they were both in business at Boston Consulting Group. In a press conference forty years later, against the dramatic backdrop of Jerusalem's old city wall, he said it was a 'moral imperative' to stop Iran, and that as President he would 'respect' Israel's decision to do so. 'We will not watch the horrors of history play out again.'[302]

The 'horrors of history' was a line deliberately echoing Netanyahu's repeated claim that Iran's Supreme Leader and its President were planning another Holocaust, this time by nuclear destruction of the Jewish nation. Addressing a meeting in the US, Netanyahu waved a letter written to Roosevelt in 1944 by the World Jewish Congress, urging the bombing of the railway lines to Auschwitz. He declaimed, 'Never again will we not be masters of our own fate, of our very survival. Never again.' It was histrionic rather than history, of course, and made credible only by the vicious language of the Supreme Leader, who responded to Netanyahu's threat in a Friday sermon in February 2012, committing the nation to pursuing its nuclear programme come what may. He described Israel as a 'cancerous tumour' that 'will be removed' (in context, by a freshly de-occulated Twelfth Imam) and declared that if America went to war against Iran 'it would be ten times deadlier for the Americans'.[303] Khamenei alternates vicious rhetoric against Israel with condemnations of 'un-Islamic' nuclear weapons, so there is no reason to take anything he says literally (or figuratively, for that matter), but his ability to provoke Netanyahu is evident – and deliberate. The Israeli Prime Minister, after all, is the son of Benzion Netanyahu, the leading Zionist historian who argued that Jews would face holocausts around every corner: 'Jewish history is in large measure a history of holocausts.'[304] His son uses this language routinely in references to the threat from Iran, and his government has encouraged the expectation of war by issuing 70,000 gas masks to a nervous citizenry, arranging to text-message the nation when the counter-attack is on its way, and planning to turn Tel Aviv's underground car parks into bomb shelters for 800,000 people.[305]

Netanyahu only demeans the memory of the Holocaust by invoking it against a nation that treats its own Jews well, and wants bombs partly because they would counter-balance those secretly possessed by Israel. The killing of six million Jews in concentration camps on the grounds of supposed racial inferiority was a policy without parallel in its wickedness, and Ahmadinejad's suggestion that it would have been more logical for the UN to have given Jews a homeland in Lower Saxony rather than Palestine is hardly evidence of his genocidal intent. Netanyahu's rhetoric depicts Jews once again as victims, and creates a climate not only of fear but of expectation that Israel will attack first – an expectation that Netanyahu may have to live up to, despite the public misgivings from leaders of his army and his intelligence services. Tzipi Livni, the opposition leader (previously responsible for 'Operation Cast Lead'), has called on Netanyahu to 'stop with the hysterical comparisons'. But they continue, as do settlements on Palestinian lands in defiance of law and of 'freeze' agreements. Netanyahu favours them, although they are a major hindrance to peace, and he opposes any emergence of a Palestinian state. In all this – and particularly in his threats to bomb in order to prevent Iran becoming 'nuclear capable', he has the support of evangelical American Christians (and former Fox News conspiracy theorist Glenn Beck) who believe that Jewish ownership of the Holy Land is a prerequisite for the Second Coming of Jesus Christ, which their prophecies say will occur in Jerusalem once Jewish hegemony is secure. Should Jesus return at the same time as the Twelfth Imam de-occulates, the two events could cancel each other out (the two might even become friends). For non-millennial rationalists, however, the pressing problem is Netanyahu's threatened attack, not Khamenei's hypothetical horror of history.

Israeli politicians have been threatening to bomb Iran since 2006, and Netanyahu and his Defence Minister, Ehud Barak, gave many to believe in 2012 that they would strike imminently. The Israel Defence Forces spend a great deal of time rehearsing and war-gaming: their 112 long-range fighter-bombers (American F-15Is and F-16Is) could, with aerial refuelling, fly over friendly Jordan and an Iraq without air defences, to drop bunker-busting bombs on Fordow and Natanz, and to attack the heavy-water plant at Arak, the uranium milling operation at Isfahan and the operational reactor at Bushehr, perhaps aided by long-distance drones and offshore submarines armed with nuclear-tipped cruise missiles.[306] They could probably shatter the 9,000 centrifuges in the main hall of Natanz, although the chamber at Fordow, 80 metres deep, might not be so easily scathed. The Israeli Security Cabinet reassuringly announced that only 300 Israeli deaths were expected from attacks by Iran and its allies – Syria, Hezbollah and Hamas – during a reprisal missile war likely to last three weeks. It has made no calculation of, perhaps because it has little interest in, the number of civilian deaths that would be suffered in Iran from an Israeli first strike. This is a crucial calculation, which has received little or no consideration. Proponents of an Israeli/US strike pretend it will be a surgical operation like Osirak or Al-Kibar, causing a few dozen deaths. On the contrary, bombing of only Natenz, Bushehr and Isfahan – the minimum of Iran's seventeen declared nuclear sites – will kill thousands of citizens. Natenz alone has about 10,000 scientists, soldiers and support staff working two shifts, so half are likely to be blown up in any 'successful' bombing raid. Worse will be the fallout: the IAEA estimates that these facilities hold 371 metric tons of highly toxic uranium hexofluoride. Release of this gas into the atmosphere after a bombing raid will blind and burn and close the lungs of people in its path (many thousands of them at Isfahan), and enter the water, soil and food chain with consequences for cancer rates and birth defects for years to come. If Bushehr, an operational reactor, is attacked, the radiation could cover the quarter-million people in the eponymous nearby city, and winds might carry it to Kuwait and Iraq and Saudi Arabia. How many Neda Agha-Soltans will die in and after and as the result of the operation so passionately advocated by Mr Netanyahu? In 'Operation Cast Lead', Israel suffered ten deaths against 1,000 dead Palestinians. It estimates that 300 Israeli deaths will result from reprisals for striking Iran: on the same calculus, is it prepared to kill 30,000 Iranians?

The Obama administration, with the help of sane voices from Israel's own military and intelligence establishment, has pointed out that any Israeli strike would not destroy the Iranian nuclear programme, or delay it for longer than 'maybe one, possibly two, years' (the estimate of Leon Panetta, US Secretary of Defense). Given that Iran now has all the necessary nuclear weapon knowledge, reconstructing the programme and building a bomb within five years would not be difficult, and public revulsion and patriotic fury over an Israeli strike would probably drive them to do so. This is, after all, a state run and managed by men who survived Saddam's poisonous gas on the battlefield, and will survive Israeli – and American – bombs with renewed determination. They will respond by closing, or mining, the Strait of Hormuz, through which a third of the world's oil passes, and possibly by attacking US military bases in Qatar, or Bahrain or the UAE, drawing America into what would be another disastrous Middle East war. Iran would remain a theocratic, merciless mullocracy, in which reformers would have even less chance of overthrowing its government, more determined than ever to possess nukes. The outrage on the Arab streets would force Egypt and Jordan to end their non-aggression agreements with Israel, making it less secure than ever.

It should not be thought, incidentally, that 'regime change' would necessarily produce a nuclear-weapons-free Iran. Mousavi, when Prime Minister, was an avid promoter of the bomb, on the basis that it would enhance Iran's prestige and security. Opinion polls have tended to show constant support for the government's hardline 'right to enrich' policy, although a recent poll, show-ing a drop in support as a result of sanctions, was hurriedly suppressed. Israelis, too, are unconvinced by Netanyahu's argu-ments for action: a considerable majority oppose bombing Iran without American support.[307] This majority may well increase as they digest the news that the war will cost them an estimated $11.7 billion, just in direct damage to infrastructure and private property from reprisal attacks, quite apart from human casual-ties.[308] And were it ever to come to a battle, Iran's population has almost doubled in the last twenty-five years and is now over 70 million, with two thirds under the age of thirty – giving it a massive manpower superiority over Israel, with a population of nearly 8 million (20 per cent of whom are Arab Israelis).[309] That population may well decline as Netanyahu's war drums beat louder: the main 'existential' threat to Israel comes from his scare campaign, which is likely to scare people into fleeing the country.

Whilst there is no doubt that the spectre of a nuclear-armed Iran would provoke proliferation, an attack on a nuclear-capable Iran would have the same consequence. The lesson of Osirak is that it persuaded Saddam that he needed nukes more than ever, and in consequence a clandestine programme came very close to success within a decade. Saudi Arabia has already threatened to obtain nuclear warheads from Pakistan, happy to sell to rich Sunnis,[310] and it is planning a civil nuclear programme from which it will have the capacity to 'break out'. A nuclear arms race across the Middle East will follow, indeed has already started: at least fifteen nuclear reactors are scheduled to be built in the next decade – in Egypt, Turkey, Jordan, the UAE, Kuwait and Saudi Arabia.[311]

Whether Israel attacks or not, and whether or when Iran 'breaks out' from its full fuel cycle, the events of 2011–12 demonstrate that proliferation is now impossible to stop. That is the result not only of Iranian diplomatic brinkmanship, but of Israeli hypocrisy in threatening aggression against a member of a Nuclear Non-Proliferation Treaty that it refuses to join. Unless or until Israel comes clean and permits IAEA inspections of Dimona and its arsenals, as a result of joining either the NPT or some other international arrangement, it will lack the moral standing to make demands on Iran, much less to attack it. 'Nuclear opacity' is no longer an option.

The most sensible solution to the encroaching problem of nuclear proliferation in the Middle East is the establishment of a nuclear-weapons-free zone in the region – a recommendation of the 2010 NPT Review Conference. Although Israel, like Iran, publicly supports the proposal, it cannot be serious so long as it insists on hiding its own nuclear arsenal (nor can Iran be serious, of course, so long as it pursues nuclear weapons). Israel pretends to support non-proliferation measures, but refuses to be bound by the NPT because this would entail inspection of its nuclear facilities by the IAEA. (It is an IAEA member, but not subject to the inspections which would be insisted upon it were it a party to the NPT.) In consequence, its policy of 'nuclear opacity' can easily be seen through. There is no reassurance that its nuclear facilities are safe or that they do not pose occupational or environmental risks, and the constitutional position – who decides when to use them and pursuant to what rules – is hidden from the Israelis themselves and covered by a pervasive media black-out, the result of official censorship that goes unchallenged. It is by no means certain that the secret instructions for using them are confined to 'self-defence', as that concept exists in law. Vanunu claimed that Israel possessed nuclear artillery shells for use on the battlefield as well as thermonuclear devices on missiles aimed at other states (although obviously these allegations cannot be verified so long as Israel remains 'opaque'). Israel is readily perceived as hypocritical in urging the US to bomb Iran for attempting to obtain a weapon that it possesses itself.

Israel's best reason for 'nuclear opacity' has been its insecurity, born of the fact that it is still unrecognised by a majority of Arab nations and indeed by the majority of the fifty-two Muslim states, with some neighbouring political groups – Hamas and Hezbollah – formally committed to its extinction. This is intolerable – as the ICJ has held, 'Israel is entitled to exist, to be recognised and to security'[312] and it currently enjoys none of these rights. But Israel's refusal to talk truthfully is preventing progress on disarmament and certainly on the proposal for a regional nuclear-weapons-free zone. In 2008 the foreign ministers of the Arab countries threatened that unless Israel admitted its nuclear weapons and committed to destroying them, they would leave the NPT.[313] They are likely to renew this threat and will probably act upon it: Israel's 'opacity', as much as the truculence of North Korea, Pakistan and India, is contributing to the end of the treaty that once provided some containment of the national urge to acquire bombs.

Israel's policy has complicated and discouraged the most hopeful international step beyond the NPT, namely a Fissile Materials Cut-Off Treaty (FMCT), whereby all state parties would agree to end the production of fissile materials for nuclear weapons. The 'Big 5' themselves have ended such production, so this treaty would impact on India, Pakistan, North Korea and Israel, and on Iran and any other states contemplating 'break-out'. It is a throwback to the Baruch–Evatt plan, which would have placed control of fissionable materials in a UN agency. The idea for an FMCT was advanced by Bill Clinton and taken up by the UN General Assembly, and actually supported (after their 1998 tests) by India and Pakistan. But Netanyahu wrote to Clinton, 'We will never sign the Treaty, and do not delude yourself – no pressure will help. We will not sign the Treaty because we will not commit suicide.'[314] The treaty was not favoured by the Bush administration, but Obama revived the idea in his Prague speech and it is the logical precursor to establishing a nuclear-weapons-free zone in the Middle East. But it is a treaty that requires verification work by an international agency – inevitably the IAEA – and Israel will not permit inspections of the premises it uses to enrich uranium to weapons grade, or to produce plutonium.

One alternative would be for the Security Council to demand universal membership of the NPT, thereby putting pressure on North Korea, India, Pakistan and Israel – the four refuseniks – to join. Netanyahu's letter to Clinton makes clear that Israel will resist that pressure, no matter how important to the peace of the world. But Israel rarely thinks of what is good for others, and may not be the best judge of what may be good for itself. If war can be averted until after the mandated departure of Ahmadinejad (in mid-2013) and the electoral demise of Netanyahu, peace might be given a chance.

At a time when, in Barbara Tuchman's phrase, 'history is still smoking' and the ashes from the gas chambers are still warm, Israel's determination to keep its nuclear arsenal has become an understandable psychological security blanket for a nation whose right to exist is still denied by some Arab powers and most viciously in the founding charter of Hamas, which calls for genocide – the hunting down and killing of all Jews. Israel has 'come by its paranoia honestly' when mullahs like Rafsanjani crassly count the millions of Muslims who will be left standing after a 'nuclear exchange' with Iran which wipes out every person (including one million Arabs) in Israel's 20,000 square kilometres. To counter that threat, Israel has positioned itself for a devastating posthumous retaliation: five Dolphin class submarines, recently delivered from Germany, equipped with cruise missiles tipped with 200 kiloton nuclear warheads, stooging for months at a time off the coast of Iran, capable of delivering a second strike that will make Tehran (and other cities) look like Hiroshima.[315] If Iran were ever to obtain nuclear weapons and use them to wipe Israel from the pages of time, can there be any doubt about the contents of an equivalent 'letter of last resort' to these submarine commanders from Mr Netanyahu? Or indeed about their own instincts for retribution after their wives and children had just been incinerated? These consequences – unlikely but certainly not inconceivable over the next century – demand action now to ensure they could never come about. It must be the sort of action that results both in Iran never getting hold of nukes and in Israel eventually agreeing to destroy its stockpile. Otherwise, the war law rule against disproportionate reprisal will have no meaning in the vicious cycle of Middle East tit for tat, providing the ultimate illustration of Auden's point:

> I and the public know
> What all schoolchildren learn
> Those to whom evil is done
> Do evil in return.

The brains behind the bomb: Albert Einstein
and J. Robert Oppenheimer

PART III

THE LAW

CHAPTER 14

WAR LAW AND THE BOMB

The Court ... notes that nuclear weapons are explosive devices whose energy results from the fusion or fission of the atom. By its very nature, that process, in nuclear weapons as they exist today, releases not only immense quantities of heat and energy, but also powerful and prolonged radiation ... peculiar to nuclear weapons. These characteristics render the nuclear weapon potentially catastrophic. The destructive power of nuclear weapons cannot be contained in either space or time. They have the potential to destroy all civilisation and the entire ecosystem of the planet.

The radiation released by a nuclear explosion would affect health, agriculture, natural resources and demography over a very wide area. Further, the use of nuclear weapons would be a serious danger to future generations. Ionising radiation has the potential to damage the future environment, food and marine ecosystems, and to cause genetic defects and illness in future generations.

In consequence ... it is imperative for the Court to take account of the unique characteristics of nuclear weapons, and in particular their destructive capacity, their capacity to cause untold human suffering, and their ability to cause damage to generations to come.[316]

International Court of Justice *Nuclear Weapons* case

It is a remarkable – if unusually unremarked – feature of nuclear history that the development of the atomic bomb was unencumbered by any reference to the law of war – that collection of rules known as 'international humanitarian law' (IHL). Prisoners in German and British camps in World War II were generally treated with careful attention to Geneva standards, with Red Cross visits and rights in the officers' mess at Colditz. There were a few notable infractions (e.g. the killing, on Hitler's orders, of POWs who took part in 'the Great Escape') and they were punished severely at the

Nuremberg trials, as the many more Japanese atrocities against POWs were punished at the war crimes tribunals in Tokyo and elsewhere. Given this attention to war law, it is surprising that the development, dropping and subsequent stockpiling of nuclear bombs was accomplished without any reference to humanitarian standards.

This phenomenon continued into the twenty-first century – the former US Secretary of Defence Robert McNamara, for a long time the leading US nuclear policy maker, said in an interview towards the end of his life that he had never been briefed on the legal aspects of nuclear weapons, and the subject is not taught in the legion of military courses in the US today.[317] The Obama administration's 2010 Nuclear Posture Review was presented with reference to policy and security considerations, without reference to human rights or international law. It came as a surprise at the 2010 Review Conference of the NPT that IHL was even mentioned in the Action Plan and the reference was brief, merely noting the 'catastrophic humanitarian consequences' of deployment of any of the many thousands of nuclear warheads stockpiled in the world today and the consequent need for all states at all times to 'comply with applicable international law, including international humanitarian law'. Even that was an achievement, by the efforts of the Red Cross and the president of the Review Conference, Libran Cabactulan (Filipino ambassador to the UN), so it is a slim reed which deserves now to be grasped.

WAR LAW

All civilisations have fought wars according to rules designed to make them marginally less bloody. Humanitarian concerns may be detected in customs of the Greek and Roman armies, attributed to the wisdom of the gods, and later there was Christian chivalry (St Augustine forbade attacks on women and the wounded) and the influences of heraldic tradition on aggressive medieval city states. The first rule relevant to the bomb emerged in 1139 from the Second Lateran Council, forbidding the use of the crossbow in wars between Christians: it was an inhumanely deadly weapon for the Middle Ages, permitting no time for last rites, hence fit for use only against the infidel. Prohibitions against poison and plague – throwing infected corpses down civilian drinking wells – and against 'pillage' and 'plunder' of the houses or lives of persons not involved in the combat soon followed. Scholars such as Grotius and Vattel, who envisioned war law in the seventeenth and eighteenth century, were at pains to identify 'just' wars and to emphasise that the rules protected non-combatants, always subject to military exigency and to the policy requirements of rulers, for whom wars, like marriages, were necessary diplomatic activities. Nonetheless, the Christian soldiers of Europe were well aware of their legal duty to give 'quarter' to surrendered opponents, to protect the lives and property of civilians and to treat prisoners of war humanely. The war ordinances of Henry V's army forbade the rape of women and the desecration of churches. Shakespeare gives Henry a pedantic Welsh captain, Fluellen, who can state with confidence that the French atrocities are 'expressly against the laws of war'. All the armies in the fields of Marston Moor and Naseby, in the English civil war, had detailed ordinances, prescribing punishment (often death) for killing prisoners of war and harming civilians – Cromwell, on his way to fight ferociously at Drogheda, hanged two of his soldiers for stealing chickens. At his trial in 1649, Charles I was accused of war crimes, including the torture of prisoners and the deliberate burning of civilian houses.

The first modern set of law rules was compiled by Dr Francis Lieber in 1863 at the direction of Abraham Lincoln, concerned that his Northern Army should not commit brutalities that would disaffect from the Union those who had followed the Confederate flag. Lieber's code – *Instructions for the Government of Armies of the United States in the Field* – remains the basic source for IHL principles, supplemented by all the treaties – most importantly the Hague Conventions of 1899 and 1907, and the Geneva Conventions of 1949 and Protocols of 1977 – and the case law from Nuremberg onwards, including the 1996 ICJ decision on the bomb. This all goes into the mix of what is described as 'customary international law', accepted as binding by states (even if, as in the case of torture, many do not actually abide by it). There is a general organising principle, known for obscure reasons as 'the Martens Clause',[318] which acknowledges the duty of all belligerents to obey the rules of customary international law 'as they result from the usages established between civilised nations, from the laws of humanity and the requirements of the public conscience'.

It must be said that the first international conferences to develop
rules for the limitation of armaments – at St Petersburg (1868) and
The Hague (1899) – were motivated less by humanitarian concern
than by the soaring costs of new weapons, especially poison gases
and the newly invented exploding bullet, although the latter were
denounced at St Petersburg because they 'uselessly aggravated the
suffering of disabled men'. But here, for the first time, potential
belligerents met to consider 'the technical limits at which the
necessities of war ought to yield to the requirements of humanity'
and promised to maintain this balance 'in view of future improvements which science may effect in the armament of troops'. The
1899 conference ended in a convention which prohibited the use
of dum-dum bullets and asphyxiating gases, and laid down the
principle (confirmed at another peace conference in The Hague in
1907) that 'the right of belligerents to adopt means of injuring the
enemy is not unlimited'. But what, then, were the limits? Poison
and dum-dum bullets, certainly, and crossbows, but otherwise
'weapons calculated to cause unnecessary suffering'. But who was
to decide what suffering was 'necessary' for military purposes – a
state with its back against the wall, reaching for a weapon 'necessary' to save it from surrender? A belligerent with an intractable
and irresponsible enemy, needing a terrifying weapon to bring a
drawn-out conflict to an end? Did the end justify the means, as a
matter of military necessity, if the belligerent with the bomb had
right on its side, in the sense that it had not started the war, or was
fighting a barbaric enemy? Roosevelt and Churchill, at Hyde Park
in late 1944, considered that use of the A-bomb against Japan was
really necessary, and gave the Manhattan scientists a year to make
it. As war law then stood, were they wrong?

Just as the Hague rules – particularly relating to poison gas
– had been ignored in the First World War, so the 1923 Hague
rule against aerial bombing 'for the purpose of terrorising a civilian population' was ignored in the Second. It was subject to an
exception that legalised bombing 'when directed at a military
objective' – and most cities – Coventry, Dresden, Tokyo, Hiroshima,
Nagasaki – had military installations, munitions factories, naval
bases or war industries of some kind, around which the houses of
workers and their families, their schools, churches and hospitals,

were clustered. By the time it was dropped, international law had simply not caught up with the bomb, other than by generalities about measures that caused 'unnecessary' suffering. If Hiroshima were never to happen again, then an explicit rule against the use of nuclear weapons should have been a priority for the new United Nations. The time was ripe: the Nuremberg judgment of 30 September 1946 had created an international criminal law, applying it to the Nazi leaders as individuals, who could not escape either by way of diplomatic immunity or by claiming that they were following the orders of a superior. Hitherto, international law had only applied between states, and individual statesmen could not be punished if it was broken. Now, with the judgment at Nuremberg, and revelations after Hiroshima and Nagasaki of the horrors of radiation poisoning, it should have been made clear that the next leader to press the nuclear button, and his military and political administrators, would be liable to the gallows, or at least imprisonment for life.

But this was not the way anyone thought, or could think after the war. The most pressing post-Nuremberg preference at the United Nations was to criminalise any future holocausts – this was done in the 1948 Genocide Convention – and to issue at the same time the non-enforceable Universal Declaration of Human Rights. When it came to restating IHL, the 1949 Geneva Conventions carefully made no mention at all of the bomb, although this was the most notable example of an offensive weapon that nobody wished to see deployed. Common Article 3 (i.e. common to all the four conventions, relating to prisoners of war, civilians, the wounded on land and the wounded at sea) prohibited military actions of the following kinds:

> Wilful killing, torture or inhumane treatment, including biological experiments, wilfully causing great suffering or serious injury to body or health, and extensive destruction of property, not justified by military necessity and carried out unlawfully and wantonly.

This specifically included 'biological experiments' but not nuclear experiments, and although the description might be applied to some future Hiroshima, 'military necessity' and the need for the prosecution to prove 'wantonness' would provide arguable let-outs for future political and military leaders who might want to press the nuclear button. In March 1949, the date of the Geneva Conventions, nobody wanted to upset the Americans, who had the nuclear monopoly – least of all the Soviets, who were about to make it a duopoly.

There were, of course, some academic commentaries – international lawyers could not, like politicians and generals, ignore the greatest contemporary challenge to international law. Their doyen, Hersch Lauterpacht, updated the leading text on the subject in 1952, writing with awkward delicacy that 'there is room for consideration' as to whether 'the destruction and suffering entailed in the use of the A-bomb' might put it 'outside the principle of the law of nations as they result from the usages established among civilised peoples, from the laws of humanity and the dictates of public conscience'. There was not much – if any – wriggle room if these principles were to be rigorously applied, but the equivocating Cambridge academic found some in the fact that the bomb had not been outlawed by international agreement, and there could be cases where 'the laws of humanity' would not be relevant – he could only instance the case of reprisal for its use by an enemy (i.e. two wrongs make a right) or, more interestingly, where the enemy 'violates rules of the law of war on a scale so vast as to put himself altogether outside the orbit of considerations of humanity and compassion'. Lauterpacht was no doubt thinking of the Holocaust, but that was not actually a violation of the laws of war because the victims were not soldiers and had not been killed as a result of combat. His vacillation ('it is difficult to express a clear view') did international law a disservice, embedding itself in the approach to nuclear weapons which was followed in the 1996 opinion on the legality of their use by the ICJ.

TREATY LAW

Meanwhile, what prospect was there of international agreement? The Baruch plan was dead, but the peaceful uses of nuclear power, especially to provide electricity, were much touted. In 1953 Eisenhower made his famous 'Atoms for Peace' speech, warning of the 'awful arithmetic of the atomic bomb' (i.e. nuclear proliferation) but offering assistance to nuclear research for peaceful purposes and reactors to nations which supported a new streamlined body, the IAEA, which came into existence in 1956 for the purposes of encouraging the spread of peaceful nuclear technology. Many countries benefited, including India, Israel, Argentina and Brazil, which would later use the benefits in attempts (subsequently abandoned by the latter two nations) to build nuclear weapons. Also profiting were the US suppliers of nuclear technology – a budding, soon to be booming, military-industrial complex. By 1960, President Kennedy said he expected to see fifty nuclear powers by the end of his term of office, which he never lived to see. What he did see, and see through, was the Cuban missile crisis.

Kennedy's old speechwriter, Arthur Schlesinger Jnr, recalls those thirteen days as 'the most dangerous moment in all human history'. Never before had two contending powers possessed between them the technical capacity to destroy the planet. Had Kennedy been an exponent of the later Bush doctrine of 'preventive war', it may all have ended in tears.[319] There were exponents of nuclear war – notably Curtis LeMay, fire-bomber of Tokyo – but the Kennedys (Attorney General Robert being the sanest influence on the President) faced them down. Under another President, it would certainly have been war, although not initially a nuclear one: the US would have destroyed the missiles, and the Soviets would probably have attacked West Berlin in reprisal, and the mind boggles at what might have happened thereafter. Khrushchev's provocation was outrageous (the warheads he placed in Cuba, over 100 of them, were later admitted to be nuclear) but he folded after a deal that removed American missiles, aimed at Moscow, from Turkey. Khrushchev and Kennedy were rational men, as were most of their advisers. The Russians had no belief in God, so wanted to live as long as possible on earth and wanted their families to survive. The Kennedys, as Catholics, might hope their sins would be forgiven but had absorbed firm doctrinal teaching about the sanctity of life and their duty to avoid ending it prematurely. There were no abiding hatreds, no death marches, no kamikaze ideas, and no hope of reocculating a Twelfth Imam to complicate their decision. MAD (mutually assured destruction) had no need to work: sanity prevailed.

The aftershock was intense, and managed not only to have the 'hotline' installed between the White House and the Kremlin but to inspire treaties by which even the 'Big 5' powers as well as potential nuclear states promised to keep their bombs away from the Antarctic, the sea bed, the moon and other orbital bodies and outer space. Most importantly in 1968 there opened for signature the NPT, which came into effect, in record time, in 1970. It has been, ever since, and now although broken still is, the only legal protection against the kind of world that was lived in at the time of the Cuban missile crisis. All states in the world are members, except Israel, India, Pakistan and North Korea, the latter having withdrawn in 2003. It became the eventual solution that Dr Evatt could not broker between the Baruch and the Gromyko plans. The deal, as we saw in Chapter 11, between the 'Big 5' nuclear states (who happened to be the 'Big 5' permanent members with a veto in the Security Council, hence their abbreviation 'P5') and all the rest was that the 'Big 5' would not use their nuclear weapons against those states which, by becoming a party, had abjured ever possessing nuclear weapons. (This means, paradoxically, that the P5 can use conventional weapons against Iran, but not nuclear weapons so long as it remains an NPT party. Israel, which is not a party, may use its nuclear weapons if and when Article 51 and the 1996 ICJ decision entitles it to use them for self-defence.)

To provide the non-nuclear states with more confidence, the 'Big 5' promised to negotiate 'in good faith' to disarm, gradually and completely. The 'Big 5' also promised to assist the non-nuclear states to realise what the treaty called their 'inalienable right' to the benefits of nuclear energy. As explained in Chapter 11, this is the paradox of the NPT – it encourages the use of nuclear energy for peaceful purposes, which entails uranium enrichment at least to 3.5 per cent and in the nature of the science up to 20 per cent, and the development of a fuel cycle – exactly the 'inalienable right' that Iran currently claims. But this would put such states 'a few twists of the screwdriver' away from nuclear weapons capability, which requires uranium enrichment to 90 per cent. There are by now over twenty state parties to the NPT which have that capability, i.e. to go from using nuclear energy for peaceful purposes to using it in a bomb, within a few months (in Japan, it may only take a few weeks) of the decision to 'break out'. That is what North Korea did in 2003, withdrawing from the NPT in order to make the nukes that it developed in secret and tested in 2006.

The NPT served as a valuable mechanism for discouraging many states from opting to make or obtain nuclear armaments in the 1970s. Russia strong-armed its satellites and puppets to sign (although it then stationed its own nuclear warheads on their territory) and the US brought pressure to bear on its own dependants (Taiwan and South Korea in particular had to be pushed to join). The treaty set an international standard – a presumption against the bomb – which informed and influenced democratic choice: 'In powerful countries the decision to forgo nuclear weapons came after prolonged internal debate, for example as in Sweden, Switzerland, Belgium, Yugoslavia, Turkey, Egypt and Spain. Even in Australia there were once powerful voices in favour of nuclear weapons.' [320] The treaty was not universally popular: in the US it was opposed by Cold War warriors who feared it would put a brake on US superiority in the arms race; in Europe and elsewhere some anti-colonialists saw it as perpetrating great-power hegemony. The first shock to the new system – India's so-called 'peaceful test' of a nuclear device in 1974 – revealed its weakness (India had never become a party) but the response was to establish the Nuclear Suppliers Group – the cartel of suppliers of material which is either unique to the production of nuclear weapons or at least 'dual use', having peaceful applications as well. These were made subject to export controls in member countries and to agreements forbidding export to facilities where IAEA inspectors are not permitted entry. This all seemed to work satisfactorily enough, until the exposure of Dr Khan's 'one-stop nuclear shop' in 2003 revealed the ease with which export controls had been bent, by bribery and the use of diplomatic bags. But in the mid-1990s, when the ICJ decided the Nuclear Weapons Case, confidence that the NPT could stop other countries from making the bomb was at its height.

True it was that the Article VI obligation on the 'Big 5' to engage

in 'good faith' moves to disarm was subject to no supervision or
schedule, and had been simply abandoned in the Gadarene-like
rush for more and more weapons to array on Cold War borders.
George Kennan, the astute US diplomat, did not exaggerate when
he admitted, 'We have gone on piling weapon upon weapon,
missile upon missile, new levels of destructiveness on old ones.
We have done this helplessly, almost involuntarily, like the victims
of some sort of hypnotism, like men in a dream, like lemmings
headed for the sea.' These US and Soviet nuclear missiles – tens
of thousands of them, some on 'hair trigger alert' (some still are,
although the reaction time is fifteen rather than eight minutes) –
kept the world insecure, until the collapse of the Soviet Union at
the beginning of the 1990s. The chink of reason that had opened
with 'the walk in the woods' at Reykjavik in 1986 seemed, by the
time of the UN human rights conference in Vienna in 1993, to be
a flood of illumination: nukes could be reduced in number, and
might, just conceivably, be reduced to zero. Saddam's near-nuclear
arsenal was demolished after the international community pushed
back and punished his invasion of Kuwait, and a Comprehensive
Test Ban Treaty was on the way, promising to freeze nuclear
arsenals and allow only for their reduction. By preventing testing, new nuclear powers would find it difficult to emerge and
old powers would find it difficult to develop more sophisticated
nuclear devices. When the Clinton administration signed this
treaty, in 1996 – subject, of course, to congressional ratification –
it seemed that the bomb's time was almost up.

THE NUCLEAR WEAPONS CASE

All that was needed, to give it a final shove, was a decision by
the world's court, the ICJ, when it was asked by the General
Assembly in 1996 whether the threat or use of nuclear weap-
ons would be contrary to international law. This would not
retrospectively embarrass the ghosts of Truman, Roosevelt and
Churchill: they had not known the facts about radiation poison-
ing, and had not been bound by the principles of the post-war
Geneva Conventions and the Universal Declaration of Human
Rights. The Court could draw on the first protocol to the Geneva
Conventions, signed in 1977, which had reiterated the banning

of weapons causing superfluous injury or unnecessary suffering, and had added prohibitions on 'methods of warfare which are intended, or may be expected, to cause widespread, long-term and severe damage to the natural environment'.[321]

It is astonishing to record that nuclear weapons went for fifty years without legal challenge, despite the clearest prohibitions on precisely the kind of weapons they were – namely those which caused 'superfluous injury', 'unnecessary suffering' and 'severe damage to the natural environment', and which failed to discriminate in their lethal results between civilian and combatant. States, of course, could not be sued because they had immunity, and so, it was thought, did statesmen, until 1998 when Pinochet was arrested in London under the Torture Convention. No serious attempt had been made to raise the issue of the bomb's legality until the 1990s, other than in mock trials of Harry Truman, which no doubt had some educative value but failed to produce other than one-sided judgments, usually because they heard only one side.

There had been one case, in a Japanese district court in 1963, which applied IHL to declare the bombing of Hiroshima illegal: it was hailed unreservedly by 'ban the bombers' (although it did not much assist their case) and derisively dismissed ('*Japanese* judges – they would, wouldn't they?') by many who had not bothered to read it. In fact, the *Shimoda* decision was a careful assessment by experienced jurists, who concluded that IHL did apply to nuclear weapons – and that itself was half the legal battle. The second half was lost, at least by the Hiroshima victims who had been plaintiffs: their damages claim against the Japanese government, for concluding the agreement with the US which had extinguished their rights to sue, was dismissed on technical grounds. But this court did not rule that possession or use of the bomb was unlawful: its finding was only that the actual attack on Hiroshima was contrary to the 1923 Hague rules on aerial bombing of *undefended* cities. This factual basis for the court's limited finding was open to question: Hiroshima was certainly (as it accepted) an important military target, which was one objective of the bombing as well as terrorising civilians (in fact, the main objective was to terrorise the Emperor and military leaders into surrender). Hiroshima had anti-aircraft batteries – silent because an attack was unsuspected:

would the bombing have been legal had they been firing at the 'Enola Gay' to protect this acknowledged military target in a defended city? The court made no distinction between the bombing of Hiroshima and the bombing of Dresden or Coventry or Tokyo – perhaps in IHL there was none, but the number of 'blind aerial bombings' by both sides throughout the Second World War showed that this deviation (or deviate interpretation of the 1923 rules, devised at a time when pilots dropped bombs by hand from Sopwith Camel biplanes) was a matter of state practice so the actual *Shimoda* decision, although it applied IHL, was lacking in logic. There are now better arguments, based on the post-war Geneva Conventions and protocols and on the gradual rise of human rights jurisprudence, that would declare the dropping of thermonuclear bombs – infinitely more powerful than 'Little Boy' – to be a crime, anywhere and anytime.

Half a century on from Hiroshima, it seemed to many NGOs and most independent non-nuclear states to be time for a definitive opinion, from the world court. As far as the 'Big 5' nuclear powers were concerned, however, no time was a good time. 'A legal ruling would interfere with the disarmament process,' they chorused, although it was difficult to see how or why it could slow down a process that had come to a virtual stop anyway. Besides, the 'Big 5' had a built-in advantage in the ICJ, namely the right as the permanent Security Council members each to appoint its own judge. The judges are nominated by states because they have served states, often as diplomats or legal advisers, or academic consultants. Many are academics – professors of international law – who lack the more robust independence of lawyers who act in court against states or for defendants. Most of the judges on the ICJ in 1996 would not have presided over a criminal trial and would not have known a human right if they fell over it, but at least they had a degree of independence, because peer pressure (bad judgments attract academic criticism) keeps them relatively honest. Honest enough for the nuclear powers to fear the result. They had to face some impressive jurists – Professor Christopher Weeramantry, for example, from Ceylon, nominated by New Zealand because of his academic brilliance. Or Dr Shahabbudeen from Guyana and Professor Koroma from Sierra Leone, independent-minded individuals who would not be cowed by claims that the case would disrupt a snail's-pace disarmament process. These were the three judges who declared that the use of nuclear weapons was unlawful in all circumstances. The Japanese judge, Shigeru Oda, had served in the air force during the war and had trained, with evident lack of success, as a kamikaze pilot. He was the only judge who thought the question too 'political' to answer.

The problem with the world court was not so much the independence of its judges, but rather their jurisprudential courage. The court still has difficulty getting its judgments accepted, and although all members of the UN must be members of the court, disgracefully only sixty-five states have been prepared to take their chances by agreeing to be bound by the optional clause that enables them to be sued by other states without their consent. And the fifteen state-appointed judges (only fourteen sat in the *Nuclear Weapons* case) know the importance of sovereignty to the sovereign states that have appointed them: they have always worked on the *Lotus* principle, called after the case in which it was first enunciated, that if international law does not clearly stop a state from acting in a certain way, then it cannot be held liable for acting in that way. However, the ICJ exists to declare international law based 'on certain general and well-recognised principles, namely: elemental considerations of humanity, even more exacting in peace than in war, and every state's obligation not to allow knowingly its territory to be used for acts contrary to the rights of other states'.[322]

This simple approach was first adopted in the *Corfu Channel* case of 1949, when Albania was ordered to pay compensation for failing in its elemental humanitarian duty to notify foreign shipping of a minefield it had secretly laid in international waters. This finding of state responsibility for creating a hazard to human life had been relied upon by Australia in its attempt to stop France from conducting atmospheric nuclear tests in the Pacific (the *Nuclear Tests* case). The question was eminently justiciable, but nine of the ICJ's fifteen judges in the case naively (or perhaps cravenly) found an excuse not to decide it: since France announced that its 1974 series of atmospheric tests was the last it would hold, 'the claim of Australia no longer has any object' and thus did not need to be adjudicated.[323] This reasoning was disingenuous: the case was of crucial and continuing importance, since atmospheric testing by other countries continued, and France was soon to dishonour the spirit of its undertaking by further testing in the Pacific, albeit underground, and in 1985 by committing an act of terrorism, blowing up in a New Zealand harbour a Greenpeace boat (the *Rainbow Warrior*) that was drawing attention to its perfidy.

The ICJ displayed the same jurisprudential funk in the face of nuclear *realpolitik* two decades later when called upon by the World Health Organization (WHO) to decide the case of the *Legality of the Threat or Use of Nuclear Weapons in Armed Conflict*. As a UN body, the WHO has the standing to request an advisory opinion on any question which arises 'within the scope of its activities'. In a piece of breathtakingly specious reasoning, the ICJ decided that since 'whether nuclear weapons are used legally or illegally their effects on health would be the same',[324] the issue was outside the scope of the WHO's activities! As one of three dissenting judges observed, noting the evidence of the health and environmental devastation wrought by the bombing of Hiroshima and Nagasaki, 'to hold as the court has done that these matters do not lie within the competence or scope of activities of the WHO borders on the unreal and smacks of cynicism, and the law is not cynical'.[325] So it was to fourteen, hopefully uncynical, jurists that the General Assembly put the question:

Is the threat or use of nuclear weapons *in any circumstances* permitted under international law? [emphasis added]

This time, the court could not wriggle out of giving an answer – it was a straightforward question of applying international law to a threat to drop, or actually dropping, nuclear bombs. It did not relate, however, to the right of states to build them in the first place, let alone acquire the capacity to build them by enriching uranium, or whether the possession by states, or certain states, could be unlawful. In the proliferating climate of 2012, these are the more urgent questions. In 1996, there had yet to be a nuclear squeak from Pakistan or North Korea, Israel was 'opaque' and India had only deviated slightly. But the question that was asked by the General Assembly was at once too broad (almost any circumstance can be conceivable, however unrealistic) and too narrow (it referred to nukes only in or in the run-up to war, and not their possession or testing or accidental explosion in a time of peace) to produce an answer which would help rid the world of bombs.

There was a risk in taking the case to the ICJ: it might decide that nuclear weapons, unmentioned by name in any of the conventions, were unique and outside the scope of IHL. This danger did not eventuate: counsel appearing for the 'Big 5' did not even take the point. The court itself made clear that IHL applies to all forms of warfare and to all kinds of weapons – those of the past, those of the present and those of the future. A few judges quarrelled with the question, but most thought it capable of an answer. The tactic of the main nuclear states – the US, UK and France – was to ask the court to use its discretion *not* to give an answer, because to do so would interfere with the political rights of states to address the question by reference to their national interests, and any opinion would have 'the potential of undermining progress already made on this sensitive subject'. It was understandable that states with nuclear weapons would want to stand above the law, but quite why this submission was endorsed by states like Finland, the Netherlands and Germany is not clear. Australia confusingly had its Solicitor General claim that any decision by the court would damage the disarmament process so the case should not be heard, but then its Attorney General (Gareth Evans) rose to make a compelling case that all nuclear weapons were illegal, a submission that, if endorsed by the court, could hardly have damaged the process of eradicating them. At any rate the majority opinion, and most of the minority judges, firmly rejected this invitation for the ICJ to demonstrate a lack of confidence in international justice.

Human rights were not much mentioned in the arguments, because they did not much matter in 1996. The ICJ dealt very briefly with the only human rights points that were advanced

– that the use of the bomb would be contrary to the right not to be arbitrarily deprived of life, and contrary to the Genocide Convention. Significantly, the court accepted that human rights law applied in war as well as peace, but said that the right to life in war depended on IHL, and that whether a bomb drop would infringe the law against genocide would depend on the circumstances. In the latter case it was obviously correct (dropping a bomb with the intent to obliterate Israel, however, would be genocide), but in the former view it was seriously mistaken. IHL (war law) is a subject which pertains to conduct in war, or in going to war. In peacetime, the right not be arbitrarily deprived of life does not overlap with IHL because the latter has, by definition, no application at all. Nuclear weapons can be 'used' in peace – if they go off accidentally or are acquired by terrorist groups (the court did not think of this). And it was not asked by the question framed by the General Assembly to think about the lawfulness of making nukes, or possessing them, or about criminal responsibility for their use. The Hague tribunals were only just getting underway to punish perpetrators of international crimes in the Balkans and Rwanda, and nobody of any importance had been arrested, let alone convicted – and the ICC did not yet exist. It is arguable (see Chapter 16) that as both human rights law and humanitarian law stand today, they incriminate those who order the bomb to be used, or order new bombs to be made.

The ICJ accepted that nuclear weapons were unique, not just in causing damage of greater degree than conventional bombs, but by the peculiar phenomenon of radiation:

> The destructive power of nuclear weapons cannot be contained in either space or time. They have the potential to destroy all civilisation and the entire ecosystem of the planet ... Ionising radiation has the potential to damage the future environment, food and marine ecosystems, and to cause genetic defects and illnesses in future generations.

When the court came to consider treaties relating to the environment, it was strong on rhetoric ('the use of nuclear weapons would constitute a catastrophe for the environment ... the living space, the quality of life, the very health of human beings, including generations unborn') but weak on application. Treaties were all very well in their way, it conceded, but they could not diminish the sovereign power inherently belonging to every state to go to war in self-defence, although the decision to use nuclear weapons in pursuit of that right should 'take into account' their environmental effect. Here the court was being ingenuous: if you are wiping out your enemies, you don't stop to worry about the fate of their plants.

So could the threat or use of nuclear weapons, inevitably and invariably and indiscriminately destructive of civilian life, with radiation effects going on through generations, ever be lawful? Obviously not, as the court was *almost* prepared to concede:

> The principles and rules of law applicable in armed conflict – at the heart of which is the overriding consideration of humanity – make the conduct of armed hostilities subject to a number of strict requirements. Thus, methods and means of warfare, which would preclude any distinction between civilian and military targets, or which would result in unnecessary suffering to combatants, are prohibited. In view of the unique characteristics of nuclear weapons, to which the Court has referred above, the use of such weapons in fact seems scarcely reconcilable with respect for such requirements.[326]

Dropping a nuclear bomb is not 'scarcely' reconcilable: this weasel word obscured the fact that it can never be reconcilable with any of the following 'intransgressible principles of international customary law' (as the court described those IHL rules):

> *The Rule of Controllability:* A belligerent cannot use a weapon with effects that are beyond its control, because that makes it impossible to judge whether the use is necessary or proportionate. The effects of nuclear weapons are in this sense unknowable – ionising radiation may linger for half a century, with consequences spread over hundreds of square miles. Even a short nuclear exchange in a discrete region – e.g. between India and Pakistan – could have a devastating impact on the world climate, causing a global famine that could kill one billion people.[327] And which way will the wind

blow the mushroom cloud? Over who knows how many states, uninvolved in the war, and their people.

The Rule of Discrimination: It is impermissible to use a weapon that cannot discriminate in its impact between military targets and combatants on the one hand and civilians, hospitals, churches and schools on the other. The latter do not merely suffer 'collateral damage' from any primary military targeting of a nuclear bomb: its effects cannot distinguish between them.

The Rule against Unnecessary Suffering: The evidence from Hiroshima proves, beyond reasonable doubt, that this rule is violated – and now we have bombs that are many times the force of 'Little Boy'. The Soviet Union at one point in the 1960s produced a 50 megaton bomb, 5,000 times the force that eviscerated Hiroshima. As the ICJ accepted, the destructive power of nuclear weapons cannot be contained in either space or time. They have a capacity to cause untold human suffering, and the ability to cause damage to generations to come.

The Rule of Proportionality: This applies to the use of any weapons whose potential impact on civilians, their property and cultural objects and on the environment outweighs the anticipated military advantage. This is always, objectively, the case with nuclear weapons, however much a particular government may think its own culture more worthy, and more worth preserving, than that of the enemy.

These rules would be breached in any use of nuclear weapons in wartime, quite apart from the effects on the environment and on the likelihood of escalation. So why did the court not give the simple answer that under no circumstances could it be lawful to drop the bomb?

It chose instead to temporise, pointing out that other banned weapons are singled out by name for prohibition, but nuclear weapons have been the invisible elephant in the conference room at all treaty drafting sessions. Moreover, states had ratified a number of conventions under which they promised not to use nuclear weapons in certain circumstances or places – in outer space, or the Antarctic – which implied that there were circumstances or places in which they *could* use them, at least for the Article 51 right to self-defence against an armed attack threatening a vital security interest. General Assembly resolutions over the years had condemned the use of nuclear weapons, but they had been passed with the dissent of the 'Big 5' and their friends, so they could not really count as strong evidence of civilisation's renunciation of nuclear weapons. Whilst the effect of a nuclear weapon – uncontrollable in space and time, unable to draw distinctions between civilians and combatants – would 'generally' be inconsistent with the rules of war law, the court was struck by hypotheticals dangled by advocates from the 'Big 5' – for example, 'a low yield nuclear weapon against warships on the High Seas or troops in sparsely populated areas' might not cause too many civilian casualties.

This somewhat fantastical scenario was presented by the UK's Attorney General, and swallowed by most of the judges. It is in fact inconceivable that first use against ships and troops in these circumstances would not provoke the victim state to reply in kind with a nuclear reprisal, with inevitable damage to the atmosphere, the oceans and the 'sparsely populated' area (which would henceforth be entirely unpopulated). Escalation would be inevitable, no matter how 'small' or 'clean' or 'low yield' or 'tactical' the first weapon to be used, because all emit lethal radiation. The US advocates urged the court to accept the scientific precision with which they could target those weapons on solely military objectives, but their 'precision targeting' came adrift a few years later in Kosovo (where their bombing from a height of 15,000 feet killed over 1,000 people), in numerous 'friendly fire' incidents and in drone killings of hundreds of civilians and innocent bystanders. Yet this was the principal US submission to the court, which should have foundered on the simple fact that if these 'low yield' nukes yielded so little, that result could be sufficiently achieved by conventional weapons, so they were unnecessary and disproportionate. The danger of finding this 'low nuclear yield' scenario compliant with war law is that it encourages the stockpiling of 'dirty bombs' which might well be used by terrorist states and their proxies to spread panic and radiation. It was a far-fetched submission: scientists say that a low-yield tactical nuclear weapon could not have a 'clean' use but the court seemed to accept the British position that some nukes might behave so well and so discriminately that their use could not be condemned.

Worse was to come. With a metaphorical sigh, the court said that 'it cannot lose sight of the fundamental right of every state to survival', and hence its 'right to resort to self-defence, in accordance with Article 51 of the Charter' might permit it to use the bomb. So, in view of what they heavily emphasised was 'the current state of international law', the majority judges (as there were seven who disagreed for various reasons, the case was decided by the casting vote of the President) gratefully clung to the literal question – they could not decide conclusively that use of a nuclear device would be contrary to international law in *all* circumstances.

These findings were incorporated into a carefully calibrated answer to the General Assembly's question. First the good news:

> The threat or use of nuclear weapons would generally be contrary to the rules of law applicable in armed conflicts and in particular the principles and rules of humanitarian law.

That sounded clear and sensible and correct, but watch out for that weasel word 'generally'. It presaged a proviso:

> The Court cannot conclude definitively whether the threat or use of nuclear weapons would be lawful in the extreme circumstances of self-defence, in which the very survival of a state would be at stake.

At this final hurdle, the judgment fell flat on its face. How could the survival of a state – a pariah state, or a failed state, or just a crummy little state like, say, North Korea, ever justify it nuking its enemies? What the court is saying is that international law might permit states to use their nuclear bombs if their backs were against the wall, even if that has come about merely by the enemy's use of conventional weapons. To take one topical example, if in a few years time Iran were attacked by Israeli bombers, and decided – the decision as to whether the survival of its theocratic state would be the theocratic state's own decision – to use a nuclear weapon in response, that might be lawful, according to this very curious paragraph which none of the seven judges who signed up to it thought was satisfactory, but they could not think of any other way to produce a decision that would satisfy everybody, or at least not dissatisfy the 'Big 5'. They were stuck in an international law system where the rights of states – and of five states more than others – were uppermost.

Only two years later, international human rights law struck a blow against this outmoded idea that states could get away with murder – by arresting General Pinochet, whose state immunity could not prevail against the duty to hunt down torturers. It was surprising that none of the judges thought to point out that dropping a nuclear bomb would inevitably inflict torture in the sense of 'cruel and inhumane treatment or punishment' on the civilian population exposed for years afterwards to its ionising radiation, its devastating effects of disease and disfigurement a form of collective punishment for whatever the government had done to deserve a nuclear reprisal. Had the case been heard a few years later, that argument would certainly have been made.

No state has the 'right' to use an illegal weapon to destroy hundreds of thousands of civilian lives, albeit enemy lives, to save its own sovereignty. This was expressly rejected as a defence in the Nuremberg trial of Krupp and other Nazi industrialists who claimed that war law could be ignored when a nation was *in extremis*:

> It is an essence of war that one or the other side must lose … the rules and customs of warfare are designed specifically for all phases of war. They comprise the law for such emergency. To claim that they can be wantonly – and at the sole discretion of any one belligerent – disregarded when he considers his own situation to be critical, means nothing more or less than to abrogate the laws and customs of war entirely.[328]

It never occurred to the judges to envision the German head of state in his bunker, ordering nuclear bombs to be dropped on Moscow and London in a last-ditch effort to avoid surrender. Having no nukes, Hitler ordered the firing of V-bombs at London

– unlawfully, because these rockets were not aimed at military targets. He would have had so much more Wagnerian pleasure had he been able to deliver nuclear bombs instead of 'doodlebugs'. Similarly, it cannot be doubted that Japan's brutal leaders would have authorised nuclear bomb drops on Russian and American invaders – fanatic nationalists, like all fanatics, would do anything to avoid surrender. It is ironic that by leaving an opening for states to use nuclear weapons in self-defence, the ICJ has legitimised their use at the very moment in a war when heads of state are most desperate, most irrational and most vengeful.

The problem with this 1996 decision is that it is simply wrong in law, which gives no 'ultimate' right to a state to preserve itself at the expense of the rights of other states and the rights to life of millions of citizens. If this is some ultra-right, a *grundnorm* of statehood, then you would expect each state to preserve it jealously – yet the great majority of states, in ratifying the NPT, promised not to acquire such weapons for use in any circumstances. The only states which are free to use nukes to save themselves from surrender are India, Pakistan, Israel and North Korea – ironically, the very states likely to prove most dangerous when cornered.

There is no basis for the notion that states have a 'right to exist' which entitles them to contravene the law by firing nukes when their governments feel seriously threatened. Demystify the concept of 'the state' and into focus comes the government of that state, invariably confusing its own demise with that of the nation. Dictators and absolute monarchs do this all the time ('*L'état, c'est moi*'). Ironically, had Colonel Gaddafi followed through on his nuclear purchases, and not given them up in 2003, he would by 2011 have had nuclear bombs which he would not have scrupled to drop on Bengazi, or even on Brussels, to save his regime from extinction (a message that will not have been lost on other dictators). To suggest that governments, confusing themselves with the state they govern, have some natural right to lash out with nukes to prevent their own overthrow is a serious mistake. Even if the ruling is read to refer to the survival of a state *qua* state, this would have provided a right for Milošević, say, to use nukes to prevent the break-up of Yugoslavia. Yet that unhappy amalgam of disparate regions had no 'right' to exist, any more than dissolved states like the USSR or East Germany, or some of the artificial states of Africa, their borders drawn at places where the English explorer met the German missionary. The last state to have its very existence threatened was Kuwait, invaded by Saddam Hussein in 1990. The international community came to Kuwait's aid not because it had a right to exist, but because the invasion was a breach of international law which challenged peace and security.

The right of a state to self-defence under Article 51 of the UN Charter is a wholly unsatisfactory basis on which to legitimise the use of nuclear weapons. The fundamental charter obligation on member states is to refrain from the 'threat or use of force against the territorial integrity or political independence of any state' (Article 2(4)). The Security Council may decide, under Chapter VII, to authorise intervention in the interests of international peace and security, and there is by now a recognised role for 'humanitarian intervention' to save civilian lives, but otherwise the only basis is the Article 51 'right of individual or collective self-defence if an armed attack occurs' against a member state. As will be explained in the next chapter, in customary international law self-defence has clear limits. Since it is grounded in necessity, the counter-attack must be solely and immediately designed to remove the threat, and must remain proportionate to that objective.

Force may be used to intercept an attack, but not to pre-empt an attack that is merely possible. It is obviously disproportionate to permit a state to launch a nuclear war when it has suffered some conventional attack, and even a nuclear attack which wipes out one of its cities could not justify a nuclear response which wipes out enemy cities. The notion of preventive self-defence stretches the *Caroline* doctrine (see next chapter) and dangerously expands the power of states to go to war whenever they feel threatened, however lacking in proof of real danger – the US, for example, is prone to leap before it looks closely, its attack on Iraq in 2003 being a prime example. If it were ever to confess to killing Iranian nuclear scientists, Israel would claim that it was justified by preventive self-defence to delay Iran building the bomb – a claim that would not stand up in any court concerned to apply the proportionality test or the proximity test.

The 'right of state survival' relied upon by the ICJ for legitimating last-resort use of nukes reminded some continental lawyers of the old German proverb 'necessity in war overrules the manner of warfare' ('*Kriegsraison geht vor Kriegsmanier*'). This might have suited Clausewitz and Bismarck, but has no place in any modern army. Few political leaders, faced with a choice between obeying international law or being defeated, would elect the honourable course: giving them an option to violate the law in order to avoid defeat is to accept that 'necessity knows no law' – and 'military necessity' reduces simply to the need to win. There must be a balance, objectively assessed, and the concept of proportionality provides it, by determining whether indiscriminate and arbitrary loss of civilian life will be caused by the weapon rather than by the circumstance of its use. The mistake made by the World Court in 1996 was to fashion an opinion meant to be all things to all people: to acknowledge that the use of the bomb was 'generally' unlawful, but that particular circumstances (indefinable ahead of time) that involved 'extreme self-defence' might permit its use. So states (at least if they left the NPT) might still make and possess the bomb without limit, but were restrained in threatening and using it to extreme situations where justification would depend on the facts and international law was not yet clear. In other words, on the very question it was asked, namely:

Is the threat or use of nuclear weapons in any circumstances permitted under international law?

the Court was giving an answer known to international lawyers (in Latin, of course) as a '*non liquet*' – i.e. 'we can't say because the law at this point in time is uncertain'. The crucial question, to be addressed in Chapter 16, is whether the law is now certain.

The ascertainment of the international law rule today would be based on facts that are very different to those presented to the court in 1996, a time of post-Cold War optimism about the effectiveness of the NPT (which had just been extended indefinitely), and the likely introduction of the CTBT. It was the year when the Canberra Commission – a collection of household names from the four corners of the world – reported that 'this uniquely favourable moment should be seized to eliminate the idea of weapons which, alone, can destroy all life on earth'.[329] The report was premised on what the commission thought was a realistic possibility of eliminating nuclear weapons: it wanted a start made by taking nuclear forces off alert and removing warheads from delivery vehicles, so as to reduce the risk of accidental or mistaken launch. Sixteen years later, these relevant steps have not been achieved (although the 'hair trigger' time to decide whether a threat is real and requires retaliation has been increased from eight to fifteen minutes). But what the Canberra Commission experts did see clearly – and was largely overlooked by the ICJ – was that 'the possession of nuclear weapons by any state is a constant stimulus to other states to acquire them'[330] and thus serves to diminish the security of all states. It pointed out that the more states that possess a nuke, the greater the danger one will explode as a result of accident or inadvertence by armed forces less capable and experienced than those of the 'Big 5', and the greater the danger of diversion to terrorists. That is certainly the position in 2012, where four countries stand outside the NPT and possess over 500 nuclear weapons between them, and Iran's footsteps towards nuclear empowerment are being followed by other countries. The comfort zone of 1996, when judges could actually conceive of nuclear powers (in some cases, their own country) using nukes in a 'humane' and discriminating fashion against warships and desert encampments, is long gone. In 2012, the Cold War has been replaced by local hot wars and the prospect of even hotter ones, in which any nuke to hand is likely to be launched, not so much by accident or mistake, but from visceral race enmity or religious hatred. The presence of nukes in so many unreliable and shaking hands means that a nuclear catastrophe, if not inevitable, is sufficiently foreseeable to make possession of the weapon by any state unlawful, because there is a customary rule of international law against first use, and any second or third use would be a disproportionate reprisal.

As if to salve its conscience, the ICJ threw into its opinion an unrequested but very valuable interpretation of Article VI of the

NPT, by which each party 'undertakes to pursue negotiations in good faith' towards 'a treaty on general and complete disarmament under strict and effective international control'. This was not a 'mere obligation', the court said, but a *legal* obligation to achieve a precise result – and the parties should get on with it. Although START treaties and other agreements have reduced nuclear warheads from 40,000 at the time of the ICJ decision to 19,000 in 2012, a treaty that requires demolition of all nukes, and makes it a crime to help build any more, is very far off. According to Global Zero, one of the best NGOs in the anti-nuclear business, the earliest practical date for a nuclear-free world is 2030. President Obama, in his Prague speech, feared that his 'ultimate goal' may not happen in his lifetime, and Hillary Clinton, perhaps in jest, spoke of moving 'toward our goal of a world someday *in some century* free of nuclear weapons'.[331]

But what has happened to this great judgment, the *Legality of the Threat or Use of Nuclear Weapons* case, this courtroom cop-out which tried to satisfy everyone? Surprisingly, at first it did, with anti-nuclear states and campaigners pleased with its ruling that the 'elementary considerations of humanity' had produced 'intransgressible principles of international customary law' which meant that the bomb was 'generally' prohibited. Nuclear weapon states – the 'Big 5' plus four – were pleased that the use of bombs was not outlawed in all circumstances and US military manuals currently give the impression that the court had decided that use of nuclear weapons is permitted.[332] It follows that possession of the bomb could not be unlawful because its use in legitimate circumstances could not be excluded. So the nuclear weapons states proceeded to plan the modernisation of their stockpiles, whilst other states saw no legal reason not to proliferate. However, like some untested and defective bomb, the judgment itself was a fizzer: it produced no immediate impetus for disarmament, and failed to persuade the US Senate that it should ratify the CTBT, which it rejected in 1999 and still rejects (President Obama did not dare to put it back before Congress in his first term). Proliferation continued, courtesy of A.Q. Khan, who seemed to have committed no offence (other than theft of URENCO's copyright) by organising Pakistan's first test, in 1998, or by supplying Iran, North Korea and Libya with the designs and the techniques for making their own nukes – a supply which restarted shortly after the judgment was delivered. There was only one comfort that could sensibly be taken from it. The court made very clear that the red line of 'intransgressible' international law was moving with the needs of humanity and the dictates of public conscience. Its opinion in the case was provisional and the rules were not set in aspic: they were based on 'the current state' of international law, a dynamic and developing doctrine. The president, Judge Bedjaoui, who gave the casting vote (the court was deadlocked 7:7) in his separate judgment detected 'a very advanced process of change' in the law, 'a current trend' towards imposing an absolute ban. The old rule was dead but the new rule had not yet crystallised. The court left the question hanging: in 1996 it was incapable of answer, but in 2012, or thereafter, might an answer be forthcoming?

President Netanyahu at the UN, September 2012,
with an aid for slow learners.

CHAPTER 15

CAN ISRAEL ATTACK IRAN? THE IGNOBLE ART OF SELF-DEFENCE

THE 'CAROLINE' TEST

It is an example of the surreal quality of international law that this – its crunch question in 2013 – must be resolved by a rule resulting from the fate of a paddle boat which was sent crashing over Niagara Falls by British soldiers in 1837. It is through correspondence over the *Caroline* incident, between the US Secretary of State Daniel Webster and the British Foreign Secretary Lord Ashburton, that the limits of what is termed 'anticipatory self defence' were settled, i.e. the extent of a nation's right to strike before it is struck at. Bizarrely, an attack on a slow boat on a calm lake 175 years ago produced the definition of the law which must now be applied to decide the legality of Israel's threats to bomb Iran's nuclear facilities (and, ironically, of Iran's right to prevent such an attack by bombing Israel first). Webster's language, which elicited a British apology, has been set in the stone of legal precedent.

At the time, the US and UK were at peace, but some Canadians rebelled against British rule and were supplied with guns and equipment by American supporters, using the USS *Caroline* to ferry them to rebels encamped on the British side of the lake. The British regarded these rebels as terrorists and had their troops seize the boat in an American port, killing two US nationals. They set the ship on fire, fixed its steering and sent it over the falls. The US protested against this attack, Britain claimed its 'inherent right' to self-defence, and an acrimonious correspondence ensued, in the course of which Britain accepted Webster's formulation of the principle that states claiming this right must 'show a necessity of self-defence, leaving no choice of means, and no moment for deliberation'. Moreover, there must be 'nothing unreasonable or excessive, since the act, justified by the necessity of self-defence, must be limited by that necessity, and kept clearly within it'.[333]

The *Caroline* case was endorsed as a correct statement of the law of self-defence by the court at Nuremberg[334] – an iconic precedent which confounds those lawyers who claim that there is no right to 'anticipatory' self-defence at all (a state must wait until it is attacked) and those 'Bush lawyers' who claim that, on the contrary, there is a right, at least for the US, to attack whomsoever it thinks might one day want to attack Americans (this they call 'preventive' or 'pre-emptive' self-defence). Webster's language is reasonably clear, requiring that the threat be 'imminent' – likely to happen very soon – and that the response to it be both necessary and reasonably proportionate. It enables sensible distinctions to be made: for example, the US was not justified, under the *Caroline* test, to conduct a 'self-defence' reprisal bombing of Tripoli in 1986, ten days after a bomb in a Berlin nightclub had killed a US soldier – this was disproportionate, further terrorist incidents were not 'imminent', the information was dubious and the attack was an exercise in revenge that did not 'defend' America. On the other hand, the *Caroline* test under Article 51 justified the attack on Afghanistan after 9/11 – the Taliban government was harbouring Al Qaeda, so the US was entitled to bomb bin Laden's training camps and his terrorist infrastructure to try to capture the criminals and remove the danger of another terrorist atrocity.

The test calls for a restraint that Israel and the US are reluctant to show: force may be used to pre-empt an incipient attack, but not one that is possible at some time in the future. 'Anticipatory self-defence' under the *Caroline* precedent means that the US would have been entitled to sink the Japanese fleet the moment it set sail for Pearl Harbor, but not to demolish it whilst it was in port merely on the grounds that it had the capacity to carry out such an attack, even if it was training, or war-gaming, for just such an event. As Yoram Dinstein, the distinguished Israeli academic, puts it,

the crux of the issue is not who fired the first shot but who embarked on an apparently irreversible course of action, thereby crossing the legal Rubicon. The casting of the die, rather than the actual opening of fire, is what starts the armed attack. It would be absurd to require the defending State to sustain and absorb a devastating (perhaps a fatal) blow, only to prove an immaculate conception of self-defence.[335]

Franklin Roosevelt put it in a homely way in his 'fireside chat' to the nation on 11 September 1941 before Pearl Harbor, explaining why he had ordered the US Navy, on convoy protection duty in the Atlantic, to open fire if they spotted German ships or U-boats: 'When you see a rattlesnake poised to strike, you do not wait until he has struck before you crush him.'

This is the common-sense position that aims to restrict the inevitable cruelty that follows from any use of modern military force. The UN Charter – the bedrock of international law – sets down the fundamental principle in Article 2(4):

All Members shall refrain in their international relations from the threat or use of force against the territorial integrity or political independence of any state, or in any other manner inconsistent with the purposes of the United Nations.

This basic rule admits of three exceptions. Principally, states *can* use force with the approval of the Security Council, under Chapter VII of the charter, whereby the council may determine the existence of a threat to or breach of the peace, or an act of aggression, and may, if it thinks that other measures (such as sanctions) are inadequate, use or authorise such force as may be necessary to maintain peace and security. (A recent example is provided by its authorisation to NATO to use 'all necessary means' to protect civilians in Libya from the Gaddafi regime's threats to massacre them.) The Security Council, of course, is often a fractured body, with a veto bestowed on the 'Big 5', two of whom (Russia and China) are reluctant to encroach on state sovereignty, especially the sovereignty of states with which they are in alliance (for this reason they have prevented UN intervention in Syria), and they would be likely to veto any attack on Iran, even if it acquired the bomb, unless there was a real likelihood that it would drop it on

Israel. This is not an unreasonable position so long as it is unlawful for Iran to possess nuclear weapons, but it is at odds with
the promises of Presidents Bush and Obama (and potentially,
Romney), who have all pledged that the US will stop Iran from
acquiring the bomb.

The second way in which an armed attack might be lawful
would be in self-defence. Article 51 of the charter declares:

> Nothing in the present Charter shall impair the inherent right
> of individual or collective self-defence if an armed attack occurs
> against a member of the United Nations.

Purists, reading Article 51 literally, exclude the *Caroline* principle
of 'anticipatory' self-defence entirely and argue that the right
arises only 'if an armed attack occurs'. This is the plain meaning
of Article 51, and reflects the over-optimistic view of delegates
in the drafting commission back in 1945, who assumed that in
their brave new UN world the Security Council could be trusted
to deal collegially with incipient threats to the peace. There is
no doubt, however, that the *Caroline* principle already existed in
customary international law, and had become part of the 'inherent right' of self-defence: it reflects the common-sense position
that a state must be entitled to nip military or terrorist attacks in
the bud – at least, once the budding process is underway.

There is a more controversial exception, based on human
rights law, which provides for 'humanitarian intervention' to
save lives threatened by a crime against humanity. The best
example is provided by NATO's bombing of Kosovo in 1999 to
prevent 'ethnic cleansing' by the Serbs under Milošević. It was
not authorised by the Security Council but was not condemned
either (a Russian motion to deplore it was heavily defeated) and
it served, at least to the satisfaction of the non-Serbian majority
of Kosovars, to save lives and liberty – even though US bombing
from 15,000 feet took hundreds of their lives. Another example is
provided by the 'safe havens' declared by NATO in Iraq to protect
the Kurds from Saddam's vengeance after the first Gulf War. If the
acquisition of a nuclear bomb is a crime against humanity (as the
next chapter of this book will contend), then there may be a legal

justification for an attack on Iran's nuclear facilities by a US-led coalition, but only if there is proof positive that it has constructed a nuclear weapon. But on the law declared by the 1996 ICJ decision, mistaken and now outdated, acquiring the bomb cannot amount to a crime against humanity, simply because it is not a crime. So long as Iran (like North Korea) leaves the NPT, and thus sheds its duty not to proliferate, the law as declared in 1996 would not stop it from building a bomb, unless it did so intending to drop it on Israel. Then the right of humanitarian intervention would arise (at much the same time as the *Caroline* right of anticipatory self-defence would become available to Israel and its allies) and at a time by which the Security Council would have a duty to act under Chapter VII to preserve international peace and security.

'OPERATION OPERA': OSIRAK, 1981

For most international lawyers, the relevant tipping point at which Israel or its ally America may lawfully bomb Iranian nuclear institutions is to be determined by the *Caroline* test. That was the main basis upon which the Security Council unanimously condemned Israel for 'Operation Opera' in 1981, its strike by eight F-16 jets on Iraq's French-supplied Osirak research reactor at Tuwaitha, just 25 kilometres from Baghdad. This reactor was not operational at the time, and was not hidden. Iraq was an NPT member, and the reactor would have come under the IAEA's most intrusive full-time inspection regime, so any furtive plutonium production would have been impossible.[336] The Israeli attack killed ten Iraqi soldiers and a French civilian – casualties that must have been foreseen. It was inexcusable, and Israel's excuse that it was 'exercising its inherent and natural right of self-defence as understood in general international law' was nonsense. It was decisively rejected by all members of the Security Council, many of them by reference to the *Caroline* principle. (Jeanne Kirkpatrick, Reagan's UN ambassador, pointed out that it failed the 'necessity' test.) The council unanimously passed Resolution 487, condemning the attack as a 'clear violation of the Charter of the United Nations and the norms of international conduct'. It said that the attack undermined the safeguards regime of the IAEA, and called upon Israel to fess up to its own nuclear stockpile and to have its facilities inspected by the IAEA. The General Assembly followed by passing Resolution 37/27, damning Israel for a 'premeditated and unprecedented act of aggression'.

Prime Minister Menachem Begin had justified the raid on a 'point of no return' principle: it was claimed that the reactor would soon go into operation close to Baghdad, after which it could not be struck without exposing citizens to radiation. This was disingenuous, given that the reactor would have been under IAEA scrutiny from the moment it commenced operation. The attack undermined confidence in the NPT system, and encouraged India and Pakistan to maintain the secrecy of their own nuclear programmes for fear that they might suffer a similar fate, from Pakistan and India respectively. Saddam Hussein reacted to the raid by calling on Arab nations to develop nuclear weapons, and thereafter did so himself in secret and with considerable success, as the IAEA discovered in 1991, after his loss in the Gulf War allowed them to inspect his progress. But what was notable (and certainly noted by Israel) was that despite the ferocity and universality of its condemnation, Israel suffered no sanctions nor any other form of punishment. There were Security Council calls for it to confess its own nuclear store and to join the NPT, but these it ignored: it was allowed to get away with a clear violation of the UN Charter.

Nonetheless, Resolution 487 and the condemnation of 'Operation Opera' does serve as a precedent for the unlawfulness of an Israeli attack today on Iran's nuclear sites. Unless... There is an ironic footnote, namely that Israel was not the first to attack Osirak. Nine months before, the Israeli chief of army intelligence had managed to persuade Iran, this revolutionary republic at war with Iraq, that the reactor would build Saddam a bomb that would one day be dropped on Tehran. The Iranians took fright, and two of their Phantom jets bombed Osirak on 30 September 1980. It is this *Iranian* incursion that should go down in history as the first pre-emptive strike against a nuclear reactor. There was no precedent set, however, and no UN condemnation, because Iran and Iraq were at war – a situation where the peacetime rules about keeping the peace do not apply. This is why the smarter apologists for Osirak, like Alan Dershowitz and Yoram

Dinstein, admit that the attack cannot be justified on the grounds of anticipatory self-defence, but suggest that Iraq and Israel were at war – indeed, had been at war since 1948 – and Osirak was a legitimate military target. It was a war that had been subject to 'inordinate prolongation' thereafter, without casualties until 1981, but which resurfaced in 1990 when Saddam fired scud missiles at Jerusalem.[337]

This is a 'nice try', but lacks reality – Israel has been in a state of enmity with most Arab countries since its foundation, but this does not mean it has been in a state of war. Saddam's scud-firing in 1991 was not a war crime (Israel was not among the coalition attacking him over his invasion of Kuwait), but a breach of Article 2(4) of the UN Charter. Any Israeli attack on Iran's nuclear faculties (it has seventeen of them) would equally be a breach of Article 2(4). Although Alan Dershowitz huffs and puffs in the Huffington Post that 'Israel has the Right to Attack Iran's Nuclear Reactors Now'[338] his evidence for the claim that Iran is already at war with Israel is decidedly shaky – an alleged arms shipment to Hamas intercepted in 2011; 'support' for Hezbollah (whose main supporter has in fact been Syria) and the bombing of the Israeli embassy in Buenos Aires back in 1992. These isolated actions do not amount to war. That much is clear from the ICJ's decision in *Nicaragua* v. *US*, which pointed out that 'frontier incidents', provocations, raids and force which does not have 'scale and effects' – including the supply to rebels of weapons and logistical support – cannot amount to an 'armed attack' sufficient to constitute a state of war.[339] There was no excuse for Osirak, and there is no existing state of war today that could excuse an attack on Iranian nuclear facilities (or can excuse Israel's assassinations of Iranian nuclear scientists).

'OPERATION ORCHARD': AL-KIBAR, 2007

Nonetheless, the proponents of Israel's right to strike remember Menachem Begin's defiant words after Osirak: 'This attack will be a precedent for every future government in Israel ... every future Israeli Prime Minister will act, in similar circumstances, in the same way.'[340] They have taken heart from the subdued – almost non-existent – international response to 'Operation Orchard', the Israeli attack in September 2007 on a nuclear reactor being secretly constructed at Al-Kibar in Syria. The US (consulted before the strike, of course) was not then confident that the reactor was part of a weapons programme because there was no evidence of a reprocessing plant or active work on a warhead. So the Bush administration turned down the Israeli request to join the strike, which was conducted with surgical precision by the Israelis although it is reported to have killed at least ten, and perhaps three dozen, workers.[341] Did this non-reaction mean that, twenty-six years on from Osirak, the damage feared from malevolent states acquiring nuclear weapons was such that the world was prepared to see the nuclear facilities destroyed without raising a legal eyebrow? Did the silence signal acquiescence, or at least a recognition that the NPT/IAEA regime did not work in relation to rogue states? This may be to read too much into the lack of reaction – the world was not made aware of the strike when it happened because Israel imposed a news black-out and the Bush administration ordered US officials not to discuss the matter. Most surprising (but also tellingly) Syria – the victim – made no complaint other than about violation of its airspace. There was a 'synchronised silence from the Arab world'.[342] For very good reasons, as the CIA revealed at a press briefing eight months later: the Israeli target was a reactor being secretly built for the Syrian military by North Korea, probably to produce plutonium for nuclear weapons.

The Al-Kibar reactor posed no immediate threat to Israel, but even after the CIA became more confident that it was part of a weapons programme and exposed the truth about the strike, only the lone voice of Mohammed ElBaradei was raised in objection, not so much to the strike as to the failure of Israel and the US, as well as Syria, to honour their responsibilities as NPT members and to provide information about the secret reactor to the IAEA. Having condemned Israel for relying on self-help and Syria for deliberately failing to declare the facility, ElBaradei announced a belated inspection. Although the site had been 'cleaned up' by the Syrians with the help of North Korean technicians, the inspectors discovered uranium particles – supporting the CIA's opinion that Al-Kibar was a secret nuclear facility constructed with North Korean experts and expertise. Once again, it became clear, the IAEA/NPT safeguards had failed: Syria, an NPT member, had deliberately and dishonestly embarked on a clandestine nuclear weapons programme, to complement the stocks of chemical weapons it had already amassed. The Assad regime, as became clear in 2012, would not have scrupled to use such weapons were its own existence at stake – the very situation in which the ICJ had said it might be lawful to use them!

The difference between the UN's reaction to Osirak and non-reaction to Al-Kibar is only partly explained by the fact that the former was a reactor openly provided by the French, in no way calibrated for weapons-grade enrichment and subject to full IAEA inspection, whilst Al-Kibar was the product of a conspiracy between Syria and North Korea (and, it has been suggested, Iran) to reprocess plutonium for weapons use. The issue is whether, given this dubious purpose, in breach of Syria's NPT obligations not to acquire nuclear weapons, Israel was entitled to attack. It is a reflection on the perceived irrelevance of international law to the nuclear issue that this time Israel offered no justification for its conduct, and the rest of the world turned a blind eye. Only the IAEA took umbrage, and that was because it had been kept in the dark. It fell to the US to attempt justification when the CIA provided details of the strike some months afterwards: it explained that the reactor was installed to produce uranium for a weapons programme, that it was soon to be fuelled, that Israel had 'considered a Syrian nuclear capability to be an existential threat to the state of Israel' and that so far as the US was concerned, 'we understand the Israeli action ... we believe this clandestine reactor was a threat to regional peace and security.' (Israel's nuclear weapons constitute no such threat, as far as the US is concerned.) It was a rehearsal for the statement that is likely to emerge from the White House after Israel strikes Iranian nuclear sites: in a reference to what has been called 'the Bush doctrine' of pre-emption, the US added, 'We cannot allow the world's most dangerous regimes to acquire the world's most dangerous weapons.'[343] Yet this is exactly what the present law allows them to do, by way of their 'inalienable right' to a fuel cycle and their entitlement to withdraw from the NPT and the IAEA as soon as they want to 'break out' into nuclear weaponry.

There can be no doubt that Al-Kibar was a covert nuclear reactor under construction, modelled on a similar reactor in North Korea. Syria failed in its duty to notify the IAEA. It tried to 'clean up' after the bombing to disguise its real purpose and has lied to the IAEA ever since by denying that real purpose. Israel could on some level be congratulated for doing the NPT – to which it is not a party – a favour. But had the US done its duty, and provided to the IAEA the intelligence it shared with Israel, there would have been demands for an inspection followed by sanctions on Syria for non-compliance. These would have worked at some stage over the next four to six years that it would have taken for Syria to have produced a bomb. Both the Osirak and Al-Kibar attacks were undertaken, in other words, years before Iraq and Syria could be expected to attain 'nuclear weapons capacity'. Neither attack could sensibly be described as necessary to neutralise an 'imminent' threat, i.e. as anticipatory self-defence. They might more accurately be described as 'precautionary', to remove a risk that could materialise at some time in the future, but that fails the *Caroline* test. It is a great risk, to be sure, in the sense that nuclear war in the Middle East would be catastrophic, but not great in the sense that it was likely to come about, given the diplomatic and political efforts that would have been made to avoid it. Nonetheless, 'Operation Orchard' succeeded, not only in destroying the reactor but in weakening the world's resolve to stick by international law, or that part of it which restricts the use of force. As a result, 'a state wishing to undertake pre-emptive action to prevent the proliferation of nuclear weapons will now believe itself less likely to meet a hostile international response'.[344]

This is unacceptable for those who want to live in a world ordered by the rule of law. The stakes are high, in respect of nuclear weapons, if they fall into the hands of the international criminals who rule Iran or Syria, yet respect for law requires such threats to be dealt with through UN instrumentalities or else under clear principles, and not by unilateral self-interested decisions taken by Israel with US support. If the ICJ had declared in its 1996 advisory opinion that the acquisition of nuclear weapons was unlawful, or that possession would amount to a crime against humanity, then a Security Council resolution approving the use of force to prevent a threat to the peace would be in order, whether or not Iran intended to use its bombs. In its absence a Kosovo-style 'coalition of the willing' to stop an ongoing crime against humanity would be justified, at least if there were no Security Council condemnation.[345] But there can be no legitimate basis for attacking a country that is exercising its 'inalienable right' to develop a fuel cycle. Thereafter, if it withdraws from the NPT, it cannot forcibly be denied its right in international law, under what is called the *Lotus* principle, to do what is not forbidden by international law.[346] Unless, of course, international law has changed and does now forbid the acquisition of nuclear weapons.

'FLEXIBLE' SELF-DEFENCE

Nukes are different: their uniquely destructive nature does make it absurd to abide by the literal meaning of Article 51, i.e. that self-defence arises only after an attack – which if it is nuclear, then nothing will arise afterwards. That leaves 'anticipatory' self-defence – but should the concept of 'imminence' in respect of nukes be more flexible than allowed by the *Caroline* doctrine? There is an alternative view, much canvassed by the lobby which wants Iran to be bombed in the interests of what it terms 'preventive' or 'pre-emptive' self defence. This is not merely an extension of the *Caroline* doctrine of anticipatory self-defence, permitting a response to a threat that is imminent, but rather a claim that the US (which generally makes it) or other nations (such as Russia and Israel, which gladly accept it) may strike first against a threat that is likely to materialise in the foreseeable future. The 'Bush doctrine' was enunciated in September 2002, in *The National Security Strategy of the United States of America*:

> We must adapt the concept of imminent threat to the capabilities and objectives of today's adversaries ... we will not hesitate to act, alone if necessary, to exercise our right of self-defense [against] rogue states and terrorists who rely on weapons of mass destruction – weapons that can be easily concealed, delivered secretly and used without warning.

This was the policy that paved the way for the invasion of

Iraq – a rogue state led by a rogue statesman with hypothetical weapons of mass destruction that the IAEA would not be given a chance not to find. But it was enunciated in the aftermath of bin Laden's announcement that Islamists had a 'duty' to obtain and use nuclear weapons, the consequences of which would be so calamitous that the risk – at least in rhetoric – seemed worth removing, irrespective of the likelihood of it ever occurring. As Richard Dearlove, head of Britain's MI6, noted after a White House meeting nine months before the 2003 invasion, 'Bush wanted to remove Saddam, through military action, justified by the conjunction of terrorism and weapons of mass destruction. But the intelligence and the facts were being fixed around the policy. The NSC had no patience with the UN route...' A route which would, if persevered with, have proved that Saddam had had no weapons of mass destruction. But the intelligence and the facts had to be 'fixed' – hence the allegation that Saddam was obtaining uranium from Niger (based on a letter which the IAEA, as soon as it was disclosed, immediately recognised as a forgery) and the 'sexed up' claim that his ballistic missiles could land on London within forty-five minutes of an order to launch them. Colin Powell regaled the Security Council with what he claimed was 'irrefutable and undeniable' evidence that Saddam was concealing WMD, and the cautious Dr Blix reported a few weeks later that his inspectors had found no such weapons, but many were 'unaccounted for'. That was enough for the Bush doctrine to permit the invasion, after which it turned out they were 'unaccounted for' because they had been destroyed years before, and Powell's 'evidence' was fabricated or 'fixed'. It has now emerged that President Bush had privately decided in January 2003 that the US would invade 'whether WMDs were found or not', in which case his war was preventive (to overthrow a malign dictator who might one day acquire weapons of mass destruction) rather than pre-emptive, to stop a malign dictator using, or transferring to terrorists, the weapons already in his possession.

Neither 'preventive' (foreclosing a risk likely to arise in the future) nor 'pre-emptive' (removing an extant risk that is not imminent) can stand as a 'flexible' adjectival expansion of the inherent right of anticipatory self-defence in the UN Charter. The

Nuremberg Court was prepared to accept the *Caroline* doctrine, permitting states to use force to avoid the threat of imminent attack, but 'anticipatory self-defence' still means there must be a real and plausible threat of an actual attack and not merely a threat that has yet to emerge. The threatened attack must be imminent, there must be no other means to deflect it (i.e. sanctions and diplomacy must have both failed) and the action must be proportionate. Moreover, the element of necessity means that there should be no non-military alternative to the proposed course of action that would be likely to be effective in averting the threat or bringing an end to the attack.[347] It is understandable that Israel and America – as the chief targets of modern terrorist movements – should wish to recalibrate the *Caroline* rule, with a more flexible interpretation of 'imminence' than the concept connoted at a time when armies and battleships took weeks to move into position. (Paddle steamers, not to mention Canadian rebels, are strikingly anachronistic.) A flexible interpretation of imminence would justify a strike on a secret facility which was actually storing nuclear bombs, if convincing evidence showed that there were plans afoot to drop or detonate them, but cannot stretch so far as to encompass the destruction of a reactor at any stage in the fuel cycle. In March 2003 there could be no 'imminence' about the threat from Saddam's WMD because their existence had not yet been verified: Bush and Blair no doubt expected in good faith that they would be found 'imminently', and Dr Blix, who shared that view, was leaving no stone (or grain of sand) unturned in order to find them. But until they were found, the threat could not be said to have emerged.

The Bush doctrine of prevention (in reality of 'precaution'), which claimed the right to respond forcibly to a threat which had not yet emerged but might do so at some point in the future, did not accord with international law and could not be brought within it by any flexible development of the concept of 'imminence'. The fatal flaw in the Bush doctrine is that 'it excludes by definition any possibility of an *ex post facto* judgment of lawfulness by the very fact that it aims to deal in advance with threats that have not yet materialised'.[348] Aggressive states and their apologists can usually say (as Israel and Dershowitz say

about Osirak) that it prevented a rogue state from developing
the bomb, but actually it encouraged Saddam to develop a bomb
in secret, and if he had not made the mistake of invading Kuwait
in 1990 he would have had one to fire at Israel in the tip of a
scud missile by the time Iraq was invaded in 2003. So far as state
practice is concerned, the great majority of states reject the Bush
self-defence doctrine, whether 'precautionary' or 'preventive' or
'pre-emptive', and 'Operation Iraqi Freedom', to the extent that
it was based upon these theories, was rejected by the Security
Council. Subsequently, the High Level Panel appointed by the
Secretary General reported that there was no such right in international law.[349]

The 2002 National Security Strategy purports to adopt the
traditional *Caroline* test of 'imminence', but promotes an altogether different test, by retaining 'the option of pre-emptive
action to counter a sufficient threat to our national security ...
the United States cannot remain idle whilst dangers gather'. This
is not anticipatory self-defence against an imminent threat. It
signals the unilateral right to use force against states hostile to
Israel which *might* develop a nuclear fuel cycle (their 'inalienable
right') and *might* be tempted at some point thereafter to manufacture a bomb (which is not illegal, according to the ICJ in 1996)
and *might conceivably* – and this is the first point at which they
would be committing an offence – either decide to use it against
Israel or deliver a nuclear device to a terrorist group for that
purpose. This so-called 'pre-emptive self-defence' does not exist
in international law. It is merely a claim by the US to go to war
whenever a sufficient danger to its interest – especially its interest
in supporting Israel – is intuited, the sufficiency of the danger to
be judged by the US alone. If it were a rule of international law,
of course, other nations would be entitled to its benefit, dangerously expanding the power of any state to go to war when it felt
threatened. This would make Article 51 'self-defence' a vigilante's
charter, a *carte blanche* for any aggressive country to respond to
a perceived (by it) threat by using force. So the Obama doctrine
is not part of international law either: it is a statement of opportunistic entitlement by the world's most powerful nation (which
may not always be the US) to attack nations which are perceived

to endanger its national interests. It is, in short, a feature of the lawless world described by Thucydides, in which the strong do what they wish and the weak what they must.[350]

The Obama doctrine has been firmly rejected by the British government: its Attorney General emphasised that 'a broad doctrine of a right to use force to pre-empt danger in the future ... is not a doctrine which, in my opinion, exists or is recognised in international law.'[351] However, powerful elements of the American political establishment regard it as essential: they laugh off the *Caroline* doctrine as a case of 'too early, too early – oops – too late'. They seek a principle that would permit the US to act alone, or in alliance with Britain and France, to stop nuclear proliferation where the Security Council is rendered impotent by disagreement with China and/or Russia. There are circumstances where the US and its allies might lawfully act, as they did to stop ethnic cleansing in Kosovo – without superpower unanimity, but at the same time without Security Council condemnation. Those who advocate this approach to 'preventive warfare' – like John Yoo, the architect of Guantanamo torture,[352] are odd bedfellows for humanitarians, and their claims to justify 'preventive war' as a form of 'humanitarian intervention' must be viewed as sceptically as Adolf Hitler's claim that he was humanely intervening in the Sudetenland. Yoo misunderstands the right of humanitarian intervention, which arises only when a crime against humanity is underway, not (as in the case of Iran's hypothetical bomb) when the crime might (or might not) be committed at some time in the future, if Iran were not only to build a bomb (which would be legal so long as it left the NPT, like North Korea), but were to decide to use it (which would not). Nonetheless, human rights law could provide a basis for NATO action without Security Council unanimity, if it were the case that building a nuclear bomb, irrespective of planning its use, was treated as a crime against humanity.

DOES IRAN INTEND TO WIPE ISRAEL OFF THE MAP?

'No President should ever hesitate to use force – unilaterally if necessary – to protect ourselves and our vital interests when we are attacked or imminently threatened,' said the then Senator, Barack Obama, in a speech on foreign policy in 2007.[353] The ex-law

professor remembered the *Caroline* correspondence and stuck to
the test of 'imminence', although it was not long before his officials
were calling for 'a more flexible understanding of imminence' to
deal with terrorist organisations. In April 2012 Obama himself
announced that the US would conduct a 'pre-emptive' strike against
Iran once it acquired a nuclear weapon – a position so flexible that
it robs 'imminence' of any meaning, given that Iran's possession of
a nuclear weapon would not be unlawful if it removed itself from
the NPT and that it has not signalled any fixed intention of dropping the bomb on Israel if it were one day to acquire it.

Those urging Obama to adopt this position speak loosely of
'Iran's declared goal of wiping Israel off the map and killing
millions of its citizens',[354] but this is not a declared goal at all. It
is a reference to a crude allusion by Ahmadinejad (at the World
Without Zionism conference in 2005) to a millennial prophecy by
Ayatollah Khomeini that Israel would one day 'vanish from the
pages of time', apparently as a result of the reappearance of the
Twelfth Imam rather than as a result of an Iranian first strike.[355]
There are plenty of rabid anti-Israeli (excused, unsatisfactorily, as
anti-Zionist) statements by Ahmadinejad, for example:

Israel is a germ of corruption which will be removed soon.[356]

The Israelis have been occupying the territories for the last sixty
to seventy years ... They have no roots there in history ... They
represent minimal disturbances that come into picture and are
then eliminated.[357]

I don't care whether the Holocaust took place or not, but it is
illogical to give a piece of Palestine for compensation.[358]

The Zionist regime will be wiped out soon the same way the Soviet
Union was.[359]

Those who think they can revive the stinking corpse of the usurp-
ing and fake Israeli regime are seriously mistaken. Today the reason
for the Zionist regime's existence is questioned and the regime is
on the way to annihilation.[360]

> Any freedom lover and justice seeker in the world must do its best
> for the annihilation of the Zionist regime in order to pave the path
> for the establishment of justice and freedom in the world.[361]

Fighting words, certainly, but from a bantam-weight: Ahmadinejad's term as President ends in mid 2013, and he has fallen out of favour with the Supreme Leader. His rhetoric falls far short of a serious threat to attack Israel, with or without nuclear weapons. Those who beat this particular drum also cite an elliptical comment by Rafsanjani that a nuclear war between Israel and Arab nations would leave Israel 'empty of people' but only cause 'serious' damage in the Muslim world – i.e. millions would be dead on both sides but that would mean a few million Muslims left standing in parts of the Middle East. Whilst both men are disgusting racists, neither is declaring war or is in any position to do so: Ahmadinejad's presidency is almost over, Rafsanjani has been relegated to run the Expediency Council, and both men are currently out of favour. Khamenei, as Supreme Leader, has been declaring the bomb 'un-Islamic,' and although he cannot be believed (in 2004 he urged on his scientists: 'We must have two bombs ready to go in January [2005] or you are not Muslims'),[362] he has not to anyone's knowledge issued a fatwa against Jews, nor is he minded to unleash a holocaust. Indeed, it is a little-known but significant fact that, outside Israel, Iran supports the largest Jewish community in the Middle East, and Khomeini actually issued a fatwa to ensure their protection! There are forty synagogues, and Hebrew schools, libraries and hospitals.[363] Netanyahu's claim that Iran wants another holocaust and is about to commit nuclear genocide can only be described (as it as has been, by Tzipi Livni) as hysterical.

WAR GAMING

Those who argue that the threat is sufficient to justify an Israeli and/or US attack can find no basis in international law. Their arguments reduce to geopolitics: the undesirability of what might happen in terms of nuclear proliferation in the Middle East. Hillary Clinton realistically predicts an arms race in the region, as Saudi Arabia, Turkey and Muslim Brotherhood-dominated

Egypt acquire bombs to counter Iran over the next five or ten years. This is an unhappy prospect, but those who believe in MAD could apply its logic to the region: in the future, all these nuclear-armed states will behave themselves for fear of triggering Armageddon. This was the argument advanced in 2012 by Kenneth Waltz in a provocative article in *Foreign Affairs*: 'Why Iran Should Get the Bomb'. It would provide parity with Israel, and diminish the provocation that might lead to a nuclear war.[364] He argues that history shows that states become more stable and cautious after going nuclear and the Iranian leadership is not so irrational as to invite its own destruction by attacking Israel: 'If Iran goes nuclear, Israel and Iran will deter each other, as nuclear powers always have.' The article served as a valuable reminder, among all the predictions in 2012 that Iran would use the bomb to obliterate Israel, that this was in fact the last thing that Iran – at least, a rational Iran – would want to do with it. The weapon, sheathed and hidden, was its best guarantee of security.

Waltz is not alone in challenging the claim that there is any 'necessity' to act now to prevent Iran from acquiring the bomb. Calm consideration of the consequences of such a strike demonstrates its downsides. Israel would once again be on the wrong side of the law, an international pariah and a magnet for terrorist attacks, with avalanches of missiles raining down from Hamas in the south and Hezbollah in the north. Iran would, in reprisal, damage the international economy and cause oil prices to rocket by closing or heavily mining the Strait of Hormuz, through which a third of the world's oil travels. However unpalatable a nuclear Iran, the consequences of a preventive strike would be immense, among them being further disregard for international law. Both Sir Michael Howard, Britain's strategic elder statesman, and John McCain have made the point – the aphorism is attributed to both of them – that 'the only thing worse than the prospect of an Iran with nuclear weapons would be the consequences of using force to stop them'.[365]

There is no guarantee that the damage would be confined to the Middle East: A US army war game ('Internal Look') leaked to the *New York Times* envisaged an Israeli first strike on Iran, to which it would respond by hitting a US naval warship in the Persian

Gulf, killing several hundred Americans, to which the US could in turn respond by bombing Tehran, and so on. Those who blithely support Israeli bombing of suspect Iranian sites overlook the fact that there are seventeen of them, some in densely populated areas near Tehran with its 9 million citizens, others underground and targetable only by 'bunker-busting' bombs that could cause widespread civilian casualties. If nuclear penetration bombs were used, of course, the damage would be much greater: each B-61-11 bomb currently in the US arsenal, and which may have counterparts in Israel, has thirty times the power of 'Little Boy', the bomb that levelled Hiroshima. No such attack is ever contemplated on India, or Pakistan, which have been suffered to build up arsenals outside the NPT, so to single out Iran for bombing will obviously appear, to those looking up from the Arab streets, unjust. Given the facts that severe sanctions did not start until July 2012, and that negotiations with the P5+1 are still proceeding in the hope of a guarantee that Iranian enrichment will not again exceed 5 per cent, an attack at this point would seem even more premature than the 2003 invasion of Iraq.

After all, what is the present state of Iran's nuclear weapons capability? In August 2012, the IAEA reported that Iran had breached Security Council resolutions and was now enriching up to 20 per cent and appeared to be stockpiling the enriched uranium in quantities for which it has no obvious use other than for the making of a bomb (its medical research reactor in Tehran does not need anything like this amount).[366] It repeated its previous comment that it had become 'increasingly concerned about the possible existence in Iran of undisclosed nuclear-related activities involving military related acquisitions, including activities related to the development of nuclear payload for a missile.'[367] The agency had received information from the security services of a number of states, and was concerned about the country's efforts, through military sources, to obtain nuclear-related dual-use equipment and designs to develop an indigenous nuclear weapon. Much of this took place before 2003 (the point at which a US intelligence report in 2007 considered that it had probably abandoned its plans to acquire nukes), but now 'there are also indications that some activities relevant to the development of a nuclear explosive device continued after 2003, and that some may be ongoing'. Moreover, 'between 2007 and 2010 Iran continued to conceal nuclear activities by not informing the agency in a timely manner of the decision to construct a new nuclear power plant at Darkhovin and a third enrichment facility near Qom (the Fordow Fuel Enrichment Plant)'.

In other words, the IAEA is now satisfied that until 2003, Iran was secretly committed to building the bomb, and had a comprehensive programme for so doing, using enriched uranium, in a bomb that would be mounted on the re-entry vehicle of a Shahab-3 missile. It has evidence that some aspects of that programme may have been revived in 2007 and may be continuing and can now confirm that Iran has begun to enrich uranium to a level of up to 20 per cent.

To summarise the position from the IAEA 2011 and 2012 reports, Iran has undoubtedly tried to develop nuclear weapons in the past and there is some evidence that it is now preparing to do so in the future. It is defying Security Council resolutions and is probably cheating on its NPT undertakings, and is certainly interested in designs for nuclear warheads (an area not covered by the NPT) but is still several years away from acquiring a few bombs. That provides no legal basis for Israel and/or the US to put civilians at risk by wide-ranging attacks on its facilities merely to 'slow down' a process that could in the foreseeable future make it capable of building some bombs, which it has no provable intention of using to commit genocide by dropping them on Israel. The answer to the question 'Can Israel attack Iran?' is clear. The *Caroline* test applies to the imminence of a threatened attack by Iran upon Israel, and not to the imminence of some development – in this case, Iran reaching 'nuclear capability' – which may (or may not) assist preparations for some such attack in the future. What will be 'imminent' in the spring or summer of 2013 is not an attack by Iran, but merely its capability to make a nuclear weapon. That gives no entitlement to Israel under Article 51 to attack Iran first, in anticipatory self-defence.

CAN IRAN ATTACK ISRAEL NOW?

The strident rhetoric from Israeli government leaders in recent years, reaching a crescendo in the summer of 2012, leaves no doubt that an attack on Iran has been planned and might soon be said to be 'imminent'. What few have noticed is that, under the *Caroline* principle read with Article 51, this would entitle Iran to attack Israel in its own self-defence, at least to the point of destroying the airbases, munitions and submarines that would be used to mount the threatened attack. Prime Minister Netanyahu and Defence Minister Ehud Barak have publicly proclaimed their determination to attack once Iran becomes 'nuclear capable', stating in August 2012 that the EU talks had failed and that time had run out: Iran was about to enter 'the zone of immunity'. This threat has been followed by the government testing an SMS system to warn the public of the missile attack which is expected in reprisal.[368] Military plans to bomb Iran's reactors have leaked, as have military exercise 'dress rehearsals' which have been held by the Israel Defence Forces since 2008. Bunker-busting bombs have been purchased from the US, as have Boeing refuelling jets which could enable the air force to travel the 2,000 kilometres to target Natanz. Few doubt, as of late 2012, that Israel is on strike readiness and is awaiting only US approval, or at least acquiescence.

Israel has always insisted that Iran will reach 'the point of no return' once it has the capacity, and the expertise, to enrich uranium in large quantities and to high-grade weapons levels. It has probably reached that point (it would take only a few months to enrich from 20 per cent to 90 per cent), so it is now a target. In late September 2012, Mr Netanyahu, addressing the UN, held up a *Looney Tunes* cartoon diagram of a nuclear bomb and declared that Iran would be capable of building it by spring or early summer 2013. Unless his rhetoric winds down, an Israeli strike on Iran will certainly be 'imminent' by then, and Iran could claim its *Caroline* entitlement to strike first. It is ironic that Israeli sabre-rattling should have reached such a pitch that Iran (or an ally) would be entitled to attack Israel pursuant to its inherent right of individual (or collective) anticipatory self-defence, under the *Caroline* doctrine of customary international law and hence under Article 51 of the UN Charter. As a matter of law, however, that is the present paradoxical position: it is Iran that is under an imminent threat of attack, whilst Israel is not.

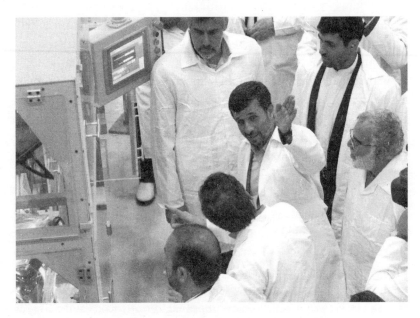

Twenty per cent enrichment and rising! President
Ahmadinejad inspects centrifuges at Natanz.

CHAPTER 16

WORLD WITHOUT NUKES, AMEN

So today, I state clearly and with conviction America's commitment to seek the peace and security of a world without nuclear weapons. First, the US will take concrete steps towards a world without nuclear weapons. To put an end to Cold War thinking, we will reduce the role of nuclear weapons in our national security strategy, and urge others to do the same. To reduce our warheads and stockpiles, we will negotiate a new Strategic Arms Reduction Treaty, and we will seek to include all weapons states in this endeavor ... [we will] immediately and aggressively pursue US ratification of the Comprehensive Test Ban Treaty ... the US will seek a new treaty that verifiably ends the production of fissile materials intended for use in state nuclear weapons...

                              Barack Obama, Prague, 5 April 2009

It was a great speech, delivered with a calm passion appropriately in the city of that philosopher-republican of peace, Václav Havel, but also of that master of multiple meaning, Franz Kafka. In September 2009, with Obama himself in the chair, the Security Council adopted Resolution 1887, resolving to create a world without nukes, and the following month Obama received the Nobel Prize from a committee which 'attached special importance to Obama's vision of and work for a world without nuclear weapons'. Suddenly, the 'Martens clause' came to mind: if the rules of IHL are made, when treaties are silent, from the usages established between civilised nations, the laws of humanity and the requirements of public conscience, then there was a much stronger case against the possession of nukes in 2009 than in 1996. The movement that the judges had then detected, but felt had not gone far enough to outlaw the threat or use of nuclear weapons in all circumstances, now seemed clear enough to justify a different opinion.

A tipping point had come in 2007, in the op-ed columns of the *Wall Street Journal,* in an opinion not by rectitudinous judges but by Henry Kissinger, George Shultz, Sam Nunn and Bill Perry – four horsemen of the nuclear apocalypse who had fought the Cold War with an invincible belief in the deterrence provided by thousands of nuclear warheads, but who now announced their conversion to the view that nuclear weapons had become a source of intolerable risk.[369] There would be accidents, and terrorist efforts to buy or build nuclear devices, but more importantly there would be unstable, failed and pariah states, whose statesmen would have a finger on the nuclear trigger. They endorsed the opinion of Mikhail Gorbachev, vouchsafed in that same year, that 'nuclear weapons are no longer a means of achieving security; in fact, with every passing year they make our security more precarious'.[370] Suddenly, there seemed no circumstances in which the bomb could properly be used: it was time to work for a world in which the mushroom cloud would be a hallucination.

This is a different world to that seen by – or presented to – the judges at the ICJ in 1996.[371] Although, on the horizon, they could descry the first '*ad hoc*' international criminal court, the ICTY, it had not yet begun work which was to destroy the claim of Serbia and of Serbian leader Milošević that they had a right to preserve the existence of 'greater Serbia' by perpetrating crimes against humanity, such as the ethnic cleansing of Kosovo. This marked the re-emergence of international criminal law, initiated at Nuremberg but which had lain inactive for half a century during the Cold War. In 1996, little attention was paid to the jurisprudence emerging from regional human rights courts – notably the European Court at Strasbourg, which protects the individual's right not to be arbitrarily deprived of life, not to be tortured or subjected to cruel, inhumane, or degrading treatment or punishment, and the right to recognition and protection as a person. These rights, which unlike IHL protect citizens in peace as well as war, are inevitably jeopardised by any use of nuclear weapons, whether owned by states or by terrorists, and whether exploded in peacetime or in armed conflict. The bombing may be of a military target, but the spread of ionising radiation for years afterwards tortures and degrades civilians within its extended radius, whilst others will be arbitrarily and immediately melted by the blast.

State leaders who acquire the bomb today (and why acquire if not to use?) can be prosecuted at the ICC for crimes against humanity. Under the Rome Statute, which accords jurisdiction to the Court (which can be triggered, in the case of non-parties, by a Security Council resolution), crimes against humanity include widespread attacks against a civilian population, pursuant to a state policy, which involve torture, extermination or 'other inhumane acts of a similar character intentionally causing great suffering or serious injury to body or to mental or physical health'. This is precisely the consequence of a nuclear explosion for the survivors. As Judge Koroma summarised the evidence in the *Nuclear Test* case,

> over 320,000 people who survived [Hiroshima] but were affected by radiation still suffer from various malignant tumours caused by radiation, including Leukaemia, thyroid cancer, breast cancer, lung cancer, gastric cancer, cataracts and a variety of other after-effects. More than half a century after the disaster, they are still said to be undergoing medical examinations and treatment.[372]

It follows that those leaders who plot to outwit the IAEA, breach their international law duties under the NPT and develop their nuclear processes to a point where they cannot be referable other than to building a bomb can be prosecuted for conspiring (or attempting, if they have gone far enough) to commit a crime against humanity. That crime not only breaches the fundamental right not to be arbitrarily (i.e. unjustly or illegally) deprived of life – which would necessarily be the case with all victims of an accidental or terrorist explosion, and all civilian victims of a first-use – but also breaches the fundamental right to human dignity. The German Constitutional Court recently invoked the right to strike down, for both reasons, a security law which required a passenger aircraft to be shot down if it were hijacked by terrorists.[373] The taking of innocent lives – and the bomb has no other purpose, in that consequences are so widespread and long-lasting that civilians are inevitably killed and tortured by its use – is a denial of humanity.

In no circumstances of their use can nuclear weapons fail to breach human rights guarantees, even in the absurd hypotheticals crafted by English lawyers for the court in 1996 – the idea that nukes might be legal if fired only at warships at sea, or at an army located in the middle of a desert. What has exploded these and similar examples is the gathering evidence of damage caused by 'safe' nuclear tests on atolls and deserts, which caused long-term contamination of the atmosphere. Some years after the ICJ decision, emerging evidence suggested that atmospheric testing may have contributed to deaths of up to 65 million people world-wide when certain cancers (especially breast cancer) were linked to the 390 nuclear bombs exploded in the atmosphere between 1951 and 1963. Soviet bomb tests, mainly in Siberia and Kazakhstan, leaked radioactive material over areas that remain out of bounds and may partly be responsible for the early deaths of over 50,000 soldiers who were stationed there before the danger was realised. [374] What of the arrogant French, and the ICJ majority judges who in 1974 refused to allow Australia's case against France to proceed because it switched to underground tests? Between 1974 and 1996, France conducted 147 of them in the Pacific – leaving a legacy of elevated rates of thyroid cancer in the people of the nearby islands.[375]

So in 2012 it cannot be maintained – as it was with straight-faced confidence in 1996 – that there are any circumstances in which a nuclear explosion, even for testing purposes in peacetime, will not breach international human rights law. This aspect was simply not considered by the International Court. It briefly noted the human right to life, but found that it was submerged in the right of civilians under humanitarian law in wartime. The two rights are different, and it is the human right that matters in most conceivable uses of the bomb, for testing or if exploded by terrorists or by accident, or simply when being constructed and stockpiled. These uses occur in peacetime, where war law – IHL – does not by definition apply. The court was asked only about the legality of the 'threat or use' of nuclear weapons, i.e. in the throes of war. It was not asked about the legality of possessing nuclear weapons, or the legality of the process of acquiring them. This falls within the domain of international human rights law.

The court in 1996 obviously could not take into account

the great leap forward in human rights law which occurred in Rome in 1998, when 120 nations signed up to the Statute of the International Criminal Court (it now has 116 ratifications). This statute defined 'crimes against humanity' in a way which would cover any person who authorised or abetted 'a systematic attack directed against a civilian population, resulting in extermination or torture, or an inhumane act intentionally causing great suffering'. The section on war crimes did not specifically mention nuclear weapons, for what seemed to delegates in Rome a good reason at the time, namely to keep the US on side, in the hope that it would support the new court. But Article 8 provided that the court should have jurisdiction over large-scale commission of war crimes, including 'attacks that killed or caused great suffering to civilians or their property' (8(2)(a)), and made an international offence of

> intentionally launching an attack in the knowledge that such attack will cause incidental loss of life or injury to civilians or damage to civilian objects or widespread, long-term and severe damage to the natural environment which would be clearly excessive in relation to the concrete and direct overall military advantage anticipated. (8(2)(b)(iv)).

This would precisely cover any use of the bomb in war, given what is known about its effects as a result of peacetime tests, but there was potential wriggle room to keep the Americans on side. The violation had to be 'within the established framework of international law' – and international law, as a result of the 1996 decision, did not at the time of the Rome Conference, which settled the ICC Statute, regard the bomb as illegal *per se*.[376] This loophole will be closed once international law accepts the obvious, namely that nuclear weapons are illegal in and of themselves, from the moment all their parts are ready to assemble.

The rise of human rights law after 1996 has been extraordinary. There was truly a 'proliferation' of jurisprudence, from the European Court of Human Rights, the Inter-American Court and the African Court on Human and Peoples Rights, about the duty of states to protect their citizens' rights to life and to live free of inhumane treatment. There has also been the advent of war crimes courts dealing with crimes in the Balkans, in Rwanda, Sierra Leone, East Timor, Cambodia, Bangladesh and Lebanon, not to mention the ICC in The Hague. They give fresh force to earlier declarations that the ICJ ignored in its 1996 opinion. For example, the UN's Human Rights Committee, a body of eighteen experts, many of them judges, had issued a ruling (described as a 'General Comment') in 1984 that 'the production, testing, possession, deployment and use of nuclear weapons should be prohibited and recognised as crimes against humanity'. These weapons threaten to take life arbitrarily and indiscriminately, especially in peacetime as a result of accident or mistake, and their very existence 'generates a climate of suspicion and fear between states', inimical to respect for human rights.[377] After the ICJ advisory opinion, other UN committees began to urge that the production of nukes was contrary to human rights law as well as humanitarian law.[378]

Moreover, the international criminal courts which became active in the twenty-first century soon delivered rulings that exposed the most flagrant defect in the 1996 decision, namely the notion that sovereignty could, if the survival of a state was at risk, justify the use of nuclear weapons. Repeatedly, in war crimes judgments relating to state leaders that picked up on decisions of Nuremberg tribunals after the Second World War, these new UN courts ruled that crimes against humanity could not be committed in purported defence of the nation, even if the perpetrator thought them necessary for the survival of his government or his state or himself. Thus Chief Hinga Norman was brought to trial in the UN court in Sierra Leone for recruiting child soldiers, although he had done so in desperate defence of the democratic government, whilst General Gotovina's claims that he was protecting the state borders of Croatia could not justify the pillage and torture of Serbs in the Krajina.

Self-defence remains an 'inherent right' of a state under Article 51 of the UN Charter, and entitles a response by force to an armed attack, but the response must not be disproportionate or calculated to inflict torture or mass murder on civilians. There can be no defence in human rights law for responding to a conventional invasion by use of a nuclear weapon, nor – and this is the point which the 'Big 5' states which cling to deterrence theory do not want to admit – can there be any right to respond to a nuclear bomb attack with more nuclear bombs? At this point, two wrongs do not and cannot make a right. In the extremely unlikely event of a war between any of the 'Big 5' powers, a nuclear response might well end the world. In less drastic and more possible future scenarios, of e.g. Iran dropping a nuclear bomb on Israel or North Korea targeting Seoul with a nuclear-warheaded rocket, the response – preferably authorised by the Security Council – would have to be limited to conventional weapons, and would be none the worse for that. A massive assault on military targets, using 'bunker bombs' to hit underground nuclear facilities, together with ground force invasions, would clearly be justified in such circumstances. The survival of a state which had opted for a first nuclear strike would not be a matter of legal or moral concern: any claim to sovereign survival would have been lost by its use of nuclear weapons.

One rule that did seem to crystallise after the *Nuclear Weapons* case was that any 'first use' of a nuclear weapon, either to initiate hostilities or in the course of a conventional war, would certainly be a crime against humanity. NFU ('No first use') commitments were given by nuclear powers at the NPT Review Conference in 1995, at least to non-nuclear parties to the treaty, with the logical proviso that the commitment would not hold in respect of any party that nuked them first. These commitments sound all very clear cut on paper, but cannot hold if the 'first nuclear strike' is from a puppet state or proxy organisation, or if ionising radiation causes massive casualties in countries neighbouring the victim state. China, India and North Korea have publicly pledged not to be the first to use nuclear weapons, whilst Israel's misleading pledge 'not to be the first country in the Middle East to formally introduce nuclear weapons to the region' can at least be read as a promise not to be first user of the nuclear weapons it has already introduced to the region. The US has gone some distance – although in order to maintain its deterrence posture, not far enough – by promising not to use such weapons against 'non nuclear weapons states that are party to the NPT *and in compliance with their nuclear non-proliferation obligations*' (emphasis added). This last condition was added so as to give it the wriggle room to nuke Iran, which has been non-compliant in so many ways. But this is all talk and must remain in the blogosphere of bluff and counter-bluff: *any* use of a nuclear weapon can never be justified, under international human rights law, even in self-defence in response to a nuclear attack.

• • •

The world in 2012 presents different factual issues to those upon which the ICJ ruled in 1996, assuming as it did that the NPT would work as a means of corralling the bomb, that the CTBT would be ratified by the US and would stop more bombs being developed, and that the weapons states would take seriously their NPT Article VI legal obligation to reduce their arsenals to zero. None of this happened. Despite (and to some extent because) President Clinton had described his signature on the CTBT as one of the most important acts of his presidency, in 1999 his Republican enemies in Congress declined to ratify it. Led by Senator Jesse Helms, the all-time American enemy of international human rights, they refused to contemplate a world in which America could not experiment with bigger and better bombs. They maintained this position throughout the Bush presidency: 'We may find at some future time we cannot diagnose or remedy a problem in a warhead critical to the US nuclear deterrent without conducting a nuclear test,'[379] said Condoleezza Rice to explain its hostility to a treaty banning nuclear tests. Despite Obama's Prague speech promise to push for ratification of the CTBT, he has not been able to raise the numbers in the Senate, whose Republican leader says, 'I will do everything in my power to see it defeated.'[380] This intransigence is catching: India's External Affairs Minister told its Parliament in 2007 that 'India has the sovereign right to test and would do so if it is necessary in the national interest'[381] and Pakistan confirmed in 2009 that it would not sign the CTBT, for the same reason as was given by Condoleezza Rice, namely the need to modernise nuclear weapons and keep them in working order. Although the CTBT has 155 state parties, it cannot enter into force until 44 states considered 'nuclear capable' when it was negotiated in 1996 have ratified it. Ratifications are awaited not only from the US, Pakistan and India, but from Israel, North Korea, China and Egypt.

Another factor that was not apparent to the ICJ in 1996 struck quite literally out of a clear blue sky on 11 September 2001 with the kamikaze attacks on the World Trade Center and the Pentagon. The generation who could still remember where they were when they heard the news that President Kennedy was shot gave way to a generation who will live with the freeze-frame forever in their minds' eyes of the passenger jets exploding their fuel tanks on the buildings that served as the buck-teeth of New York. It was not long before the fear began to grip of terrorists achieving a purpose even more grandiose than 9/11 by obtaining and exploding a nuclear device or a 'dirty bomb'. This fear was stoked by Osama bin Laden's much-publicised quest for an Islamic bomb,[382] but was over-egged: Al Qaeda, even when it flourished, failed to recruit nuclear physicists (although it did meet with Dr Khan's networkers). The real fear was that states would divert nuclear know-how and materials to terrorist proxies like Hamas and Hezbollah, which had no shortage of suicide bombers to deliver them.

The US acted with commendable speed and largesse to buy up the nuclear weapons in the regional arsenals after the break-up of the Soviet Union – the Global Threat Reduction Programme spent $400 million on dismantling nuclear and chemical stockpiles in eastern Europe. More significantly, concerns about nuclear terrorism brought agreement (brokered jointly by Russia and the US) in 2005 on an international convention to suppress it, by making it an international crime for anyone not in the established military forces to possess, threaten or use radioactive material or a nuclear device with the intention of causing death, injury or damage to the environment.[383] At long last, and only under the impetus of Al Qaeda, the crime that Baruch and Evatt had urged in 1946 came to pass, sixty years later, although only in respect of individuals from 'non-state actors' i.e. terrorist groups and movements. But if it was a crime for a non-established military force to possess a bomb, what entitled any military force to possess it? The Convention for the Suppression of Nuclear Terrorism was supplemented by the Convention on the Physical Protection of

Nuclear Material and Nuclear Facilities (2005), the preamble of which noted that 'illicit trafficking, the unlawful taking and use of nuclear material and the sabotage of nuclear material and nuclear facilities' had become 'a matter of increased national and international concern'.

The 1996 advisory opinion had been predicated on a belief in the NPT, but all too soon its cracks began to show. In 1998, two of the refuseniks – India and Pakistan – tested their rival bombs. The IAEA inspection regime was exposed as ineffective in 2003 when its inspections could provide no conclusive reassurance that Saddam had *not* reactivated his nuclear programme, thereby providing an excuse for the invasion of Iraq. Later that year its competence was again called into question by Gaddafi's confession that Libya had neared completion of a nuclear bomb without alarming the IAEA. It was similarly flummoxed by the North Korean nuclear test in 2006: its inspections had not detected the advance before the North Korean withdrawal from the NPT in 2003 ended their rights of access. To speak of the IAEA having 'rights' of access is a misnomer (see Chapter 11): it can negotiate enhanced inspection rights with particular parties or it can have them bestowed by resolution of the Security Council, but it cannot, if a state party denies co-operation, open locked doors or inspect particular suspect facilities. This makes nonsense of any claim that it operates an exhaustive inspection regime, when a state party (e.g. Iran) refuses access to facilities, whilst a non-state party has no obligation at all to allow IAEA inspectors to enter the country. The IAEA has adopted an 'additional protocol' giving it greater powers over member states to collect information on their nuclear plans and obtain speedy access to their suspect locations, but seventy-two 'non-nuclear' states have thus far failed to bring the additional protocol into force. The effectiveness of inspection inevitably depends on intelligence (the IAEA is beholden to the CIA and to the intelligence services of states that are prepared to inform – not always accurately – on their enemies) and on permission for physical access to suspect locations, which is usually withheld if the suspicions are correct.

• • •

There can be no doubt that the acquisition of nuclear weapons by a government headed by international criminals is dangerous to the peace of the world. That would be the case not only with Iran, but also with a government so puerile and irresponsible as that of North Korea's, or so excitable and vulnerable to terrorist attack as Pakistan's. Iranian nuclear weapons capacity will provoke a nuclear arms race in the Middle East (Egypt, Saudi Arabia and Turkey, for a start) and in south east Asia. A nuclear war in these regions could affect the whole planet. The only way forward is to adopt a comprehensive approach by recognising that the further acquisition or possession of nuclear weapons, as well as their testing or use, is unlawful, and that all existing nuclear weapons states are under an obligation to reduce their numbers, gradually, to zero. That is what the NPT set out to achieve, but failed from the outset when Nixon and Kissinger protected Israel and later when China would not contemplate Chapter VII force against North Korea, and when irresponsible governments in India and Pakistan pandered to populist sentiment and, in Pakistan's case, allowed Dr Khan to behave like some nuclear Johnny Appleseed. That a brutal government like Iran can follow in their footsteps is a wake-up call to the world: unless there is a universal agreement to achieve these ends, backed in the last resort by force, there will be no end to nukes.

Iran is simply the most striking example of the illogic of international law's old approach to nuclear weapons, namely its failure to treat the bomb as morally wrong in itself. It outlawed the dum-dum bullet, for expanding and causing death with maximum suffering. The bomb's infinitely greater capacity for cruelty through ionising radiation effects on humans should have branded the weapon as the ultimate instrument of torture and screamed out 'never again' after Hiroshima. But this daemonic power has proved too tempting for the 'Big 5', and too attractive for excitable democracies like India and Pakistan, and for security-craving Israel, and for malevolent authoritarian states like Syria and Libya, Iraq, Iran and North Korea. The NPT was a temporary fix after the Cuban missile crisis, but was crafted to deal with the Cold War and not beyond. The 'Big 5' betrayed their obligation to disarm, whilst the others envied and copied them.

The only point at which the law might have asserted itself was in 1996, when the ICJ failed to find the obvious, namely that nuclear weapons are *always* (and not 'generally') incompatible with IHL. But that law has progressed, in the sixteen years since the *Nuclear Weapons* case, and has been supplemented by the international human rights law now dispensed by regional courts in Europe, Latin America and Africa and by the UN war crimes courts for the Balkans, Rwanda, Sierra Leone and Cambodia and the ICC itself. It cannot now be doubted that in view of the uncontrollable effects of a nuclear explosion and the long-term consequences of radiation poisoning, the weapon causes unnecessary suffering, cannot distinguish in its lethal effects between combatants and civilians, and (in the words of Geneva Protocol I) 'may be expected to cause widespread, long term and severe damage to the natural environment'. As the Red Cross described them, to the 2010 Review Conference on the NPT,

> nuclear weapons are unique in their destructive power, in the unspeakable human suffering they cause, in the impossibility of controlling their effects in space and time, in the risks of escalation they create and in the threat they pose to the environment, to future generations and indeed to the survival of humanity.

The '*opinio juris*', one of the infuriating Latin phrases international lawyers use when they examine the weight of opinion about whether a new rule of international law has emerged, has moved since 1996 towards a norm that prohibits the acquisition of nuclear weapons. It does not require the immediate emptying of existing arsenals – the law does not have retrospective effect. But it would criminalise any decision by non-nuclear states like Iran to 'break out' from a full nuclear fuel cycle to build nuclear weapons. By trespassing over this legal 'red line', by producing all the elements necessary for a bomb in a programme that can have no other purpose, Iran would be inviting a Security Council resolution to ramp up sanctions, and failing that, to authorise e.g. NATO to stop it by force.

In other words, international law has now changed, from the position in 1996 that use of nuclear weapons was in some circumstances permissible (so their very possession would be lawful) to the position in 2012 that acquisition of new nuclear weapons, by any state, is unlawful. The law is now what the UN Human Rights Committee, back in 1984, prematurely said that it was, when making a general comment on the 'right to life' guaranteed by the Human Rights treaties:

> The designing, testing, manufacture, possession and development of nuclear weapons are among the greatest threats to the right to life ... the production, testing, possession and deployment and use of nuclear weapons should be prohibited and recognised as crimes against humanity.[384]

Whether this opinion, shared at the time by the General Assembly (which has regularly passed motions to endorse it, although with some opposition), has now, twenty-eight years later, become a rule (or 'norm') of international law depends on a law creation process unlike that of national states, where parliaments pass statutes or dictators proclaim orders which are interpreted by courts and enforced by police. International law has no police force. Its treaties are honoured because states generally find it convenient to honour the promises they make to each other, and to behave as other states think it right to behave in their dealings with each other, according to generally accepted principles adopted by international tribunals and leading jurists. It is the interplay between these factors that can produce a new or altered 'customary' rule, 'custom' being made up of state practice (what governments have done and intend to keep on doing) and what is termed the *opinio juris* – what governments feel they are obliged to do (even if, in practice, or in secret, they do the opposite). If that moral obligation is strong, then it forms part of the *jus cogens* – rules 'accepted and recognised by the international community of States as a whole from which no derogation is permitted'.[385] There is a duty, owed to the whole international community, to obey the rule, and a correlative power, in the members of that community, to enforce such a 'peremptory norm from which no derogation is permitted'.[386]

It is notable that 'state practice' (which includes state non-practice), drawn from general statements, diplomatic correspondence, international conference resolutions and actual conduct, has virtually created a norm against *use* of nuclear weapons. As the US *Nuclear Posture Review Report* put it in 2010, 'it is in the US interest and that of other nations that the nearly 65 year record of nuclear non-use be extended forever'. That can only be achieved if international law prohibits possession, and it has moved in that direction in relation to future possession by currently non-nuclear states. It has begun to treat Iran as if its acquisition of a nuclear weapon would be illegal. Even China and Russia have agreed to the imposition of sanctions for its refusal to stop enriching uranium, and in meetings in Istanbul, Baghdad and Moscow the P5+1 have demanded that it should abjure steps that might make it nuclear capable. Well might Iranian diplomats intone their mantra about their 'inalienable right' to enrich: this was not acceptable to the 'Big 5' plus Germany and plus most other nations. Nor were North Korea's nuclear tests in 2006 and 2009, which incurred the inevitable condemnation of, and some sanctions from, the Security Council. Israel has not broken cover by conducting a nuclear test for fear of drawing attention to the unacceptability of its nuclear hypocrisy, and the *opinio juris* has in recent years hardened against any new country acquiring the bomb – one reason why criticism of the strike on Syria's reactor at Al-Kibar was so muted was because it was recognised as a surgical removal of the wherewithal for Syria to commit a future crime. North Korea aside, there have been no recent nuclear tests, and no defence of the necessity to carry them out since Condoleezza Rice gave this as a possible reason for the Bush regime's refusal to ratify the CTBT – a reason rejected by the Obama administration. At the same time, there has been increasing support for the IAEA in its watchdog role as sniffer-out of clandestine proliferation, on the assumption that there would be something wrong about a state party to the NPT developing a weapons capacity, whether or not it withdrew from the treaty before doing so. The main nuclear-armed states – the US and Russia – have in the START treaties accepted a duty gradually to reduce their arsenals, and their decision has been applauded by enemy and ally alike. If state practice now treats the acquisition of new nuclear weapons as if it were unlawful then, as a matter of customary international law, it already is.

Moreover, the recent decisions of UN courts have emphasised that the rules of IHL – including the ban on weapons that cause unnecessary suffering and which kill civilians and destroy the environment – are *erga omnes*, i.e. all states have a 'legal interest' in their observance and consequently a legal entitlement to demand their respect.[387] As the Red Cross points out, in its study of the customary rules of IHL, this duty to ensure respect imposes a requirement on states to 'do all in their power to ensure that international humanitarian law is respected universally'. That duty is primarily entrusted to the Security Council, but when it declines to act, states could use such force as may be in their collective power against a country found to be making nuclear bombs. Under human rights law, where crimes against humanity are ongoing (and illegal possession is a continuing offence) there is a 'right of humanitarian intervention' to use force to bring such crimes to an end – as with Milošević's ethnic cleansing in Kosovo and the 'safe havens' forcibly established by the US and UK in Iraq to protect the Kurds from Saddam's revenge. If acquisition of a nuclear weapon by a state that does not already possess it is now an international crime, as this book contends that it is, then it must be a legitimate exercise for other states, preferably with but otherwise without the backing of a Security Council resolution, to stop that crime in its tracks. Not as a matter of self-defence, but as part of the duty to ensure respect for international law.

The Red Cross would like to exclude the use of force as a means of ensuring respect, but that is pacifism on principle, ignoring the sad fact that sanctions do not always – or often – work. Once Iran starts to assemble nuclear bombs, only force will stop it. As an international war crimes court (the ICTY) pointed out in the *Kupreškić* case, human rights and humanitarian norms do not impose synallagmatic obligations (i.e. obligation of one state towards another) but 'they lay down obligations towards the international community as a whole'. Norms such as the prohibition of the use of weapons that cause superfluous injury or unnecessary suffering are of such a character that all states are entitled to take action to prevent their acquisition, and are obliged to take action to prevent their use. In this calculation, the legality of an attack on Iran's nuclear facilities by any state or alliance of states after a Chapter VII Security Council resolution had been disobeyed notwithstanding the severest sanctions would simply depend on whether there was evidence (the burden of proof being upon the attacking states) that Iran, having achieved a full nuclear fuel cycle, had decided to 'break out' and had reached the point of no return – the point at which all necessary components for a weapon are ready to assemble. This would put the 'red line' much further back than Israel would wish, and probably further back than Obama's elliptical statement about preventing (at what point?) Iran from acquiring nuclear weapons. In reality, there would be a period of months if not years before a bomb could be constructed after a 'break out' decision, followed by problems with delivery systems for the untested weapons, so the danger of it being used in this period is negligible. There would need to be clear proof that the decision had been taken – proof capable of being presented and tested in public – and any consequent attack would have to be proportionate to the objective of removing or destroying Iran's weapons production – dismantling Frankenstein's monster on the slab, as it were, before the electricity charge could bring it to life.

If the world is to proceed on the basis that the acquisition of nuclear weapons is now a crime, it must also heed the legal interpretation of Article VI of the NPT given by the ICJ in 1996 and largely ignored. This article imposes a legal duty to disarm, or at least to negotiate a convention that provides deadlines for the stages that would lead gradually to complete disarmament. Article VI has, very belatedly, been taken up by the Obama administration in conjunction with Russia, and the START agreement envisages initial reduction to 1,550 warheads each. But there has been silence from China and France, and the UK – strapped for cash as it is – has already earmarked an obscene £25 billion for the refurbishment of its Trident nuclear submarine fleet, which will probably cost three times as much. There must be no backsliding of this kind, and the Security Council must force the NPT recalcitrants – North Korea, Israel, India and Pakistan – to take part in a gradual reduction alongside the 'Big 5'. All nine arsenals quite clearly threaten international peace and thus are subject to the Security Council's Chapter VII powers. In August 2012, an Islamic militant attack on a Pakistani air force base where nuclear warheads were stored brought home just how dangerous they are – over 100 of them – in a country riddled with terrorists whose people still revere A. Q. Khan as a national hero. North Korea cannot be trusted at all, India is quietly developing a nuclear-armed fleet and Israel is planning for some of its untested nukes to be launched from submarines. Non-proliferation arrangements having broken down, the only way forward is back, to the total prohibition backed by criminal sanctions envisaged in 1946 by the Baruch and Evatt plans.

There are different ways of achieving this goal in a world with 19,000 nukes. The most satisfactory and comprehensive solution would be to replace the NPT with a Nuclear Weapons Abolition Convention, ratified by 193 states (all those at present in the world). This would make it an international crime for any state or person to design, develop, manufacture, stockpile, trans-fer, use or threaten to use a nuclear device, or to design, adapt or use a missile, torpedo or other vehicle to deliver a nuclear device. Any such allegation would be furnished by a strength-ened IAEA directly to the ICC Prosecutor, who would be entitled to bring an indictment at his or her own discretion, subject to approval by the judges of the court. There would be no need for a Security Council resolution, because that would enable the 'Big 5' to veto any investigation or prosecution of an ally, which was the reason why Baruch in 1946 was insistent that the UN should remove the superpower veto. His argument is much more powerful today when the Security Council cannot agree to take any action to stop the killing in Syria, and has been disastrously irresolute in dealing with North Korea. Cutting out the Security Council would require an amendment to the ICC Treaty, which gives the court jurisdiction over non-parties to its own treaty (such as Iran, North Korea, Pakistan, India, Israel and the US) only upon a reference from the Security Council. The conven-tion would need to establish the IAEA as a much more powerful verification body – one that could have its detectives enter any state at any time with the right to inspect any site or facility and to require disclosure of information in response to their enquiries. The Nuclear Weapons Abolition Convention would become the treaty foreshadowed by Article VI of the NPT, by including deadlines for destruction of all existing nuclear devices, under the supervision of the verification body, gradually over a period of, say, twenty-five years.[388]

Alternatively, until such a treaty were to come into force, the Security Council could pass a resolution declaring that nuclear weapons are a violation of international law, authorising force against any non-nuclear state that has been discovered attempting to make them and directing gradual elimination by those nations that already possess them – a 'first in, last out' process, perhaps, in which North Korea would be the first to lose its nuclear arsenal and the US the last. The next review conference for the ICC – due in 2016 – could add, to the list of war crimes within the court's jurisdiction, the crime of acquiring, testing or using a nuclear weapon. Such an amendment had very substantial majority support at the Rome Conference in 1998, but was taken off the agenda in a failed effort to keep America and Israel on side. America has – at least in the words of President Obama – accepted the need for complete nuclear disarmament, and an Israel post-Netanyahu may come to recognise that its own future is better assured by a nuclear-free Middle East. The problem for any solution relying on the present Security Council, however, is that it is likely to take a nuclear weapons explosion before it can be galvanised into agreement. A less dramatic way to force its hand would be for the General Assembly to refer the issue back to the ICJ, to obtain a ruling that the law has changed since its unsatisfactory decision in 1996.

For the present, the world should proceed on the basis that nuclear weapons are self-evidently illegal. No matter what politicians, generals, diplomats and scientists may say, the reasons are so blindingly obvious that they will have no defence, if they help their state to acquire missiles, to future prosecution in The Hague for a crime against humanity. The reason was given, simply but compellingly, by the chairman of the 2010 NPT Review Conference:

No amount of legal hair-splitting or operational obfuscation can change the fact that of all the weapons ever conceived by the mind of man, nuclear weapons are inherently indiscriminate, far beyond proportionality, cause unimaginable unnecessary suffering, and are inescapably and grievously harmful to the environment. It is a weapon where the notion of control is meaningless and the idea of military necessity is absurd. Nuclear weapons are the apex of man's genius at finding ways to destroy his fellow human beings.[389]

After Nagasaki: a boy stands to attention whilst
he waits to lay his brother on a funeral pyre.

EPILOGUE

This book has been an attempt to bring the debate about nuclear weapons back to the most fundamental of human rights, the entitlement of every individual not to be deprived arbitrarily of his or her life and not to be subjected to the inhumane treatment and torture caused to survivors by ionising radiation. These rights are 'intransgressible', as the International Court of Justice described them in 1996, and are inevitably put in jeopardy by any state which possesses a nuclear device in the knowledge that its very possession will provide a constant stimulus for other states to acquire this weapon the destructive power of which is uncontainable in space or time. It is unnecessary to dilate on the impact of the bomb – pictures of Hiroshima and of its victims provide evidence enough, updated by a reminder that today's nukes, even those built from scratch or from the designs of A. Q. Khan, are many times more powerful. Nor has it been necessary to dwell on nightmare scenarios, such as nuclear terrorists running around New York or Mumbai with suitcases containing grapefruit-sized packs of HEU, capable of devastating three square miles of the city.[390] This is a risk, as of course is explosion by accident or as a result of a misunderstanding or in the course of a political upheaval. It is a simple and obvious calculation that the more countries that have nukes, especially if uninspected for safety by the IAEA, the greater the risk of such a catastrophe. As for deterrence theory, in today's world the doctrine simply lacks logic. As Barry Blechman puts it,

> when our enemies are either unaccountable dictators with doubtful devotion to their citizens' welfare and distorted knowledge of the world around them, or terrorists with no return address, the

threat of inflicting mass civilian casualties in response to a nuclear
attack is neither practical, nor moral, nor likely to be effective.[391]

Iran wants a bomb, for power and prestige, but not to drop on
Israel: the prospect of some dying or demented Supreme Leader
giving that order, and having it obeyed by grasping Revolutionary
Guards, is low – as low perhaps as the prospect that Iran would
want to impress the Muslim world by firing a nuke in anger at
France in revenge for cartoons of the prophet in *Charlie Hebdo*.
These minute risks, even if estimated as low as 1 per cent, are not
risks worth running, either by Israel or by the world. It is a bad
point, but one always made in debates over Iran's intentions, that
its government is rational. This is the refrain of Kenneth Waltz,
doyen of deterrence theory, and of distinguished professors of
international relations, for example: 'There is little evidence to
suggest that leaders of so-called "rogue states" who now have (or
may soon have, as in the case of Iran) oversight of nuclear inven-
tories are any less rational than their US and Soviet cold war
counterparts were.'[392] There is a vast amount of evidence, which
I have summarised in the first part of this book, that the leaders
of Iran are about as rational as a group of serial killers, and it is
their criminality, rather than their rationality, that matters, if and
when they acquire a weapon of demonic destructiveness. They
are mullahs without mercy, without the slightest spark of human
feeling for those people and states they regard as their enemies.

That is why Iran must be stopped, not because the mullahs are
irrational but because they have committed unrequited atrocities
in the recent past, and may commit them again. Perhaps they
will be stopped, for a few years at most, by an American/Israeli
strike, once the cat and mouse game Iran is presently playing
with the Security Council and the P5+1 diplomats comes to an
end. In one respect, Mr Netanyahu is right, in his unprecedented
intervention in the US election, challenging President Obama
to lay down a 'red line' beyond which the US bombing of Iran
would begin. Of course, Netanyahu wants the 'red line' to be
drawn at the point when Iran achieves 'nuclear capability' (a
position he expects it to attain by Easter 2013). The White
House wants no line at all, preferring to leave Iran in the dark

about whether or when it will strike, in the hope of a sanctions-driven solution. But Iran is entitled to know where it stands: like any potential criminal, it deserves to be advised about the law so that it may decide whether or not to break it. And that is the problem – there is no clear rule because the law, as last declared, remains in the *Lotus* position: the case that decided that a state is entitled to do whatever there is no law against doing. That is a reason for the Security Council or the General Assembly to seek an urgent advisory opinion from the ICJ as to whether (and if so at what point) international law gives Israel and the US the right to attack Iran. This is a legal question, and deserves a legal answer. The US has a poor record of compliance, but the moral force of an ICJ decision on the issue would carry some weight. The question could also be referred to the court by the board of governors of the IAEA: it could hardly be said that the bombing of IAEA-inspected sites (with IAEA inspectors and equipment perhaps inside at the time) is outside the scope of the agencies' activities. Since the policing of the NPT is also part of the IAEA activities, it could also ask the World Court to rule on whether Iran's 'inalienable right to enrich' has been alienated by its misconduct (see pages 219–221).

The proposed bombing of Iran will top the international news agenda in 2013. Its proponents pretend it will be like the Israeli strikes on Osirak and Al-Kibar – an overnight surgical strike with a handful of casualties. But the truth is that there are likely to be thousands of deaths, if not from the bombing then from the radiation (if the operational reactor at Bushehr is hit) and from the 371 metric tons of highly toxic uranium hexafluoride stored at Isfahan and Natanz and other declared sites, which if released into the atmosphere will choke and burn the humans in its path (a path that may lead through cities). The only scientific study of the likely consequences of bombing Iran's major facilities draws on Bhopal and Chernobyl as comparators and estimates tens of thousands of deaths from exposure to highly toxic chemical plumes and radioactive fallout:

Between 3,500 and 5,000 people at Iran's four nuclear sites would be killed or injured as a result of the physical and thermal impact of the blasts. If one were to include casualties at other targets, the total number of people killed and injured could easily exceed 10,000. At Isfahan alone, anywhere between 240,000 and 352,000 people could be exposed to toxic plumes. Similarly, a strike on Bushehr would not only expose the 240,000 residents of Bushehr to fallout, it would eventually contaminate much of the Persian Gulf. Major cities, business centres and trading routes throughout the region would be at risk. The environmental and economic costs of strikes on the facilities would be in tens of billions of dollars, and that is assuming that there will be no war.

The human cost of bombing Iran demonstrates the danger of the West being stampeded by Israel into an attack that would not be forgotten or forgiven by the Iranian people, who are the best and only guarantee of their country's future – once they work out how to take it back from the mullahs who have put them at such risk by this nuclear gambit, partly to distract from their brutal human rights record. That record is never put on the table by the P5+1 and EU diplomats. Before any question of sanctions relief should be considered, there must be an acknowledgement of the regime's crimes, a truth commission at least to identify the whereabouts of the bodies of their victims, and compensation to their families. Before any compromise is reached – and for all it will jangle Israeli nerves, the eventual compromise may be a fuel cycle that enriches up to 5 per cent but is subject to ultra-intrusive IAEA inspections to ensure that it does not divert – there must be recognition and justice for those this state has unlawfully killed.

• • •

What is clear is that dealing with the challenge of Iran's potential 'breakout', and the breakouts by other countries which are sure to follow, should not be left to the US, and much less to Israel. The only 'red line' that Iran cannot cross must be drawn by international law. That is either through the exercise of anticipatory self-defence on the *Caroline* principle, a right which would only arise if Iran could be proved to have both the bomb and the intention of dropping it on Israel. There is an alternative, however, once it is accepted that possession of the bomb is an international crime. That would justify action against Iran without evidence that it intends to nuke Israel – the legal red line would be drawn at the point when Iran actually has the bomb in its possession. In law, that would be the point at which it has all components prepared and ready to assemble, with an intention to assemble them.

This assumes, of course, that possession of a nuclear weapon is by now the crime against humanity that the Human Rights Committee in 1984, and the General Assembly in a number of resolutions, have declared it to be. But if the US is to rely on either argument, it must heed the words of its own Justice Robert Jackson, as he opened the Nuremberg trial in 1945: 'If certain acts of violation of treaties are crimes, they are crimes whether the US does them or Germany does them, and we are not prepared to lay down a rule of criminal conduct against others, which we would not be prepared to have invoked against us.'

At the UN on 25 September 2012 President Obama warned of the dangers of a nuclear-armed Iran and referred to 'a coalition of countries' (presumably including the UK, whose people have not been consulted) that will join the US to 'do what we must to prevent Iran obtaining a nuclear weapon'. But any such attack on Iran attracts a reciprocal duty on the US and its allies to treat nuclear weapons as if possession of them were illegal under international human rights and humanitarian law, and to proceed to negotiate the disarmament convention required by Article VI of the NPT 'in good faith', a phrase which requires a commitment that has not hitherto been apparent.

There are, of course, many obstacles in the path of complete disarmament, most obviously the problem of how to deal with states that cheat. That is why it is essential to begin the quest for a world without nukes by establishing a legal architecture for the disarmament exercise. The General Assembly could make another reference to the ICJ, this time asking the question whether, today, possession of nuclear weapons infringes international law, and whether the nuclear parties to the NPT have been in compliance with their Article VI duties (they haven't), and what is now required of them to deliver on the guarantee of 'complete' disarmament. Of course, as the Canberra Commission pointed out, whilst a legal regime must establish the basic architecture for a nuclear-free world, it must be recognised that a legal regime 'supports but does not bring about such a world'. That will only happen if there is sufficient public awareness of the new dangers of a post-proliferation world to mobilise governments and non-government organisations alike to produce the kind of consensus that brought the Landmines and Cluster Bomb Conventions into force. That is why human rights organisations should begin their lobbying and campaigning to ban the bomb, on the basis that it is contrary to the right to life and the right not to be subjected to inhumane treatment and torture.

But where have all the protestors gone? Whatever happened to the 'Ban the Bomb' movement, so vital in the 1960s, which seems to have gone into occulation? Professor Lawrence Freedman has noted that the very absence of nuclear war for so many years has inculcated complacency: 'In a strange way, a sort of confidence that the weapons will not be used provides a degree of comfort that time is available for an orderly progress to abolition'.[393] Will it really take another Hiroshima, an accidental explosion or a terrorist dirty bomb, to generate the necessary impetus for international agreement on a legal regime that really does ban the bomb? How else can policy makers, and the people for whom they make policy, be jolted out of the mind-frame set by Cold War propaganda that lots of nukes actually protect their security, simply because there has not been a nuclear war since 1945? For all the Nobel Prize-winning talk about disarmament, for all the lip service to Article VI compliance, in 2009 not one of the states with nuclear weapons had a single official, let alone any government department or inter-agency group, working on how to decommission its nukes.[394] In the absence of a nuclear weapon accident or use by one proliferating state or other, the only way that this complacency will be jolted is if the mullahs actually manage to make a bomb. That would be a wake-up warning for the world, and is the strongest argument in favour of letting them go right ahead.

The only alternative is to bring nuclear disarmament out of the papers of policy wonks and into the streets and the protest movements. That does not mean dusting off duffel coats from the Aldermaston marches: CND in the 1960s was before the time when NGOs influenced governments. If ever there was a human rights issue in the world today, it is the appalling prospect of Iran with nuclear weapons. That would make it the tenth state in the world with weapons that imperil the most fundamental right of all, not to be arbitrarily deprived of life. So why does this issue never feature in the campaigns of Amnesty International and the reports of Human Rights Watch (HRW)? Why have I found no international human rights law textbook (and there are many) with 'nuclear weapons' in the index? This extraordinary over-sight is explicable only on the basis that 'disarmament' has been detached from 'human rights' – they have separate departments at the UN which do not appear to talk to each other. Ironically, both Amnesty and HRW have issued short statements complaining about how international concern over Iran's nuclear programme has overridden any concern about its human rights violations, but neither have made the link and pointed out the danger of a human rights violator getting the bomb, or indeed the danger of the bomb to human rights. It is an issue that they must now take up, for their passion and their legal precision are desperately needed to find answers when foreign policy and diplomacy have failed. If human rights means anything, it must mean campaign-ing to switch off the lights of this perverted science which have brought so many nukes into the world, and now threaten to bring more.

ACKNOWLEDGEMENTS

My interest in the human rights situation in Iran was first aroused by Roya and Ladan Boroumand, who asked me to investigate the prison massacres of 1988 and whose foundation published my report, on which I have drawn for my description of these appalling events. (I should make clear that my comments and historical analysis are not necessarily shared by Roya and Ladan or by their foundation.) I repeat my thanks to the witnesses who came forward for interview by myself or my assistant, Jen Robinson, who helped me with great skill, dedication and discretion. Over forty former prisoners or relatives of the victims were interviewed at my chambers in London, and in Washington, Amsterdam, Paris, Cologne, Frankfurt and Berlin, and I met others at a seminar held by Oxford's School for Socio-Legal Studies in 2011. Some have been reluctant to be named, and I have respected their wishes. I am grateful to Anne Applebaum for inviting me to participate in a seminar at the Legatum Institute in 2012, and to Firouzeh Mirrazavi at the Iran Review for keeping me updated with the view from Tehran. Lionel Nichols, Toby Collis, Nodoka Kikuchi, Dr Simona Tutuianu and Emlyn Clay provided expert research and assistance, and Judy Rollinson worked tirelessly on the manuscript. At Biteback, my thanks to Sam Carter, Hollie Teague and Iain Dale, and at Random House (Australia) to Catherine Hill, Nikki Christer and Fenella Davidson. My agent Caroline Michel brought us all together, and my family suffered my absence both from its bosom and from gainful employment, as my deadline, and Israel's red line, both approached at the end of the summer of 2012.

CHRONOLOGY

847 AD	At age five, the Twelfth Imam 'occulates'.
1837	Sinking of the USS *Caroline*.
1863	Lieber Code for the conduct of soldiers in wartime adopted.
1899	First Hague Convention.
1906	Introduction of democratic constitution for Persia.
1907	Second Hague Convention.
1914	H. G. Wells's *The World Set Free* published.
1921	General Reza Khan seizes power.
1926	Reza Khan crowned as Reza Shah Pahlavi, marking the beginning of the Pahlavi Dynasty. Mohammed, his eldest son, proclaimed Crown Prince.
1935	Persia renamed Iran.
1941	Shah deposed by occupying British–Russian forces in favour of his son.
1945	
6 August	'Little Boy' explodes over Hiroshima.
9 August	'Fat Man' explodes over Nagasaki.
14 August	Emperor Hirohito broadcasts Japanese surrender.
24 October	UN Charter becomes effective.
1946	Baruch plan proposed. Dr H. V. Evatt appointed first chair of Atomic Energy Authority.

1948

9 December   Convention on the Prevention and Punishment of the Crime of Genocide.

10 December   Universal Declaration of Human Rights proclaimed.

1949   Geneva Convention.

Korean War: General MacArthur requests nukes.

1951   Majlis votes unanimously to nationalise the oil industry. Mohammad Mossadegh becomes Prime Minister. United Kingdom imposes blockade in reprisal.

1953   Eisenhower's 'Atoms for Peace' speech at UN.

Military coup (backed by CIA and MI6) removes Mossadegh then Shah returns to rule with military support.

1956   Establishment of the IAEA.

1961   Ben-Gurion promises Kennedy that Israel will not develop nukes at Dimona.

1963

5 June   Ayatollah Khomeini criticises the Shah and is arrested. Several hundred protesters are killed by security forces.

1964

November   Khomeini is exiled from Iran after six months of house arrest.

1967   Arab–Israeli Six-Day War. Israel considers first use of nuclear device.

1968   The Treaty for the Non-Proliferation of Nuclear Weapons (NPT) opens for signature (enters into effect in 1970).

1968   Iran becomes signatory to the NPT.

1970   Iran ratifies the NPT.

1971   Celebrations at Persepolis. Arrest, trial and execution of eleven MEK student leaders.

1972   The Shah announces a programme for forty nuclear reactors.

1974	India's first test of its nuclear bomb. A. Q. Khan offers expertise to Pakistan.
1977	Promulgation of the First Protocol to the Geneva Conventions (Protocol I).

1979

4 January	Shah appoints his long-time opponent, Shapour Bakhtiar, as Prime Minister. Bakhtiar dissolves SAVAK, and restores freedom of the press.
1 February	Khomeini returns. Hailed by the masses as the saviour and new leader. Demands Bakhtiar's resignation.
5 February	Establishment of the Provisional Islamic Revolutionary Government, with Mehdi Bazargan as its Prime Minister.
1 April	The Islamic Republic of Iran established by referendum. Day declared as 'the first day of the Government of God'.
4 November	Armed students storm the US embassy in Tehran and take a hundred hostages.

1980

24 January	Abolhassan Bani-Sadr is elected President.
22 September	Iraq launches several strikes against Iranian airfields, starting the Iran–Iraq War.
30 September	Iran bombs Iraq's Osirak reactor.

1981

7 June	Israel bombs Iraq's Osirak reactor.
20 June	Massive street demonstrations by MEK supporters in favour of Bani-Sadr; many killed by Revolutionary Guards.
22 June	Bani-Sadr flees to Paris with Rajavi.
28 June	Bomb at the Islamic Party headquarters. Seventy killed. 'Reign of Terror' against MEK begins.
October	Rafsanjani calls for extermination of 'hypocrites', i.e. the MEK. Ali Khamenei is elected President. Mir-Hossein Mousavi is Prime Minister. Jafar Nayyeri is appointed a religious judge.

1984

8 February	Amnesty International charges Iran with large-scale abuses of human rights including over 5,000 executions since 1979.

1985

10 October	President Khamenei begins a second four-year term.
23 November	Ayatollah Hossein Ali Montazeri is selected by a special assembly as Ayatollah Khomeini's successor as Supreme Leader.

1986

1986	A. Q. Khan visits Iran. Pakistan and Iran in secret deal for nuclear co-operation.
June	Rajavi and MEK expelled from France. They move to Camp Ashraf on the Iraq border, under the protection of Saddam Hussein.
5 October	The *Sunday Times* publishes Mordechai Vanunu's details of clandestine Israeli nuclear weapons programme.

1988

28 March	Mordechai Vanunu sentenced to eighteen years' prison for treason and espionage, twelve to be served in solitary confinement.
March	Saddam uses chemical weapons against the Kurds and the Iranian army.
June	Ayatollah Khomeini appoints Majlis speaker Ali Akbar Hashemi Rafsanjani Commander-in-Chief of the armed forces.
3 July	USS *Vincennes* mistakenly shoots down Iran Air flight 655, killing all 290 passengers and crew.
20 July	Khomeini broadcasts his bitter acceptance of a truce with Iraq ('more deadly than drinking poison').
25 July	The MEK launch their 'Eternal Light' invasion with Iraqi air cover.
28 July	Khomeini's fatwa orders the execution of all 'steadfast' MEK prisoners.
29 July	MEK retreats to Iraq.
29 July –10 August	Death Committee hearings and executions take place in Evin and Gohardasht and at least twenty provincial prisons.
5 August	Chief Justice Mousavi Ardebili announces public demands 'to execute all MEK without exception'.
15 August	Montazeri calculates that between 2,800 and 3,800 prisoners have been executed in the first ten days of the fatwa.
26 August	The Death Committees reconvene to begin the 'second wave' of killings.
2 September	Amnesty International issues 'Urgent Action' in response to reports of the prison killings.
October	Reynaldo Galindo Pohl, UN special representative

for Iran, reports to General Assembly that 200 MEK massacred in Evin prison assembly hall and 860 buried in a mass grave.

1989

January   Rafsanjani admits that 'less than one thousand' have been executed. Pohl reports to the Human Rights Commission, listing names of over 1,000 victims.

14 February   Fatwa on Salman Rushdie and his translators and publishers.

May   Death of Khomeini. Replaced as Supreme Leader by Khamenei. Rafsanjani becomes President.

November   Pohl report to the General Assembly confirms that mass executions of political prisoners took place in 1988.

1990   Kazem Rajavi assassinated in Switzerland.

December   Amnesty International report alleges 'perhaps thousands' of executions of political prisoners.

1991   Assassination of Shapour Bakhtiar in Paris.
               IAEA 'discover' Iraqi plans for the development of nuclear weapons.

1992

17 March   Iran sets off bombs at Israeli embassy in Buenos Aires, Argentina.

1994   Iran pays $3 million to A. Q. Khan for nuclear weapons assistance.

18 July   Iran sets off bombs at Jewish community centre in Buenos Aires, Argentina.

1995

17 April   NPT Review Conference calls for a Middle East nuclear-
–12 May   free zone.

1996

8 July   ICJ hands down advisory opinion on *The Legality of the Threat or Use of Nuclear Weapons*.

November   Report of Canberra Commission

1997   Opening of NPT additional protocol (as of today only 117 nations have brought into force).
               Mohammad Khatami wins presidential election ('Tehran Spring').

Mohammed ElBaradei of Egypt elected as Director General of the IAEA.

1998
17 July   Rome Statute creates International Criminal Court. (ICC jurisdiction begins 1 July 2002.)
Pakistan tests six nuclear weapons. India tests its 'Big Bomb'.

1999
January   Iranian Ministry of Intelligence admits responsibility for the 'chain murders'.

2002   MEK press conference reveals Iranian clandestine nuclear weapons programme at Natanz.
September   Bush administration releases US National Security Strategy, approving 'preventive' self-defence.

2003   Iran agrees to suspend nuclear activities and ratifies NPT additional protocol.
Colonel Gaddafi gives up Libya's nuclear weapons programme and exposes the A. Q. Khan network.
10 January   North Korea withdraws from the NPT.
19 March   US invasion of Iraq.

2004   A. Q. Khan televised confession; pardoned and placed under house arrest.

2005   Mahmoud Ahmadinejad elected President.
13 April   Adoption of the International Convention for the Suppression of Acts of Nuclear Terrorism.

2006
3 January   Iran informs IAEA of its decision to resume nuclear research and development.
April   Ahmadinejad announces enrichment to 3.75 per cent LEU.
4 July   North Korea's first nuclear test.
31 July   UN Security Council Resolution 1696 calling on Iran to suspend all enrichment-related and reprocessing activities including research and development.
23 December   UN Security Council Resolution 1737 reiterates demand that Iran suspends nuclear weapons activity.

2007
24 March   UN Security Council Resolution 1747 calls upon all

states and international financial institutions not to enter into new commitments for grants, financial assistance and concessional loans to Iran.

6 September   Israeli bombing of Syrian Al-Kibar reactor ('Operation Orchard').

2008   The foreign ministers of the Arab countries threaten to leave the NPT unless Israel admits to its nuclear weapons and commits to disarmament.

2009
5 April   US President Obama gives Prague speech, committing to seek a world without nuclear weapons.
25 May   Second North Korean nuclear weapons test.
12 June   Ahmadinejad wins second-term presidency in election many believe to have been rigged.
15 June   Mass 'where is my vote' protests.
20 June   Massacre of political protestors, including Neda Agha-Soltan.
20 December   Ayatollah Montazeri dies in Qom.

2010
9 February   Iran announces it will enrich to 20 per cent LEU.
8 April   New START Treaty between US and Russia signed (effective 5 February 2011).
May   NPT Review Conference.
November   Assassination of Iranian nuclear scientist.

2011
November   IAEA report announces 'credible' evidence of recommencement of Iranian nuclear weapons programme.

2012
February   Ahmadinejad publicly announces enrichment to 20 per cent.
April   US President Obama says US would conduct a 'pre-emptive' strike against Iran to prevent acquisition of nuclear weapons.
June   The White House admits complicity in the 'stuxnet worm' virus attack on Iran's nuclear computer systems.
1 July   OECD discontinues purchase of oil from Iran.
August   IAEA reports that Iran may not have suspended its enrichment-related activities at Natanz and Fordow facilities.
               Taliban militants storm Minhas air force base where some of Pakistan's nuclear warheads are stored.

13 September	IAEA adopts a resolution condemning Iran over its nuclear programme.
16 September	Netanyahu challenges Obama to lay down a 'red line'.
Late September	MEK to be removed from the US terrorist list.
	Ahmadinejad, at UN, says Israel 'will be eliminated'. Denies any interest in nuclear weapons.
	Obama says that a 'US-led coalition' will stop Iran from building nukes.
27 September	Netanyahu 'blinks' at UN. Resets red line to spring/ early summer 2013.
3 October	Demonstrations in Tehran bazaar against Ahmadinejad and economic malaise. The rial reels.

THE TREATY ON THE NON-PROLIFERATION OF NUCLEAR WEAPONS (EXTRACTS)

...

Considering the devastation that would be visited upon all mankind by a nuclear war and the consequent need to make every effort to avert the danger of such a war and to take measures to safeguard the security of peoples,

Believing that the proliferation of nuclear weapons would seriously enhance the danger of nuclear war,

...

Declaring their intention to achieve at the earliest possible date the cessation of the nuclear arms race and to undertake effective measures in the direction of nuclear disarmament,

...

Recalling the determination expressed by the Parties to the 1963 Treaty banning nuclear weapons tests in the atmosphere, in outer space and under water in its Preamble to seek to achieve the discontinuance of all test explosions of nuclear weapons for all time and to continue negotiations to this end,

...

Desiring to further the easing of international tension and the strengthening of trust between States in order to facilitate the cessation of the manufacture of nuclear weapons, the liquidation of all their existing stockpiles, and the elimination from national arsenals of nuclear weapons and the means of their delivery pursuant to a Treaty on general and complete disarmament under strict and effective international control,

...

ARTICLE I

Each nuclear-weapon State Party to the Treaty undertakes not to transfer to any recipient whatsoever nuclear weapons or other nuclear explosive devices or control over such weapons or explosive devices directly, or indirectly; and not in any way to assist, encourage, or induce any non-nuclear-weapon State to manufacture or otherwise acquire nuclear weapons or other nuclear explosive devices, or control over such weapons or explosive devices.

ARTICLE II
Each non-nuclear-weapon State Party to the Treaty undertakes not to receive the transfer from any transferor whatsoever of nuclear weapons or other nuclear explosive devices or of control over such weapons or explosive devices directly, or indirectly; not to manufacture or otherwise acquire nuclear weapons or other nuclear explosive devices; and not to seek or receive any assistance in the manufacture of nuclear weapons or other nuclear explosive devices.

ARTICLE III
1. Each non-nuclear-weapon State Party to the Treaty undertakes to accept safeguards, as set forth in an agreement to be negotiated and concluded with the International Atomic Energy Agency in accordance with the Statute of the International Atomic Energy Agency and the Agency's safeguards system, for the exclusive purpose of verification of the fulfilment of its obligations assumed under this Treaty with a view to preventing diversion of nuclear energy from peaceful uses to nuclear weapons or other nuclear explosive devices...
...
4. Non-nuclear-weapon States Party to the Treaty shall conclude agreements with the International Atomic Energy Agency to meet the requirements of this Article either individually or together with other States in accordance with the Statute of the International Atomic Energy Agency...

ARTICLE IV
1. Nothing in this Treaty shall be interpreted as affecting the inalienable right of all the Parties to the Treaty to develop research, production and use of nuclear energy for peaceful purposes without discrimination and in conformity with Articles I and II of this Treaty.
2. All the Parties to the Treaty undertake to facilitate, and have the right to participate in, the fullest possible exchange of equipment, materials and scientific and technological information for the peaceful uses of nuclear energy...

ARTICLE V
Each Party to the Treaty undertakes to take appropriate measures to ensure that, in accordance with this Treaty, under appropriate international observation and through appropriate international procedures, potential benefits from any peaceful applications of nuclear explosions will be made available to non-nuclear-weapon States Party to the Treaty on a non-discriminatory basis and that the charge to such Parties for the

explosive devices used will be as low as possible and exclude any charge for research and development...

ARTICLE VI
Each of the Parties to the Treaty undertakes to pursue negotiations in good faith on effective measures relating to cessation of the nuclear arms race at an early date and to nuclear disarmament, and on a treaty on general and complete disarmament under strict and effective international control.

ARTICLE IX
3. ...For the purposes of this Treaty, a nuclear-weapon State is one which has manufactured and exploded a nuclear weapon or other nuclear explosive device prior to 1 January 1967.
4. For States whose instruments of ratification or accession are deposited subsequent to the entry into force of this Treaty, it shall enter into force on the date of the deposit of their instruments of ratification or accession...

ARTICLE X
1. Each Party shall in exercising its national sovereignty have the right to withdraw from the Treaty if it decides that extraordinary events, related to the subject matter of this Treaty, have jeopardized the supreme interests of its country. It shall give notice of such withdrawal to all other Parties to the Treaty and to the United Nations Security Council three months in advance. Such notice shall include a statement of the extraordinary events it regards as having jeopardized its supreme interests.
...

Note: On 11 May 1995, in accordance with Article X, paragraph 2, the Review and Extension Conference of the Parties to the Treaty on the Non-Proliferation of Nuclear Weapons decided that the Treaty should continue indefinitely.

ENDNOTES

PREFACE

1   Geoffrey Robertson, *The Massacre of Political Prisoners in Iran, 1988: Report of an Inquiry* (Washington, DC: Abdorraham Boroumand Foundation, 2010), p. 1.

2   Ibid., pp. 1–2.

INTRODUCTION

3   Physicians for the Prevention of Nuclear War, August 2010.

4   Encyclopædia Iranica, 'Islam in Iran vii. The Concept of Mahdi in Twelver Shi'ism', www.iranicaonline.org/articles/islam-in-iran-vii-the-concept-of-mahdi-in-twelver-shiism.

5   Quoted in Chris Patten, *What Next? Surviving the Twenty-First Century* (London: Allen Lane, 2008) p. 125.

6   Daniel H. Joyner, *Interpreting the Nuclear Non-Proliferation Treaty* (Oxford: Oxford University Press, 2011) p. 5.

7   Gareth Evans and Yoriko Kawaguchi (co-chairs), *Eliminating Nuclear Threats: A Practical Agenda for Global Policymakers* (Canberra: International Commission on Nuclear Non-proliferation and Disarmament, 2009) para. 5.15 (p. 52).

CHAPTER 1: BACKSTORY

8   Ian Black and Saeed Kamali Dehghan, 'Iran lays claim to British Museum's Cyrus Cylinder', *The Guardian*, 15 September 2010.

9   See Con Coughlin, *Khomeini's Ghost* (London: Macmillan, 2009), p. 129.

10 Gertrude Bell, *Persian Pictures* (London: Ernest Benn, 1928).

11 See Stephen Kinzer, *All the Shah's Men: An American Coup and the Roots of Middle East Terror*, 2nd edn (New York: Wiley and Sons, 2008), p. 95.

12 Christopher de Bellaigue, *Patriot of Persia: Muhammad Mossadegh and a Very British Coup* (London: Bodley Head, 2012), p. 107.

13 Ray Takeyh, *Guardians of the Revolution: Iran and the World in the Age of the Ayatollahs* (Oxford: Oxford University Press, 2009), p. 242.

14 For Taleqani's equivocal relationship with Khomeini, see Hamid

Dabashi, *Theology of Discontent: The Ideological Foundation of the Islamic Revolution in Iran* (Somerset, NJ: Transaction, 2006), pp. 267–70.

15   The numbers killed on 5 June 1963 have been wildly over-estimated ('thousands') by the Islamic Republic, to assist its demonisation of the Shah. Emadeddin Baghi, 'Figures for the Dead in the Revolution' (Emruz, 30 July 2003) calculates that a total of 3,164 were killed between 1963 and 1979 under the Shah. Even this is said to be an over-estimate, for example by former UK ambassador Sir Denis Wright. However there is no doubt that many more were tortured by SAVAK.

16   Abbas Amanat, *Apocalyptic Islam and Iranian Shi'ism* (London: I. B. Tauris, 2009), p. 192.

17   Ervand Abrahamian, *Tortured Confessions: Prisons and Public Recantations in Modern Iran* (Berkeley: University of California Press, 1999), p. 112.

18   See 'How my cellmate became a torturer in God's name', *The Times*, 10 August 2010.

19   See Ervand Abrahamian, *The Iranian Mojahedin* (New Haven, CT: Yale University Press, 1989), p. 89 *et seq.*

20   Abrahamian, *Tortured Confessions*, p. 106.

21   Said Amir Arjomand, *The Turban for the Crown: The Islamic Revolution in Iran* (Oxford: Oxford University Press, 1988), p. 137. Also see Khomeini's speech at the cemetery of Qom on 9 March 1979, *Sahifeh Nur*, vol. 5 (Ministry of Islamic Guidance, 1983), p. 185.

22   Coughlin, *Khomeini's Ghost*, p. 170.

23   See Dr Abdolkarim Lahiji, 'The Judiciary in Iran', paper for Legatum Seminar, 14 May 2012.

24   'Case Concerning US Diplomatic and Consular Staff in Tehran', *IJC Reports* (1980), 3 para. 91.

25   See Fakhreddin Azimi, *The Quest for Democracy in Iran: A Century of Struggle against Authoritarian Rule* (Cambridge, MA: Harvard University Press, 2008), p. 363.

26   Ibid., p. 143.

27   See Abrahamian, *The Iranian Mojahedin*, p. 220. Lingering suspicion still attaches to a pro-Soviet faction with the Islamist regime, since the most senior casualty, Beheshti, was the most powerful anti-communist among the mullahs.

CHAPTER 2: REVOLUTIONARY JUSTICE

28   *Kayhan*, 4 July 1981, p. 4, reporting Ayatollah Khomeini's speech for the families of those killed at the bombing of the Islamic Party headquarters. A fuller version, published on the same day in *Ettela'at*, can be read as a blood-curdling incitement to punish by

death (the punishment God had set for them) the MEK, who are 'corruptors who wade into the street and scare believers' by their Marxist-influenced interpretation of Islam: 'They and we are not alike ... They believe in class war. They think there is no day of resurrection and there is nothing beyond the material world. But you don't. The day they prevail, you (God forbid) shall be their sacrificial lamb.'

29 *Ettela'at*, 4 July 1981. The Chief Public Prosecutor of the Islamic Republic, Hojatoleslam Mousavi Tabrizi, clarifies in a speech on 21 September 1981 the fate of dissidents mentioned by Ayatollah Khomeini: 'If they arrest them, they will no longer wait for months whilst they [the arrested] eat, sleep and use up the resources that belong to the people. [Instead,] they will be prosecuted in the streets. [Thus,] whoever held a [Molotov] cocktail in his hands and stood opposed to the institution of the Islamic Republic was prosecuted on the spot. When they are arrested and by the time they are brought to the Public Prosecutor's office, they are already tried and their sentence is execution.'

30 Report of Friday Sermon, *Jomhuri Eslami*, 4 July 1981, p. 8; *Ettela'at*, 4 July 1981, p. 10.

31 See Sayyid Muhammad Rizvi, *Apostasy in Islam* (http://www. al-islam.org) and sources cited therein.

32 Chief Revolutionary Prosecutor Mousavi Tabrizi, *Jomhuri Eslami*, 15 December 1981, p. 12.

33 Abrahamian, *Tortured Confessions*, p. 125.

34 So I am informed by a number of survivors of the 1988 massacres who were arrested after participating in the Mojahedin demonstration of June 1981.

35 On 27 July 1981, Tehran radio announced that MKO central council member Mohammad Reza Sa'adati had been executed – apparently summarily (reported by NYTimes/Reuters).

36 Takeyh, *Guardians of the Revolution*, p. 242.

37 Abrahamian, *Tortured Confessions*, p. 170.

38 'Islamic Revolutionary Prosecutor General: 90% of active MKO members arrested', *Jomhuri Eslami Daily*, 21 February 1982.

39 Abrahamian, *Tortured Confessions*, p. 186.

40 *Jomhuri Eslami*, 8 January 1983, p. 5.

41 *Jomhuri Eslami*, 9 August 1982, p. 12.

42 *Kayhan*, 18 February 1985, pp. 1–2, reporting Minister of Intelligence Reyshahri (often translated as Minister of Information).

43 *Ettela'at*, 20 January 1982.

44 See Coughlin, *Khomeini's Ghost*, pp. 234–5.

45 Dilip Hiro, *The Longest War: The Iran–Iraq Military Conflict*, rev. edn (London: Paladin, 1990), pp. 244–5.

46 Khomeini's letter to Montazeri (1986) in *The Political Memoires*

of Reyshahri, p. 255, as quoted in Iraj Mesdaghi, *Neither Life nor Death, Volume 3: Restless Raspberries*, 2nd edn (Stockholm: Alfabet Maxima Publishing, 2006), p. 82.

47 *Resalat,* 20 July 1987, p. 10, reporting a speech by Ayatollah Eslami.

48 Mesdaghi, *Neither Life nor Death*, pp. 66, 100.

49 Several statements made to me confirm this and I do not believe MEK denials. As an avid reader in my youth of World War II prison memoirs, I recall that there does not seem to have been a Stalag in which some hidden radio was not surreptitiously tuned to the BBC. Even the Baader-Meinhof gang, the most heavily guarded of terrorists, followed the fate of hijackers demanding their release via smuggled transistors. Many MKO members were engineering students. They were buoyed by what they heard, but there is no evidence at all that their radios were two-way or that they were receiving commands from Iraq.

CHAPTER 3: THE 1988 MASSACRE

50 Hiro, *The Longest War*, pp. 242–3.

51 The numbers of casualties are disputed. See Baqer Moin, *Khomeini: Life of the Ayatollah* (London: I.B. Tauris, 1999), p. 278, which suggests that the casualties may have been in hundreds on both sides. The then Minister of Intelligence, Mohammad Mohammadi Reyshahri, gives the figure of 3,400 Mojahedin killed, wounded or captured. See M. Mohammadi Reyshahri, *Memoirs* (Tehran: The Centre for Islamic Revolution Documents, 2007 (in Persian), p. 171.

52 The fatwa itself is undated, but internal evidence from the Montazeri memoirs has pin-pointed this date.

53 See Baqer Moin, *Khomeini: Life of the Ayatollah* (New York: Thomas Dunne, 2000), pp. 287–9.

54 *Kayhan*, 6 August 1988, p. 15.

55 Amnesty International, 'Urgent Action: Death Penalty', 2 September 1988.

56 Hossein Ali Montazeri, *The Diaries of Ayatollah Montazeri* (Los Angeles: Ketab Corporation, 2001) (in Persian), p. 347.

57 National Council of Resistance of Iran (NCRI), 'The Massacre of Political Prisoners' (1999). In 2001 in its publication 'Crimes against Humanity', the NCRI estimated 30,000 deaths nationwide, although this figure is not convincingly explained and seems highly exaggerated.

58 NCRI, 'Crimes against Humanity'; see also *The Diaries of Ayatollah Montazeri*, pp. 352–3.

59 NCRI, 'Crimes against Humanity', p. 22.

CHAPTER 4: DEATH TO THE ATHEISTS

60 *The Diaries of Ayatollah Montazeri*, pp. 637–8.

61 Iran Human Rights Documentation Center (IHRDC), *Deadly Fatwa: Iran's 1988 Prison Massacre* (New Haven, CT: IHRDC, 2009), pp. 25–6.

62 Ibid., p. 30.

63 Ibid.

64 *Ettela'at,* 1 September 1988, p. 14.

65 *Ettela'at,* 7 September 1988, p. 2.

66 *Kayhan,* 11 September 1988, p. 14.

67 Ibid.

68 Nima Parvaresh, *An Unequal Battle: A Report of Seven Years' Imprisonment 1983–1990* (Paris, 1995) (in Persian).

69 IHRDC, *Speaking for the Dead: Survivor Accounts of Iran's 1988 Massacre* (New Haven, CT: IHRDC, 2010).

70 Monireh Baradaran, 'Evin Prison: Summer 1988', *The Plain Truth: Memoirs of the Prisons of the Islamic Republic of Iran* (Independent Association of Iranian Women, 2006) (in Persian).

71 Amnesty International, 'Iran: Violations of Human Rights 1987–1990', MDE 13/21/90, 1 December 1990.

72 *Kayhan,* 18 February 1985, pp. 1–2.

CHAPTER 5: MOURNING FORBIDDEN

73 IHDRC, *Deadly Fatwa*, p. 54.

74 Amnesty International, 'Iran: Preserve the Khavaran Grave Site for Investigation into Mass Killings', MDE 13/006/2009, 20 January 2009.

75 See Iran Research Group, *Iran Yearbook 89/90* (Bonn: MB Medien and Bucher Verlagsgesellchaft, 1989)

76 See NCRI, 'Crimes against Humanity', p. 81.

77 IHRDC, *Speaking for the Dead*, witness statement of Sepideh, para. 39.

78 See Amnesty International, 'Iran: Violations of Human Rights 1987–1990', p. 13.

79 See NCRI, 'Crimes against Humanity', p. 99.

80 IHRDC, *Speaking for the Dead*, witness statement of Sepideh, paras 34–5.

81 Ahmad Mousavi, *Goodnight Comrade* (Spånga, Sweden: Baran, 2005) (in Persian).

82 See 'Iran: Double Standard?' *The Economist,* 29 August 1998, p. 45.

83 Amnesty International, 'Iran: Political Executions', UA235/88, MDE 13/14/88, 2 September 1988.

84 See Reynaldo Galindo Pohl, Interim Report Annexed to Note by the Secretary General, ECOSOC Report, 'Situation of Human

Rights in the Islamic Republic of Iran', A/43/705, 13 October 1988 ('Interim 1988 Report'), paras 5–11, p. 59.

85   Iran Research Group, *Iran Yearbook 89/90*, (Bonn: MB Medien & Bücher), note 3.

86   *Resalat,* 7 December 1988, pp. 2, 11.

87   *Kayhan,* 25 February 1989, p. 16.

88   The Baha'i faith was founded in Iran in 1844 and is now its largest non-Muslim religious minority. Whilst reaffirming the core ethical principles common to all religions, the founder of the Baha'i faith, Baha'u'llah, was also said to have revealed new laws and teachings to lay the foundations of a global civilisation. The central theme of the Baha'i faith is that humanity is one family and the time has come for its unification into a peaceful global society. After 1979, its adherents were treated as apostates and have been subjected to continual discrimination and repression.

89   Reynaldo Galindo Pohl, 'Report on the Situation of Human Rights in the Islamic Republic of Iran', 28 January 1987, E/CN.4/1987/23, para. 82(b). No Red Cross representatives were allowed to visit prisons in Iran until 22 January 1992: just two months later on 21 March 1992, all Red Cross representatives were expelled from the country. See Reynaldo Galindo Pohl, 'Report on the Situation of Human Rights in the Islamic Republic of Iran', 28 January 1993, E/CN.4/1993/41, para. 168.

90   Reynaldo Galindo Pohl, 'Report on the Situation of Human Rights in the Islamic Republic of Iran', 25 January 1988, E/CN.4/1988/24, paras 82(7), 82(8).

91   Pohl, Interim 1988 Report, para. 47.

92   Reported in *Kayhan,* 6 August 1988, p. 15.

93   Pohl, Interim 1988 Report, paras 69, 71.

94   Reynaldo Galindo Pohl, 'Report on the Situation of Human Rights in the Islamic Republic of Iran', 26 January 1989, E/CN.4/1989/26, paras 15–18.

95   See ibid., paras 6–10. The Iranian diplomats who blindsided Pohl in this period were Ambassador Mahallati in New York and Ambassador Sirous Nasseri in Geneva. The latter is now a businessman in Europe and the former resides in the US.

96   Abrahamian, *Tortured Confessions*, p. 221.

97   One prisoner, Monireh Baradaran, in her memoirs *The Plain Truth*, pp. 543–4, tells how she later met Pohl and discovered that he had been introduced to fake 'prisoners' in Evin, who had (unsurprisingly) praised their humane treatment.

98   Reynaldo Galindo Pohl, 'Report on the Situation of Human Rights in the Islamic Republic of Iran', 6 November 1990, A/45/697, para. 230.

99   Ibid., para. 240.

100 Ibid., para. 136.

101 Ibid., para. 142.

102 Ibid., para. 215.

103 Amnesty International, 'Iran: Violations of Human Rights 1987–1990', p. 14.

104 Professor Pohl seems to lose interest in the massacres: his report of 13 February 1991 makes no reference to them, despite the fact that Amnesty International published its detailed report just two weeks previously. See Pohl, 'Report on the Human Rights Situation in the Islamic Republic of Iran', 13 February 1991, E/CN.4/1991/35. In 1992, Pohl reports that 164 executions of political prisoners have taken place in 1992: see Pohl, 'Final Report on the Situation of Human Rights in the Islamic Republic of Iran', 28 January 1993, E/CN.4/1993/41, para. 281. In the course of this year, the Iranian government officials realised that Pohl was obtaining his information on political executions from the government-controlled local media, which had been reporting the boastful statements of judicial authorities. So they took action to curtail reporting – a leaked government document expressed satisfaction that 'all of the sources used by Galindo Pohl to provide documented and irrefutable reports was therefore neutralised': see Pohl, 'Interim Report on the Situation of Human Rights in the Islamic Republic of Iran', annexed to Note by the Secretary General transmitting the Pohl Report to the General Assembly, 8 November 1993, A/48/526, para. 92.

105 Azar Nafisi, *Reading Lolita in Tehran: A Memoir in Books* (London: Fourth Estate, 2003), p. 239.

CHAPTER 6: GETTING AWAY WITH MASS MURDER

106 See Geoffrey Robertson, *The Tyrannicide Brief: The Story of the Man Who Sent Charles I to the Scaffold* (London: Vintage, 2006), Chapter 10.

107 Holinshed, Shakespeare's source, mentions no such incident. The only justification ever suggested has been that the English army was vastly outnumbered by their French prisoners, who, if they had lived, might have fought another day and won. See Theodor Meron, *War Crimes Law Comes of Age* (Oxford: Clarendon Press, 1998).

108 See ibid., p. 120, and Francis Lieber, *Instructions for the Government of Armies of the United States in the Field*, Arts 28, 133.

109 Military and Paramilitary Activities in and against Nicaragua (*Nicaragua v. USA* (judgment)) ICJ Rep 1986, p. 14, para. 218.

110 *Velásquez-Rodríguez* v. *Honduras*, Inter-American Court HR (ser. C) No. 4. (1998), para. 157.

111 *Schedko* v. *Belarus*, Communication No. 886/1999, 28 April 2003.

112 *Tas* v. *Turkey*, Application No.24396/924 (2000), para. 80.

113 See *Velásquez-Rodríguez* v. *Honduras.*

114 See *Prosecutor* v. *Mitar Vasiljević,* Case No. IT-98-32-T (ICTY), 29 November 2002, para. 227.

115 Imposing the death penalty for religious or political affiliation (or non-affiliation) is considered to violate the restriction of the death penalty to the 'most serious crimes'. See, for example, Concluding Observations of the Human Rights Committee: Libyan Arab Jamahiriya, UN document CCPR/C/79/Add.101, 6 November 1998, para. 8 and Concluding Observations of the Human Rights Committee: Sudan, UN document CCPR/C/79/Add.85, 19 November 1997, para. 8.

116 *Öcalan* v. *Turkey,* No. 46221/99 ECHR 2005, paras 148–9.

117 See, for example, Concluding Observations of the Human Rights Committee: Sudan, UN document CCPR/C/79/Add.85, 19 November 1997, para. 8.

118 Michael A. Newton and Michael P. Scharf, *Enemy of the State: The Trial and Execution of Saddam Hussein* (New York: St Martin's Press, 2008).

119 See Geoffrey Robertson, *Crimes Against Humanity: The Struggle for Global Justice,* 4th edn (London: Penguin, 2012), pp. 720–27.

120 *Prosecution* v. *Kvočka et al,* Case No. IT-98-30/1-A, Appeal Judgment, 28 February 2005, paras 285–91; see also Trial Judgment, Case No. IT-98-30/1-T, para. 45.

121 See, for example, *Batı v. Turkey* (No.33097/96;57834/00) ECHR, 3 June 2004, paras 114 and 117; *Mammadov v. Azerbaijan* (No.34445/04) ECHR, 11 January 2007, paras 66, 68–9; Nigel S. Rodley, *The Treatment of Prisoners under International Law,* 3rd edn (Oxford: Oxford University Press, 2009), p. 96.

122 *Selmouni v. France* (No. 25803, 1994), European Commission of Human Rights Report 1999, paras 96–97.

123 See Philippe Sands, *Torture Team: Deception, Cruelty and the Compromise of Law* (London: Allen Lane, 2008) p. 30.

124 See, for example, the website of Iraj Mesdaghi: www.irajmesdaghi.com.

CHAPTER 7: GLOBAL ASSASSINS

125 Takeyh, *Guardians of the Revolution,* p. 56.

126 Geoffrey Robertson, *The Justice Game* (London: Vintage, 1999), pp. 159–60.

127 Salman Rushdie, *Joseph Anton: A Memoir* (London: Jonathan Cape, 2012), pp. 245 (Khamenei), 195 (Rafsanjani).

128 Ibid., pp. 326, 429.

129 'Iran adamant over Rushdie fatwa', BBC News, 12 February 2005.

130 Testimony by former Ministry of Intelligence official Messbahi at *Mykonos* trial: Roya Hakakian, *Assassins of the Turquoise Palace* (New York: Grove Press, 2011), p. 273.

131 IHRDC, *No Safe Haven: Iran's Global Assassination Campaign* (New Haven, CT: IHRDC, 2008), pp. 5–6.

132 Ibid., p. 16.

133 Ibid., p. 17.

134 Ibid., p. 21.

135 Ibid., p. 24.

136 Ibid., pp. 27–9, and see Hakakian, *Assassins of the Turquoise Palace*, pp. 116–17.

137 Hakakian, *Assassins of the Turquoise Palace*, pp. 271–2. Messbahi defected because he had been warned by Saeed Emami, his friend in the Ministry, that Fallahian was out to get him – perhaps because in 1984 he had deliberately bungled an order to have Iran's foremost comedian, Hadi Khorsandi, killed: he set up the assassination in London then tipped off MI6, apparently because he enjoyed the target's jokes (see pp. 264–5). This may explain why Emami was made the scapegoat for the 'chain murders'.

138 IHRDC, *Murder at Mykonos: Anatomy of a Political Assassination* (New Haven, CT: IHRDC, 2007), p. 18.

139 IHRDC, *No Safe Haven*, p. 32.

140 Abdorrahman Boroumand Foundation, *Terror in Buenos Aires: The Islamic Republic's Forgotten Crime against Humanity* (July 2009), p. 10.

141 William C. Rempel, 'Recruiting a Political Assassin', *CA Times*, 25 November 1994.

142 IHRDC, *No Safe Haven*, pp. 39–47.

143 See ibid., and 'Extracts from the Instruction Relative to the Double Assassination of Shapur Bakhtiar and Sorouch Katibeh', http://www.iranrights.org/english/library-91.php.

144 Abdorrahman Boroumand Foundation, *Terror in Buenos Aires*, pp. 4–5.

145 David Adams, 'Argentina to expel Iran envoys over bombing links', *The Times,* 10 August 1994; Ian Brodie, 'CIA confirms Tehran's role in bombing of Jewish targets', *The Times*, 12 August 1994.

146 Hugo Mon, 'The Shadow of Iran in Argentina Takes On a Suspicious Shape' in Cynthia Arnson *et al.* (eds), *Iran in Latin America: Threat or 'Axis of Annoyance'?* (Washington, DC: Woodrow Wilson International Center for Scholars, 2009), p. 51.

147 Larry Rohter, 'Argentine judge indicts four Iranian officials in 1994 bombing of Jewish center', *New York Times*, 10 March 2003.

148 Abdorrahman Boroumand Foundation, *Terror in Buenos Aires*, pp. 14–16.

149 See Muhammad Sahimi, 'The Chain Murders: Killing dissidents and intellectuals', Frontline, 5 January 2011, http://www.pbs.org/wgbh/pages/frontline/tehranbureau/2011/01/the-chain-murders-killing-dissidents-and-intellectuals-1988-1998.html.

150 Ibid.
151 Ibid.
152 Takeyh, *Guardians of the Revolution*, p. 212.
153 Ibid., p. 215.
154 Giles Whittell, 'US "foiled Iran plot to kill ambassador"', *The Times*, 12 October 2011.
155 Bill Condie, 'Israel vows vengeance on Iran as blasts raise fears over world terror campaign', *The Times*, 15 February 2012, p. 25.
156 Jason Burke, 'Iran was behind bomb plot against Israeli diplomats, investigators find', *The Guardian,* 18 June 2012.
157 It is now enshrined in Article 7 of the ICC statute. There can be no doubt that it was an international law crime at the time of the assassination campaign: the ICTY held in the *Tadić* case a few years later that it was a freestanding international crime needing no connection to any particular war.
158 G. A. Res 51/107, UN GAOR, 51 Sess., UN Doc A/RES/51/107.
159 Decree to assassinate Manouchehr Ganji, signed by Prosecutor General of Iran, 17/3/93, in translation, in IHRDC, *No Safe Haven*, Appendix 5.
160 *Shahintaj Bakhtiar v. Islamic Republic of Iran* (US District Court, District of Columbia, 17 July 2008, Judge Henry Kennedy Jnr).

CHAPTER 8: CRUSHING THE GREEN MOVEMENT
161 Quoted in Hakakian, *Assassins of the Turquoise Palace*, p. 112.
162 Ali M. Ansari, *Crisis of Authority: Iran's 2009 Presidential Election* (London: Chatham House, 2010), pp. 14–16.
163 Afsaneh Moqadam, *Death to the Dictator! Witnessing Iran's Election and the Crippling of the Islamic Republic* (London: Bodley Head, 2010), p. 24.
164 See IHRDC, *Impunity in Iran: The Death of Photojournalist Zahra Kazemi* (New Haven, CT: IHRDC, 2006).
165 IHRDC, *Violent Aftermath: The 2009 Election and Suppression of Dissent in Iran* (New Haven, CT: IHRDC, 2010), p. 9.
166 Moqadam, *Death to the Dictator!*, p. 47.
167 Ibid., p. 79.
168 IHRDC, *Violent Aftermath*, pp. 25–7.
169 Dabashi, *Theology of Discontent*, p. 50.
170 See IHRDC, *Violent Aftermath*, pp. 46–8, from the account of Maryam Sabri.
171 Dabashi, *Theology of Discontent*, p. 149.
172 Ansari, *Crisis of Authority*, pp. 63–5.
173 Moqadam, *Death to the Dictator!*, p. 113.
174 IHRDC, *Violent Aftermath*, p. 76.
175 Martin Fletcher, 'Tehran regime turns the screw on BBC by targeting families back home', *The Times*, 6 October 2011.

176 Ansari, *Crisis of Authority*, p. 75.
177 IHRDC, *Violent Aftermath*, p. 9.
178 Ibid., p. 91.
179 Martin Fletcher, 'Pray for my captors, detained lawyer tells son in secret letter', *The Times*, 21 May 2011, p. 42; 'Prisoner of Conscience', *The Times*, 14 September 2011, p. 8.
180 Hugh Tomlinson, 'Tehran gives human rights lawyer 18-year sentence', *The Times*, 7 March 2012, p. 13.
181 Martin Fletcher, 'Torture and Exile, the fate of lawyers supporting Ashtiani', *The Times*, 8 October 2011, p. 49.
182 Laura Dixon and Martin Fletcher, 'Stoning widow beaten into TV confession, says lawyer', *The Times*, 13 August 2011, p. 11.
183 Martin Fletcher, 'Ashtiani a shadow of her former self after six years spent waiting for death', *The Times*, 7 February 2012, p. 29.
184 Hugh Tomlinson and Martin Fletcher, 'UN to investigate abuses as stoning verdict is upheld', *The Times*, 25 March 2011.
185 Amir Taheri, 'A life depends on the battle for Iran's soul', *The Times*, 6 November 2010.
186 Azar Nafisi, 'Iran's Women: Canaries in the coalmine', *The Times*, 27 November 2010, p. 28.
187 In a rare capitulation to Western pressure, the minister was reprieved in September 2012.
188 Reza Khalili, 'Iran Human Rights Head: Execution, Eye Gouging, Cutting off Hands and Feet "Beautiful and Necessary"', PJ Media, 6 June 2011.
189 Dabashi, *Theology of Discontent*, p. 74.

CHAPTER 9: HIROSHIMA
190 Paul Ham, *Hiroshima Nagasaki* (Sydney: HarperCollins, 2011), pp. 425–7. Burchett's experience caused him to develop an abiding hatred of America, which unbalanced his later journalism – a fault that should not detract from a courageous scoop.
191 Tom Zoellner, *Uranium: War, Energy and the Rock that Shaped the World* (New York: Penguin, 2010), p. 29.
192 Robertson, *Crimes against Humanity*, p. 29.
193 Zoellner, *Uranium*, p. 37.
194 Joseph Cirincione, *Bomb Scare: The History and Future of Nuclear Weapons* (New York: Columbia University Press, 2007) p. 1.
195 Ham, *Hiroshima Nagasaki*, p. 107.
196 Andrew J. Rotter, *Hiroshima: The World's Bomb* (Oxford: Oxford University Press, 2008), p. 77.
197 Zoellner, *Uranium*, p. 80.
198 Joseph M. Siracusa, *Nuclear Weapons: A Very Short Introduction* (Oxford: Oxford University Press, 2008), pp. 20–21.
199 Ibid., p. 20.

200 Ham, *Hiroshima Nagasaki*, Appendix 4, pp. 520–21.
201 Rotter, *Hiroshima*, p. 124.
202 Ham, *Hiroshima Nagasaki*, pp. 199–200.
203 Rotter, *Hiroshima*, p. 226.
204 'Six Power Committee and Draft Atomic Policy', *Canberra Times*, 3 July 1946.

CHAPTER 10: PROLIFERATION
205 Hans J. Morgenthau, 'Death in the Nuclear Age', *Commentary*, September 1961, p. 233.
206 A good account of the building and testing of Soviet nukes is found in Peter Pringle and James Spigelman, *The Nuclear Barons* (London: Michael Joseph, 1982), Chapters 4, 15.
207 Patten, *What Next?*, p. 125.
208 See Geoffrey Robertson, 'Who wants Diego Garcia? Decolonisation, Torture and Indigenous Rights in the Indian Ocean' (2012) 36 UniWALR 1.
209 See David S. Yost, 'The US Debate on NATO Nuclear Deterrence', *International Affairs*, vol. 87, no. 6 (2011), p. 1420.
210 Ibid., p. 1413.
211 Verghese Koithara, *Managing India's Nuclear Forces* (Washington, DC: Brookings Institution Press, 2012), p. 3.
212 Zoellner, *Uranium*, p. 118.
213 Bill Keller, 'Nuclear Mullahs', *New York Times*, 9 September 2012.
214 See Sumit Ganguly and S. Paul Kapur, *India, Pakistan and the Bomb: Debating Nuclear Stability in South Asia* (New York: Columbia University Press, 2010), pp. 76–8.
215 Rotter, *Hiroshima*, p. 290.
216 Victor Cha, *The Impossible State: North Korea. Past and Future* (London: Bodley Head, 2012), p. 285.
217 UNSC Resn 1874 of 2009; UNSCR 1695 and 1718 of 2006.
218 Cha, *The Impossible State*, p. 272.
219 Ibid., p. 224.
220 James Wirtz and Peter Lavoy (eds), *Over the Horizon Proliferation Threats* (Stanford: Stanford University Press, 2012), p. 49.
221 Ibid., p. 57.
222 Mohammed ElBaradei, *The Age of Deception: Nuclear Diplomacy in Treacherous Times* (London: Bloomsbury, 2011), pp. 166–7.
223 Mohammed ElBaradei says that A. Q. Khan claimed that senior officers in the Pakistani army instructed him to co-operate with North Korea and Iran: ibid., p. 175.
224 Gordon Corera, *Shopping for Bombs: Nuclear Proliferation, Global Insecurity and the Rise and Fall of the A. Q. Khan Network* (London: Hurst, 2006), p. 47.

225 Ibid., pp. 103–5.

226 Ibid., p. 161.

227 Christopher O'Clary, 'The A. Q. Khan Network – Causes and Implications', Master's thesis, December 2005, p. 1.

CHAPTER 11: THE NPT PARADOX

228 Steven L. Spiegel, Jennifer D. Kibbe and Elizabeth G. Matthews (eds), *The Dynamics of Middle East Nuclear Proliferation* (Lewiston, NY: Edwin Mellen Press, 2002), p. 67.

229 ElBaradei, *The Age of Deception*, pp. 178–9.

230 Statute of IAEA, Art XII(A)(1).

231 Elli Louka, *Nuclear Weapons, Justice and the Law* (Cheltenham: Edward Elgar, 2011), p. 110.

232 Hassan Beheshtipour, 'Breaking the deadlock over Iran's nuclear talks', Iran Review, 22 September 2012.

233 'Doubts surface over nuclear inspector: is Watchdog at risk of a WMD re-run?' *The Guardian*, 23 March 2012.

234 Ibid.

235 See David Leigh, *Betrayed: The Real Story of the Matrix Churchill Trial* (London: Bloomsbury, 1993).

236 See Robertson, *The Justice Game*, p. 313.

237 See Trevor Findlay, *Unleashing the Nuclear Watchdog: Strengthening and Reform of the IAEA*, (Waterloo, ON: Centre for International Governance and Innovation, 2012), pp. 62–3.

238 Daniel Joyner, 'Iraq's nuclear programme and the legal mandate of the IAEA', Jurist, 9 November 2011.

239 Daniel Joyner, *Interpreting the Nuclear Non-Proliferation Treaty* (Oxford: Oxford University Press, 2011), p. 5.

240 ElBaradei, *The Age of Deception*, pp. 12–13.

241 George W. Bush, 'Speech on Weapons of Mass Destruction Proliferation', National Defence University, Washington D.C., 11 February 2004.

242 'North Korea statement on withdrawal from nuclear pact', *The Guardian*, 10 January 2003.

243 Joyner, *Interpreting the Nuclear Non-Proliferation Treaty*, p. 124.

244 See US Dept of State, 'New START Treaty entry in force', Press Release, 5 February 2011.

245 Joyner, *Interpreting the Nuclear Non-Proliferation Treaty*, p. 118.

CHAPTER 12: IRAN'S NUCLEAR HEDGE

246 See Saira Khan, *Iran and Nuclear Weapons: Protracted Conflict and Proliferation*, (Abingdon: Routledge, 2010), p. 48.

247 Ibid. See also Takeyh, *Guardians of the Revolution*, p. 242.

248 Takeyh, *Guardians of the Revolution*, p. 105.

249 Khan, *Iran and Nuclear Weapons*, p. 57.

250　See Corera, *Shopping for Bombs*, p. 69.

251　Alireza Jafarzadeh, *The Iran Threat: President Ahmadinejad and the Coming Nuclear Crisis* (Basingstoke: Palgrave Macmillan, 2007), p. 135.

252　Ibid., p. 139.

253　David Albright and Andrea Stricker, 'Iran's Nuclear Program', in Robin Wright (ed.), *The Iran Primer: 'Power, Politics, and US Policy'* (Washington, DC: US Institute of Peace, 2010) p. 77.

254　ElBaradei, *The Age of Deception*, p. 118.

255　Ibid., p. 116.

256　Jafarzadeh, *The Iran Threat*, pp. 162–3.

257　Albright and Stricker, 'Iran's Nuclear Program', p. 79.

258　Jafarzadeh, *The Iran Threat*, pp. 164–5.

259　Ryan Mauro, 'UN nails Iran and Syria', FrontPageMagazine, 6 June 2011.

260　Rebecca Lowe, quoting former weapons inspector David Albright in 'Iran: From Prince to Pariah', *IBA Global Insight*, June 2012, p. 21.

261　The argument is made by Daniel Joyner, 'Iran's nuclear program and the legal mandate of the IAEA'.

262　Cited by Wyn Q. Bowen and Jonathan Brewer, 'Iran's Nuclear Challenge: Nine Years and Counting', *International Affairs*, vol. 87, no. 4 (2011), p. 923.

263　Ibid., p. 930.

264　Shahram Chubin, 'The Iranian Nuclear Riddle after June 12th', *Washington Quarterly*, vol. 33, no. 1, (2010), p. 167

265　Jahangir Amuzegar, 'Myths about Iran: The West doesn't get it', *Prospect*, June 2012, p. 22.

266　Ariel Levite, 'Never say never again: Nuclear reversal revisited', *International Security*, vol. 27, no. 3, (2002), p. 69.

267　See Mark Fitzpatrick, 'Iran can be stopped', *Prospect*, April 2012, p. 26.

268　Olli Heinonen and Simon Henderson, 'What we know about Iran's nukes', *Wall Street Journal*, 10 September 2012.

269　See Patrick Seale, quoting David E. Sanger, 'What is Obama's game plan?', Iran Review, 5 June 2012.

270　See his report, 'The Situation of Human Rights in the Islamic Republic of Iran', A/66/374; A/HRC/19/66.

271　See US Executive Order 13553 and UN Resolution A/Res/66/175 and EU Council regulations no. 359/2011 (14 April 2011).

272　Quoted in Hassan Hakimian 'The last straw for Iran's economy', *World Today*, April–May 2012, p. 28.

273　See Meghan L. O'Sullivan, 'The role and potential of sanctions', in Robert D. Blackwill (ed.), *Iran: The Nuclear Challenge* (New York: CFR Press, 2012), p. 15.

274　See 'The state of Iran', *The Economist*, 20 August 2011, p. 45.

275 Trita Parsi, *A Single Roll of the Dice: Obama's Diplomacy with Iran* (New Haven, CT: Yale University Press, 2012), p. 3.
276 Ibid., p. 4.
277 Ibid., p. 102.
278 Ibid., p. 101.
279 James Mackenzie, 'France's Sarkozy raises Iran sanction threat', Reuters, 27 August 2009.
280 ElBaradei, *The Age of Deception*, p. 310.
281 Martin Fletcher, 'Iran claims nuclear breakthrough that puts it one step away from the bomb', *The Times*, 16 February 2012.
282 David Blair, 'Iran puts on show of defiance', *Daily Telegraph*, 16 February 2012.
283 'Iran's nuclear theology: Bombs and truth', *The Economist*, 19 May 2012, p. 60.
284 Minister of Foreign Affairs of the Russian Federation, official website – 1225-21-06-2012.

CHAPTER 13: THE PROBLEM WITH ISRAEL
285 See 'A license to kill: Israeli undercover operation against "wanted" Palestinians', Human Rights Watch, 1 August 1993.
286 See 'Report of the United Nations Fact Finding Mission on the Gaza Conflict (Goldstone Report)', UN Doc. A/HRC/12/48.
287 Harriet Sherwood, 'Israel subjecting Palestinian children to "spiral of injustice"', *The Guardian*, 26 June 2012.
288 Avner Cohen and Marvin Miller, 'Bringing Israel's Bomb out of the Basement', *Foreign Affairs*, September–October 2010, p. 33.
289 See Avner Cohen, 'The Yatza Affair', in *Worst-Kept Secret: Israel's Bargain with the Bomb* (New York: Columbia University Press, 2010), p. 135.
290 Cohen and Miller, 'Bringing Israel's Bomb out of the Basement', p. 34.
291 Ibid.
292 Joseph Lelyveld, 'The alliance that dared not speak its name', *New York Review of Books*, 28 October 2010.
293 Related in Sasha Polakow-Suransky, *The Unspoken Alliance: Israel's Secret Relationship with Apartheid South Africa* (New York: Pantheon, 2010).
294 Cohen and Miller, 'Bringing Israel's Bomb out of the Basement', p. 132.
295 '"Cindy" unmasked: The honey that snared Vanunu', *Sunday Times*, 22 July 2012, p. 25.
296 Uzi Mahnaimi, 'Assassin plucks Iran's nuclear "flower" in double bomb attack', *Sunday Times*, 5 December 2010, p. 33.
297 Marie Colvin and Uzi Mahnaimi, 'Israel's secret war', *Sunday Times*, 15 January 2012.

298   Saeed Kamali Dehghan, 'Sketch cameras roll as Tehran basks in the limelight', *The Guardian*, 31 August 2012.

299   'The sabotaging of Iran', *FT.com Magazine*, 11 February 2011.

300   Michael Evans, 'Obama issues plea for patience amid "loose talk of war" with Iran', *The Times*, 5 March 2012.

301   Harriet Sherwood, 'Netanyahu tries to raise the heat on Obama over Iran', *The Guardian*, 17 September 2012.

302   Harriet Sherwood, 'Romney pledges unity with Israel over Iran', *The Guardian,* 30 July 2012, p. 13; Sheera Frenkel, 'Romney says he would back strike on Iran', *The Times*, 30 July 2012, p. 29.

303   'Israel and Iran – closer to take-off', *The Economist*, 11 February 2012, p. 49.

304   Quoted by David Remnick in *The New Yorker* in 1998. See Tobias Buck, 'Obituary for Benzion Netanyahu', *Financial Times*, 5 May 2012.

305   Vita Bekker, 'Israelis gear up amid threat of war', *Financial Times*, 1/2 September 2012.

306   'Briefing: Attacking Iran', *The Economist*, 25 February 2012.

307   Mehdi Hasan, 'Netanyahu may want war on Iran, but his people don't', *The Guardian*, 30 April 2012.

308   'Israeli economy stands to lose $11.7 billion in any Iran war', *Daily Star* (Lebanon), 21 August 2012.

309   David Blair, 'Iran, Syria, North Korea: Is the world sitting on a tinderbox?', *Sunday Telegraph*, 15 April 2012.

310   Hugh Tomlinson, 'Saudi Arabia threatens to go nuclear "within weeks" if Iran gets the bomb', *The Times*, 10 February 2012.

311   See Eric S. Edelman *et al.*, 'The Dangers of a Nuclear Iran', *Foreign Affairs*, January–February 2011, p. 70.

312   Advisory Opinion Concerning Legal Consequences of the Construction of a Wall in the Occupied Palestinian Territory (9 July 2004), ICJ, separate opinion of Justice Rosalyn Higgins, p. 18.

313   Avner Cohen and Marvin Miller, 'Bringing Israel's Bomb out of the Basement', *Foreign Affairs*, September–October 2010, p. 31.

314   See Cohen, *Worst-Kept Secret*, p. 233.

315   See Ron Rosenbaum, *How the End Begins: The Road to a Nuclear World World III* (London: Simon & Schuster, 2011), p. 154.

CHAPTER 14: WAR LAW AND THE BOMB

316   Legality of the Threat or Use of Nuclear Weapons, 1996, ICJ 226, pp. 35–6.

317   See ABA, *Nuclear Weapons and International Humanitarian Law*, 20 April 2012, convened by Jonathan Granoff, President Global Security Institute. Presentation by Professor Gary Solis, former head of law of war programme at West Point military academy.

318   Martens chaired a sub-commission at the 1899 Hague conference,

and is remembered for pointing out, against those who argued that the laws of war should be kept vague, that 'to leave uncertainty hovering over these questions would necessarily be to allow the interests of force to trump over those of humanity'. J. B. Scott, 'The Conference of 1899', *Proceedings of the Hague Peace Conferences* (International Peace Conference, 1907), p. 507.

319 Cirincione, *Bomb Scare*, p. 29.

320 David Fischer, *Stopping the Spread of Nuclear Weapons: The Past and the Prospects* (London: Routledge, 1992), p. 7.

321 Several nuclear-armed states did express reservations about these sections of the protocol applying to nuclear weapons, subject to the position of such weapons under customary international law.

322 The *Corfu Channel* case (*UK* v. *Albania*), ICJ Rep 4, 1949.

323 The *Nuclear Tests* case (*Australia* v. *France*), ICJ Rep 253, 1974, para. 53.

324 Legality of the Threat or Use of Nuclear Weapons, ICJ (8 July 1996), para. 2 HRJL 17 (1996).

325 Ibid., Dissent of Judge Koroma, p. 6.

326 Legality of the Threat or Use of Nuclear Weapons, Advisory Opinion, ICJ 226, 8 July 1996, p. 78.

327 Alan Robock and Owen Brian Toon, 'Local Nuclear War, Global Suffering', *Scientific American*, January 2010, pp. 74, 79.

328 The Krupp Trial, 10 L. Rep. TrialsWarCrim 69, 139, 1949.

329 *Report of the Canberra Commission on the Elimination of Nuclear Weapons* (Canberra: Department of Foreign Affairs and Trade, 1996), p. 285.

330 Ibid.

331 Quoted by Peter Weiss, 'Taking the Law Seriously: The Need for a Nuclear Weapons Convention', *Fordham International Law Journal*, vol. 34, no. 4 (2011), p. 783.

332 See Charles J. Moxley Jr, John Burroughs and Jonathan Granoff, 'Nuclear Weapons Compliance with IHL and the NPT', *Fordham International Law Journal*, vol. 34, no. 4 (2011), pp. 672–3.

CHAPTER 15: CAN ISRAEL ATTACK IRAN? THE IGNOBLE ART OF SELF-DEFENCE

333 The *Caroline* case (1841) 29 BFSP 1137–8 (1842) BFSP 195–6.

334 'International Military Tribunal (Nuremberg): Judgment', *American Journal of International Law*, vol. 41, no. 1 (1947), pp. 172–333.

335 Yoram Dinstein, *War, Aggression and Self-Defence*, 5th edn (Cambridge: Cambridge University Press, 2011), p. 204.

336 Richard Wilson, 'Incorrect, incomplete and unreliable information can lead to tragically incorrect decisions', available at http://www.physics.harvard.edu/~wilson/publications/OSIRAK(2).

337 See Dinstein, *War, Aggression and Self-Defence*, p. 49.
338 Alan Dershowitz, 'Israel has the right to attack Iran's nuclear reactors now', Huffington Post, 16 March 2011.
339 *Nicaragua* v. *US* (Merits) ICJ Rep 14, 1986, 126–7.
340 Menachem Begin, 'Face the Nation', CBS, 15 June 1981.
341 David Makovsky, 'The silent strike', *New Yorker*, 17 September 2012, p. 34.
342 Leonard S. Spector and Avner Cohen, 'Israel's Airstrike on Syria's Reactor: Implications for the Nonproliferation Regime', *Arms Control Today*, July/August 2008.
343 Andrew Garwood-Gowers, 'Israel's Airstrike on Syria's Al-Kibar Facility: A Test Case for the Doctrine of Pre-Emptive Self-Defence?', *Journal of Conflict and Security Law*, vol. 16, no. 2 (2011), p. 268.
344 Christine Gray, 'The Use of Force to Prevent the Proliferation of Nuclear Weapons', *Japanese Yearbook of International Law*, vol. 52 (2009), p. 101.
345 See the author's argument on the rights of humanitarian intervention in Robertson, *Crimes against Humanity*, 4th edn (London: Penguin, 2012), pp. 733–45.
346 The SS *Lotus (France* v. *Turkey)* 'The *Lotus* case' 1928 PCIJ Series A, No. 10.
347 This is the formulation in *Principles of International Law on the Use of Force by States in Self-Defence* (London: Chatham House, 2005), p. 7, drawing upon the ICJ Advisory Opinion in *Nicaragua* v. *USA* (Merits) 1988 ICJ Rep 14.
348 Ibid., p. 9.
349 UN Doc A/59/565 (2004), paras 187–91.
350 See Michael Howard, 'The Bush doctrine: it's a brutal world, so act brutally', *Sunday Times*, 23 March 2003.
351 Lord Goldsmith, Advice to the Prime Minister, 7 March 2003.
352 Robert J. Delahunty and John Yoo, 'The "Bush Doctrine": Can Preventive War Be Justified?', *Harvard Journal of Law and Public Policy*, vol. 32, no. 3 (2009), p. 843.
353 'Remarks of Senator Obama to the Chicago Council on Global Affairs', Press Release, 23 April 2007.
354 Dershowitz, 'Israel has the right to attack Iran's nuclear reactors now'.
355 See Behnam Gharagozli, 'War of Words or a Regional Disaster? The (Il)legality of Israeli and Iranian Military Options', *Hastings International and Comparative Law Review*, vol. 33 (2010), p. 203.
356 Ibid.
357 'Defiant Ahmadinejad says Israel will be "eliminated"', *Sydney Morning Herald*, 25 September 2012.
358 BBC News, 14 December 2005.

359 Associated Press, 12 December 2006.
360 'Ahmadinejad brands Israel a "stinking corpse"', AFP, 8 May 2008.
361 'Ahmadinejad: World forces must annihilate Israel', *Jerusalem Post*, 2 August 2012.
362 Gharagozli, 'War of Words or a Regional Disaster?', p. 234.
363 Ibid., p. 228–9.
364 Kenneth Waltz, 'Why Iran Should Get the Bomb: Nuclear Balancing Would Mean Stability', *Foreign Affairs*, July–August 2012.
365 Quoted by Max Hastings, 'Bombing Iran may appear justified, but would be sheer madness', *Daily Mail*, 7 March 2012.
366 Heinonen and Henderson, 'What we know about Iran's nukes'.
367 All quotes in this paragraph are from the IAEA report, 'Implementation of the NPT Safeguards Agreement and the Relevant Provisions of Security Council Resolutions in the Islamic Republic of Iran', GOV/2011/65, 8 November 2011.
368 'US insists diplomacy has time amid Iran drumbeat in Israel', *Express Tribune*, 14 August 2012.

CHAPTER 16: WORLD WITHOUT NUKES, AMEN

369 Henry Kissinger et al., 'A world free of nuclear weapons', *Wall Street Journal*, 4 January 2007, p. A15.
370 Mikhail Gorbachev, 'The nuclear threat', *Wall Street Journal*, 31 January 2007, p. A13.
371 'The growing appeal of zero', *The Economist*, 18 June 2011, p. 69.
372 Legality of the Threat or Use of Nuclear Weapons, ICJ 226 at 567 (Koroma J, dissenting), 1996.
373 BVerfG – Federal Constitutional Court, *Neue Juristische Wochenschrift*, vol. 59, no. 11 (2006), p. 751.
374 The evidence is summarised in Andrew Gillespie, *A History of the Laws of War, vol. 3: The Customs and Laws of War with Regards to Arms Control*, (Oxford: Hart, 2011), pp. 122–4.
375 Emma Young, 'France keeps its atomic testing secrets', *New Scientist*, 4 February 2006.
376 See Geoffrey Robertson, *Crimes against Humanity*, 4th edn (London: Penguin, 2012), pp. 519–20.
377 HRC General Comment 14, which follows UN General Assembly Resolution 1981 26/921 to the effect that the use or threat of nuclear weapons would be a crime against humanity.
378 See, for example, the resolutions on the right to life, passed by the UN Sub-commission on the Prevention of Discrimination and Protection of Minorities, Resn 1996/14 (13 August 1996) and Resn 1997/36 (28 August 1997).
379 Jonathan Medalia, 'Comprehensive Nuclear test Ban Treaty:

Background and Current Developments', Congressional Research Service, 3 August 2011.
380 Ibid.
381 Ibid., Indian Minister Pranab Mukherjee, 16 August 2007; Pakistani Foreign Ministry spokesman, Abdul Basic, June 2009.
382 Steve Coll, *Ghost Wars* (New York: Penguin, 2005), pp. 491–2.
383 International Convention for the Suppression of Nuclear Terrorism, 44 ILM 815, 2005.
384 UNHCHR, General Comment 14, UN Doc CCPR/C/21/Add.4, 14 November 1984.
385 Vienna Convention on the Law of Treaties, Article 53.
386 *Barcelona Traction* case (1970) ICJ Reports 3, at p. 32.
387 See ICTY: *Prosecutor* v. *Anto Furunžija*, Case No. IT-95-17/1-T, Judgment (10 December 1998), para. 47; *Prosecutor* v. *Kupreškić*, Case No. IT-95-16, Decision on Defence Motion to Summon Witness (3 February 1999), para. 48.
388 There are various drafts of a Model Nuclear Weapons Convention: one, lodged by Costa Rica with the UN and prepared by various NGOs, is UN document A/C.152/7.
389 Ambassador Libran Cabactulan, Transcript of Speech to the American Bar Association, Spring Meeting – Section of International Law, 20 April 2012, American Bar Association, Nuclear Weapons and International Humanitarian Law.

EPILOGUE
390 An example given by the 'Report of the Canberra Commission on the Elimination of Nuclear Weapons', p. 26.
391 Barry M. Blechman, 'Why We Need to Eliminate Nuclear Weapons – and How to Do It', in Barry M. Blechman and Alexander K. Bollfrass (eds), *Elements of a Nuclear Disarmament Treaty* (Washington, DC: Henry L. Stimson Center, 2010), p. 21.
392 Andrew O'Neil, 'Extended Nuclear Deterrence in East Asia: Redundant or Resurgent?', *International Affairs*, vol. 87, no. 6 (2011), p. 1450.
393 See Lawrence Freedman, 'Nuclear Disarmament: From a Popular Movement to an Elite Project, and Back Again?', in George Perkovich and James M. Acton (eds), *Abolishing Nuclear Weapons: A Debate*, (Washington, DC: Carnegie Endowment for International Peace, 2009), p. 145.
394 Perkovich and Acton, *Abolishing Nuclear Weapons*, p. 14.

PICTURE CREDITS

INDEX